PREFACE

This is the story of a few Americans who at a desperate time early in the war were by their country thrown into the worst hell hole on earth, and then promptly forgotten at home. There at a strategic port on the Red Sea, they were to do what little they might to assist the British, who were hanging on by their fingernails only, to keep the war from being lost till America might disentangle herself from her peacetime follies and get ready to fight.

This is no story of high strategy, of valor on the field of battle, of thundering guns either naval or military. It is the tale of men in the war zone just behind the lines, never themselves given the satisfaction of firing a gun, who fought under and over the sea against the unseen enemy in a naval base already captured from him, to make that naval base usable again as the last spot from which the crucial war in the Mediterranean might be supported when all else was lost under Rommel's attack.

This is the story only of that naval base and of the men in it. It makes no pretense of covering the record of what was achieved by others, American Army officers in the Middle East, who together with me of the Navy, all of us under the command and skillful leadership of Major General Russell Maxwell, U.S.A., fought in support of the British to help stave off defeat till our country was ready to fight offensively.

It will be observed that in this book, some Englishmen (mostly civilians) figure who failed to measure up to the high standard set by most of their countrymen in that time of crisis. Let no one jeer at Britain for this. For every such Englishman, there was one American at least in Eritrea who never saw beyond the dollar sign, his personal comfort, or his personal aggrandizement; so that the rest of us, struggling in desperation to carry through in Massawa what must be done if disaster were not to overwhelm us all, often had good cause to reflect bitterly that if these, our countrymen, had actually been in the pay of Hitler or of Mussolini, they could not have served them more effectively.

Some passages in this book may seem bitter. They probably are. Those days of 1942, save for our few brief moments of triumph, were with us always lived in bitterness and torture, and often in despair that we should ever survive to see our homes again. Some of us didn't; others came back broken men. This book is written in the spirit in which it was lived. Men stewing in the caldron that was Massawa in the summer of 1942, facing in addition the terrors of unseen enemy mines and bombs placed below the sea for our destruction, were little given to tolerant acceptance of the interferences of those others who from the cool comfort and safety of the high hills, threw monkey wrenches into the works in Massawa. Bitterly we flung them back into the teeth of those who hurled them. We weren't liked for it. But I had no apologies then for our lack of calm acceptance of those interferences, and I have none now.

For the little handful of Americans (mostly civilians) who loyally and self-sacrificingly struggled and suffered at my side in a critical moment in history, I have the deepest affection and regard. I have here attempted to set down some little part of what they achieved and what they suffered. For the others (grossly overpaid) who in the luxury and cool comfort of the high hills inland in Eritrea, far above Massawa and the steaming Red Sea coast, enjoyed themselves free of all restrictions and taxes of wartime America, while they interfered with us, I had and have the utmost contempt. So had my men in Massawa.

Lest anyone be led astray, I must say here that this is a story written almost wholly from memory four years after the events set down. I kept no diary then. I had neither the time nor the energy left for one, and besides, keeping personal diaries was strictly forbidden to any of us. But my memory is good and what happened is indelibly burned into it.

A few names among hundreds of all nationalities, to my great regret, I do not now recall. To those few who are not here mentioned by name for that reason, I humbly apologize. It is further possible that some of the minor conversations attributed to one man may have taken place with another instead.

All dates have been carefully checked against such data (as would pass the censorship rules) in my letters home as might serve to date the event. I believe there are few errors there.

As regards the conversations, I make no claim that they are verbatim reports of what was said. There were no stenographers in Massawa to take them down. The more vivid statements, especially those at critical moments, made such an impression on me that till I die, I shall not forget them. They are correctly set down. As regards the other conversations, they faithfully record the gist of what was said, set down here in such words as best suit the situations involved.

That this story is wholly free from errors, I cannot believe. That to others in Eritrea some things may have seemed different, is wholly natural. Their point of view was not mine.

But this is the story of those days, of that place, and of the men (and a few women) of many nationalities as seen through the eyes of the American Commanding Officer who lived himself through every minute of it and was in as good a position to observe as anybody, and far better able, on the spot, to judge than those who were not.

A final word concerning the title of the author. The title "Commander" is here used on this book because every other book he has written has appeared under that title, first conferred on him by special act of Congress in recognition of earlier service to the Navy. The author fought through the late war in three separate campaigns overseas as a Captain, U.S.N.R.

EDWARD ELLSBERG

UNDER THE RED SEA SUN

CHAPTER

1

THE NIGHT OF DECEMBER 7, 1941, I was on a train bound for Washington. Early next morning found me camping on the doorstep of the Navy Department, seeking to be re-enrolled in the Navy for active service.

After nearly thirty years in the regular Navy and in the Naval Reserve, I was a civilian at that moment. I had the year before resigned my commission as Commander in the Naval Reserve that I might be free to speak for armament against the Axis without compromising the then official efforts of the Government to preserve its neutrality, which involved situation need not be gone into here.

Being just over fifty and therefore in that physical group whose services were, to put it mildly, not much sought after, I was not in a very good position to get the chance I craved to hit back at the Axis, now that war had started, with something more than words.

Fortunately for me, on that Monday morning of December 8, 1941, Admiral Robinson, Chief of the Bureau of Ships, shocked by the reports pouring in of the wreck that Japanese bombs and aerial torpedoes had made of our battleships in Pearl Harbor, decided that regardless of age, any former officer versed in salvage might still be useful. So on his flat order to that effect and to expedite matters, escorted by my classmate, Captain Rosendahl of lighter-than-air fame, I was soon circulating through various offices, medical and otherwise, on my way towards being sworn in again as an officer of the Navy.

Here came a technical hitch. I had last resigned from the Navy as a commander, which rank had been bestowed on me some years before by special act of Congress as a reward for earlier salvage efforts. But under the law, no one coming from civil life could be first enrolled in the Navy in a higher rank than that of lieutenant commander. Would I take that lesser rank, or did I prefer to wait a possible change in the law, now that we were actually at war?

So far as I was concerned, with that burden of my fifty years weighting down my chances, I was willing to take any rank which offered a possibility for an active part in helping to roll Hitler, Hirohito, et al. into the gutter. Before any red tape experts might have opportunity to tie knots in Admiral Robinson's orders, I said, "Yes, any rank at all."

So before the gloomiest day the Navy Department had ever witnessed came to its close, I was sworn into the service again. For the fourth time in my naval career I became a lieutenant commander, which rank I had first temporarily achieved in my youth in World War I, nearly a quarter of a century before.

I took the oath amidst a flood of disastrous confidential reports pouring in from Hawaii on the haggard top command: "Battleship *Arizona* completely destroyed by magazine explosion under bomb attack." As an ensign long years before, I had assisted at the *Arizona's* launching. "*Nevada* sunk." Well I remembered her first commissioning. "*West Virginia* sunk." I had taken part in her first trials. "*California* sunk." "*Oklahoma* capsized and sunk." "*Tennessee* badly damaged, blazing from bow to stern." As a lieutenant, years before, I had helped build the *Tennessee* and had ridden that superdreadnought down the ways on her first dip into the sea.

Only Pearl Harbor itself, cluttered with the sunken hulks of torpedoed battleships and with the skies blotted out under a pall of smoke rising from the blazing hulks of those bombed warships still afloat, was a more dismal spot than the Navy Department as I held up my right hand and somberly swore to defend the United States against all its enemies. With a global war tossed suddenly into its unready lap, with its major fleet a funeral pyre for my old shipmates, now treacherously slaughtered, the United States had enemies enough on every sea to warrant the gloom on each face, from admiral to ensign, I saw about me there in Washington.

What next for me? An odd situation immediately developed. The obvious assignment for anyone as a salvage officer was Pearl Harbor. But by a freak, there was in Pearl Harbor that Sunday morning of December 7, a senior salvage officer of the Navy on his way by air to the Middle East, due that very morning to continue his journey by Clipper westward to the Red Sea. Naturally enough, the Clipper, in the face of a sky full of Japanese bombers, had not taken off. And the

Navy with one of its few experienced salvage officers providentially on the spot, hastily canceled by radio his orders to the Middle East and assigned him the sunken mass of wrecks still blazing all over Pearl Harbor.

But that reassignment left what the day before had been the Navy's major salvage problem, hanging in the air. It was into this vacuum, so to speak, that I had thrust myself as a volunteer for active service, and the task was promptly offered me.

Would I go to the Red Sea, where the greatest mass of wrecks in the world (not excluding Pearl Harbor) then lay? Or, considering my age, might I prefer a colder climate, Iceland, where a much smaller but still important salvage problem due to U-boat warfare existed and would, no doubt, grow?

I chose the Red Sea.

CHAPTER

2

THE NEXT FEW WEEKS WERE HECTIC ones. While what scant resources the Navy and the nation had in the way of divers, equipment, and repair materials were being rushed to California for work at Pearl Harbor, I had to organize a salvage force to go to the Middle East. There were now no salvage ships available for my task. There were no divers, there was no salvage personnel, there was no equipment.

To top off all, I learned there was a further handicap. As the project had been originally authorized while the country had been at war with nobody, it had been laid out under Lend-lease conditions. The intention was to have the work done, not by men in the armed forces of the United States, thus compromising our neutrality, but by civilians hired by a civilian contractor under naval direction for the salvage work.

This particular task was part only of a gigantic Lend-lease operation. Under overall Army supervision, civilian contractors and their employees were to cover the entire Middle East with airfields, ordnance depots, and support bases, both land and sea. These were intended originally to back up British arms afloat, ashore, and in the air, in their desperate struggle in the Libyan Desert to throw back Rommel and the combined German-Italian effort to isolate Russia from the world on its southern border, to lay India and the East open to Axis land attack from the west.

Now with Japan assaulting from the opposite side and threatening to form a junction through rebellious India with its Axis partners, the strategic importance of the area suddenly was intensified enormously. But with what slight forces we had under MacArthur already facing overwhelming Japanese strength in the Philippines, with the British and Dutch empires in the Far East crumbling like houses of

[4]

cards, and with our fleet battered into impotence at Pearl Harbor, the situation had undergone a sharp transformation. Dazed Washington awoke suddenly to the bitter realization that it was unable to furnish to the Middle East the men and materials it had so confidently contracted, out of its seeming abundance, to supply short weeks before.

Under these conditions, we of the Middle East project were ordered to proceed as before laid out, with civilian personnel, in spite of all the drawbacks involved in their use under war conditions. In the holocaust which had so unexpectedly enveloped us, our trifling existing armed forces, whether on sea or land, were already being mobilized to save Hawaii and even America itself from threatened invasion.

We did the best we could. Under the overall direction of Major General Russell Maxwell already in Egypt (who commanded the entire project and to whom I was ordered to report for duty), those involved, both Army and Navy, proceeded to gather up what scraps they could obtain for the work in hand.

My part got under way under particularly depressing circumstances. I was informed by the Navy Department that other than my own assignment, the Navy was in no position now to lend aid to the Middle East task. No other naval officers, trained or untrained in salvage, were available for assignment to me as assistants. No naval enlisted personnel, salvage or otherwise, were available for detail then, nor were any to be expected later. For help, if any, I must look to the Army, where naturally enough it did not exist, or to such civilians as I might hire before the Navy, badly pressed itself for salvage men, snapped them up for its own overwhelming problems.

In the Navy Department I was handed my orders. I was directed to report in Egypt to General Maxwell, commanding the North African Mission, to act as Officer in Charge of the Red Sea salvage operations and as Commanding Officer of such naval bases as might be established there. With that piece of paper as the solitary aid the Navy was able to lend then or ever to the project, I left the Navy Department and reported myself to the Army for duty.

One thing only lightened the gloom of my complete lack of any naval assistance. Rear Admiral Bruce, giving me my orders, informed me that in view of the importance of my double assignment, the Navy Department was promoting me immediately to my former rank of

[5]

commander. This, he thought, might help me somewhat in my dealings both with the Army and with the British, where, no less than in the Navy itself, rank was not wholly ignored.

What was intended? I learned quickly enough from my Army associates in the Mission. Prime Minister Churchill, master of Allied strategy, had put his finger on the Middle East as the crucial area in this war.

There a century and a half ago, Napoleon, in an earlier effort to make himself ruler of the world, had sought to crash through Egypt and Syria to India until Admiral Lord Nelson had crushed his fleet and his hopes at Aboukir Bay. There in World War I, Kaiser Wilhelm II and the Turks combined had sought the same object till stopped by Lawrence in Arabia and Allenby in Palestine. There Hitler and Mussolini now, with their joint forces under Rommel, ace commander and military idol of the totalitarians, were preparing to drive eastward through Libya toward Egypt, the Suez Canal, and the overland route to India and the East.

Britain, already strained to the breaking point by Dunkirk and the aerial blitz of England by Goering's bombers, by her disastrous rout in Greece, and her bloody defeat on land and sea at Crete, was fighting now in the Libyan sands a last-ditch battle. At all hazards, she must avoid the certain ruin that would follow the irruption into Egypt and then into Iran and India of Rommel's legions and all that would ensue.

For that meant making of the Mediterranean an Axis lake. It meant the loss of the priceless oil fields of Irak and Iran to the Nazis who most of all needed oil for their war machines, and would no longer have to stage a major campaign to wrest Baku from Russia to get it. It meant the severance of the solitary supply line into southern Russia via the Persian Gulf, through which both we and Britain were pouring aid through Iran to the hard-pressed Russians fighting desperately to stem the Nazi armies driving on Moscow, and that severance meant the collapse of the Soviets.

Lastly, it meant the loss of India, the loss of all contact with the Far East, the loss of all possible bases and routes for the supply of China which was holding in combat and away from us, the bulk of the Japanese army. Briefly, the loss of the Middle East meant the swift loss of the war and it meant a totalitarian and Axis world.

To back up Britain for the coming blow in the fall of 1941, and to save Russia, Averell Harriman, President Roosevelt's agent, had arranged as a Lend-lease project the North African Mission which was intended first only to provide the bases from which hard-pressed Britain might fight. But now that we were in the war, these were bases from which we also might fight when the day came that we had mustered some land and air forces to fight with, provided meanwhile we could keep Britain hanging on by her fingernails till that day came.

CHAPTER

3

SPECIFICALLY, MY JOB WAS TO create a naval base at Massawa in Eritrea on the Red Sea and to salvage the wrecks there. The salvage was partly to clear the harbor of Massawa, partly to recover the priceless ships the Axis had scuttled, for further Allied use.

Massawa, thoroughly sabotaged by the Axis, lay two-thirds the way down the Red Sea from Suez toward Aden. It had the best harbor in all the Red Sea and practically the only one suitable for a naval base able to support operations in the eastern Mediterranean.

Ancient Massawa lay on the hot Red Sea coastal desert, athwart the traffic stream passing via Suez between Europe and Asia. The north coast of the Red Sea bordering Arabia has no harbors at all. The south coast has only two, Port Sudan in the Anglo-Egyptian condominium of the Sudan, and Massawa in Eritrea, far superior to Port Sudan in natural facilities, in strategic location, and in protected berthing space for large ships.

In 1881, Italy had bought a foothold on the arid Eritrean coast line from the impoverished Turks who saw no value in it at all. This was the first step in the crack-brained Italian dream of building up again an African empire. Suffering even then from the delusions of grandeur which later were to flower fully under Mussolini, Italy had then set out from Massawa to conquer the hinterland, Ethiopia. However, at Adowa, in 1896, the spears and guns of Ethiopian warriors had slaughtered King Humbert's army and put an abrupt period to Italian ambitions in East Africa. Not again for forty years did Italy venture away from the barren Eritrean coast line.

But in the early 1930's, Mussolini, deluded by the screaming mobs before the Palazzo Venezia that he was Caesar reincarnated, destined to revive the glories of vanished Rome, started again on the path of

[8]

East African conquest.

Italy was bled white to provide the gold poured into the ancient slave-trading Arab village of Massawa to convert it into a modern port from which a new Ethiopian campaign might be launched and supported. And even more important, from Mussolini's viewpoint, to build in Massawa a strong Italian naval base. From that, submarines, destroyers, cruisers, and novel fast motor torpedo boats could dominate the vital Red Sea route.

It was Mussolini's belief this would blackmail Britain into keeping her hands off while Ethiopia was being overrun. Otherwise she ran the risk of having her exposed lifeline to the East severed by that well-protected Italian hornets' nest planted in the north harbor of Massawa, invulnerable behind extensive mine fields, reefs, and sheltering islands to any attack from seaward by Britain's fleet.

The scheme had worked. After years of preparation, during which Italian matrons had been stripped even of their wedding rings to get the gold to pay for it, Massawa had blossomed into a modern harbor. Everywhere sprouted massive stone quays, electric unloading cranes, substantial naval shops, warehouses packed with naval stores, airfields, submarine piers, mine and torpedo depots, coast defense guns, and—most sinister of all—a magnificent automobile highway leading inland over the mountains toward the Abyssinian frontier.

In the fall of 1935 came a three-pronged attack. First, in Geneva, Fascist orators poured out poisonous sophistries to benumb the conscience of the world. Next, from Massawa, Italian submarine flotillas straddled the trade routes to the East to point up the unwisdom of British interference. Then in Ethiopia Mussolini's cowardly legions assaulted the natives with poison gas from planes against which the guns, the spears, the shields of Haile Selassie's valiantly resisting warriors were no defense.

So Mussolini (though not without great difficulty due to Fascist incompetence even in so unequal a battle) had conquered. And after the conquest, in preparation for the economic exploitation of Ethiopian resources, Massawa, the solitary Italian outlet to the sea from that rich plateau, had been developed even further as a port.

Thus matters stood when Adolf Hitler, in 1939, thrusting unceremoniously into the background Europe's first loudspeaker for totalitarianism, started World War II. Promptly into Massawa harbor had rushed for sanctuary such German vessels in Red Sea or Indian Ocean waters as could get there. In Massawa, safe under the neutral and friendly Italian flag, they were to await the overthrow of Britain.

In the spring of 1940 came Dunkirk. Mussolini, fearful that he might miss even the crumbs of the French and British debacle, plunged uninvited by Hitler into what was left of the conflict, lest he get no glory or loot at all in the death of world democracy. Put pending the dying gasp of Britain, which at sea was still potent, every Italian vessel east of Suez had rushed also for the protection of the mine fields of Massawa before Mussolini took the plunge. There in safety they awaited the swift capitulation of the defeated French and British.

France surrendered. But to the incredulous amazement of both dumbfounded dictators, the irrational British not only refused to recognize their crushing defeat and the hopelessness of further resistance to Fuehrer and Duce, but even, where they could, took the offensive. Churchill, true to his 1940 promise to Mussolini that if Italy came into the struggle Britain would tear Italy's empire to shreds, started in to make good his words by attacking in East Africa.

Ethiopia and Eritrea were most vulnerable to British assault, and so long as Britain held Suez, incapable of support from Italy. And, therefore, it came about while England itself was being bled to death and burned to ashes by Hermann Goering's Luftwaffe, that Britain herself was setting the grand pattern for later victory in the Pacific islands and North Africa by isolating a given body of enemy troops from its home forces and then concentrating on them the necessary strength to wipe them out.

The soldiers of Britain's empire, South African, East Indian, Sudanese, Scotch, and the English themselves, aided by a Free French legion, attacked East Africa from west, from south, from east, while Britain's navy blockaded from the north on the Red Sea. At Cheren, the gateway to Eritrea from the Sudan, Scotch, Bengalis, and Sikhs, scaling unscalable heights at night guarding the rocky pass, in one of the most brilliant assaults in all military history, swept the Italians from the heights and smashed a path into Eritrea.

The badly routed Italians fled southward into Ethiopia, soon to surrender there, while the British swept forward into Asmara, capital of Eritrea, and looked down from its mountain plateau onto coastal Massawa, forty airline miles away and 7000 feet below.

[10]

As a military measure, the Italians on the coast, with the mountainous terrain between favoring them, could have put up a fierce defense of Massawa. But there was no fight left in the cowardly Fascisti; sabotage was more in keeping with their character. While they parleyed for surrender terms with the British advancing slowly through fields of land mines, they carried through the most widespread program of organized destruction yet seen in any war.

In the three harbors of Massawa and in its off-lying islands lay a fleet of some forty vessels, German and Italian. Freighters, passenger ships, warships, crowded every berth, while in addition, in the north harbor were two irreplaceable floating steel dry docks.

A tornado of explosions swept the Massawa waterfront as exploding bombs, strategically placed far below their waterlines, blew out the sides and bottoms of ships by the dozens. The priceless floating dry docks received special attention, fourteen heavy bombs being planted in them to insure not only their sinking but their total destruction. The invaluable machinery in the naval shops was smashed with sledge hammers. Electric cranes were tipped into the sea. Everything in the way of destruction that Italian ingenuity could suggest to make Massawa forever useless to its approaching conquerors was painstakingly carried through.

Finally, placed as carefully as possible, bow to stern, strings of large ships were scuttled in rows to block the harbor entrance. When the last bomb had gone up and the last ship had gone down, the Italian admiral commanding rubbed his hands in satisfaction over such a mass of scuttled ships as the world had never seen before. Then he surrendered Massawa and its smashed naval base as being not worth even one shot fired in its defense.

Massawa fell in April, 1941, useless to the entering British.

Such was the situation in far-off Massawa when, in the autumn of 1941, the threat to Alexandria from Rommel's Afrika Korps attacking from Benghazi made it imperative to get another naval base from which British Mediterranean forces could operate in case Rommel immobilized Alexandria as a base by air attack. Massawa, smashed as it was, was still the only possible large harbor close enough for support, far enough away to be safe from short range Stuka bombers.

Britain badly needed Massawa in operation. But Britain, with its own coasts strewn with wrecks and struggling to keep its home har-

bors open against constant German aerial mining, had not the men nor salvage ships to spare for Massawa. Neutral America assumed the obligation. But hardly had we assumed it than we found ourselves at war and in worse case for men and ships than Britain herself, if that were possible.

CHAPTER

4

M Y FIRST NEED WAS DIVING GEAR AND salvage equipment to work with, and machinery to replace the sabotaged outfits of the Massawa naval shops. My second was divers. My third was salvage mechanics and salvage masters. And my fourth was salvage ships from which to work. With America mobilizing for its own defense, getting these things for the Red Sea, remote from any theater of war on which American eyes were fixed, was a nightmare. Aided by W. E. Flanagan, a small package of pure TNT, I started in. Without Flanagan's fiery activities, little would have been procured at all.

Naturally enough all the salvage gear and salvage equipment already in stock in America was moving toward Pearl Harbor. All I could do, even with the high priority I had, was order what I needed from overburdened manufacturers, to be delivered at seaboard in two to four months (if I was lucky), ready for shipment to Africa, which would take several additional months. So I made up long lists of diving gear, air compressors, tools of all kinds, underwater cutting torches—thousands of items—and had the purchase orders placed for the best possible delivery.

When it came to getting machinery to replace that the Italians had smashed in the Massawa naval shops, I was in as bad case. There was none, and every existing shipyard in the United States, plus the dozens of new ones, were all screaming for shipyard machinery for instant use. Here also there was nothing to be done except to order a complete set of machinery for shipyard shops to be fabricated and trust to my priority to give me my share of what was turned out, when months later, the swamped manufacturers completed some.

Next came divers. Diving is a peculiar trade, and divers are scarce animals even in peacetime American economy. What few the Navy had as enlisted men, whom I had once worked with, were en route to Pearl Harbor, barred to me. Via every possible channel I proceeded to track down all known civilian divers in the United States.

I found that practically every one was already employed on America's pre-war defense plans, mostly on underwater work in connection with new naval dry docks being excavated on all our coasts. Not even the seductive inmates of Oriental harems were more jealously guarded by their lords and masters from predatory males than were these civilian divers from any contact with seekers after their services elsewhere.

Just for an attempted discussion with their contracting employer as to whether two divers out of over a dozen working on a pair of dry docks at the New York Navy Yard, might not be released for a navy job elsewhere, I was violently denounced and threatened with a court-martial by the Navy captain in charge. In the ensuing fiery tête-à-tête, regardless of the justice of my cause, my new three gold stripes cut only a sorry figure as against his four. I got no divers there.

Still nothing daunted by this rebuff, from Maine to Florida, from New York to California, I wrote, telephoned, telegraphed, and rushed across the country to interview any civilian who claimed to be a diver not already working on a naval project. On the whole Atlantic Coast I got one. But in Hollywood, of all places, comparatively speaking I hit the jackpot. There, working for various movie studios, I found four men with records as divers, who, apparently only because the prospect I had to offer seemed even more outlandish than what they were then doing in the world of make-believe, signed up with me.

So I had five divers. Not many, compared to the minimum of thirty or forty needed to cover my task effectively, but at least something to start with.

Salvage mechanics were just as non-existent, but there, at any rate, I could hope to train any good mechanic for the task. The Army's Middle East contractor thoroughly searched the entire field, hired thirteen for me and promised to get at least fifty more.

Salvage masters, to direct the individual operations on each ship, were even harder to find. Those few unemployed but qualified by experience and able to make the physical grade, the Navy was swallowing. The rest were already under Navy control by a salvage company to which the Navy had given a contract for all war salvage along our own coasts.

In all America I was able to locate only two competent prospects for salvage masters, both rugged individualists once employed by large salvage corporations, but now lone wolves. That both were unable, due to age or other physical causes, to get by the Navy's medical officers, was the only reason they were left to me. I snapped them up before the Navy might lower its physical standards, and snatch even these two. Bill Reed, getting far along in years and blind in one eye from diving, and Edison Brown, younger but with a weakened pair of legs probably from the same cause, were my sole recruits.

Then, while I was struggling to get men, there was always before me the problem of getting salvage ships. This turned out to be the most hopeless of all. What I needed was three or four vessels, small enough to work handily over and alongside sunken wrecks, big enough to make the voyage of 13,000 miles around Africa to the other side of the world. Large ocean tugs would suit best, but there were none available.

My acquisition of Brown as a salvage master eased one of my problems, and for a brief time looked as if it might also ease the salvage tug problem. Brown owned his own salvage vessel, an old converted tug called the *Retriever*, which had voyaged some thousands of miles in the Pacific. Practically his whole crew of eleven men, including one good diver, Buck Scougale, volunteered to ship with me, and were all promptly engaged. Brown offered to sell me the *Retriever* also for the job, and as I urgently needed ships, I agreed to buy her for his use at Massawa, subject only to one condition: Brown had to deliver the *Retriever* in the Red Sea before he got paid for her.

Brown thought that over a while, then shook his head. He doubted he could keep the old *Retriever* afloat till she got to the Red Sea. So he sold her locally in Los Angeles and I agreed that the first suitable tug I got, he and his crew were to have. Then hastily departing from Los Angeles, I continued my search for salvage ships.

In my travels, I scanned every piece of floating junk offered, from Cuba to Newfoundland and in the Pacific, which from its size gave even a scant hope of use. Ancient trawlers serving as molasses boats in Cuba; ancient yachts, converted to houseboats in Florida; ancient lighthouse tenders long since condemned and sold out of service— all these I examined, in spite of the fabulous prices asked, for nothing

[15]

else was remotely obtainable.

But all had to be rejected. Either the rusty hulls would certainly disintegrate once they hit the open sea, or the decrepit machinery could by no stretch of the imagination last out a thousand miles of ocean voyaging, let alone the 13,000 miles required.

One vessel I had, though it gave me slight comfort. My predecessor on the assignment, before there was any war and before he had set out by air for the Red Sea only to end his trip at Pearl Harbor, had contracted for a small Pacific Coast lumber-carrying steamer, the *W. L. Chamberlin Jr.,* of 3000 tons displacement. She was suitable (after radical changes) for a base supply ship and a floating repair shop, but she was much too big and unwieldy for salvage work herself.

This white elephant was in San Diego, being outfitted for the purpose, and I had about concluded that we should have to work from rowboats and rafts based on the *Chamberlin,* when Providence at last lent a hand.

I received a telephone call from Rear Admiral J. W. S. Dorling, Royal Navy, Chief of the British Naval Mission in Washington, to see him there. He knew, of course, better than anyone else, that I was seeking salvage ships for the Middle East, and how urgently they were needed there. Dubiously he offered me a ship for the job, such as it was.

It seems that months before, he had been ordered from London to contract for half a dozen small harbor tugs of a standard American design to be built at Port Arthur, Texas, for emergency salvage serv- ice in England. The first one was rapidly approaching completion; it had been scheduled to be finished in late January, 1942. But the British crew, sent over to take this first ship back to England, looking now at their tiny craft actually in the water, had decided they could never safely get across the stormy north Atlantic with her, especially in winter time, and the whole lot were rejected. That left Admiral Dorling with six tugboats in various stages of completion on his hands and no longer any use for them. If I thought I could use one, he would make me a gift of the first tug completed.

I looked at the blueprints. The tugs certainly were small, of only 78 tons net register, about the size of the tiny caravels in which Columbus had discovered America. They were just under 100 feet long, but because of their harbor design, their freeboard was trifling, much less than that of Columbus' caravels—the squat decks of these tugs were hardly three feet clear of the waterline amidships. But they had General Motors diesel-powered electric drives of 1200 horsepower and stout welded steel hulls. Tiny they certainly were, even for harbor work, but they were powerful and they were new. After the mass of rusting junk fit only for the scrap heap, the paper-thin hulls and the antediluvian machinery I had been inspecting, these new tugs positively intoxicated me.

Could I use one? I was desperate. Hastily I assured Admiral Dorling they were exactly the right size (which was true, for if they had been any bigger he would never have been able to offer one to me, and if they had been any smaller, hard up as I was, even I should never have dared attempting to send one on a 13,000-mile voyage over the open sea).

But while I had any luck, I determined to press it hard. Certainly I could use one. Still, while he was giving them away, why stop at taking one? Promptly I told Admiral Dorling I would take three.

Dorling was willing enough but he had already half promised the other five to our Navy for use as tugboats in American harbors. He would see what he could do. Finally, he was able to effect a compromise, giving me the first and third tugs done, and our Navy the rest. So I came into possession of two cockle-shells, already named by the British the *Intent* and the *Resolute,* titles which I hoped might prove good augury on their coming odysseys. Hurriedly I despatched a telegram to my new salvage master, Brown, in Los Angeles, saying I had a ship for him, and directing him to proceed immediately with his crew to take over the nearly finished *Intent* and sail with her the moment she was outfitted, probably in late February.

I scanned again the blueprints of the two tiny tugs that now were mine, then the map. Thirteen thousand miles by sea from Port Arthur, Texas, around the Cape of Good Hope to Massawa! Heaven help us all!

CHAPTER

5

My feverish search for men, for materials, for ships, had taken some weeks. But by the end of January, I had at least the rudiments of what was wanted for salvage and the machinery on order for the rebirth of the naval base.

I was then ordered by the Army to depart by air for Massawa via Egypt, to get acquainted with the situation on the ground. Meanwhile, Mr. Flanagan, my energetic assistant, would hire what additional men he could for me and attend to the forwarding of my ships and my materials.

Transportation by air in those early dismal days of the war turned out to be not so certain. I was given a high enough priority for an assured seat in a military plane (there were no others) going east for the Atlantic hop, via Brazil to Africa. But day after day in early February went by with no notice to report for departure.

Unofficially I soon learned the reason. So desperate was the Army need for fighter pilots in the far Pacific that every Army pilot of any flying experience at all was being gathered for combat there in a last-ditch attempt to stem the Japanese torrent flooding the Philippines and Indonesia, and threatening to engulf Australia. The result was that the new four-engined Fortresses, the only planes capable of carrying passengers, being ferried east to India and Australia over the south Atlantic, were of necessity going out with immature Army pilots who had barely completed their training courses.

Under these conditions, the number of Fortresses that crashed en route was startling (or perhaps it wasn't). However, since several Government missions flying as passengers in these planes had been lost with them, a secret order had gone out excluding further passengers till something could be done to reduce the crash rate.

Barring a miracle, and none were being worked in favor of the unready United States in those days, my departure by air seemed uncertain and my safe arrival in Africa that way even more so. It was a considerable relief then to learn that the Army had chartered a merchant vessel and its crew to sail February 16 for West Africa, carrying personnel for its various projects in the Middle East. Since I was now with the Army, I might go on her or by air as I chose. Naturally, as a sailor I chose to go by sea.

The *S.S. Pig's Knuckle* (to give the ship the nickname by which she was soon unaffectionately known by some of her passengers) was of 5600 tons gross register, small as passenger liners go, built sixteen years before for the coastal run between Florida and Boston. Heavily wrapped in overcoats and burdened down with our hand baggage, we boarded her in a cold, drizzling winter rain on the scheduled sailing day, February 16, to find her a madhouse. She was still cluttered with shipyard mechanics engaged in finishing fitting her out with guns, with black-out screens, life rafts, extra lifeboat davits and extra boats for her first wartime cruise.

The start of the voyage was inauspicious. The passenger list was about 380, divided about equally between Army personnel (both officers and enlisted men) and civilians under Army contract for the Middle East projects. This was somewhat over the 300 passengers the ship was designed to accommodate, but the overcrowding was not bad. What was bad was that the ship, with all the workmen on her and with a newly shipped crew, was unready to receive any passengers.

To make that matter worse, many of the civilian passengers, under no discipline at all, either from celebrating their departure or drowning their grief over it, came aboard badly drunk. Between the drunks and the workmen banging away with hammers till midnight on the superstructure, rushing to finish their job, the situation on the ship was not such as to create a favorable first impression on those sober enough to pay some attention to the vessel and her crew.

Still less was this impression improved when the shipyard men (against the captain's protests) cleared off in the middle of the night, leaving the boat deck a cluttered mess of partly rigged and hardly usable lifeboats, in miserable shape for lowering. This situation her surly seamen (mostly just shipped) very unwillingly and very ineffectively tackled.

What seemed to be the whole Nazi U-boat navy had taken advantage of the combined golden opportunities of our unreadiness for war and the chance to shift from the wintry north Atlantic, where weather and the British patrols together made submarine operations difficult, to the Gulf Stream where they were easy. U-boats by the dozen had descended a few days before on our shores. As they were sinking American ships along our unprotected southern coast in sickening numbers, the immediate usability of our lifeboats was an important factor in our lives, though from the slovenly fashion in which the merchant seaman went at readying them, one would never have guessed it. Our ship was just as likely (perhaps even more so) to be torpedoed the moment she poked her nose into the Gulf Stream south of Cape Hatteras as out in mid-ocean a week or two later.

In that shape, on the afternoon of February 17, having been hung up by fog from midnight till noon, we got under way for the lower harbor. In bitterly cold weather, we slid slowly past the Battery for our last look at Manhattan and shortly were passing St. George on Staten Island.

A lump rose in my throat. There, anchored off St. George, lay the *U.S.S. Texas,* just in from convoy duty in the Atlantic. Twenty-seven years before, as an ensign just out of the Naval Academy, I had joined the battleship *Texas,* then newly commissioned. Enviously I gazed at my old ship, grimly effective in her modernized rig for a leading part in the war, looking the very symbol of disciplined power, so different from the ill-manned tub I now knew I was aboard.

We dropped anchor ourselves in Gravesend Bay, where an ammunition barge came alongside to transfer to us the ammunition for our newly installed guns. Getting that aboard with freezing spray coming over constantly to interfere, a task for the Armed Guard seamen the Navy had put aboard for the guns' crews, took the rest of the day.

Next morning, still in freezing weather, we swung ship around the Ambrose Channel Lightship to calibrate magnetic and radio compasses. By early afternoon we were under way at last (so we thought) for Africa, headed south, steaming by ourselves. But we were escorted at least by a Navy blimp, the K-6, which circled slowly overhead to detect any lurking U-boats. Further to bolster our confidence, Ensign McCausland of the Navy, in charge of the Armed Guard, promptly posted his men at war stations, and to be sure they were ready for action, test fired all his guns.

For a ship of our size, we were well armed. We had a 4-inch gun (evidently removed from some World War I destroyer) on our stern, a 3-inch high angle anti-aircraft gun on our forecastle, two .50-caliber anti-aircraft machine guns on the superstructure aft, and two more .30-caliber anti-aircraft machine guns on the bridge. Against a possible Nazi air raider or any U-boat trying to overhaul us from astern in a surface attack with guns, we were well protected.

But against a submerged attack with torpedoes by a U-boat (when our guns would be useless), we were as helpless as a lamb. Our slow speed (thirteen knots) would allow any U-boat which ever sighted us from ahead to get into torpedo firing position submerged and undetected. And we were of such moderate size as ships go, that one torpedo meant our doom. I began to take a deep interest in our lifeboats and their condition.

For us, our only safety lay in a strong convoy of destroyers or in our keeping far away from every area in which the U-boats were reported operating. But except for the blimp, we had no convoy. Still I found soon there was little cause for immediate concern. We weren't really going to sea—yet.

A few hours' run down the Jersey coast and we ducked into Delaware Bay for the night, there to anchor till daylight. Then down we went through the Delaware-Chesapeake Canal, safely landlocked from U-boats, into Chesapeake Bay. Down that we steamed, still landlocked, past Annapolis to Hampton Roads, where again we anchored to await a calibration of our newly installed degaussing system, intended to protect us against magnetic mines.

By now I was acquainted to some degree with both the ship's officers and with my shipmates for the voyage. Senior on board for the Army was Major General C. L. Scott, an ex-cavalry officer, now of the mechanized forces, going to Egypt to study British (and Nazi) tank tactics at close range.

Aside from General Scott, all the Army officers aboard were destined for General Maxwell's Middle East Command, ranging from Colonel Earl Gruver through all ranks down to the junior second lieutenant, Jerbi, going out as dental officer for the Mission. With them came a collection of Army non-coms of all grades and a few privates, to bring the Army personnel up to about 200 all told.

Of the 180 civilian passengers carried, a few were supervisors for the contractors and the rest were mechanics and clerical personnel destined for various parts of the project, though none were my own salvage men. My personnel, particularly the mechanics, were supposed to come out with the salvage ships as their crews.

General Scott promptly got his military passengers and their routine strictly organized to lend a hand in emergency both to the Armed Guard and to the ship's company in handling boats. But the civilian passengers, governed by the top supervisor for the contractor, were left free to rest themselves on the voyage.

In Hampton Roads, on the morning of February 20, while we were awaiting our turn on the degaussing calibration course, the first friction on the ship arose. As a vitally interested passenger who had some knowledge of the subject, I pointed out to General Scott, the senior officer aboard, the scandalous condition our lifeboats were still in, improperly stowed and questionably rigged for lowering, and with a new crew which seemed to know little about the boats and from their lack of attention to them, to care even less. I suggested a lifeboat drill, with all the boats actually swung out while we were at anchor, to test their readiness in an emergency.

This seemed reasonable enough and important to the general, who sent Colonel Earl Gruver, acting as his Chief of Staff for the voyage, to the skipper with a request for a full dress lifeboat test.

Colonel Gruver, a quiet, very self-possessed, dark-complexioned officer, set off on his mission to the bridge in his usual imperturbable manner, while General Scott and I discussed the pros and cons of degaussing belts as protection against the new magnetic mines the Nazis would sooner or later (later, we hoped) lay off all our harbors. This was an intricate subject so that we hardly noticed how long Gruver had been gone when he suddenly entered the general's cabin, very red in the face, in spite of his dark complexion.

"That skipper of ours is certainly a belligerent boy, General," reported the colonel. "I had hardly presented your compliments to him and made your request, when the captain practically exploded in my face to tell me the lifeboats were none of the general's business, nor of any other passenger's, either!" Gruver looked significantly at me. "But I stayed with him, sir, in spite of his bullying, and there'll be a lifeboat drill at 11:00 A.M."

There was, and it turned out as I had suspected. Three of the ship's largest lifeboats absolutely refused to lift out of their chocks and go overboard. It developed the boat falls on two of these had carelessly been rove off backwards. On the third boat, a davit was improperly assembled. It would take hours to reverse the wire boat falls on the lowering drums and to refit the davit before those three boats could be used.

The other eleven boats were, with some difficulty, broken out of their chocks and dropped flush with the rail, ready to take on passengers, in about five minutes. Not good, but not bad either, provided our ship, if torpedoed, stayed afloat and on a reasonably even keel for five long minutes, which could hardly be counted on.

After this fiasco, I had hoped nothing further would be required for the ship immediately to cure the entire boat situation, but it turned out otherwise. True, the chagrined mates turned to, to re-reeve the improperly rove off falls and to refit the davit so all the boats could be swung out, but no attention went to checking or stowing properly the oars and equipment each boat would badly need in a hurry if ever it went overboard. I was amazed that the crew was so little concerned regarding their instant effectiveness in an emergency, especially now that war and torpedoes had multiplied radically the possibility of that emergency arising.

However, when nothing was done by the crew to overhaul the boat gear, General Scott detailed a squad of soldiers, aided by a group of carpenters and riggers among the passengers, to do the job themselves. Whatever the captain thought of this concern of his passengers for their own safety, in spite of his previous outburst to Colonel Gruver over the lifeboats, he now said nothing as the passengers turned to on what was the crew's work. At any rate, by next evening, when we had concluded all our degaussing tests and anchored just inside Cape Henry preparatory to final departure, the boats were all properly stowed at last and ready for use, so that if the worst happened, at least we would not have to swim.

CHAPTER

6

Early Sunday morning, February 22, 1942, with every passenger wearing a life jacket (which by General Scott's order he was to wear or keep at hand night and day the rest of the voyage), we stood out between the Chesapeake Capes, bound for Africa at last. On our itinerary as laid out on departure from New York, we had been scheduled to make a stop at Trinidad for refueling. But because of strong U-boat attacks of the last few days inside the Caribbean off Aruba and Trinidad, the routing was now changed by the naval authorities in Norfolk. The ship was directed to proceed to San Juan, Porto Rico, instead, for an intermediate refueling.

Since in addition, this change would keep us away from the dangerous Florida coast, in which area the unopposed Nazi U-boats were running wild, with another sinking reported only the night before off Jupiter Inlet, and several blazing oil tankers, set on fire by torpedoes, reported drifting northward, abandoned and helpless in the Gulf Stream in plain sight of shore, it is easily understandable with what relief this change in routing was greeted by the passengers.

We stood out in the face of a freezing wind past Cape Henry, bound southeast to clear Cape Hatteras, steaming by ourselves, unconvoyed, and with the knowledge now that we should have no convoy at any stage, for the Navy had no destroyers to spare for escorts. Our safety was to depend solely on our ability to avoid attack or on our guns and our Armed Guard crews in case we failed in avoidance. As one sailor who had considerable knowledge of submarines to another, I went to see our skipper for a discussion on how best he might minimize the danger of U-boat contacts.

I found the skipper rather difficult to talk to. He had a distrust (not uncommon among merchant officers of that day or before) of all naval officers as being not really practical seamen and perhaps with exaggerated notions also of their own importance and abilities. Furthermore, this particular skipper turned out to be an irascible individual, with whom no one, not even his own mates, could take a point of view even slightly differing from his own, without evoking instantly a most bellicose attitude which made further discussion of the subject unpleasant, if not impossible.

He was a large man physically, round-faced, red-faced, and apparently nearing sixty. But in spite of all his years, he had evidently never learned that authority comes from a quiet inner assurance of superior knowledge and capability and not from blustering.

In background, I learned that he had put in his entire life at sea in the coasting service. Never apparently (till the voyage he was now engaged on) had he been off soundings on an open ocean voyage (nor had his ship, which he had captained for the last sixteen years).

Still, as diplomatically as I knew how, seated comfortably in the captain's cabin over the mid-morning coffee, I opened the subject of submarines and their operating limitations in attack. On this subject I certainly could claim more knowledge than the captain and could inform him how he might take advantage of those limitations in avoiding contact. In particular, I told him I was gratified by our new destination, San Juan, which would help by taking us far away, in that winter season, from the warm coastal areas and the traffic concentrations which joined to make the Florida coast most attractive just then for U-boat operations.

"Well, you're wrong on our route, Commander," announced the skipper. "I'm following the Florida coast down to Cuba, then along the Cuban coast to Porto Rico."

Had the skipper heaved his cup of hot coffee into my face, I could not have been taken more aback. Incredulously I stared at him. Take a longer and very roundabout course through dangerous coastal waters to Porto Rico rather than the direct and safer route over the open sea? I could hardly believe my ears.

Then slowly the situation dawned on me. The skipper was like the old milk wagon horse, which all its life, day after day, had followed the same prosaic milk route till it was second nature. So when it was finally taken out for a Sunday joy ride hauling a buggy, it still persisted obstinately in dragging the buggy over the milk route, making every stop, ignoring the driver's frantic tugs at the reins, trying to get

[25]

it out into the country.

I saw it all. No more than with that milk wagon horse was it possible to get the skipper off the old familiar route. To the skipper, the route down the coast to Miami was also second nature—for thirty-five years, more or less, he had traveled it voyage after voyage. No war and no U-boats were going to get him and his ship off the route he knew, into strange waters.

I sank back into my chair, smothered my astonishment. I had to get the skipper to change his mind. Sure that I had correctly estimated his motives and that no harping on the U-boat dangers along his intended course would do anything but antagonize him and stiffen his ill-advised disregard of those dangers, I took another tack.

As casually as I could, making as light as possible of the U-boat situation, I pointed out that sooner or later to get to Africa we were bound to have to leave the waters the captain knew, for the open ocean. And it might just as well be sooner, for he was not going to gain what he thought in hugging the coast.

With a savage war at sea already raging, all the coastal lighthouses which made practically a broad White Way of the Florida coast, were surely now extinguished to avoid aiding the U-boats. Without those friendly lights the Florida coast would be strange and dangerous ground to him, not the familiar waters he had piloted over so many years. And to that argument, I added what others I could on saving fuel and saving time by the shorter route.

What finally convinced the skipper, I don't know—probably it was the vision of that well-known Florida coast suddenly become the unknowable. At any rate, after much pondering he reluctantly agreed to head directly for San Juan, and with a sigh of deep relief, I thanked him for the coffee and immediately left his cabin. It seemed an unpropitious time to go generally into submarine dangers, of which the captain apparently was deeply contemptuous, lest he become enraged and reverse his decision on the course.

I got hurriedly out of the captain's cabin to find that I was just in time to attend divine services which were being held that Sunday morning at eleven in the main dining room. Having something to give thanks for, I went below to attend.

I found Major Abraham Goff of the Army—long, lanky Abe Goff, in physique and warm human sympathy for everybody not a bad counterpart of Honest Abe himself—officiating extemporaneously as chaplain, with some thirty or forty mixed soldiers and civilians as his small congregation. Recollecting the old maxim that the faith of the sailor has always been in inverse ratio to his faith in his ship, I could only judge that if more of our 380 passengers knew as much about our ship and her officers and crew as I now did, the attendance would be greater. Reverently I bowed my head as Major Goff, impromptu chaplain, led us in prayer.

CHAPTER

7

As we stood southeast away from the Capes before a moderate westerly breeze, the freezing chill of the air began to moderate and by afternoon it began to seem there were some signs that we were leaving winter behind. At this I had no regrets (then) as, since leaving New York, I had already picked up a bad cold in the head. Besides, I was getting quite tired of going about all the time in a heavy Navy overcoat, which was a damned encumbrance to a life jacket, especially if one had suddenly to go overboard.

But if the weather was getting better as the afternoon wore on and darkness fell and in our wake, America disappeared over the horizon, the war situation and the danger on the sea seemed to grow worse. The air waves crackled with news of mounting disaster. Into the radio room came reports of new torpedoings off Jupiter Inlet, Florida, calls from distant ships in distress, gruesome reports from shore of burning and derelict tankers drifting with the current, lighting up the evening skies like mammoth torches.

By supper time we were well clear of Cape Hatteras and standing across the Gulf Stream into warmer weather, on the deep sea at last. Every other vessel had vanished from sight and we were alone on the ocean. I sniffed the warm air, went into my cabin to throw aside my overcoat for the last time for months to come, and beginning to feel much safer, though I still clung to my life jacket, I went below to supper.

Meals on our ship were nothing to look forward to. Because of a greater passenger list than the dining room could accommodate, we ate in two sections, with an interval between sittings to clear up and reset the tables. That situation never bothered me, for, as one of the senior officers, I dined in the first section. What bothered everyone was that the steward's department was as slovenly and lackadaisical as the deck force—the cooking was atrocious, the service the same.

In spite of the fact that the Army was paying the steamship line $650 apiece as the passage for everybody aboard from general through civilians down to privates (which is considerably more than a first class passenger fare on an expensive luxury liner), the food served would have suited better a laborers' camp in the backwoods. Our meals alternated mainly between unappetizing stew, corned beef and cabbage, frankfurters and sauerkraut, and pig's knuckles and cabbage.

This last dish was evidently the chief cook's favorite. It was served so frequently that as the passengers' disgust with the ship grew, she was shortly nicknamed the S.S. *Pig's Knuckle*, which, I may say, aptly characterized her.

More pig's knuckles for supper. As the weather had warmed up considerably outside, they were even less inviting than usual. I made a wry face and turned to. We could live on frankfurters, pig's knuckles, etc., and surely before the war was over, we should fare worse. But what irritated all hands was the fact that with the ship being paid a huge sum for first class fare for everybody, the operators had nevertheless provisioned her for fourth class immigrants.

The slapdash stewards carelessly slung on the food, served on none too clean dishes. There was no point in complaining to the purser about the service—it had already been frequently done, only to bring from the purser and the chief steward both, the plaintive reply that they had no control over their assistants and could get no discipline into them. Any attempt, so the purser claimed, to insist on decent service from the men hastily shipped as stewards before the ship sailed, would result only in a sitdown strike from his unruly assistants and no service at all. Since this lined up with the situation on deck, it seemed entirely possible.

With these conditions, I made as short work of my unappetizing supper as possible, grabbed up my life jacket from beside my seat, and started from the dining room to make way for the second sitting. Fast as I was, most of the other passengers were faster. I had to push my way out through a mob of grumbling ex-diners already clustered in front of the ship's canteen window, endeavoring there to buy from the purser something to top off their unsatisfactory meal.

Thrusting aside heavy black-out curtains hung here and there in the passages to prevent the slightest gleam of light from showing outside should one of the promenade deck doors be opened, I reached my cabin. There I grabbed an orange from the shrinking store of fruit I had brought aboard in New York, and donned my life jacket.

With that securely tied on, I went inboard and forward through the central passage, ducked between a pair of black curtains hung as a light trap inside the door to the deck, and turned the knob to open the door. Immediately the passage light behind me went out, so thoroughly had the ship been rewired to make effective the black-out system installed just before sailing. I pulled the door wide open, stepped through, and closed it.

For a moment, in the darkness on deck, I saw nothing. Then as my eyes adjusted themselves to the night, I looked about. It was a gorgeous evening, warm enough in the Gulf Stream current to make an overcoat unnecessary. In the sky, Orion and Sirius glowed brilliantly dead ahead across the waves, while a gorgeous half moon was just setting in the ocean on our starboard side. In a few moments the moon was gone, leaving us veiled in the warm darkness of the night. The scintillating stars above and the slight phosphorescence of the waves breaking in foam against our advancing forefoot were the sole objects visible.

Standing beneath the starboard wing of the bridge, my eyes now well accustomed to the night, I looked aft down the promenade deck past the outer cabin doors and ports. Not a trace of light showed anywhere through the locked outer cabin doors or their newly screened ports. Whatever else might be said about the S.S. *Pig's Knuckle,* certainly the shipyard mechanics had done a beautiful job in blacking her out for wartime service.

No lurking U-boat, prowling on the surface at night when she herself was invisible, was going to be able to pick us up by a stray gleam and then, shrouded in her own invisibility and aided by her surface speed which far exceeded ours, close on us for a sudden torpedo attack and our destruction.

Satisfied that at least one thing on the ship was "tops" for war service, I stepped out from under the bridge wing for a better look at the stars. Hardly had I turned my eyes upward, when involuntarily my uneaten orange dropped from my agitated fingers and bounded overboard. There over my head on our beautifully blacked-out ship, was the starboard running light burning brightly in the night, shining for all to see miles away!

Hastily I ran across the deck to take a look at the port light. There it was, full on also, its red radiance glowing even more brilliantly in the darkness than its green mate to starboard.

I dashed up the ladder to the bridge to advise the captain. After all the money and labor that had been spent to black out the ship, and the dire penalties threatened any passenger who should even dare to smoke out on deck after dark, now, on our first night at sea in dangerous waters, some dumbbell of a quartermaster had neglected to pull the switch on the running lights and they were advertising our presence far and wide to all U-boats in our area!

"Where's the captain?" I demanded as I bumped into the mate on watch on the darkened bridge.

"In his cabin, sir," came the prompt reply.

I fumbled in the gloom for the knob on the door leading aft from the bridge to the captain's cabin, found it, knocked once, and swung it open. Like every other door, it was light-screened off. I closed the door, and sidled through the curtains, blinking involuntarily in the bright light suddenly greeting me.

In a chair, reading, was the skipper. He looked up at me, surprised.

"Captain," I said hurriedly, "someone's forgotten to pull the switch on the running lights! We're steaming with the brightest lights on the ship full on in the middle of your black-out!"

The skipper glared up at me, his red face instantly growing even redder with anger than his glowing port side light. Anger at such negligence I had expected of him when he heard the news. But what he said floored me.

"Nobody's forgotten anything!" he snapped out. "Those lights are on by my orders, and they're staying on!" Abruptly he dropped his eyes to the book he was reading. So far as he was concerned, all discussion was over.

The running lights on by the captain's orders on a troop ship steaming through U-boat infested waters? What kind of madhouse was our country sending us to sea on?

Had it not been for all that had gone before, I should have imagined I was crazy myself before I believed my ears as to what I had just heard. The lights on by the captain's orders? But it was all of a piece with the unusable lifeboats, the proposed suicidal course via the Florida coast, and all the lesser idiocies I had already observed. There was nothing for it but to cajole the skipper somehow to turn out those lights. So ignoring my brusque dismissal, I asked mildly enough why he thought the Government had spent so much on an elaborate black-out system if it wasn't a wartime necessity?

The skipper, mad as a hornet over having his decision questioned, glared up at me again, but apparently as I was a passenger he could not throw me offhand out of his cabin, and some answer seemed required. I was flabbergasted to learn from him he was doing it because he was in nowise afraid of U-boats, that even if torpedoed he was sure his ship could not sink because she had some six watertight bulkheads.

But running without lights! That went against the grain. He might get into collision with another ship. He might lose his license as a master for a violation of the Rules of the Road. Never would he do it!

I nodded gravely as he blustered at me what he would not do. At least I had him talking now, and I was learning something of his antiquated inhibitions. Running without lights was nothing to a naval man. We did it often in close formation even in peacetime. Merchant officers in convoy would swiftly learn (many had already) in this war to get as used to it as we and think as little of it.

So diplomatically, as casually as I could, I went to work on him. After all, I had been trained by the Navy, among other things, as a naval architect, I told him. I had worked on ship designs, had built them, had operated them, had helped salvage and repair them when they were in trouble in war and in peace. Then I had been a torpedo officer once, and I had a thorough knowledge of torpedoes and what they had done and could do to ships—warships, passenger liners, freighters.

I could assure him that modern German torpedoes with the heavier warhead charges the Nazis now were using would tear such a huge hole in the side of his little ship that his few bulkheads might just as well not be there so far as saving her from quick foundering was concerned. Did he know what U-boat torpedoes had done to the British *Athenia,* a vastly bigger and safer passenger ship than his, on the very first day of this war in Europe? And to God alone knew how many more large British ships since in this war, not to mention the sad case of the huge *Lusitania* in the last war?

And if all that did not satisfy him, he might consider the recent cases of our tremendous battleships resting now on the bottom in Pearl Harbor, built with hundreds of bulkheads each (as against his trifling five or six) for the very purpose of protecting them against torpedoes. I knew them and their maze of bulkheads by heart. What had Japanese torpedoes done to them in spite of all their bulkheads?

Admiral Farragut at Mobile Bay might have been warranted in damning the torpedoes of the Civil War period and going ahead to attack nevertheless, but I could assure him that it wasn't being done any longer. Every modern naval commander had a very healthy respect for torpedoes and acted accordingly, so did every informed merchant officer. A proper dread of torpedoes was with them a mark of intelligence, not of cowardice.

As regards the collision danger of which the skipper was so afraid, now that we were away from the coast and heavily traveled routes and not steaming in convoy with other ships, to me it seemed negligible. At any rate, the probability of a collision as compared to the probability of getting torpedoed was trifling.

Certainly, of these two possible hazards, our skipper as a prudent captain was going to choose the lesser. And as regards the danger to his license, I could assure him that running without lights was normal in wartime. Regardless of what happened running blacked out, his license was in no danger. But there was plenty of danger to his license should any survivors ever appear before an inquiry to testify that he was torpedoed running with lights on.

"And that, Captain," I concluded, "is about all I know on this situation. Now that you've been informed also, I leave it to your own sound judgment. Whatever decision you make, goes with me."

Of course, while I didn't say so, I knew well enough it had to go with me, whether I liked it or not, since with the radio in the captain's hands and no private messages permitted, there was no possible way of getting him overruled by shore authorities. But I felt rather sure now of the captain, whom I had fairly well swamped with data he couldn't even argue over. His ignorance of ship damage in wartime was extensive. And I was certain that my final gesture of saving his face by resting everything on his own sound judgment would get him.

Still standing, I looked down at the skipper for the decision. I didn't get it. Befuddled but still obstinate, glaring angrily at me for having intimated he might lose his license if he didn't comply, he muttered finally:

"I'll see. Maybe when we get far out at sea, I'll turn 'em off."

"Thanks, Captain, for listening." I turned to go. "It's all up to you now," and I vanished through the door, to take station out on the darkened forecastle where I could watch those ill-omened lights. I wondered how long it would take for the captain's fears over losing his license for carrying lights to overcome his habits of a lifetime.

Ten minutes later the running lights suddenly went out. In a complete black-out now, the *S.S. Pig's Knuckle* steamed on through the night.

CHAPTER

8

Morning dawned, to find the ship
for the first time in her career well out on blue water and off soundings, far away from lighthouses, from buoys, from lightships, from
landmarks, from near-by radio beacons, from every piloting aid by
which her position had always before been plotted up and down the
coast. Now it was up to her officers to fix her position by celestial
navigation.

It was a beautiful day for it, with a moderate breeze, a following
sea, and the sun in a clear sky on the port side shining over seas of
a deep blue tinge running right out to a sharply cut horizon.

Normally on a merchant ship, one mate only does the navigating,
but here all four mates were clustered on the port wing of the bridge,
sextants glued to their eyes, shooting the sun for our 8:00 A.M. position. Close at hand, the quartermaster stood with a watch to mark
time for them when they called to him.

From the near-by boat deck, I was watching them, when the skipper
accosted me, more affable than I yet had seen him on the voyage.

"Commander," he invited, "wouldn't you like to borrow my sextant
and navigate yourself? You're welcome to it."

"Thanks a lot, Captain, for the offer. Glad to take you up. I like
navigation." I accompanied him to his cabin, got his boxed sextant,
carefully extracted the instrument from the box, screwed the sun
telescope into the eyepiece, checked the index correction, and adjusted
the shade glasses. Then I took my stand with the mates, braced my
feet to steady me on the slowly rolling deck, and got three closely
spaced shots at the sun, for which the quartermaster noted the time
each time I sang out,

"Mark!"

With my altitudes and times, with the chronometer correction, and with the 8:00 A.M. dead reckoning position from the chart for data, I retired to my stateroom, lugging also copies of Bowditch and the 1942 Nautical Almanac borrowed from the skipper, to work with. Since only a Bowditch was available, I had to work out the sights by the old Marc St. Hilaire method, accurate enough, but tedious. Being somewhat rusty also over the formulas, this took me rather longer than usual. But with my morning position finally worked out and checked over twice to make sure there were no errors in the figures, I took it up on the boat deck to compare it with the positions of the four mates.

I found the second, third, and junior third mates all together in the second mate's stateroom, still struggling with the problem, literally sweating over their formulas and figures. The first mate was nowhere around; evidently he had locked himself up in his own cabin for work in seclusion.

I left the three mates worrying over their calculations, the while I wandered out on the boat deck again and into the radio room to learn what was new. There was plenty. About 6:00 A.M. the operator had picked up a signal from a vessel about fifty miles to the southwest of us, reporting she was being chased by a submarine and calling for help. Since then he had heard nothing further from that ship.

The radio operator handed me a sheaf of other messages. There was a report of a sinking off Bethel Shoals; radio calls from another ship being tracked by a U-boat off Jupiter Inlet; a report from shore of a wreck drifting on its side off Jupiter Inlet; and finally, a general warning to all ships to keep clear of the Florida coast. I read the reports, handed them back to the radio operator. Evidently the unchecked U-boats were having a profitable morning along the Florida coast. I was certainly glad the *Pig's Knuckle* wasn't there, though I understood that even in February the swimming isn't bad along the Florida beaches.

I went back to see how the navigation stood. The second mate had given up completely; the third mate and the junior third had finally worked out something from their sights. I compared their positions with mine.

The results were positively ridiculous—from our three positions, the ubiquitous *S.S. Pig's Knuckle* was simultaneously at 8:00 A.M. at three widely scattered points on the ocean. Two of these positions were certainly crazy, and perhaps they all were, for none agreed very well with our morning position by dead reckoning alone. Our dead reckoning position, of course, might itself be badly in error, for during the night we had crossed the Gulf Stream, the swiftest ocean current on earth, with uncertain effect as to where the drift of that current had carried the ship.

What was wrong with us? The second mate confessed he was too rusty on navigation to work out his position at all. He was out of it. Had the chief officer announced his results, I asked, against which the remaining three of ours might be checked? No, it seemed the first mate was still locked incommunicado in his own room.

Hastily then I scanned the work sheet of the third mate. His trouble was obvious. He had made a mistake in the time equations and was off on the wrong foot from the start.

I turned from his work sheet to that of the junior third mate. He also had bungled some figures, so his position was clearly erroneous also. Both the third mate and the junior third turned to on corrections, but the discovery of their blunders gave me little satisfaction. My own position was too far away from the dead reckoning point to suit me. The dead reckoning might be wrong, but not that badly, for at least an allowance had been made in it to take account of the normal Gulf Stream drift. Something else must be haywire.

I looked again at all the computations spread out before us. Then I noted a strange thing. While all of us had taken our shots at the sun within a minute or two of each other under beautiful horizon conditions, our observed altitudes of the sun were in nowise consistent with one another. According to our sextant readings, the sun had been in four different places in the sky at once just before 8:00 A.M., and that couldn't be, of course. Either the eyes of all of us were badly defective or there was something wrong with the sextants. Probably the latter was the trouble. I turned to the second mate.

"I used the skipper's sextant. Do you know how long since it's been adjusted?"

"Commander," replied the second mate, a well-meaning, hardworking officer, but rather slow in figures, "to tell you the truth, I don't know. I been on this bucket seven years now, and in all that time, there ain't never been a sextant used aboard her till today. I never even had mine aboard before, and for all I know, there hasn't been a sextant on board of her in them seven years till we shoved off for this voyage. That's how I've forgotten what navigation I had to learn to get my license. This ship's never been navigated at sea; she's always been piloted on soundings. How long since the captain's sextant's been adjusted? I don't know. I ain't never seen it in use till today."

I listened, open-mouthed. What a ship to send to sea! First the lifeboats, then the course, then the running lights, now the navigation! It was obvious there wasn't a really competent navigator on board her. Certainly the three mates before me weren't, and the first mate couldn't be any better than they or he would long since have come out of his stateroom to plot his morning position on the chart.

Seven years, and not a sight taken on the ship! Probably there never had been one taken on her since the day, sixteen years before, when, fresh from the builder's yard, the present skipper came aboard to commission her.

I picked up the captain's sextant, took it out on deck, glanced at it horizontally to test the index mirror, then vertically to check the horizon mirror. Both mirrors were out of adjustment. So were the mirrors on the second mate's sextant, and those of the third mate's. None of these three had obviously been checked for a long time. All were inaccurate. The sextant of the junior third mate (who had more recently got his license) was a new and much more modern instrument than the others; it was perfect.

So all the sights we had before us to work on were taken with faulty instruments and were worthless except those of the junior third mate. After I had helped him correct his computations, he came out with a position which seemed reasonable, and that, by default, went down on the chart as our 8:00 A.M. position, since the second mate, the third mate, and I threw all our useless data into the wastebasket, and if the first mate ever worked out a position, he never exhibited it.

I got the instrument tools out of the skipper's sextant box, and went to work on the reflecting mirrors, so that soon I had his sextant properly adjusted to give accurate readings. At the request of the second and third mates, I readjusted theirs also, so for further navigation, we could at least rely on our sights. What results the mates might get in their computations from that point on, I could look forward to only with doubt. I had accepted the captain's offer to use his sextant only as a lark for one sight; now I saw that I had better keep on navigating.

We were having other troubles also. From practically the first day out of New York, the decks had been neither swept nor washed down. With 380 passengers using them, and some of the seasick ones none too successful in getting to the lee rail in time, the decks quickly resembled a pigpen. Routine sweeping and washing down were urgent, but the chief officer, a mild-mannered, inoffensive person of slight build and general futility in exercising his authority as first mate and executive officer on the ship, got exactly nowhere with his sullen deck force in getting it done. Neither did the skipper's blustering have any better results.

The recalcitrant seamen claimed they were overworked; unless they were paid overtime for it, the wash deck gear could go hang for all they cared. Neither the captain's bullying nor the chief officer's pleading had any effect on them and the filthy decks soon became unbearable.

In this predicament, the passengers voluntarily took over. Squads of men, both soldiers and civilians, manned the wash deck hoses and the brooms. Regularly from the first few days out they washed down the decks each morning and swept down twice a day to keep the ship livable, while the idle deck force, contemptuous of their officers and unconcerned about the passengers, lounged about below, reading their seamen's journals full of articles on how valiantly merchant seamen everywhere were co-operating to win the war. Very possibly on other ships, they were.

Meanwhile, in the week since departure from New York, practically every passenger on the ship, civil and military, had come down with a bad cold in the head, and an increasing number were laid up with flu. The army surgeons aboard were tearing their hair, fearful of what an influenza epidemic might result in at sea. Inhalers, drugs, and attempted segregation of the flu cases seemed to be doing no good.

After supper, strolling for exercise on the darkened promenade deck, I bumped into Major Curtin of the Army, who had been detailed by General Scott to act as Safety Officer for the voyage. It was his job (assisted by a number of tough sergeants) to see that no one ever appeared outside his stateroom without his lifebelt; that black-out screens were kept in place; that no smoking occurred on deck after sunset; and that all hands turned out at lifeboat muster, which was now to be held daily.

On this occasion as we strolled down the deck, since we both had

[39]

colds the conversation turned quickly to that and the inability of the Army surgeons to check it. I suggested to Curtin that if aboard ship, with all its facilities, his surgeons could do no better than that, the troops were going to have a terrible time with disease when they ran up against field conditions ashore in Africa, which were reported pretty bad.

Major Curtin stopped, looked around, noted some seamen near us, then took me by the arm and led me aft to the stern. There, with only the muzzle of our 4-inch gun over our heads and the foaming wake of the ship directly beneath us, we were certainly alone. Still, Major Curtin drew close to me, lowered his voice.

"Don't worry about Africa, Commander. I'll let you in on something. It's not our doctors, it's our ship that's the trouble! The surgeons have just put their finger on the source, and it's going to be cured damned quick tomorrow morning."

"The ship?" I asked dubiously. I knew plenty was wrong with the ship and her crew, but what could they have to do with an epidemic of flu and colds?

"Yes, it's the damned *Pig's Knuckle* that's causing it. But keep what I'm telling you dark tonight. Our surgeons have tracked it down to the dining room and the galley. Those lousy stewards below haven't been washing the dishes or the silver at all between sittings—just scraping the plates, rinsing 'em in cold water, and putting everything back that way for the second sitting. And even for the first sitting each meal the dishes don't get washed in water hot enough to sterilize 'em; just a dip in lukewarm water, then a lick and a promise with a dirty dishrag to make sure the germs get well spread around. No wonder everybody on the ship's got a cold, and more and more of 'em every day are going flat on their backs with flu!"

Major Curtin paused a moment for breath in his indignation, took a second look around to see no one had come within hearing, then continued:

"When they found that out, our senior surgeon and I went to see the chief steward about it. No luck. The chief steward said he couldn't get his men to wash the dishes, let alone sterilize 'em. Too much work. Then we went to the captain about it. He passed, too. Said it was useless to try. What in hell's the matter with the officers on this ship, I don't know. Either they're worthless or the crew's got 'em buffaloed, or both, maybe. Anyway"—he lowered his voice to a whisper—"on the general's orders, I'm doing something about it for the Army. Get down to breakfast early tomorrow and you'll see something."

Being thus tipped off, I was first on hand in the dining room a little before seven next morning, when the first sitting was supposed to breakfast. The dining room was empty. There wasn't a sign of food in sight. There wasn't a plate, a knife, a fork, or a spoon to be seen on any table.

The only person visible was the very agitated chief steward, running his hands through his hair, eyeing fearfully the closed doors leading forward from the dining room to the galley.

I went to my place, sank into my seat, scanned the empty table before me. Then I looked at my watch.

"Steward!" I sang out to the only other person in the room with me. "Here it's seven o'clock and nothing for breakfast. What's the matter with you?"

Unsteadily and apparently shaking with fear, the ashen-faced chief steward stumbled over to my table.

"Look!" I growled, indicating the table. "No plates, no silver, no food, no steward, no nothing! This is a hell of a way for you to run a ship!"

"It's not my fault, Commander," he mumbled tremulously. "The Army! They won't let me. With guns, too! Look in there!" And he pointed fearfully to the closed galley doors.

I rose, strode over to the nearest door, pushed through it. There, dimly seen through clouds of steam filling the room, was Major Curtin, his back to the doors, blocking the exits, with four Army sergeants beside him, and each with an unlimbered .45 Colt automatic trained on the cowering stewards before them!

Major Curtin twisted his head swiftly to see who had intruded, then swung it back again.

"Morning, Commander. Breakfast may be a little late this morning," he apologized. "These boys have just been persuaded it would be a good idea to wash all the dishes, so there'll be no service till they're through. They're so anxious to do a good job now, they've decided to sterilize 'em, too, in boiling water while they're at it, so there may be quite a delay. Sorry."

All over the galley, the stewards, with their eyes shifting constantly from those unwavering muzzles and the menacing faces of the squad of grim sergeants between them and escape, to the huge steaming kettles, were busy plunging everything in sight in the way of dishes and silver into boiling water. Evidently Curtin was right about the delay, but I guessed it would be the last one. From the looks on the faces of the stewards, I judged they had been persuaded also it would be a good idea to wash the dishes henceforth after each meal without further argument.

And so it turned out. But for the rest of the cruise, an armed sergeant was always present in the galley at dishwashing time just to see there was no backsliding. And our epidemic of colds and flu swiftly subsided.

CHAPTER

9

Our third day at sea, February 24, commenced with the wind blowing fairly hard, and shortly it had risen to a strong gale with about a 50-knot wind from ahead. The waves built up rapidly to give rise by early afternoon to unusually steep seas, with a remarkable breaking effect on their sharp crests. There was no rain, but the spray, cut sharply from the wave crests by the howling gale, drove like buckshot into the skin, drenched everything on deck.

Soon the ship was pitching heavily, driving headlong in the seas and pounding hard each time her bow slapped down in the troughs. Naturally, with all this, the rails were soon lined with seasick passengers, and the dining room got very little patronage the rest of that day and the next, which helped in allowing the stewards to get accustomed to the new order of cleanliness below.

But the greatest benefit of the storm was noted in the radio reports. Submarine attacks ceased as if cut off by a knife. Not for two days while the storm lasted was there a single report of a torpedoing. Evidently the U-boats found the remarkably steep seas not to their liking, either for surface or submerged attack. Probably they were too busy ensuring their own safety to bother about endangering anyone else's. Nevertheless there were two radio reports during the storm that the skipper relayed to me with great relish—two collisions had occurred off the coast.

There was quite an "I told you so" grin on the skipper's countenance as, without comment, he showed me these. But as none of the vessels involved had sunk and there were no details in the reports beyond their approximate locations, it was obvious the skipper didn't know whether lack of lights or the storm was responsible, or even whether the collisions had occurred at night, and neither did I. So

I grinned back and said nothing either. I noted that our running lights stayed out though, regardless of those two collisions, however much the reports of them may have bolstered the captain's ego.

On our fifth day at sea, in fine weather with only a slight wind, we steamed on, expecting to make San Juan harbor in the very early afternoon. In view of that, I took a careful set of morning and noon sights to determine our position, which I communicated to the skipper. But he decided to ignore it in favor of the junior third mate's position, which placed us considerably to the eastward of my observations. The third mate had a position which placed us far away from either of these, and where the first and second mates thought we were, I never learned. Setting his course from the junior third mate's morning position (in which the captain seemed to have most faith, though I advised against it), we kept on, headed for San Juan.

At about 2:00 P.M., the high mountains of Porto Rico, a very large island stretching for a hundred miles in an east and west direction across our course, loomed up on the horizon ahead of us. Still keeping the course intended to take us into the harbor, the ship held on towards land. But as we got close enough to pick up the shore line through glasses, I noticed increasing uneasiness on our skipper's beefy countenance.

He had reason enough for it. The city of San Juan, Morro Castle towering above it on the seaward cliff and its lighthouse, all easily visible far out at sea to incoming ships, were nowhere in sight! Nor could he spot anything else, recognizable on the chart to fix its position. Before us in both directions stretched only a barren coast, void of all charted landmarks.

Very agitated now by this mishap, the skipper nevertheless obstinately held his course unchanged, still hoping on close approach to pick up something identifiable to show him where he was. But finally there was no help for it. He had to ring up "Stop" on the engine room telegraph lest the ship drive hard upon the unknown shore now close ahead.

A more ridiculous (if it had not been serious) scene I never saw on a ship's bridge. There ahead of us certainly was the island of Porto Rico. But where were we? And which way, east or west, should the ship head to get to the city of San Juan?

His face glowing red with anger, the outraged skipper glared questioningly for the answer at his four mates who had landed him in that predicament. The cowed mates, rightly enough uncertain of their navigation, couldn't agree. Some dubiously suggested east, some thought west would be better.

"Captain," I volunteered in this dilemma, "I'm sure my morning longitude sight was good and my figures O.K. That placed us much further west than the position you used. I advised then a more easterly course. Go east now and you'll find San Juan about an hour's run from here."

He did, and we did. About fifteen miles eastward down the coast, approximately the distance I had figured we were off the true course, we picked up the entrance to San Juan.

From that point on, the skipper was in his element. If there was anything he knew, it was piloting. Once there were buoys and lights in sight to take bearings on, no one could beat him. Very skillfully, relying hardly at all on the local pilot we picked up outside, he conned his vessel through the torpedo nets and the narrow channel, fringed with surf breaking on reefs close aboard, into the harbor and neatly laid her alongside the wharf.

But far from any thanks for my assistance in our safe arrival, it seemed to me from the skipper's distant behavior from the moment he headed the ship east, that I had now only his strong ill will. I had been a witness on the bridge to that exhibition of gross incompetence in the deep sea navigation of the *S.S. Pig's Knuckle.*

Our overnight stay in San Juan, while the ship was being refueled alongside the wharf, was memorable, but not pleasantly so. The weather ashore was hot and humid, more noticeably uncomfortable as we had just come from winter.

I went into town only to buy a book of modern navigation tables. In addition I picked up a few charts of the South Atlantic and a Nautical Almanac for 1942. With these as my own property and the occasional use of one of the mates' sextants, for it was perfectly evident I was no longer welcome to use the captain's, I figured that I could keep on navigating on my own, the while I taught the mates, of whom three at least were eager for help, how to navigate accurately themselves.

Most of the larger shops were soon closed, as we had landed late in the afternoon. But still open, especially near the water front, was a plethora of dives proclaiming themselves in Spanish and in English to be "Night Clubs," with gaudily painted but still ugly and unattractive native "hostesses" swarming about them as lures. From inside each of these places came the most infernal racket of jazz bands, struggling to outdo adjacent competitors in noise.

Finally, Porto Rican rum seemed to be on sale everywhere, cheap as compared to New York prices. So far as I could guess, as I sauntered back to the ship with my new navigational equipment, it was already being guzzled in enormous quantities by my fellow passengers, civilians as well as soldiers, judging by their uncertain gait from "night club" to "night club."

Back on the nearly deserted ship, I turned to at once in my stateroom on boning up on the thin volume of Ageton's tables I had managed to buy ashore. Ageton's tables and his method gave a much quicker and simpler means of solving the trigonometric problems involved in celestial navigation than I had learned in my youth.

But even Ageton required some practice to develop the familiarity with the tables necessary for speed. Consequently I was still involved in working out by this newer method the sights of the sun I had taken much earlier north of Porto Rico, when 11:00 P.M., which was the zero hour for the expiration of shore leave for the passengers, struck. From then on, singly and in small groups, the sightseers began to return and very shortly, perforce, I had to give up further study.

A more hideous and disgraceful night was never experienced on any ship as those drunks, overflowing with Porto Rican rum, staggered aboard—some fighting drunk, some roaring drunk, some singing drunk, and some just drunk. Hour after hour the deafening hullabaloo kept up, started afresh by a continuous stream of late comers each time Major Curtin and his overworked sergeants managed to subdue momentarily some of the most obstreperous of the already on board cases.

The drunken soldiers, Curtin and his M.P.s managed to quell. Even when drunk, the soldiers still had instinct enough left to recognize the danger of bucking their sergeants. But the drunken civilians were hopeless. They were free and equal citizens of the United States, drunk as lords, and recognized no authority at all. Short of strangling them, there was no way of quieting them.

All through the night, the ship echoed from bow to stern with an ear-rasping uproar from shouting, screaming, singing, fighting drunks that would have shamed a pack of hyenas. No one slept on the S.S. *Pig's Knuckle* that night.

Morning came at last and with it relative quiet. Worn-out drunks were strewn prostrate everywhere, in deck chairs, in the passages, on the deck. The M.P.s cleaned up by heaving the now dead-to-the-world celebrants indiscriminately into the nearest staterooms to sleep off their stupors.

The ship, topped off with fuel, made ready to sail at noon. A check on the passenger list, however, showed one man still missing. So instead of sailing, the ship's whistle began to shriek, in the thin hope the noise might waken our missing passenger ashore. It did. Half an hour later he sauntered slowly down the dock, his leisurely gait an added insult to the chafing officers aboard. Explaining casually only that he had been asleep ashore till the whistle roused him, he ambled over the gangway and we immediately cast loose, an hour late.

That delay promptly caused trouble then and more later. Hardly had the ship cleared the wharf, and started to swing her bow towards the harbor mouth, than two huge Pan-American flying boats came in from seaward and straightened out, flying low over the water, for a landing inside the harbor. To avoid a possible chance of fouling them, either in the air or in the long lane of clear water they needed to come down on, our skipper had no option but to drop anchor suddenly to hold us clear.

As soon as both flying boats had landed in clouds of flying spray, come about, and taxied away to their berths, clearing the harbor, the clatter of chain links banging over the wildcat forward announced our anchor was being weighed. But before it came aweigh, the clanging of chain coming in suddenly ceased, and we remained anchored for almost another hour before the anchor was at last heaved up into the hawsepipe. It was 2:00 P.M., nearly two hours late, when the vessel finally sailed from San Juan.

On February 27, ten days out of New York, we stood out of the harbor. We headed due north for some time, then east-northeast, to get well off the coast before turning eastward for our normal course. The naval authorities in the port had warned us before departure that a U-boat had been reported that morning working in the Anegada Passage east of the island of St. Thomas.

Several Navy patrol planes and a destroyer were being sent to search the area, and at least keep the U-boat submerged and immobilized during the day. Still, as we would now pass that way at night, it was advisable to give the coast as wide a berth as possible off Anegada Passage.

When we were about two hours out of San Juan and straightened away on our eastward course, I learned in strange fashion what had caused the delay in weighing anchor. Up on the bridge where I was chatting with the third mate over my newly acquired navigation tables, came a swarthy, heavy-set seaman, demanding to see the captain. While a messenger went for the captain, the mate whispered to me that this man, chosen apparently for his obstreperousness, was the union delegate, representing all the strange assortment of "seamen" that made up our motley crew.

As soon as the captain appeared on the bridge, with no preliminaries, the delegate faced him with an air of obvious insolence and announced,

"The crew's all decided I've gotter tell you the ship's gotter turn back right away to San Juan."

At this outrageous demand, the captain was struck dumb. For once I was sorry for him. It had certainly come to a sad pass in the American merchant marine when a seaman, a crew's delegate or not, dared brazenly to order a ship off a voyage and back to port.

When finally the skipper came to sufficiently to speak, he asked, "What for?"

"We talked it over and decided that the feller what got his mitt jammed in the wildcat when we was weighin' the anchor oughter be taken right back to San Juan and put ashore in the hospital there."

At this point, the third mate whispered to me that another able seaman had carelessly jammed a finger between chain and wildcat while the chain was coming in. The delay to the ship in San Juan had occurred from an instant stop of the heaving process till the chain was carefully wedged free of the wildcat to clear him. Now he was in the sick bay for treatment of his torn finger.

Here at least I had to admire the skipper for his restraint, though I felt his actions were governed considerably by his knowledge that as matters had been going lately at sea, ship's officers got little backing from authorities ashore in disputes with their organized crews. In case any member of the crew, from cabin boy up, cared to make an official complaint, a ship master was more likely to find himself permanently without a ship, as had lately happened to the unfortunate skipper of the *City of Flint,* than to find his authority or his judgment backed up. I held no brief for our captain, who had been unable to get his crew, either on deck or below, to do the ordinary ship's work, so that the problems had been sloughed off on the passengers who had solved them in various ways, but nevertheless no one could help sympathizing with him now.

It was my turn to look with astonishment at that brash seaman, unabashedly telling the captain what he and the crew, none of them with the slightest knowledge of surgery, had decided must be done. Turn a troop transport at sea in wartime, with the ship's own surgeon and an oversupply of military surgeons aboard, all capable of treating any wound, back to port to treat an injured finger. What gall!

The captain, with difficulty restraining his wrath, though it was plain from the swelling arteries in his temples that he was near apoplexy, turned from the seaman before him to the quartermaster.

"Tell the ship's surgeon to come up on the bridge. Then ask General Scott if he'll send the senior Army surgeon up here, too."

The quartermaster slid down the ladder. The captain abruptly turned his back on the insolent delegate before him, lest he burst a blood vessel, strode to the far wing of the bridge, grabbed his binoculars and started to scan the empty sea ahead. The third mate and I walked to the other wing of the bridge, leaving the delegate grinning alone near the helmsman. Self-satisfaction was written all over his smiling countenance.

"This finger business is all a smoke screen," muttered the third officer. "That bozo doesn't care any more about that other sailor's smashed finger than the king of Dahomey does. I see through his game. If the ship goes back now, it's so late she can't sail again till tomorrow morning, and it'll give him and his mates another go tonight in San Juan at the cheap rum and the cheap whores there! Did you notice he waited to complain till we were well out, not when we might have landed anybody and then kept right on going?"

Very possible, I thought. At any rate it sounded more rational than the reason given.

In a few minutes, the ship's doctor, a retired Navy surgeon of long experience gone back to sea in the merchant service for the war emergency, clambered up the bridge. He was followed by a major in the Army Medical Corps.

The skipper came back amidships, faced his seaman.

"Tell the doctors what you want."

[49]

"We want the ship put back to San Juan to land that man with the busted finger for treatment in the hospital there."

It was now the turn of the two surgeons to look in puzzled astonishment from the seaman before them to each other.

"What for?" asked the ship's doctor. "I've already operated on that finger, got the bones set, splinted, and bandaged, and there's nothing more anybody or any hospital could do right now. Don't you agree, Major?" he asked the Army man. "You watched the operation."

"I don't understand you, my man," said the major, wrinkling his brows questioningly at the sailor before him. "Your shipmate can't get better medical attention in the world anywhere than he's getting right here. There are four surgeons aboard and only one minor accident case for them to work on. Landing him's ridiculous."

At that "my man," the seaman stiffened up as if insulted. Apparently a crew's delegate expected to be addressed in a more respectful manner, though I noted that he had ostentatiously omitted any title at all when addressing his captain. But he said nothing till the doctor had finished, then he growled sullenly,

"That's what you say. Now I'm telling you for the crew, turn the ship around and land that man."

The skipper grew still redder, but his only answer was to turn to the Army surgeon.

"Will you recommend to General Scott, Major, that I put the ship back to port so's this patient can be transferred to a hospital for treatment?"

"I will not! No doctor could. This is the damnedest 'Alice in Wonderland' performance I ever heard of! You can leave me out of it!" and with that the major swung angrily and left the bridge.

The skipper turned back to the delegate.

"You heard what both the doctors said. That man will be treated aboard, I'm not turning back."

"What them doctors say ain't nothin' to me. You put this ship around or the crew—"

"Get off the bridge now," exploded the skipper, "or I'll have you thrown off!"

The startled sailor, cut off in the middle of his "or else," gazed a moment at the irate captain. There was no question the skipper was through palavering. For once, he was in a fine position in case the crew's union back home made an issue of it. It was wartime, the War

[50]

Department was bound to back him up ashore. And right now before the crew tried to start trouble on board if they didn't like his decision, they would doubtless recall that episode in the galley a few days before when some of them had looked down the muzzles of the M.P.s' Colts.

To save his face, the interrupted seaman started to mumble again his demand.

"Get!" shouted the exasperated skipper, moving toward him.

The delegate "got."

Leaning over the port wing of the bridge, gazing down at the waves as the ship steamed on eastward, I reflected on what I had just witnessed and what had gone before. It began to look as if that Army surgeon had hit the nail squarely on the head. This cruise of the S.S. *Pig's Knuckle was* right out of "Alice in Wonderland."

CHAPTER

10

THE REST OF OUR VOYAGE WAS MORE of the same, with variations—some ridiculous, some serious.

Our first night out of San Juan, while north of the Anegada Paspage, the bow lookouts reported two torpedo tracks crossing our stem. Nothing hit us, but there was consternation enough aboard. About midnight the second evening, the general alarm sounded from the bridge turning out all hands in their lifebelts to stand by the lifeboats, while the ship, with guns ready for action, suddenly reversed course, and ran full speed away from some undetermined object spotted in the darkness ahead in our path.

The food stayed bad, the crew sullen, the captain more so. This latter was not helped any when four days later, approaching the Equator, we were chased by a warship which might have been an enemy raider but turned out to be one of our own cruisers on South Atlantic patrol looking for enemy raiders camouflaged as merchantmen.

What thoroughly upset our skipper was the bawling out he got from the warship captain for answering a signal to identify himself by hoisting the *Pig's Knuckle's* confidential war code call letters instead of her ordinary merchant code flag identification. Had our pursuer been an enemy, sang out the warship captain angrily through his bull-horn when close aboard us, this would have put him in possession of a secret code call which he could have used later to decoy other Allied ships.

On we steamed over the Line towards our next refueling stop, Recife, in the state of Pernambuco, Brazil. I ran a navigation school for the three junior mates, which the skipper looked on with obvious but silent disapproval, though the mates took the instruction enthusiastically.

Meanwhile, I also navigated myself, using my own equipment and the third mate's sextant. The skipper's sextant, at his request, had gone back to his custody, where it went out of service again. Evidently he regretted the generous gesture by which he had started all this in offering me the instrument and inviting me to navigate when I pleased, though he never openly said so to me. In this delicate situation, all my positions went down on the chart as the third mate's, which I believe the skipper suspected, and it went decidedly amiss with him. He still said nothing to me, but went at it obliquely. Calling the third mate into his cabin, he told the mate to tell me to stop navigating. This the third mate refused to do on the grounds that first it was the captain, not he, who had asked me to navigate, and second, the instruction was doing the mates (as well as the ship) a good turn. The skipper became quite violent over this refusal, and the mate came out of the cabin, determined to quit the ship at the first opportunity, sure now that the captain had a knife out for him.

On March 8, nine days out of San Juan, we made the Brazilian coast, coming in from seaward some sixty miles north of Recife. The landfall, based on a fine set of star sights I had got just before sunrise and worked out together with the third mate, was beautiful. We picked up Cape Blanco exactly on the bearing and at the time predicted—an occasion notable by its complete difference from our lubberly landfall at Porto Rico, but it was marked on the bridge mainly by a complete silence on the part of all hands there.

In sight of land and with known lighthouses again to guide him, the skipper became less sour as with his usual skill he piloted down the coast. Pernambuco harbor, an unusually difficult one to approach because of off-lying reefs and an involved outside system of buoys, he took his ship into in a manner to arouse any seaman's admiration— a performance which made the skipper himself positively genial as we came in and anchored inside the breakwater, preparatory to docking for refueling.

But the geniality swiftly went sky-high. Someone, either the captain, the purser, or the ship's operators back in New York, or all of them together, had blundered. Our arrival in Recife was a complete surprise to Recife—no berth had been assigned, no fuel oil had been ordered there to await our coming. And with oil in foreign ports in wartime scarce and strictly rationed, this last was serious. The local oil representatives merely shrugged their shoulders—all their fuel oil

[53]

was allocated, they could let go of none of it to any ship without proper papers. And the poor *S.S. Pig's Knuckle*, in keeping with all else in connection with her, had none at all, proper or otherwise.

For two days, we lay idle in Recife while the choleric captain burned up the cables to far-off New York, and the purser kept out of sight. Still, to most of the passengers, the captain's troubles were a blessing. Here was a large city for a liberty, cooler, though it was close to the Equator, than San Juan, far more inviting. Had there been a repetition of San Juan, however, given two days ashore, our passengers would have torn both the ship and Recife to pieces, ruining forever our relations with Brazil.

But this time in port, General Scott was prepared. Rigorous warning went out to every passenger as to dire penalties, should there be a duplication of that outrageous night in San Juan. And as preventative medicine, Major Curtin's M.P.s went ashore armed, with orders to pick up and return to the ship immediately any passenger seen on the streets unduly happy.

As a result of this, there was relative peace in Recife and on the ship during our stay. Some disgracefully drunk cases were picked up and taxied back alongside by the M.P.s, but we were spared another night of hideous screeching.

On our third day in port, we finally started fueling about 9:30 A.M. Sailing time was set at 6:00 A.M. next day, March 11, in preparation for which Major Curtin had all the passengers carefully rounded up and checked in on board the night before. But when 6:00 A.M. on March 11 came round, we did not get under way. To the great chagrin of the skipper, who had been riding General Scott the day before over delaying the ship on account of passengers, several of the crew were missing. Not till 9:00 A.M., three hours late, did we shove off, even then leaving a quartermaster and an oiler who had apparently decided to desert the good ship *Pig's Knuckle*, ashore in a foreign port.

We cleared Recife, and shortly were out on the broad South Atlantic, headed at last for Lagos in Nigeria, on the coast of West Africa, our final destination. The events in Recife had made the skipper more peevish than ever; no one could speak to him from then on without getting his head snapped off. This situation was in nowise improved by various alarms of sightings of both enemy surface raiders and U-boats—perhaps true, perhaps false. We ran from everything as a matter of prudence.

The weather stayed fine, and though we were running just a hair south of the Equator with the sun practically dead overhead at noon, giving maximum summer conditions, the air felt unusually comfortable. Certainly the climate at sea with us was far superior to summer weather I had experienced in New York, Washington, or Boston, where I had often sweltered with the thermometer around 90° F.

Major Goff and I, he from Idaho and I from Colorado, in both of which western states the weather is always perfect, pondering this phenomenon our second day out of Recife, became curious as to what the temperature really was there under the Equatorial sun. Ordinarily I should have solved this problem simply by a look at the bridge thermometer, but that ship's instrument had been broken no one knew how long before (certainly long before we left New York) and never replaced. So I couldn't help.

Major Goff, however, took care of the matter in routine Army style. Near by on deck was a sergeant. In the Army, sergeants are the solution to everything.

"Anderson!" sang out the lanky major. "Get us a thermometer!"

"Yes, sir!" With no ado and no questions asked as to where he might find one, Sergeant Anderson, like Major Rowan delivering the message to Garcia, set off to obtain a thermometer.

By and by, he returned with a fever thermometer, evidently from the sick bay.

"This may not do, Major," he apologized, handing it to Goff, "but it's the best I could get."

The fever thermometer would read no lower than 94°, and it turned out the temperature on deck was considerably lower than that. Going back to the sick bay to return the clinical thermometer, I saw a small thermometer secured to the bulkhead, which with the surgeon's permission I removed and took out on deck. The temperature there turned out to be 84° F., amazingly low for Equatorial summer, indicating that there are far more uncomfortable spots on earth in summer than right on the Equator.

Meanwhile, our troubles continued. While bringing liquor on board the ship had been strictly forbidden, still with the experience gained in prohibition days in the art of bootlegging, evidently some of the passengers had smuggled aboard plenty. The amazing situation developed that the senior civilian on board, the top supervisor for our Middle East contractor, was so continuously drunk at sea that the surgeon had reported him on the verge of delirium tremens. After investigation of this by a board of officers belonging to the Mission, he was relieved of his authority and ordered to be sent home immediately we got to Africa. It became clearer, how with such a man in charge of them and setting the pace, our civilians had shown so little self-restraint.

In his place, Mr. Patrick Murphy, construction superintendent for the contractor, a man grown gray in the construction business, took over and brought some order back into the lives of his unruly charges. But Murphy had a hard crowd to deal with, especially as there was still plenty of bootlegged hooch, both Porto Rican and Brazilian, stowed away aboard. Finally Murphy brought his troubles to me. He had everybody under control but one man, an ironworker by the name of Bill Cunningham.

"This Cunningham's a tough hombre, Commander," explained Murphy. "When he's sober, he's as fine and accommodating a worker as you'll ever see. But once he gets some liquor in him, he's a wild man, spoiling for a fight. And he's got fists like iron!" Murphy shrugged his shoulders hopelessly, then continued,

"I'm round sixty now, and none too well for that. If I was younger myself, I'd take care of him. He's drunk right now and down in the starboard lower passage, looking for a fight. I could send the M.P.s down there and he'd get it. But when it was over, half a dozen of them M.P.s would be busted up and Cunningham'd be so busted up, too, he'd never be worth a damn to me. He's a terror in a scrap, and I don't want any. Now you're an officer, Commander. Maybe he'll listen to you. He's worth saving for that African job if we can only get him there whole, and then keep him sober."

My naval training had taught me it's useless to enter an argument with a drunken sailor. The only safe thing to do is to slap him into the brig and talk to him when he's sobered up and recognizes authority.

But from what Murphy said, slapping Bill Cunningham into the brig meant a battle royal which would ruin him for our purposes, and well I knew that we had very few good ironworkers. In Massawa, one would be worth his weight in gold.

Dubiously I told Murphy I would see what I could do, though I didn't know Cunningham. While I had little faith in my ability as a lion-tamer, still it was possible that Cunningham might be awed by a naval uniform. If not, I was sure that I could run faster than any drunk.

So I went below alone to the passage indicated on the lower passenger deck, to find all the stateroom doors on both sides of the passage closed and presumably locked. In solitary possession of the passage, clad solely in shorts and a sleeveless undershirt which exhibited only too well his powerful shoulders and his brawny muscles, clutching in one fist a bottle of rum and banging with the other on the closed doors, was a man shouting drunkenly,

"Open them doors, you bastards! Come on out an' fight!"

Evidently here was Cunningham.

At the noise of my footsteps, he ceased pounding, looked round toward me, then braced himself, ready to fight.

"Your name Cunningham?" I asked brusquely.

"Yeah. Wot's it to you?" Uncertainly his bloodshot eyes scanned me from my feet to my brass hat. He didn't know who I was.

"Lots. I'm in command in Massawa. You headed there?"

"Sure. I'm gonna work there."

"Well, you're not. You're fired! You're a damned disgrace to the United States. I don't want any drunken bums like you in Massawa. As soon as we get to Lagos, your trip ends! That's all of Africa you'll ever see. You're going right back home on this ship! How's that suit you?"

Cunningham's bleary eyes stared into mine. Steadily I stared back. My staccato phrases in discharging him so peremptorily had momentarily, at least, taken his mind off fighting and his befuddled brain was evidently struggling with the new idea as he gazed at me.

"How's that suit you?" I reiterated sharply.

"Naw. I wanna go to Massawa. Had enough o' this damned ship. Doan wanna go home on her," he mumbled finally, dropping his eyes.

"Well, you're going to! You're fired! You get that? I can't use any bums like you. But if you think you can do better, quit this damned drinking right now. Then come see me the day we're due in Lagos and maybe I'll reconsider. That's only maybe, remember! I won't

[57]

promise anything." I paused a moment to let that sink in, then snapped out,

"Which is your stateroom?"

Still further confused by the sudden change of subject, Cunningham shuffled uneasily, dropped his fighting stance, and started solemnly to scan the closed stateroom doors.

"That one," he announced finally, pointing uncertainly with the bottle to the fourth door down.

"As a start, then, get into that room and stay there till you're sober!" I ordered.

Cunningham's drunken eyes came angrily back to mine. With those shoulders he might have broken me in two, but I gazed back unflinchingly. For a long minute we stood glaring at each other. Whatever then motivated him, I never knew. Perhaps it was fear over the loss of the chance of ever seeing Africa. Perhaps it was his dread of the long trip home in the *Pig's Knuckle*. At any rate, without a word he shuffled off into his stateroom, leaving me in possession of the empty corridor. I went back up on deck, and told Pat Murphy quiet now reigned below.

CHAPTER

11

AT 11.5 KNOTS, OUR NORMAL CRUIS-
ing speed, leaving a little power in reserve for emergencies, we
steamed on due east for Africa, keeping a little to the south of the
Equator. Lookouts were doubled, the Armed Guard crews kept always
on the alert at the guns. It was hereabouts in the South Atlantic the
year before that Nazi raiders had caught and sunk two merchant ships,
the *Zamzam* and the *Robin Moor*, with particularly brutal attacks
on their passengers and crews, seeing we were then neutral.

It was amazing how out of the world we were on our last leg from
Recife to Lagos. We never received any radio news reports, for the
ship's radio set was kept constantly tuned only to the emergency S O S
wave length and consequently could receive neither any long or short
wave news broadcasts.

As for private portable receiving sets, of which several had been
brought aboard by passengers, all had been gathered up and locked
away on General Scott's orders. Such sets in receiving, reradiate sufficiently to act as short range sending sets themselves, giving off a
signal which a U-boat not too far off can pick up with a direction
finder and thus track down. So as completely cut off from the world
as in the old sailing ship days, and at a speed not much faster, we
headed for Lagos.

The weather stayed remarkable—blue skies, blue water, clouds of
flying fish, with at night a gorgeous phosphorescent wake, burning
stars—and no moon. This last was especially appreciated, as with no
Wacs, no Waves, and no other women aboard, we had no need of a
moon, and its absence made everybody feel better since it completed
our black-out perfectly.

But the weather was our only bright spot. In the dining room,
the unending round of stew, frankfurters, and pig's knuckles, all

served as usual with soggy potatoes and awash spinach, more unpalatable than ever under tropic skies, kept the ship true to her nickname. Then the skipper began running with all the huge steel cargo doors in the side of the ship's hull down near her waterline, swung wide open, ensuring her prompt capsizing in case of torpedoing. A protest by General Scott against the most serious jeopardizing of the safety of a ship at sea in wartime I ever heard of, brought nothing but a wisecrack from the skipper in answer to Major Curtin who carried the general's request that they be kept closed as a matter of elementary safety.

In fact, the offended skipper went on from wisecracks to inform the major in ordinary times he would be warranted in locking up General Scott, the major himself, Colonel Gruver, and some other officers he named (oddly enough he omitted me) for their interference with his ship, but he was generously refraining. The fact that these were not ordinary times seems to have eluded the skipper altogether. Had they been, the Army would not have chartered the ship, the general and the rest of the Army passengers would not have been aboard on their way to war, and none of us, including the captain himself, would have been there in the South Atlantic in danger of being torpedoed.

So Major Curtin only laughed at the skipper's gesture of magnanimity in refraining. It was as obvious to him as it was to the skipper, that locking up the general, with 200 armed troops at his back, for endeavoring to ensure the safety of his troops and himself, was something not lightly to be undertaken by anyone.

Eight days out of Recife, found us on March 19 in the Gulf of Guinea, center of the slave trade in the old days. We were just north of the Equator, heading northeast for Lagos and only 346 miles from it.

We had already traveled 6500 miles in the thirty-one days we had been at sea since leaving New York, and only one thought animated all hands on our last day out—if our luck held for just one more day, we should get to Lagos and say good-by forever to the *Pig's Knuckle*. Personally, I regretted the ill-advised moment in which I had canceled my chance to go by air—a trip in a Flying Fortress piloted by even the least experienced of the Army Air Corps' newest flyers would have been more competently run and far less nerve-racking. And it would have taken only four days at most, instead of the thirty-one we had already been on the ocean in our roundabout wanderings.

Our last night at sea found the skipper fearful of something at last —an air attack! U-boats and their torpedoes he disdained, but apparently planes and their bombs, menacing his upper decks directly, were something else with him. At any rate, he requested of General Scott that the military lookout be doubled during the night to watch for planes, and I volunteered for one of the watches.

From midnight on till 4:00 A.M., I stood a sky watch atop the pilot house but sighted nothing at all except a lovely array of stars, most of them never visible in northern latitudes, which of itself repaid the effort and the loss of sleep. Aside from that, it enabled me to size up leisurely the best stars for morning sights.

I was very anxious to see that the ship made a good landfall this last time. A good landfall was imperative for us, as the Guinea coast each side of Lagos was covered with uncharted British minefields for the benefit of any U-boats which might try snooping in the vicinity. It was no shore to come blundering up against blindly as we had at Porto Rico, looking for landmarks to tell us where we were; not at least if we wanted to get into Lagos still afloat.

I selected two stars, the planet Venus in the east and the star Shaula of the constellation Scorpio bearing south. Both of these were of a magnitude bright enough to remain visible in a sextant even when approaching dawn lighted the horizon sharply enough for use. And these two stars made practically a right angle with each other in the sky, so that the lines of position I could get from sights of them would intersect almost perpendicularly and give me an excellent "fix" for the ship.

With that determined and no enemy planes showing up, I went below when my watch ended at 4:00 A.M., got the third mate's sextant (as well as the third mate who turned out to help) and went back on the boat deck.

By now I had confidence enough in the navigational ability of both the third mate and the junior third (both of whom had worked diligently on navigation the past few weeks) to trust them on their own to get the ship back safely to New York from Africa. But this last position was unusually important and I felt safest doing it myself.

Between 4:32 A.M., when the horizon began to show up in the east, and 4:49 A.M., when the increasing dawn started to fade out even my bright stars, I obtained a fine set of sights of both Venus and Shaula.

These, swiftly worked out by Ageton's method, gave us for 4:49 A.M. (ship's time) a sharp "fix" for the ship. The intersection of my lines of position placed us then in Latitude 4° 43.3′ North, Longitude 2° 07.7′ East, just 129 miles from Lagos.

The third mate, with no further ado, entered this on the chart as his early morning position. From it, run up to 7:00 A.M., the skipper then changed course some 10° more to the westward, and with the ship speeded up to her maximum, 13 knots, headed (so he hoped) directly for Lagos.

Meanwhile, I turned in, clothes and all, to catch up on my lost night's sleep. Hardly, it seemed, had I even closed my eyes when a knocking on my stateroom door woke me again. I glanced at my watch. Only seven o'clock. Who wanted me that early when I had been up practically all night?

I looked up and there in the open doorway stood Bill Cunningham. I rolled out of my bunk, sat up on the edge of it.

"You said to come to see you the day we got to Lagos, Commander," announced Cunningham in a voice strangely soft as compared to his husky frame. "Here I am."

He was certainly bright and early. I rubbed my sleepy eyes, looked him over. He was sober, and from his clear eyes and skin, had evidently been so for some time. The change in his manner, his voice, and his appearance since the day I had last seen him below in the corridor, was remarkable. He was as mild and inoffensive a person now as one might ever see.

"All right, Cunningham, you remember what I said when I fired you. How about it?"

"I ain't had a drink, Commander, since that time. I want to go to Massawa, and if you'll only give me another chance, I'll try my best to stay sober. I can't promise you I'll never take another drink, but I can promise I'll do my damnedest to stay away from it. I'm not looking for any trouble or any fights with anybody. All I want is to go through with what I started. Don't send me home."

That was an honest enough statement. Looking into Cunningham's deeply serious face, no one could doubt he meant it.

"That's fine, Cunningham; I'll take you at your word," I assured him briefly. There could be no gain in long lectures on the evils of drink. "You try your best and that's good enough for me. All right, you can go with us. And good luck to you on the job." I rose and shook his hand warmly.

He thanked me wholeheartedly but uneffusively and in only a few words, and left. I rolled back into my bunk to see no more of Bill Cunningham for months to come.

A little later, I was roused by the heat, for as we approached the Guinea coast and the sun got higher, it began to get uncomfortably warm. I rose again, stripped, and soused myself in the shower to cool off. Then down to breakfast, with a feeling of thankfulness that shortly I should say farewell to that dining room and all its unpleasant memories.

Up on deck again, even in a light khaki uniform, it was hot. The breeze happened to be from dead astern and about force 2, matching our own speed, so that effectively we were traveling in dead air, with no movement relative to us to cool us off. But since it was just as uncomfortable on deck as inboard, I soon retired to my stateroom to pack my bags, preparatory to departure.

About 2:00 P.M., as expected, we picked up low-lying land ahead. Still steaming on for a short time without the slightest change in course being needed, we hit the entrance to the harbor between the long outlying breakwaters squarely on the nose, a beautiful landfall!

This was perfection, which I had scarcely dared to hope for in deep sea navigation. But that something at least within hail of perfection was necessary in making Lagos, soon became evident.

As a grim reminder of what was now going on in the world, lying not far to the westward of the channel entrance were the topmasts of a large ship protruding from the water—just the tips of her two masts with some shrouds showing above the waves, and nothing else. The pilot (a very black native of Nigeria who boarded from a small pilot boat at the channel entrance to take us up the river to Lagos) laconically informed us of what had happened.

Those were the masts of a vessel which had recently made the mistake of coming close in, too far to the westward. Then when the error was realized, and she had found where she was, she had steamed directly east for the breakwaters, only to hit a defensive mine en route and founder finally, unsuccessful in her struggle to get into the shallow harbor before she went down.

I scanned the tips of those masts with professional interest. Apparently the ship was down in about fifteen fathoms of water. Too bad I hadn't one of my salvage ships with me. Here right at the western gateway to Africa was a job for us. But I knew I had no need to worry about jobs. If what I had heard of Massawa were only half true, we should have a plethora of wrecks to work on.

All hands were now crowding up on deck, intensely relieved. Discarded life jackets went sailing helter-skelter onto the boat deck, to land nobody cared where any more. We were inside the breakwaters at last, safe from any further wartime perils of the sea. Now all eyes were turned eagerly on Equatorial West Africa, opening before us as we entered the river up which Lagos in Nigeria lay.

White sand beaches fringed the river mouth. Palm trees were everywhere, and the river banks as we stood on were lined with lovely white tropical homes, a yacht club, the Government House, and such other appurtenances of British colonial life as we'd read about.

Passing the Government House, the guard and band (very soldierly looking blacks in white uniforms but with bare feet) were paraded in our honor and an American flag hoisted alongside the British, while the band ashore played both "The Star-Spangled Banner" and "God Save the King." As we had no band, we could answer this welcoming gesture only by dipping our colors and cheering wildly.

Within half an hour, we were being breasted in by tugs against our berth, a very modern pier. Our thirty-two-day voyage was ended safely—no thanks to the *S.S. Pig's Knuckle* and her *Pinafore* crew.

CHAPTER

12

As we had known all along, we were due to cross Africa to our Middle East stations by air. Once the ship was tied up, the sole topic of conversation was how soon the planes would start us on our way, as Lagos was hot, humid, and worst of all, malarial. This was the fever coast of ill fame, where in the old slave trading days, no white man could stay a night without contracting malaria, where a stay exceeding a few months was sure death from malarial fever.

Before leaving America, together with all the other Middle East personnel, I had been immunized by the Army Medical Corps against everything possible—smallpox, typhoid, tetanus, yellow fever, cholera, and typhus—a series of shots, which though spread over several weeks, had kept me decidedly groggy till departure.

But against malaria, the Army had no inoculation. Each of us was armed with a package of quinine tablets, but that was no preventative —it would merely mask and mitigate the symptoms once malaria was contracted. Our only defense, so our surgeons assured us, was to stay behind screens once night had fallen and the malarial mosquitoes were abroad, and to sleep under mosquito nets, with which all of us had been provided.

Under the circumstances, although to some degree the swampy mosquito coast had been cleaned up, getting out of Lagos in a hurry was desirable. General Scott sent his aide ashore immediately to check up on the air transportation situation.

It turned out to be not bad. The Army Air Corps was running all air transport across Africa with Pan-American planes and pilots doing the actual flying. Having been warned by cable of our coming, though not of the exact day of our uncertain arrival, Pan-Am had arranged to mass all its transport planes at Lagos for the movement. But even so, with 379 passengers landed all at once to take out, the departure would take three days, starting with one plane in the morning while the others were being assembled for later despatch.

Since this was an Army movement, it goes without saying that priorities in departure were naturally to be in order of rank. Civilian rank (due to executive position) was, however, also equally recognized, with the planes taking off alternately with soldiers and with civilians. The first plane out next morning was scheduled to carry military passengers.

Early next morning found General Scott and the fifteen top ranking officers (including me) going over the side to the pier, bound for the airport outside Lagos, clad in our lightest weight khaki, for it was already (or still) hot. Without regret and without ceremony, we bade farewell forever to the S.S. *Pig's Knuckle* and all she stood for, to us seemingly only a long drawn out nightmarish dream from which at last we had escaped by waking.

Hopefully, the moment our feet touched the pier ridding us of her finally, our faces turned eastward across Africa and what opportunities in the war lay before us there in the Middle East.

It was only a short ride in a car to the Lagos airfield, a flat, wide, well laid out plain, baking under the Equatorial African sun, the first of many such fields I was soon to be acquainted with.

We were on time for our early morning take-off, but our plane wasn't. Something wasn't right with its engines, and the mechanics were still struggling with them. Meanwhile, the sun rose higher, and in spite of the protection of the airfield office into which we promptly fled for shade, we began to swelter.

Finally, the perspiring Army Air Corps major running the field came in to tell us the plane, specially rushed to Lagos for the first trip, could not be tuned up sufficiently well to take off that day for the 3000-mile flight across Central Africa. Our faces fell at that lugubrious announcement. Back to the *Pig's Knuckle* for another day? It was unbearable!

But hastily he revived our sunken feelings. A regularly scheduled land flight was due in about 9:00 A.M. from the cross-Atlantic air terminus at Roberts Field in Liberia, westward of us. Considering all the rank he had before him and the circumstances, he would bump all the passengers off that plane and give it to us for our eastward trip. We should be delayed only a few hours. The incoming passengers he would forward, depending on their priorities, as rapidly as he could.

This was better. While we sympathized with those coming in who would find themselves unexpectedly held over in Lagos a day or more, still we shed no tears over them. If they had been lucky enough somehow to get across the ocean to Africa by air in a few days, while we had suffered a month on the same passage, it was only the natural law of compensation that they, rather than we, should bear the burden of this mishap.

At 9:00 A.M. on the dot, the plane, a twin-engined Douglas transport, appeared over the field, circled to a landing, and then taxied up to a stop in front of the airfield office. The port side door was swung open, and the passengers started nonchalantly to debark to stretch their legs (so they thought) a few minutes before taking off again for the interior of Africa.

With eagle eyes we, already on the field out under the sun again, scanned their necks and their shoulders as one by one those unsuspecting passengers emerged. All Army men, except one naval lieutenant and one very insignificant-looking civilian clutching an umbrella. And, thank God, from their collar or shoulder insignia, not a general, not a colonel, not even a major in the crowd! There would be no serious trouble in bumping off that lot.

The Air Corps major bustled up to the descending passengers.

"Sorry, gentlemen!" he announced. "There'll be a delay here for all of you. Get back in the plane and bring out your belongings. You're going no further in this plane!"

We got back into the office out of the sun, content to leave arguments and protests to the airfield manager, of which he immediately got plenty. But some of the more indoctrinated Army juniors and the Navy man, looking over the general's stars, my brass hat, the eagles, and the silver and gold oak leaves liberally sprinkled over the waiting group in the office, took it more philosophically.

Protests or no protests, however, within half an hour the plane had been emptied of all the incoming passengers and their baggage, our bags stowed on board in the nose of the plane in their place, and we were invited to embark. General Scott first, so he might choose where he pleased to sit, then the rest of us, clambered through the door into the khaki-colored plane bearing the Army Air insignia painted prominently on its wings. All sixteen of us were carefully checked off inside the plane, both by the airfield manager and Colonel Gruver, to make sure none were missing and no unauthorized passengers were with us, then the manager descended and the door was slammed to, sealing us in.

The plane had stood half an hour already on the field, absorbing heat both from the overbaked ground beneath and the sizzling African sun overhead. Since all insulation and interior sheathing had been stripped from its aluminum shell to lighten it for war service, it was literally an oven inside once the door was closed.

We expected momentarily that the chocks would be pulled from the wheels and we should take off to cool ourselves in flight, but it didn't happen. Instead, minute after minute for another half hour went by and we stewed. I couldn't stand it any longer. After a few minutes, off came my khaki jacket, wringing wet with sweat. A little later, off came my khaki shirt, even wetter. Still we remained on the ground. Casting dignity to the wind, off came my undershirt then, completely soaked through. Meanwhile, my fellow passengers were doing likewise, and I think we should next have started stripping off our trousers had not the door of the plane been suddenly opened from the outside. To the cry,

"Another passenger! Flat orders to send him! You're off now!" there was literally tossed through the opened door, followed by his bag, the insignificant little civilian who had previously been bumped off the plane, still, of all things, clinging to his umbrella! Behind him, the door was slammed to again and secured.

Simultaneously with that, the chocks were jerked free of the wheels and we taxied over to the runway. Swabbing our faces vigorously to clear our eyes of sweat so we could see out, all of us were so engrossed in watching the ground whiz past while our plane hurtled down the runway and lifted smoothly into the air, we gave no more than a swift malevolent passing glance at the cause of our delay as he picked himself off the deck and sidled inconspicuously into the end seat next the door.

Even after we had straightened away in flight and were steadily climbing, all hands were fully occupied for some time in trying to dry their dripping torsos, a hopeless task, as no one had anything dry at hand to work with. Gradually as we rose into higher altitudes, with the hot earth dropping away beneath us and the cooler air rushing by at 160 miles an hour to wash away the heat from our plane, it became comfortably cool inside, so we stopped perspiring.

But the plane kept swiftly climbing till we were at 9000 feet long before we or our belongings had opportunity to dry out. As we rose toward 9000 feet, to us it became colder and colder. Whether we liked it or not, to keep from freezing, back one by one went on our soaked undershirts, our dripping shirts, our wet jackets. Finally we were driven to slipping on our overcoats, which we hadn't worn since leaving Cape Hatteras, but which now fortunately we were carrying with us inside the plane, since we couldn't stow the bulky things in our bags. Thus clad, we sat shivering for some time till the heat of our bodies at last dried out everything between our skins and our overcoats.

All this took nearly the first hour aloft. Not till then did I pay much attention to the interior of the plane. When reasonably dry, I began to look around. Our plane was a standard Douglas twin-engined transport, stripped completely and outfitted for Army service. Gone were the upholstered bucket seats, the interior sheathing. We could look directly at the aluminum ribs, the outer aluminum shell, all the tiny rivets holding the plane together.

For our seats, instead of the athwartship chairs, nicely upholstered for comfort, there ran along each side simply a long, low aluminum-topped bench, molded into seat bottoms, but naturally with no give to the aluminum. Other than these two benches, the inside of the plane was completely barren of fittings. This plane was the prototype of hundreds of others I was to see before the war was over, unarmed, lightened as much as possible, intended only to carry as many troops or paratroopers and their fighting equipment as it could lift off the ground.

Having satisfied my curiosity as to our plane, I looked casually aft along the port side. There, huddled on the end of the bench next the door, sat the added passenger who had been the cause of our sweltering delay. (I was myself seated well forward on the starboard side.)

He must have been quite an important civilian in spite of his half-pint size. And he must have had quite an unusual priority to have managed to hold the plane till he could get the airport manager over-ruled and himself reinstated on a full plane once he had been bumped off. That no one of our own group had been bumped off at the last minute to make room for him when reinstated, was probably due only to the fact he weighed so little, it made no difference to the plane.

Now for the first time, I took a good look at him, then looked again in astonishment. There could be no doubt of it, our very important passenger was a Hindoo! Except that he had more on, all light linen, he was a dead ringer in appearance, age, and manner for Mahatma Gandhi, and certainly weighed no more, not over seventy or eighty pounds at most. Perhaps, considering what had happened, he was the Mahatma!

I nudged the Army captain seated alongside just abaft me, and asked him to look and see if he saw what I saw.

He took a look, and his eyes bugged out. Excitedly he turned again to me.

"Why, I know that Hindoo! I was on the Clipper bound westward across the Pacific for the Middle East that got hung up in Honolulu the day they bombed Pearl Harbor. And that Hindoo was with me, bound home for India. Of course, the Clipper ended its voyage then and there, and how that Hindoo wept all over the place! Now I'll be damned if I'm not with him again in a plane bound east this time for the Middle East, while he's still headed for India. But it's wartime now. How'd he ever wangle an air priority across the Atlantic?"

That, of course, I wouldn't know. It was all quite a coincidence, not to mention very curious. My seat mate jumped up, walked all the way aft down the passage, greeted our Hindoo fellow traveler most cordially. It turned out to be the same Hindoo, sure enough, but he seemed to be far more interested in solitary meditation over that umbrella clutched now between his bony knees than in renewing a casual acquaintance with an American. Their conversation swiftly languished.

My companion came back a little crestfallen.

"It's the same Hindoo, all right, but he doesn't seem to want to talk any more. I asked him how he was lucky enough to get a priority going this way in wartime, and he shut up like a clam, so I left him. Funny little duffer, isn't he?"

I agreed he was, and then lost interest in him, for now, having left the coast and the green valley of the Niger behind us, and having cooled the plane off, the pilot was flying at lower altitude, 5000 feet, and giving us a better view of the country. We were heading northeast for Kano, 400 miles inland from the coast, our first stop, and we were not too far away from it.

The terrain below had changed from the dense green along the coastal belt to more open, drier country with only straggling vegetation, and then became rather barren.

Soon we dropped very low and started circling for a landing over Kano, a very ancient market city on the southern edge of the Sahara Desert. Kano, with a native population of 100,000, from the air was startling. All over the place were what appeared to be huge, sprawling, flat-roofed apartment houses heavily built of mud, resembling very much the Indian pueblos of our own Southwest, except they were decorated with gaudily colored tiles. Surrounding the whole city, and perhaps explaining how it had managed to survive some thousands of years, were tremendous mud walls, some forty feet thick. The brown mud of which everything seemed to be built, looked as if a heavy rainstorm would dissolve the whole city, but presumably it rained very little, if at all, thereabouts.

We came down for a smooth enough landing and were taken promptly to the Officers' Mess of the Air Force for lunch. We stayed in Kano only long enough for lunch, but even in that brief time, two things struck us forcibly. One was the temperature. It was hot, 105° in the shade, but as it was dry, it was bearable. The other was the tall black natives, striding along with heavy burdens skillfully balanced on their heads, clad in white robes of the cut of flour bags (which on close inspection many of them were, brand names and all). Never had I seen such utterly black Negroes; they were so black they seemed to have almost a bluish tinge.

After a swift take-off (no waiting in the sun this time), we headed for Maiduguri, 300 miles further to the eastward and our stopping place for the night, since no night flying was being done along that lonely route fringing the southern Sahara. The scenery was more of what we had passed over approaching Kano—tiny native villages composed of round thatched huts, sparse vegetation, and nothing of any great interest.

I had a headache, eyestrain I thought, brought on by the glaring sunlight, and the afternoon air over eastern Nigeria was rather bumpy which made most of the Army passengers seasick. None of us were sorry when a few hours later we dropped down on Maiduguri airfield on the eastern edge of Nigeria, ending our first day's air voyage, though it was still only late afternoon.

An airways bus, driven by our own pilot, took us all, passengers and plane crew, from the hot airfield to the Pan-Am station some miles away, where at least there were palms about to give some shade.

There was a village of Maiduguri near by, which we had glimpsed from the air, but all hands were quite content to stay at the station. There the buildings, of typical Central African architecture, were built for comfort only and that was all we were interested in. Every building in the compound was the same—one-storied, with thick mud walls, rather high, and over all a heavily thatched roof, sharply pitched, projecting considerably beyond the walls to shade them, and clear of the side wall tops by several feet so that an open space for ventilation was left all around the building. Undoubtedly it was needed.

What took our eyes most on arriving, however, was a shower bath, pointed out to us by the pilot. It was primitive, but effective. Atop a fenced enclosure some twenty feet square and eight feet high, stood four fifty-gallon ex-gasoline drums, connected to impromptu shower heads. The water supply was simple—no pumps, no pipes, no valves, no meters. Half a dozen black boys with buckets on their heads brought the water, four more blacks alongside the drums overhead poured it into them, and there you were.

We were all hot, sticky, and uncomfortable. Sightseeing in Maiduguri could go hang. Immediately we had dumped our bags and ourselves into the open-topped, mud-walled rooms assigned us in the main quarters building, we were all stripping. In a few minutes, clad only in towels and shoes and carrying our own soap, we were all trekking through the hot dust to the shower a hundred feet away. There, four at a time, we reveled under the coarse sprays while the grinning black boys overhead poured on the water.

By the time all of us had dressed again in dry clothing extracted from our now available bags, the sun had set and it was cooler. Outside in the dust, native merchants, scenting trade, were spreading their wares for display—leopard skins, python skins, elephant tusks, ivory souvenirs, and native weapons of all kinds. Since I had no place within my scanty plane allowance to carry an ounce more, I refrained from purchasing anything, though some magnificent boa constrictor skins were insistently offered.

Tiring of the traders' persistency, I turned away back to the quarters, just in time to glimpse something odder even than the huge boa constrictor skins unrolled a moment before at my feet. Now that all the Westerners had cleared it, there in solitary state was our Mahatma Gandhi, fully clothed, carrying a towel, heading for the shower enclosure, and wonder of wonders, still carrying his umbrella! Did he intend, I speculated, to hold that over him while he stood beneath the spray?

About an hour later, dinner was announced as served in a separate mud-walled building, some distance from the quarters. While it was to be nothing special, only the regular evening meal for the Pan-Am and the Army airfield personnel who far outnumbered us, we needed no second urging to be on time.

Dinner was served by barefooted black boys clad in the usual white flour sacks, simply but effectively tailored with three holes cut in them for head and arms, but it was far better served than by the surly white stewards we had left on shipboard. And what a dinner! Creamed spinach soup, fried chicken, roast beef, some delicious native vegetables, excellent mashed potatoes, and real apple pie with cheese! Shades of the unlamented *S.S. Pig's Knuckle!* How we fell on that dinner!

But our Hindoo companion disdained it. Apparently nothing they served (or its cookery) came within the boundaries of his religious taboos, and not till a can of sliced peaches was brought and opened in his presence, did he deign to take anything at all.

Darkness fell quickly. As we were due to make an actual early dawn take-off for a long flight next day, I turned in at 8:00 P.M. Rather than sleep in the room assigned which still retained quite a bit of the heat absorbed during the day, I elected to use one of the narrow iron beds set up in the open outside, where it was already cooler.

Fully clothed, I crawled into the bed beneath the netting. Then I saw that that all-important mosquito net, draped from outriggers at head and foot, was solidly tucked in under the mattress all around me before I undressed and slipped into my pajamas. Of course, to anyone with reasonable experience in a Pullman upper berth, this last was no trick at all.

I dragged the sheet over me, then very shortly a blanket also, for it was remarkable how cool it soon got there in the open, once night had fallen. I gazed upward through my mosquito netting at the brilliant Equatorial stars, then swiftly went sound asleep for the first time in over a month. Here in the African desert was a comfortable bed, so different from those on the *Pig's Knuckle,* where the pillows, to mince no words, literally stank, and the mattresses were hard as rocks.

At 4:30 A.M., still in complete darkness, we were all turned out to dress hurriedly and breakfast before departure. The breakfast matched the dinner—pancakes with real maple syrup, and delicious coffee. That finished, just as the first indications of dawn appeared, we were herded back in the airways bus.

Hastily the pilot counted noses in the early twilight to make sure he had everyone, then slammed the bus door. Meanwhile, Colonel Gruver, just as anxious to ensure none of our party was missing, was doing the same. As the pilot threw in the clutch and started, Colonel Gruver sang out,

"Pilot, wait! You've left a man. That Hindoo is missing!"

Instead of stopping, the pilot only shifted into second, then into high. When finally the bus was well under way, he half turned his head to answer,

"That's O.K. He's staying over in Maiduguri on business. Don't bother."

That certainly seemed odd. What business could our Hindoo, having moved heaven and earth to get aboard our plane in his urgent desire to get speedily back to India, suddenly have discovered in the God-forsaken village of Maiduguri to cause him to abandon the plane in Central Africa? But in view of the pilot's curt reply, no one commented any further and we moved swiftly on to the airfield.

In the dim twilight, we took off, from several thousand feet aloft soon to witness the sunrise, abrupt in its suddenness in the clear, dry desert air. When the plane had finally been leveled off, the co-pilot took over and the pilot came back into the passenger compartment, apologized to Colonel Gruver.

"Sorry to have cut you off that way in the bus, Colonel, but I couldn't discuss that Hindoo while we were still on the ground."

"Oh, that's all right, pilot, no apologies needed," Colonel Gruver assured him. "I was just afraid you'd forgotten him and the plane would be hung up again while somebody had to go back for him. But what'd he want to stop in Maiduguri for? He didn't show any signs of having business there last night up to the time he turned in."

"He stayed there on business, all right, Colonel, but it wasn't of his own choosing." The pilot swung about to take in General Scott and the rest of us. "Along about 11:00 P.M., when everybody was asleep, a coded radio message came in from British Army Intelligence. It said to seize that Hindoo suddenly before he could destroy anything, search him thoroughly, report results, and then hold him incommunicado in Maiduguri for further instructions. Well, since this is British territory, the airfield manager sent into the village for the head of the British constabulary to do the job. He came out with a couple of limey assistants and you should have seen him work." The pilot paused, apparently recalling the scene admiringly.

"That lad knew his stuff. He got that Hindoo asleep, so he certainly had no chance to destroy anything, and got him and all his belongings out of there into the airfield manager's office without waking up anybody else. Then they searched him thoroughly, and I mean thoroughly—went through everything he had and didn't find a damned thing of interest. After that they stripped him and looked in his mouth, his ears, his nose, between his toes, under the soles of his feet. He came through that as innocent a Hindoo as you'll ever find. Then they nailed him with the goods. How do you think?"

Nobody hazarded a guess; we couldn't imagine.

"By his umbrella! Of course, that constable had gone over the umbrella one of the first things he did—opened it, closed it, found it had a solid wood shaft and handle, no hollows in it to hide anything. But when he couldn't find anything anywhere else, it struck him the Hindoo certainly set store on that umbrella—he'd had it with him in his bed when they grabbed him. So the constable went back to the umbrella. It had a long metal ferrule over its wood tip; nothing unusual in that, but he thought he'd see. So he worked off the ferrule, and there it was! Wrapped round the tip of the umbrella under the ferrule were long thin strips of paper covered with fine writing, some in German, some in Hindoo. It took two men to hold that half-portion Hindoo when they found that!

"Well, they took that Hindoo and all his stuff off to the hoosegow in Maiduguri to await developments, and I went back to sleep. And that's the business that's holding him in Maiduguri. He won't be flying the rest of the way with us."

So there, sequestered in the hands of the British Intelligence on the edge of the desert in Central Africa, we left our Hindoo and his secret Nazi instructions, weeping even more copiously, I imagine, than when his other plane, stopped halfway round the world from us by Japanese bombs falling on Honolulu, had also failed to carry him further along toward India and sedition.

CHAPTER

13

THE PILOT, WITH THAT EXPLANATION off his mind, started back for his controls. Just before he ducked through the forward door, he turned and added,

"We're over French Equatorial Africa, which is in the hands of the Vichy French and they'd intern you if we landed. So we've got a long nonstop hop to make on this leg all the way to El Fasher in the western Sudan before we can come down. But that Vichy crowd have got no planes to bother us while we're in the air, so I'm going to fly low now. We're passing over the Lake Chad country, which is the best wild animal spot in Africa, and maybe you'll see some of 'em."

In a rather swift descent, we came down to 800 feet. Below us was only desert country—nothing green whatever, with only the African version of sagebrush and desert trees, and the bare earth looking very dry and burned. A couple of lions (startled by the roar of our engines, no doubt) bounded madly away through the brush. We spotted a few gazelles and some half dozen ostriches, then crossed a small river with a few crocodiles basking in it. The river seemed out of place, for Heaven knows where the water might come from; the multitude of fine dry river beds we saw, all of sand, seemed more in keeping.

That was all, for it was too uncomfortably hot that low down to stay long, and shortly the pilot took us up to 5000 feet again and continued eastward, with the country below getting more barren and sandy.

The hours dragged on with the plane droning steadily eastward and our aluminum seats getting harder and harder. Having no other use for our overcoats, we soon were all using them, folded up, for cushions to sit on, while monotonously, mile after mile, we sped across the dead plain below.

Some hours out, the ground, still barren, began to get somewhat mountainous and we rose to 7000 feet. Then up we went still higher, to clear a mountain range with peaks rising to 9000 feet, with their ridges clearly visible not far below us—jagged, burned very brown, no vegetation on them. Nor any snow either, for they all looked too hot for that.

The air became quite bumpy and the plane began to bounce round in lively fashion. Whoever invented the old saw about riding on air as the ultimate in smoothness had obviously never been in a plane with air currents beneath him rising off hot mountain peaks.

We got over the mountains safely and settled into straighter flight. All hands breathed somewhat more easily. Had we crashed anywhere, even the Vichy French and their internment would have been welcomed to save us all from dying of thirst, for the caravans we spotted creeping along beneath us were few and very far between.

Once again we had desert country to fly over, but soon we reached the western Sudan and there was friendly territory beneath us— friendly, that is, politically only, for the desert looked no more inviting. Then briefly we encountered some more mountains, not so bad this time. Shortly beyond them must have been some water, for there below was the little town of El Fasher on the western fringe of the Sudan, where several important caravan routes crossed to justify its existence. We had flown 900 miles since leaving Maiduguri.

We came down on the airfield for a stop to have lunch while the plane refueled. It was hot, as usual. At this field, run by the British, there was no such meal as we had had at the Pan-Am stations. Food was evidently scarcer and strictly rationed. A couple of sandwiches and some warm water had to suffice.

Meanwhile, at El Fasher I got a grim reminder of why I had not got off by air from New York. On the field were the burned remains of a Flying Fortress. Just off the field at Kano had been the crushed wreck of another. How many of these early Fortresses had not even made Africa, I never learned.

We took off shortly for our last eastward leg to Khartoum on the Nile. We hurdled some more mountains, flew over more desert, and finally in the late afternoon came down on the airfield, the largest we had yet seen, outside Khartoum. We had covered 1400 miles since dawn.

When the plane taxied to a stop and we emerged, I gasped as if I had stepped directly into a blast furnace. At the first whiff of that blistering air, involuntarily I stopped breathing. We had thought we had been hot before, but we had met nothing like that Khartoum field. We rushed for the nearest building to get out of the sun and of that dry, baking heat that seemed to shrivel the lungs.

Khartoum was the air crossroads of Africa. Eastward ran the route to Arabia and India. Part way along that course lay Eritrea, where the regular flights never stopped. Southward ran the route to Durban and Capetown. Northward a thousand miles was Cairo, where I was to report to General Maxwell before proceeding to my station. We would stay overnight in Khartoum and the next morning separate, some few going on to Eritrea in other planes, General Scott and most others going to Cairo.

Very soon the sun set, and with its disappearance the desert sands cooled off and the air quickly lost its burning heat. Once it was dark, Major Goff and I went into Khartoum to see the famous city where, at the junction of the Blue and the White Niles, Chinese Gordon had been killed and Lord Kitchener of Khartoum had made history in avenging him.

Khartoum itself was something of a disappointment. It was a modern enough European city of fair size, about half the population of Kano. But it was neither Egyptian nor Sudanese in architecture and about as exciting as Main Street, with its street cars and its cinema showing an American movie.

The one compensation which the major and I got for our twenty-mile ride over terribly dusty roads from the airfield was a view by flashlight (Khartoum was blacked out) of a statue of Chinese Gordon astride, not a horse, but a camel. This was the first equestrian statue I ever saw which could claim any real novelty. It stood boldly out in the little beams of our flashlights against the night sky, a really magnificent bronze.

Next, though we searched carefully in the black-out, we could find no statue of Kitchener in Khartoum, where he won his fame and his title. Possibly if he had fallen victim to a fuzzy-wuzzy spear near by instead of to a German U-boat in far distant waters, it might have been otherwise.

So back we went to the airfield to turn in after a fatiguing day. Our quarters, adjoining the airfield, were in what we were told was a girls' college before the war. We slept in one of the ex-dormitories. They must have had those native girls living on a high spiritual plane in that college. The narrow beds, reminiscent of Queen Nefertiti's long-gone day, had only rope for springs and the pillows consisted of short cylindrical rolls packed hard with straw, which gave me a pain alternately in each ear as I rolled from side to side.

We were under way early for Cairo and glad to get high up into the air before the sun really got to work. For some distance north we followed the Nile, to get a startling impression of how that river *is* Egypt. Only a narrow strip, rarely as much as a mile wide, along either bank was green. Outside that strip the hot sands came in on both sides to a sharp line of demarcation between desert sand and irrigated fields. For almost a thousand miles we saw that—the thin ribbon of green, intensively cultivated bordering the Nile, running through the desert on each side.

Away from where the Nile waters the land, is the most terrible desert on earth from Khartoum north to Cairo. The deserts we had crossed coming from Lagos across Central Africa were as nothing to this. I could well believe that nowhere else on earth or in the sea or in the air could one find an area so absolutely devoid of any form of life whatever—no birds, no animals, no men, no vegetation. Here was only burning sand—sand in ripples, sand in ridges, sand in waves, sand dunes, barren rocks bordered with sand, scorched mountains with never a bit of green on them rising from seas of sand with rivers of sand flowing down their sides like glaciers, and vast clouds of fine sand thousands of feet up in the shimmering air, drifting over the sand below—everywhere desolation, aridity, and sand.

We made a brief stop at Wadi Halfa, where the Nubian Desert meets the Nile, for lunch. It was nearly as hot on the ground as at Khartoum. Then we continued on, flying high above the Nile to arrive finally in mid-afternoon at the Heliopolis airport on the outskirts of Cairo, when we came down.

Since leaving Khartoum, we had flown directly north over a thousand miles, about the distance separating Miami from New York. The change in latitude to the north produced a similar change in temperature. When we descended, on March 23, from the plane at Cairo in Latitude 30° North, outside the tropic zone, it was to encounter what might have been mild summer weather in any American city.

General Russell Maxwell, U.S.A., Chief of the North African Mission, Commanding General of all American forces in the Middle East, was at the airport to greet General Scott. For the first time, I also met him and looked over my new commanding officer with considerable interest.

What struck me immediately was his square chin, setting off his rugged features. Evidently from that chin, and the keen, searching eyes above it, General Maxwell was a man of firm decisions and no nonsense. Aside from that, he was broad-shouldered, almost stocky, though only of medium height, all of which seemed to add to the resolution of his face. It became quickly evident, as he greeted us at the plane, that he was quite a reserved person, not much given to casual conversation, though this impression may have been accentuated by the fact that obviously he had plenty on his mind and was seeking action, not words, from his newly arrived assistants.

The two generals drove off together. Colonel Chickering, Chief of Staff for the Mission, going off with them, told me General Maxwell wanted to see me next morning at headquarters. With that, all the other incoming officers and their bags were loaded into Army cars and driven into Cairo.

The Army billeting officer had done as well as he could in crowded Cairo, overflowing with British staff officers and men on leave from the near-by British Eighth Army, to house us temporarily. I was directed to the Hotel Continental, where I was told there would be room for me. There was. Three Army officers and I, lest some of us sleep in the streets, accepted gladly a room meant for two, and drew lots to see who should sleep in the two beds and who on the floor. I drew a bed.

Next morning I reported as directed to General Maxwell at the Mission headquarters, a large Egyptian residence hastily turned to office use with no changes.

The discussion was brief. The general had had no opportunity as yet to visit Massawa himself. I should find things there in bad shape; the climate also was reported as terrible. Had I read these things in the preliminary reports on that station? I had. The British were in possession of the country, but unable, due to lack of man power and materials, to rectify matters. It was important to get something done at Massawa immediately. The situation on land in Libya was deteriorating rapidly. Rommel had overrun El Agheila, just recaptured Benghazi, and was driving eastward. It was hoped to stop him at Tobruk, to the west of which the Eighth Army was now fighting delaying action in the desert. Tobruk had before held against a long Axis siege; it was believed it could again. However, there was no certainty of it; besides, Rommel might elect to by-pass Tobruk and drive immediately on to Egypt.

As regards the British naval situation in the Mediterranean at the moment, General Maxwell knew it was bad, but gave me no details. I might get them when I left by a visit to British naval headquarters in Cairo, just around the block.

All in all, the Middle East picture was far worse than when I had left the United States in mid-February. I must get to Massawa immediately and, utilizing what I might find on hand there, do anything that might be done, not waiting for my own men and materials. The need was urgent.

I suggested to General Maxwell that it would be well if I went to the British naval base at Alexandria a day or two to get acquainted with the British officers there with whom I should later have to work, and learn their needs.

"No," said General Maxwell decisively, "get on to Massawa. Leave tomorrow. The British have a Navy captain in Massawa. He can tell you what they need. In two or three weeks from now, when you've got things started in Massawa, you can come back to visit Alexandria. Meanwhile, before you leave, come and have dinner with me tonight."

"Aye, aye, sir." I saluted and left, to walk directly to the near-by British naval headquarters, as General Maxwell had advised, to report my coming to them and get what information I might from the naval staff there in Cairo.

If General Maxwell had painted a gloomy picture of the land situation, which the world in general knew from the position of Rommel's advancing Afrika Korps, it was nothing to the gloom of the naval picture, which was a deep secret, completely unknown to the world at large, and probably even to the enemy.

I listened with a sinking heart as the background against which Massawa must be made to work, was outlined to me by British naval officers.

Britain no longer had a battleship fleet in the Mediterranean to oppose the powerful Italian battle fleet composed of certainly four and possibly five or six dreadnoughts.

While it was then completely hush-hush, the British Mediterranean battleship fleet which had dominated that sea since the war began, in 1939, was no more—not a single battleship left in service. Their flagship, the superdreadnought *Barham,* had been torpedoed late the preceding November by a submarine while operating with her two sisters, the *Queen Elizabeth* and the *Valiant,* off Tobruk, and had swiftly gone down with vast loss of life, over 800 men. It was believed the enemy was unaware of this, or at least not certain of her sinking. The British, in the face of Axis reports, were not admitting her loss. Her consorts, the *Queen Elizabeth* and the *Valiant,* had been withdrawn to Alexandria harbor, there to lie in safety behind submarine nets, pending further operations at sea.

Then disaster had struck the remaining two battleships in spite of all conceivable precautions. Only a few weeks after the loss of the *Barham,* a picket boat patrolling the submarine nets across Alexandria harbor, just after midnight had come across a couple of men in bathing suits perched atop an unused mooring buoy. This was curious; it was hardly normal for anyone to be out swimming in the harbor in the middle of the night. The boat picked them off the buoy, and seeing that the swimmers were obviously neither English nor Egyptian, took them aboard the nearest moored warship for interrogation, while it departed to resume its picketing. The vessel happened to be the battleship *Queen Elizabeth.*

The swimmers turned out to be Italians, which was disquieting. But if that turned out to be disquieting to the naval officers interrogating them as to what they were doing swimming in the harbor at night, the two swimmers seemed also greatly disquieted at finding themselves unexpectedly aboard an enemy warship. Still, in spite of that, they kept their mouths shut, other than to admit they were Italians, which they could hardly deny.

After some futile questioning, leading nowhere, and anxious to lose no time in the face of probable peril, the captain of the *Queen Elizabeth* ordered his First Lieutenant to get out a hogging line and sweep the bottom of the ship from bow to stern with it, to see if they could catch and dislodge anything which might have been attached to their hulls by those two ill-omened swimmers. Then he signaled the *Valiant,* advising her to do the same.

Meanwhile, there were the two bathers, obstinately mute, though agitated visibly enough even on deck. Perhaps below, they might become sufficiently more agitated to explain what their swimming party meant.

So they were separated and sent below, one forward and one aft, to compartments just above the double bottoms, with an armed marine stationed at the open hatch just overhead each. Each bather was informed in Italian that whenever he wanted to talk, the marine would bring him up on deck again.

Then commenced a battle of nerves. On deck both battleships, in the darkness working parties broke out hogging lines, dropped them over the bows, time after time carefully swept the drags aft under the hulls, feeling for obstructions. Below, the marines anxiously watched their prisoners, pacing in gradually increasing nervousness the small compartments far below the waterline into which they had been dropped.

Nearly three hours elapsed. On deck, the first sharp concern had subsided. The drags had caught nothing. Perhaps those Italians, enemy agents though they probably were, were merely spies from the heterogeneous foreign population of Alexandria, swimming out from shore to scout the fleet at close range. How else, in view of the nets and the close patrols, they could have got into the harbor was incomprehensible. Below, the marines reported their charges still mute, except that occasionally in pantomime, they asked what time it was.

At about a quarter of five in the morning came a break. Almost simultaneously, both marines sang out that their charges, suddenly frantic, were begging to be taken up, eager to talk.

Hurriedly the prisoners were rushed up on deck to meet the captain again. They talked volubly now; it was almost impossible to stop them. In a mad torrent of Italian, gesticulating wildly, they begged to be taken off the ship. They had secured a huge mine to her bottom amidships; in fifteen minutes it would go off and blow the *Queen Elizabeth* to pieces! And a similar mine was under the *Valiant!*

The captain of the *Queen Elizabeth* took the astounding news more coolly. There were, thank God, no magazines in that vicinity but to him it made no difference if there were. He had no intention of abandoning ship, only of saving her. He had just fifteen precious minutes to work in.

Instantly the news, with instructions, was signaled to the *Valiant.* While the message was going over, on the *Queen Elizabeth* the General Alarm bells started to ring, the bugles blared to turn out all

[84]

hands. Bos'n's pipes shrilled, followed by the hoarse calls.

"Secure everything below! Close all watertight doors! All hands on deck!"

In the boiler rooms, oil fires were hastily extinguished; in boiler and engine rooms, all steam lines secured. All over the ship men were madly dogging down every watertight door in every bulkhead, every watertight hatch in every deck, every airport in the sides of the ship's hull, coming up as they secured the openings, leaving no one below and nothing open.

In less than ten minutes the entire crew, well over a thousand men, were mustered on deck in the darkness, with below them the darkened and deserted hull of the *Queen Elizabeth* sealed up, bulkheads, decks, and sides, as it had never been since the day she was commissioned.

In excruciating silence, the seamen waited in the night as the last five minutes till five o'clock dragged endlessly by. Was it perhaps only a hoax? Or was it real? And if it were real, what would that mine do to them? Each man's imagination had free rein. Not one of them but had already seen in the Mediterranean what mines, torpedoes, and bombs had done to other ships. Only three weeks before they had all been present when torpedoes had set off the magazines of the *Barham,* tearing her to bits as she sank, killing most of her crew. Had there been a mad rush overboard from the *Queen Elizabeth,* no one could have blamed the crew. But silent, dogged as always, those British seamen kept their ranks, waiting for five o'clock.

It was no hoax. At five o'clock a terrific underwater explosion shook the 31,000-ton *Queen Elizabeth;* a few seconds later a similar shock hit the *Valiant.* Both vessels trembled as if struck by titanic sledgehammers, then started to settle rapidly in the water. In each, a vast hole had been torn in her bottom beneath the central boiler room, crushing the massive boilers up against the heavily armored protective deck overhead as if they had been only eggshells.

Had the crews been caught unaware, both ships would undoubtedly have sunk, total losses. But with no one killed, no confusion, all hands forewarned, and all openings already sealed up, their crews were ready once the explosions were over. Instantly, they went below with flashlights to get what machinery was still intact fore and aft of the damage, going again to battle leakage. The flooding was confined principally to the ruptured boiler rooms amidships.

Even so, both vessels sank bodily till their low after decks were nearly awash. Hardly a few feet of their sides remained above water after the explosions. In this parlous position, their crews below fought desperately to keep the water from spreading; only a slight margin of buoyancy remained between them and complete disaster.

They succeeded. When dawn broke over Alexandria harbor, there were the *Queen Elizabeth* and the *Valiant* still afloat, still erect, with no visible damage, and except to someone passing close aboard to note their extraordinarily slight freeboard, looking as if nothing had happened.

It was imperative to maintain the illusion that nothing *had* happened, that Britain still had at least two effective battleships in the Middle East. Some half dozen other Italians in peculiar semi-diving masks, had meanwhile been picked up elsewhere in the harbor or on the beaches inside the nets. It seemed that all the Italians directly engaged in this ingenious and hazardous operation with tiny submersible boats which had somehow got over or under the nets to attach the mines, had been captured. None had escaped; evidently only by air reconnaissance could the enemy judge now what success these men had had in destroying Britain's all-important battleships.

So to carry out the illusion to air observers, who could never detect their low freeboards, life went on as usual on deck both battleships —the bands played, the crews were mustered for inspection at normal hours, small boats came and went on their ordinary schedules. The ruse had succeeded. There was not the slightest evidence now, three months later, that the enemy had any knowledge of the startling success of his daring attack.

But that hardly lessened the gloom of the British officers to whom I was talking. Only a few cruisers, some destroyers, and some submarines now remained as their whole Mediterranean fleet. They had not a heavy ship left to defend themselves with, nor to attack the Italian Navy convoying supplies to Rommel's advancing army.

Not for a year at least would either the *Valiant* or the *Queen Elizabeth* be able to enter battle again. By truly herculean efforts, they had expelled water enough from the *Valiant,* the less damaged of the two, to get her on their large floating dry dock in Alexandria for emergency repairs to her bottom only, so she might safely float while she was being taken elsewhere, out of the war zone.

Only that week, with her smashed boilers still smashed, able to steam on her remaining boilers at hardly ten knots, the wounded

Valiant had been taken off the dry dock to make way for the still more damaged *Queen Elizabeth*. The *Valiant* would shortly proceed at slow speed through the Red Sea to Durban in South Africa, there to receive some further patching to enable her to limp across the Atlantic to the United States for real repairs.

Meanwhile, the *Queen Elizabeth's* bottom repairs would be rushed on the dry dock in the hope they could at least get the hole patched and the ship away from Alexandria before Rommel got close enough for his Stuka bombers to stop it. But all this was keeping their large dry dock tied up with these two ships only for over six months. This left the Alexandria naval base with only one smaller dock available for cruiser or other ship repairs and they were falling far behind. How soon could Massawa get going and lend a hand?

I had to shrug my shoulders. I hadn't the slightest idea.

To deepen my gloom, the British captain to whom I was talking informed me sympathetically,

"I understand, Commander, your new station's a bloody hell-hole. In fact, though I've never been there myself, I'm sure of it. To help you, we sent a commander in the Royal Navy to Massawa a month or so ago to await your coming, which we'd been told was to be by air from America. He was to act as liaison officer between you and the Royal Navy. That month in Massawa, partly in February and the rest in March, has browned him off already. He's now in a military hospital high up in the Eritrean mountains, broken mentally and physically, though it's reported he'll recover in time. But then he'll have to be sent home to England."

He paused while apparently he sized me up as to how I might stand it, then shook his head dubiously. I wasn't so young nor any physical marvel either. Abruptly he asked,

"How old are you, Commander?"

"Fifty, sir."

"Really?" He lifted his eyebrows. "Our medical chaps who've surveyed the spot have recommended only men *under* fifty be sent there for work. They don't think anybody that old can stick the course."

"Well, Captain," I assured him, "Americans can stand lots of heat. We're used to it more than you. America gets much hotter than England. Ever been in Washington in the summertime?"

"No," he admitted, "but Massawa's unique on earth. So far as temperature goes, they tell me the next stop's Hades. Well, be that as it may, we're sending you a relief liaison officer. He's shoving off for Massawa in the morning by air, but right now he's in another office here getting his instructions. Just a moment; I'll bring him in and introduce him."

I waited. In a few minutes he returned with a Royal Navy commander in tow. Briefly he introduced us, then with a clipped,

"Cheerio! Good luck to you both in Massawa!" he departed, leaving us alone.

I looked over the new liaison officer. Evidently he was some years younger than I. Apparently the Royal Navy had taken great care on that point. But other than that, I was not impressed by the man on whom I must depend in all my contacts with the British. He was bigger than I, tanned enough by the African sun, but decidedly nervous. I learned from a brief conversation he felt he had already been through too much for his new and decidedly unwelcome assignment.

It seemed that some time before, he had been beached when his ship was lost. That, I now knew, was not unusual in the Mediterranean. Then he had been assigned to go to Benghazi as Naval Officer in Charge (NOIC, in British parlance) of that newly captured port in western Libya. But before he could report in Benghazi, Rommel had recaptured it and there was now no need for a British NOIC in Benghazi, nor from the looks of things in Libya, would there be there or elsewhere in Libya for a long time, if ever. That had left him available when the liaison officer already in Massawa had so speedily cracked up, and he had been given the job. He had done his best to get out of it, but unsuccessfully. It appeared the swift dissolution of his predecessor in Massawa, whom he knew well, had made a deep impression on him.

As a last straw, he appealed to me for aid. Couldn't I help keep him from going to Massawa? He just knew he couldn't stand it there; nobody could, with the summer season just coming on. Even the Italians, he assured me, when they had the place, used to lock it up and flee to the mountains for the summer. Couldn't I save him from it, he pleaded?

All this, somewhat hysterically put, was, I thought, a strange request to make of a foreign naval officer who had come a long way to go to that same station. Massawa, I reflected, must be something if it could make a naval officer of considerable experience bare his naked soul to a stranger he had met only the moment before.

Regretfully I had to tell him I could do nothing. I had no voice in the assignments of the Royal Navy; none to speak of, even in my own Navy. I went where I was sent, and I presumed he should have to, also; like good sailors, we would both do the best we could. Still, inwardly I regretted his assignment, and if I had possessed any power to get it changed, I should certainly have used it. This man was licked before he started by his terror of Massawa; yet on him I should have to depend in all my contacts with the British in getting Massawa going that summer, when he had no faith at all in the possibility.

Telling him I hoped to get a place next morning in the plane for Eritrea in which he already had a seat reserved, so that we might talk matters over at greater length, I left him. He stood there disconsolate, so wrapped in his fears he was wholly oblivious to the ridiculous figure he was asking me to cut before some British admiral, pleading to have a British officer younger than myself spared an ordeal I, an officer in a foreign navy, was undertaking without complaint.

From the Royal Navy offices, in no very cheerful state of mind after all I had heard, I went directly to the U.S. Army Transportation Officer in Cairo with my orders to depart for Eritrea, to get passage there. It turned out our Army was not flying the route from Cairo to Asmara, capital of Eritrea, but the British had a daily plane, not a large one, which ran that route, going via Port Sudan. It was part of a private line, British Overseas Airways Corporation, operating, however, under the supervision of the British Army in the same way Pan-Am in Africa ran under the direction of our Air Corps. The transportation officer said he would immediately get in touch with the British authorities and arrange my flight.

He tried, but he didn't succeed. It appeared that the BOAC plane for Asmara next morning was not only loaded with British military passengers with top priorities, but so were all their planes for over a week to follow. It was too late to do anything for the plane the next day; regarding those following, provided the joint British-American military staffs were willing to bump someone off in my place, a place might be made in a few days.

Somewhat disgruntled at this state of affairs, the Air Corps captain doing the inquiring dropped the telephone and turned to me.

"How urgent is your trip, Commander?"

"You'll have to put that up to the Chief of Staff, Colonel Chickering," I replied. "All I know is that General Maxwell ordered me to get along to Massawa, four bells and a jingle. He wouldn't even let me take a day or two for a visit to Alexandria."

The air officer was about to call Colonel Chickering to put some heat on BOAC in my favor, when the very Pan-Am pilot with whom I had flown all the way from Lagos, happening to be waiting in the transportation office, broke in.

"Captain, I think I can fix this for you. I'm flying my plane back west to Accra via Khartoum in the morning, and we haven't got much of a load going to Khartoum. I'll fly the Commander to Khartoum. There he can transfer to one of those special Pan-Am planes headed east for Asmara that are carrying the men from his ship in Lagos through to Eritrea; there'll be lots of them coming through. Their last hop from Khartoum to Asmara isn't very long. They can always carry an extra passenger on that jump they wouldn't dare to haul on the long hops coming east from Lagos. How does that strike you?"

The transportation officer looked at me. I thought it over hastily. The trip via Khartoum was roundabout, but it looked certain. Tomorrow afternoon I would be in Khartoum; the second morning, after a few hours' flight, I would be in Asmara, capital of Eritrea. Whereas on the small BOAC planes, Heaven alone knew who their few passengers might be over the next two or three days and what priorities they might have—possibly whole planes full of Hindoos clutching umbrellas with trick priorities that nobody dared touch, bound for India.

"I'll take you on that," I said. "It sounds fine to me."

The transportation officer wrote out the necessary papers, one for passage to Khartoum, another for my trip from Khartoum to Asmara. The pilot warned me to be sure to be at the Heliopolis airport at 6:00 A.M.; he was taking off early as he meant to get all the way to El Fasher that day. I assured him I'd be there and thanked him heartily for his help.

I took a brief stroll around Cairo the rest of the afternoon to find it completely unaffected by the war, except favorably. Things you couldn't buy anywhere else in the world you could buy freely in Cairo —provided you had the price. Even automobile tires. And there was no gasoline rationing for private cars, which were running wild all over the place.

The war was being fought all around Egypt, had already been fought on Egyptian soil, and apparently shortly would be again. But the Egyptians weren't doing any fighting themselves in defense of their country—they were just cashing in. If the British lines held, well and good. With the payroll of the whole British Eighth Army and its supply being spent in Egypt, never in its history had Egypt been so prosperous.

If Rommel broke through, so much the better. The Egyptians, for some strange reason, seemed ready to welcome him with open arms. God knows what they expected at the hands of Hitler, but it was evident they must have been promised plenty. Officially, Egypt was neutral. (I had to show my passport to get into the country, an odd situation for an officer in a war zone.) Unofficially, the country seemed to be playing both sides against the middle, forcing the Allies to supply it freely with articles for general consumption which Allied citizens at home couldn't get at all. And apparently from the eagerness with which they were awaiting Rommel, they expected to do even better with the Axis. I have no doubt at all that the period from 1940 through 1942 (after which the war drifted away from Egypt) will long be remembered in that country as the Golden Age.

Evening came. It was cool in Cairo in the evening. For the first time since leaving the American coast, I put on a blue uniform again when I drove to the outskirts of Cairo for dinner with General Maxwell.

The dinner party was small—General Maxwell, Colonel Chickering, Lieutenant Sumner Gerard of the Navy, who was the general's personal aide, a few other Army officers on his staff, and the American Naval Attaché in Egypt, Commander T. V. Cooper, whom I had known since we were both midshipmen thirty years before.

The general proved to be a cordial host, but he had apparently had a tough day and said little, content to listen. He had heard something of the voyage of the *Pig's Knuckle* from General Scott—it sounded unbelievable, probably just a landlubber's tale. Was it really so?

It was, unfortunately, I had to inform him, and it came about as a result that the whole evening was mostly devoted to our odyssey across the Atlantic, since all the others had come over earlier by air and were keenly interested in what they had missed by sea.

The party broke up early, since I had a daybreak date at the plane and the others were weary enough themselves. Commander Cooper drove with me back to town, a long ride, mostly along the Nile bank. It seemed so cold after all the heat I'd been through, I turned up the collar of my blue jacket, and if I'd had my overcoat, I would have worn it with pleasure.

Commander Cooper, who was more warmly dressed, said regretfully,

"I should have warned you, Ellsberg. There's a chill in these Cairo nights that gets you after a warm day. Be careful the next time you go out."

I thanked him for the caution and we rode the rest of the way in silence. This seemed advisable once we were in the city, for Cairo was completely blacked out, its sole concession to wartime. The way the thoroughly heedless Egyptian drivers tore about in the black-out with no lights on their cars save practically invisible blued-over pinpoints, took everybody's attention in the car. We didn't want to be smashed ourselves or to murder any Egyptians on foot whose dark skins stood out none too well in the black-out. It was with considerable relief that I finally safely disembarked at the Hotel Continental.

C H A P T E R

14

AS SCHEDULED, I TOOK OFF FROM THE Heliopolis airport early next day in the Douglas transport for the flight southward to Khartoum. There were no other passengers in the plane; mostly it was loaded with freight—captured enemy ordnance material going back to the United States for examination and test.

The trip was dreary enough. My second view of that thousand miles of terrible desert from Cairo to Khartoum was as depressing as the first.

In the early afternoon we got to Khartoum. Once on the ground, I bade good-by to the Pan-Am pilot, who refueled immediately for his westward hop to El Fasher, while I lugged my bags out of the plane and struggled with them across the burning field to its edge, where I wangled a ride in an R.A.F. station wagon to the transportation office. This was in the group of ex-college buildings some little distance from the runways.

As I gasped for breath in the heat and the dust on that Khartoum field, I began to wonder if my judgment hadn't completely decayed from age or something. I had had a chance in the beginning to go to Iceland instead of to Africa; had I possessed the slightest vestige of intelligence, I should have seized it. If Khartoum was like this, how, I wondered, could Massawa possibly be worse, even though it was so reported?

I got to the transportation office, dumped my bags into it and went up to the desk to present my papers for passage to Asmara.

The R.A.F. lieutenant running the desk looked at my papers, then looked blankly at me.

"I say, Commander, someone in Cairo's been pulling your leg. We've got no flights scheduled out of here for Asmara!"

"No regular ones, Lieutenant; I understand that," I explained. "But there are a lot of special flights going through here from Lagos to Asmara with a whole shipload of Army files and civilians who landed in Lagos with me a few days ago. I'm to go on one of those."

"Oh, those!" He shook his head pityingly. "My word, were they banking on those? Really, now, that's too bad. Your Pan-Am chaps did a better job on their transport than they'd expected and their last plane flew out of here on that mission this morning. There won't be any more."

I gazed at him, stricken. No more special Pan-Am flights to Asmara? Had I come a thousand miles from Cairo only to bake again needlessly in the heat of Khartoum?

There was nothing for it but to backtrack to Cairo and make a fresh start from there via the BOAC planes to Asmara. But in that also, I was in trouble. I had now no orders calling for transportation from Khartoum to Cairo and without them the sympathetic R.A.F. man could do nothing for me. He suggested I see the airfield Commanding Officer.

Miserably I dragged myself out of the transportation office and went looking in the heat for the C.O. It was a vast airfield and everywhere I went, the C.O. seemed one jump ahead of me. Finally, when night had fallen, I caught up with him in the dining room.

Sympathetically he also listened to my sad story. But all he could do, he declared, was to wire my situation to transportation headquarters at Cairo, and ask for orders and a priority assignment. It was now so late, it was hopeless to expect he could catch anyone at Cairo in time to act on the matter that night, so he might put me on a plane in the morning. The very best I could hope for, if in Cairo they assigned me a high enough priority, was a place the second morning following in the plane coming north from Capetown, bound for Cairo.

Two more nights and another whole day in Khartoum! I could have chewed nails at the prospect. But instead, I begged him only to get the wire off immediately and make it as strong as he dared. He promised.

Wearily I straggled over to a dining table, sat down. My khaki uniform was covered with dust, my face was dry and burned, my eyes ached from the glaring sands. Very evidently a navy cap, in spite of its brass-visored elegance, was not the thing to wear in Africa. I promised myself the moment I returned to Cairo I should lay in a pith sun helmet and a pair of sun glasses for future wear, regardless of whether or not the uniform regulations permitted such non-reg headgear. And I was terribly chafed between the legs also. I decided to add shorts to my purchases—no more long navy trousers for me. I was going to be comfortable, or at least as comfortable as I could, little as my rig in the future might look like a naval officer's.

A Sudanese servant—tall, black, stately, robed all in white—set my dinner down before me. It wasn't a bad dinner, but at the sight of it, I was suddenly made aware that my stomach had been feeling queer. I didn't have any desire to eat. Instead, without touching anything, I rose from the table and went to the airfield sick bay, looking for the surgeon.

The British doctor, military, of course, looked me over, took my temperature, asked me where I'd been, where and what I'd eaten, how long I'd been in Egypt, had I felt chilled any night? I told him.

"Gyppy tummy," he announced without hesitation. "Most new-comers get it right away. Sometimes it's from eating native food, but you haven't. Most cases, like yours, are from a chilled abdomen, due to night exposure after a hot day. Must have been that ride you had last night in Cairo with no overcoat. Well, not much I can do for you. It's a beastly bother but you'll get over it after a while; everybody does. Take this every few hours; it may help a bit," and he gave me a small bottle of medicine.

I managed to get a servant to cart my bags from the transportation office to the room assigned me in the girls' ex-dormitory, similar in all respects to the one I'd had my first night there. Then I made haste to locate the nearest toilet.

My spirits drooped when I discovered it. Modern plumbing did not exist in that part of Egypt. The sanitary facilities were of the out-house type made famous by "The Specialist." Here, however, they were a little more elaborate, being built of brick, and with plenty of chloride of lime at hand. But the little row of hot brick cubicles was at least 200 feet from my room. That would be bad. Forlornly I sat down to cogitate. Just my luck to be trapped with "Gyppy tummy" for thirty-six hours at least in such a place.

For that night, all the next agonizing day in the heat, and the second night following, I was not away from one of those brick cubicles for more than fifteen minutes at any one time. I practically wore a path in the hot brick pavement from my cubby-hole of a room to the nearest cubicle. Seriously I considered abandoning my useless bedroom and staying there all the time—my brief intervals away hardly made worth while the constant trekking back and forth, but the odors and the flies, despite the chloride of lime, deterred me.

"Gyppy tummy" indeed! That was much too flip a name for it; it warranted something far more impressive, for it was worse to endure than any of the ancient plagues of Egypt the Bible sets forth. Had Moses only smitten the Egyptians with this plague first, he could have spared himself all the trouble of bothering with the many minor plagues he had to use; undoubtedly the Egyptians would have been so preoccupied with it, the Children of Israel could have gone forth from Egypt at their leisure, wholly unmolested.

Only one ray of light brightened my sad state next day—just before noon I was informed radio orders had come through for me from Cairo with the ultimate in top priorities. The C.O. assured me that with that, regardless of who was on next morning's plane from Capetown and Durban, a place would be made for me going north.

It was. When the plane showed up from the south about the middle of the next morning, I was on hand on the Nile bank, for this plane was a huge British flying boat. Wan, weary, and bedraggled from little sleep and much internal tumult, I was hurried by a motorboat through the swirling waters of the Nile rising rapidly to flood stage, to where the moored plane was breasting the current, and thrust aboard.

Nobody aboard disembarked. I found the inside of that flying boat already jammed with South African troops headed for the Libyan battle front. They crowded together a bit and made room for one more. In a few minutes, with vast sheets of spray shooting by on both sides, we lifted from the Nile and took to the air.

For the third time within five days I found myself surveying the interminable sands between Khartoum and Cairo. I liked them no better on greater acquaintance than on first view—in fact, I was thoroughly sick of that desert, as well as being sick anyway. I had a miserable trip north, not helped any as this flying boat, in spite of all its massiveness, had a continuous vibration I had not noted in the Douglas land planes I had recently been in. This vibratory motion added, if that were still possible, to the uneasiness of my already completely uneasy insides.

Between the relative lateness of our start and the slow speed of that flying boat, it was much too late when I finally got into Cairo to do anything that day about getting out of it again, or even to get to the billeting officer for a room assignment.

In the faint hope they might by chance have a room, I went directly, bags and all, back to the Hotel Continental. The clerk there dashed my hopes. They had not a single room vacant; they were fuller than ever. So were all other hotels. The clerk, however, had a suggestion. The three Army officers I had previously shared a room with at the Continental still had the same room, and it being towards dinner time, should be in it now. Perhaps they might let me into that overcrowded room again. He would call their room and see. They would.

I went up and almost threw myself on their necks for their generosity, regardless of the fact that this time it would be my turn to sleep on the floor. At least this night I should be near a decent toilet; a bed would not have been of any great use to me.

CHAPTER

15

PROMPTLY WHEN IT OPENED IN THE morning, I was on hand in the Army Transportation Office, to relate to the Air Corps captain there how our elaborate plan to get me to Asmara had blown up because Pan-Am had turned out to be too efficient. He seized his telephone and went to work on BOAC again.

After considerable haggling and a great deal of stress on international relations, he finally hung up and faced me triumphantly. BOAC had agreed to take me next morning; their car would call for me at the Continental at 7:00 A.M. He wrote out my transportation order, and I left.

I had the day free in Cairo, since I decided it was the part of prudence to keep away from the North African Mission Headquarters, where they thought that days before I had already arrived in Massawa and had turned to there. There was no better way for the moment to help the war effort than to devote that day to myself, so I went shopping for equipment, by now my case of "Gyppy tummy" having somewhat subsided.

Cairo, a huge modern city that could hold up its head when it came to shops with New York or London, proved the best place in the world for my purpose. It was overrun with military tailors, all English firms, that were quite accustomed to British officers from the Eighth Army dashing into Cairo from the desert and out again the same day. I had no trouble at all in finding a firm, which, measuring me for three pairs of khaki shorts, promised faithfully that the completed shorts would be delivered to my hotel that night (and they were). In another equipment shop—this proved more trouble, since they were getting scarce—I picked up a fine khaki-colored pith sun helmet. In an optical shop, I found some American-made sun glasses.

There was only one odd feature in all this—the tailors insisted on all cash in advance with order, no checks, no C.O.D.s, no credit. Not, they assured me, that they doubted my word or my good faith, but so many officers were getting killed at sea or in the desert, it was an infernal nuisance collecting from their relatives overseas, and they had given up trying. Cash now, if you don't mind, and thank you so much.

This took all the rest of the morning. I went then to Shepheard's Hotel for lunch, being very wary now of where I ate anything in Egypt. After lunch, in my new sun helmet, I sat a while on the terrace in front of Shepheard's, watching the endless flow of burned and weary British soldiers, kit bags and bedding rolls draped over their shoulders with the thick dust of the Libyan Desert all over them, streaming into Shepheard's for a drink, and (they hoped) a chance at a bath.

About the middle of the afternoon, I returned to the Continental, feeling that a nap would do me some good. I stopped at the desk for the room key. The clerk, together with the key, handed me a sealed envelope with my name on it which had been left for me an hour or so before. I looked at it, puzzled. Who, in Cairo, save my three Army roommates who had no need to leave notes at the office, knew I was at the Continental?

I tore open the envelope, read hastily the typed blue slip enclosed:

BRITISH OVERSEAS AIRWAYS CORPORATION
To: COMMANDER ELLSBERG, Continental Hotel, Cairo.

We regret to inform you that you will not be traveling tomorrow morning on our service to Asmara.

I stared at that blue slip of paper incredulously. Whether the news itself or the suave language in which the bitter pill was conveyed seemed the more unbelievable to me, I could not determine. But it made no real difference. I swore fluently, tossed the room key back at the astonished room clerk, and dashed out of the hotel, bound for our Army Transportation Office. Was I never going to get to Massawa?

Furiously I thrust that blue slip of paper under the nose of the transportation officer who had a few hours before arranged my passage.

"They can't do that to us, Captain!" I exclaimed.

He read the slip, flared up more angrily even than I.

"I'll say BOAC can't do that to the United States!" He grabbed his telephone, started hastily to dial a number, while beads of sweat began to gather on his forehead. "If General Maxwell finds out we haven't got you to Asmara yet, he'll tear this office to pieces!"

There followed the longest and the hottest telephone conversation over a plane seat that had yet taken place in Africa, involving everything from breaches of faith among allies through reciprocity and hands across the sea to the allurements of Lend-lease, spiced with dire threats of what General Maxwell would do to BOAC when he heard of it.

Finally, after listening for a moment, the Air Corps captain hung up the telephone, wiped the sweat off his brow, and announced grimly,

"Be ready at your hotel at seven. They tell me now to tell you, 'Commander Ellsberg will be traveling tomorrow morning on our service to Asmara.' And damned intelligent of them to have come to that conclusion, or they couldn't have got a seat on one of our planes from now on for Churchill himself!"

I shoved off next morning, March 29, from the Heliopolis airport in the BOAC plane, a small, low-powered, twin-engine affair, compared to our Army's Douglas transports, and seeming even smaller relatively since it had not been stripped inside. It had all its peacetime sheathing and its original athwartship bucket seats, seating ten.

Of the passengers aboard, six were R.A.F. fighter pilots bound for Port Sudan, where we were to stop en route, there to pick up some American fighter planes and fly them back to Libya. The other passengers, except me, were British military officials, bound for Eritrea or Arabia. For whom it had been intended to bump me off, or who finally was left off the plane when I was reinstated, I never learned. Nobody mentioned the subject.

We flew at first due south down the Nile again some 300 miles to Luxor, where we stopped briefly to refuel. By now I had seen so much of the Nile, I felt I might qualify as a river pilot on it without further experience. From Luxor, leaving the Nile, we took off in a southeasterly direction for Port Sudan on the Red Sea, about 500 miles away.

This leg, mainly over the Nubian Desert to the eastward of the Nile, was new to me. It was as barren as the Egyptian and Sudanese deserts I had so often just seen, but much more rocky and less sandy, with its rocky plateaus so cut by wind-blown sand they resembled vast river systems, except there was no sign of water anywhere.

About halfway on this leg, we crossed the boundary from Egypt into the Sudan. The dividing line could have made little difference to anyone, since the entire region thereabouts was worthless even to desert Arabs, and was wholly uninhabited. Roughly around noon, we spotted the Red Sea ahead, shimmering in the heat below and shortly came down on a stretch of desert sand bordering it, where lay Port Sudan.

It seemed to me as we emerged for lunch from our plane that the field at Port Sudan was hotter even than that at Khartoum, but in this I may have been mistaken. What made it seem so was that the heated air rising from the burning sands could literally be seen like the wavering pattern in moiréed silk, dancing sinuously upward in quivering streams.

At the far end of the field from where we landed—there were no special runways on the field, it was simply all hard sand—stood a row of six fighter planes, wing to wing, spaced not very far apart. The six R.A.F. pilots who had come with us as passengers, immediately they had landed, started posthaste on foot for those planes, eager to get out of Port Sudan. As they ran, they strapped to their backs the parachutes they had previously been carrying.

With difficulty, as they went by me, I restrained the involuntary cry that rose to my lips,

"For God's sake, wait! Get a boat or you'll all drown!"

For if I were to believe the clear evidence of my own eyes, all of those fighter planes stood submerged in deep water almost to the under sides of their wings—there all about them was a considerable lake, with its blue surface ruffled gently into ripples glistening beneath the sun!

I choked back my warning. Of course, it couldn't be so, even if unmistakably I were looking directly at a lake. Nobody would put land planes in a lake for a take-off. However real it seemed, that lake *must* be imaginary, a desert mirage effect, the first such I had seen.

It was, of course. In a minute or so, it seemed as if all the pilots had suddenly been swallowed by the water, only their heads remaining visible to me above the rippling surface.

While I stood rubbing my eyes (which made no difference at all in clearing them of this incredible scene), the pilots clambered up out of the water into the cockpits of those planes, started their engines which needed no warming up, revved them up once or twice to try them, and all together in wing to wing formation started off. For a moment it appeared as if their planes were breasting the waves. Then they burst clear of the mirage onto the near-by sand, picking up speed in startling fashion.

It was clear at once why they were taking off abreast. A vast cloud of sand thrown up by the propeller race, rose in the wake of each plane; very obviously, no pilot wished to be caught in that choking mass of fine sand and dust by taking off even a little behind one of his mates.

So in beautiful formation, all six planes (apparently American Tomahawk fighters) roared across the field, circled once at low altitude over it while they retracted their landing gear, and then shot across it not a hundred feet up, heading westward. How fast they were going I couldn't tell—so amazingly fast, anyway, that as they whistled by in the air, I could hardly turn my head fast enough to follow as they swooped directly over and swiftly shrank into tiny dots which vanished in the west.

After a very brief pause for a very skimpy lunch, we re-embarked in our own hot plane and hurriedly took off for higher altitudes, partly to cool off, partly to gain the height we needed to clear the Eritrean mountains a hundred miles ahead.

We headed almost south, quickly losing the Red Sea behind us and flying inland as we rose. In an hour we were over the border into Eritrea, well away from the coast, and flying at 11,000 feet, with a mountain range about 10,000 feet high not much below us. But these mountains were not so barren as those of the southern Sahara, perhaps because they were higher, more likely because they were closer to the sea and trapped some of its moisture.

In another hour, we were over the mountains and well inside Eritrea at last, coming lower over what seemed a vast plateau which lay green and inviting beneath us, 7000 to 8000 feet above the sea, stretching away southward into Ethiopia. There, nestling on the fringe of the plateau, was Asmara, by its appearance from the air a sizable European city.

We came down smoothly on the airfield, a very modern one laid out by Mussolini and seemingly now run by our Air Corps. I was in Eritrea at last!

[102]

I descended from the plane, stretched myself luxuriously. Here for the first time in Africa I was on an airfield which at midday was comfortably cool—in fact, that late March day in Asmara reminded me of similar early spring weather in my boyhood home in Colorado at an altitude only moderately lower.

I was met at the field by an Army officer from the Mission headquarters in Eritrea to escort me into the city, and also, to my surprise, by my new liaison officer, the Royal Navy commander I had last seen in Cairo five days before. Since he had got away from Cairo on schedule, I had expected he was, of course, long since in Massawa.

I looked questioningly at him as we all got into an Army car for the five-mile drive into Asmara. He did not keep me long in the dark as to his presence. He had not yet been to Massawa. He had no intention of going there to report till he saw me again. Even more wrought up than when I had seen him at Admiralty House in Cairo, he began once more on the same theme. Now that he was only seventy miles by road from Massawa and had learned more about it both from British military officials in Asmara and paroled Italian officers there, he was even surer he could not stand it in Massawa. Couldn't he remain in cool Asmara, 7500 feet above that steaming Red Sea coast, and act as liaison officer from there?

I assured him that was a matter for the British naval authorities in Massawa to pass on; however, so far as I was concerned, it wouldn't do. If there was to be a liaison officer, I wanted him close at hand; otherwise I was better off without one.

Nervously he mulled over that thought. Then in desperation, he made a final appeal,

"Commander, tell Captain Lucas—he's the Royal Navy NOIC in Massawa—he'll have to get me quarters up in the hills about thirty miles outside Massawa. It's cool there. I just *can't* live in Massawa! For God's sake, promise me that!"

I tried to show the poor devil his request was ridiculous, and that in making it, he should only get himself in bad with his seniors in the Royal Navy. But he was so obsessed with his phobia of Massawa, logic had no appeal to him—neither had war needs nor the effect on his naval career. He just couldn't go to live in Massawa—he would die there! And till he had a favorable answer, he wasn't going to Massawa to report!

Finally, to quiet him, I promised I should bear his message to Captain Lucas, Royal Navy, whom, of course, I had never met, but whose reaction I could safely forecast. However, it wasn't my funeral. If my liaison officer insisted, in spite of all my warnings, I should oblige him. And with that, I turned my back on him, to speak to my Army companion who had been listening in silent astonishment to all this.

Very soon we were rolling through the streets of Asmara and down the Viale Mussolini, as fine and broad a city boulevard as one might hope to see anywhere. New modern and modernistic business buildings lined it on both sides—some so new the Fascisti had not had time, when they brought their ill-advised war upon their heads, to finish them. Still, uncompleted as they were, they also were in use.

We dropped my liaison officer at the hotel where the British Army had billeted him, glad to be rid of him. Then we drove to the government building, formerly Fascist, now occupied by the U.S. Army as headquarters for the Eritrean branch of the North African Mission. There I reported to Colonel L. J. Claterbos, Engineer Corps, U.S.A., who, as representative of General Maxwell, headed all the Mission activities in Eritrea. I had last seen him in New York in early January, just prior to his taking off for Africa in one of the first Army Fortress flights. He had been in Eritrea well over two months already, and I judged from my first sight of him that already he had been through the mill.

Colonel Claterbos was a huge person, well over six feet, with massive shoulders and a set of features looking as if they had been roughly carved out of granite, that matched his tremendous form. In his day (it happened to overlap mine at Annapolis) he had been an outstanding player on Army's football team; one look at his still athletic figure made it easy to guess why.

But since our parting in January, the lines in his creased face had deepened appreciably, his voice had hardened beyond description; very evidently there had been plenty of trouble in Eritrea.

We greeted each other cordially, then immediately got down to business. The naval end of the Massawa venture was mine; everything else there and elsewhere in Eritrea Colonel Claterbos had directly on his own shoulders. Nothing had yet been done regarding Navy matters in Massawa, awaiting my arrival; as regards other matters, Claterbos had more than had his hands full in a projected air base at near-by Gura (to be built), projected ordnance shops, motor transport shops, living quarters, ammunition depots, all the construc-

[104]

tion work required to transform Eritrea into a vast military base for Middle East operations. But the men promised for the projects had arrived only in driblets and in far smaller numbers than promised or needed—he was short of officers and men, the contractors were far short of mechanics, though to balance that they had an oversupply of civilian executives and supervisors, and nobody had any tools or equipment to speak of to work with yet.

As regards my naval project, he knew my situation with no naval assistants at all. As soon as he had any, he would assign me a few younger Army officers—I could do what I might to train them in unfamiliar duties. Respecting workmen, a fair share of the mechanics who had come by shipboard with me would also be assigned to the projected housing for the naval base and Pat Murphy would be sent there in charge of them. Of course, so far as salvage in Massawa went, there could be none of that till such time as my salvage forces arrived —he had no men at all who could help me there.

Finally, not much was expected of us in Massawa. It was hot there already (it always was, even on Christmas Day) and the season was rapidly coming on when all work in Massawa usually ceased for the summer. He hoped we might, in view of the war urgency, get a couple of hours' work in in the early morning at sunrise and a couple of hours more in the evening about sunset—the American civilian workmen would, of course, have to be paid for a full eight-hour day regardless of that or he could get none of them to go to Massawa at all, since on the Asmara plateau they could make a day's pay in comfort, even in July.

Aside from the few American workmen available, I might hire all the Eritrean natives I wished—they weren't good for much, but they stood the heat better—and if I could use any, he would do what he could to get me as many Italian prisoners of war as I wanted. Some of them were good mechanics; since they were prisoners, it might be possible to keep them working somewhat longer hours than the Americans.

That was about everything Colonel Claterbos had to suggest. He assured me of his cordial co-operation, and of his assistance in every way within his limited means, and I felt sure he meant it. Then he turned to face a long line of waiting favor-seekers—American, British, Italian, native—while I left to be driven to my billet for the night, the Army Officers' Mess in Asmara.

I washed some of the dust of Port Sudan from my frame, put away the sun helmet and khaki in which I had traveled from Cairo, and put on a blue uniform and my naval cap. So dressed, I went out for a brief stroll in cool Asmara before dinner.

Asmara was something. All the wealth that could be wrung out of impoverished Italy had been lavished on producing there on the plateau bordering Abyssinia a Fascist showplace. There were, I was told, 40,000 Italians in Asmara, not to mention 100,000 Eritreans who didn't count. All the Italians at least were out for a stroll also on the Viale Mussolini and most of them were in uniform.

Not even in Rome, when I had been there in 1936, just at the close of Mussolini's Ethiopian adventure and the start of his sub rosa campaign to help Franco in Spain, had I seen so profuse and so gorgeous a display of the products of the Italian military tailors' art—the Fascisti might have proved themselves the world's worst soldiers (exceeded in general worthlessness only by the Fascist sailors), but their tailors, having such excellent clothing dummies on which to hang their creations, had risen to the heights.

Apparently every Italian officer captured in the East African campaign the year before was out, magnificently caparisoned, strutting along the Viale Mussolini that afternoon. I had heard these officers had all been paroled by the British and were now free to live privately anywhere in Asmara, but at sight of them, I could hardly restrain a gasp.

I was unarmed, so was every other of the few British and American officers forming a drab blotch on that otherwise brilliant military spectacle. But every one of these prisoners of war was armed—clinging to his waist was an automatic pistol protruding from its holster! There were enough armed Italian officers in sight easily to take over the country in view of the few soldiers the British had left in Eritrea and the slight handful only that I knew we had. What kind of topsy-turvy war was this where conquerors went about defenseless while their prisoners roamed the streets at large, armed?

At dinner that evening in the Officers' Mess, where I met practically all the army officers stationed in Asmara, I had my answer from Major Goff, who had beaten me there by some days.

"It's all a matter of Italian honor, Commander," he explained. "An American can hardly understand its nuances. Brigadier Kennedy-Cooke, British Military Governor here, had to explain it to me twice before I took it in. You see, when the Italians surrendered their forces to General Platt after he'd smashed them at Cheren, they insisted on surrendering with the honors of war. So long as there wasn't any more fighting, nobody gave a damn what they surrendered with. Well, when Platt and his troops had moved back to Libya and they brought all the Italian officers who promised to behave into Asmara as paroled prisoners of war, imagine what happened! The sensitive Italian P.O.W.s claimed that as they had surrendered with the honors of war, precedent all the way back to the Crusades gave them the right to retain and to wear their side arms. And as swords have now gone out as symbols of chivalry, they claimed the right to wear pistols instead as side arms! Unless they retained and wore their pistols, their honor as soldiers would be grievously wounded. Of course, the British just couldn't bear the idea of wounding their soldierly honor, so they acquiesced. They did insist that the honorable P.O.W.s agree to leave the cartridges out of their automatics, and maybe they do, but nobody ever searches one to see whether his pistol is loaded or not. Neither you nor I nor Brigadier Kennedy-Cooke wears a gun, because as a matter of honor we want to show the Fascisti in this captured country we're not afraid of them; but the Fascisti think their honor requires them to wear guns to show us God knows what! Who cares? It's all very honorable. We've got Eritrea, they've got their honor, and everybody's happy!" He shook his head sadly, then added,

"First the *Pig's Knuckle,* then this cockeyed country letting a prisoner go around with a gun! Nobody in Idaho will ever believe me again when I try to tell 'em about it. They'll only look at me skeptically and say,

"'Abe, you used to be a solid citizen and we trusted you. But you've sure turned into a Baron Munchausen since you went away to war.'"

CHAPTER

16

After breakfast in the morning, I spent a little time with the Army finance officer, arranging my personal accounts, then slightly after nine, my bags were loaded into an Army car and I started alone for Massawa. It was March 30; I had been under way for Massawa since February 16.

My driver for the trip was an Italian prisoner of war, an ex-enlisted man evidently, who had no honor to preserve, since he wore no pistol. It was a strict Army rule that no American officer should be permitted ever to drive a government car himself; only the driver assigned to the car might drive it. Since in Eritrea there were insufficient enlisted men for such service, various P.O.W.s had been impressed for the job, and I had one. Had I known what I was in for, I should have walked the seventy miles to Massawa, leaving only my bags to go in the car.

About five miles out of Asmara, we ran off the 7500-foot plateau and started down the precipitous mountain road to the sea. That beautifully paved road was a triumph of Italian engineering, and for scenery it was marvelous. In thirty miles by road (less than ten miles in a straight line) we dropped 7000 feet. The switchbacks cut into the solid rock of the mountainsides were terrific—regularly as we came to one of those hairpin turns, I was certain we were going to take off straight into empty space. In one spot, Nefasit, within only an airline distance of perhaps half a mile but a vertical drop of Heaven alone knew how many feet, there were seven hair-raising switchbacks.

All this would have been enjoyable to me since I grew up in Colorado and liked rugged mountains and mountain scenery, had it not been for my driver. He drove like mad down that mountain road. I doubt that we ever went below fifty miles an hour, and I am certain we never dropped below forty, even on the worst switchbacks.

I expostulated from the back seat, but it was hopeless. I knew no Italian, the driver knew no English. In what little I could remember of my Spanish, I ordered him to slow down, I was in no hurry to get to Massawa. Evidently my involved Spanish phrases did not register. There was no effect.

"Lento! Lento!" I shouted next, trying single words this time, while the tires fairly shrieked and I smelled burning rubber as we hurtled round a switchback.

There was no slow down. Instead, I caught something in Italian which, from the intonation, I judged was meant to convey to me there was no cause for alarm, everything was all right. We speeded up on the ensuing brief stretch of straight road, heading for the next turn. It wasn't all right, either with me or with those priceless tires, which were irreplaceable 13,000 miles from home.

"No pronto, no pronto!" I tried again in Spanish negatives, hoping to make my meaning clearer. No answer. We skidded sickeningly round that mountain hairpin like a racing car, straightened away for the next stretch with hardly any speed lost. We had before us now perhaps half a mile of steep but straight downgrade to go until the next turn. The Italian P.O.W. must have concluded he had not wholly succeeded in making the foreign officer understand. Now he seized his opportunity to make himself understood beyond any doubt. To my horror, he let go the wheel entirely, turned round and with both hands gesticulating meaningfully started to explain in Italian again apparently that everything was under control!

I seized both his wildly waving wrists, twisted him sharply round forward, and let go. Possibly he understood from that that the crazy American for some strange reason had no desire to listen. He grasped the wheel again. Thank God, we were still on the road!

Completely limp, I subsided; it was safer. Had I had a pistol, I should have shot that P.O.W. in the back of the head on the next straight stretch and dived over the back of the front seat, trusting to bring the speeding car to a stop before it crashed the mountainside or dropped off the bordering precipice. But failing a gun, I didn't dare try taking control; in the struggle for the wheel it was certain we should plunge off the road.

For thirty nerve-shattering miles this went on while we dropped from 7500 feet to 500 feet above the sea. As a final aggravation, in Eritrea we were under the British Rules of the Road—that is, all traffic keeps to the left—and try as I would consciously to keep that in mind, subconsciously I could not escape the terrifying impression that always we were hurtling down those mountains on the wrong side of the road, bound to crash head-on into the next car we met toiling up those grades.

While still some five miles from the end of our drop, we raced through the mountain village of Ghinda, 3000 feet above the sea, forty miles by road from Massawa. There, I knew, it had been planned long before I left America, to have the contractor build a housing project large enough to take all Americans working in Massawa. The idea was to haul them to Ghinda in buses each night so they could sleep in cooler mountain air, and each morning transport them back to Massawa for their day's work. The last thing I had done before I left New York was to order the twelve large buses which were to do the transportation job.

As we raced through Ghinda I noted that on a relatively flat spot (still very hilly, however) construction work on that housing project had already started. Some graders were already leveling off various plots for foundations. That was about all I could take in as we whizzed by, but from there on, I took especial note of the rest of the road over which twice a day our large buses were to transport hundreds of American workers, including me, when months hence, the project should be finished.

When at last we emerged on the flat desert, a few hundred feet above sea level, which stretched away about thirty miles to Massawa, I knew the whole housing project in Ghinda was utterly impracticable. It might have looked a fine idea in far-off New York; on the ground its absurdity seemed to me immediately apparent.

To try to negotiate that mountain road regularly with a fleet of large buses was simply courting disaster—even far more careful drivers than the one I had could not possibly avoid accidents, especially since of necessity the mountain end of the journey would each day start and finish in the darkness. Undertaking such a transportation feat could only result in about a month in no workmen at all—half would be dead, the other half would be in the hospital, and the buses would be masses of crushed junk lying at the foot of some precipice. Enough smashed Italian military trucks lay strewn already bordering that road to make the prediction fairly safe.

When finally we leveled off on the desert, even though our speed promptly jumped far above sixty, I breathed a sigh of relief. No matter how bad Massawa proved to be, the less I saw of that road to Ghinda and Asmara, the happier I should be. My leg muscles, till then tensed to jump for my life from whichever side of the car offered at the moment the best chance, gradually relaxed. We had made it safely.

I settled back against the cushions and began to think a little less malevolently of Mussolini than I had during the ride. After all, he had built that road up those precipitous mountains for one purpose only, the invasion of Abyssinia. To the Italians bound for that war the road was perfectly all right and in nowise alarming—whether one got killed on the road or by Haile Selassie's warriors beyond it, what difference? And the road had even one advantage—if you got killed there, you could count on not being castrated, which was something an Italian couldn't be too sure of avoiding if ever he got to Abyssinia. It had happened before to them at Adowa, in 1896.

We raced along over flat desert country extending from the foot of the mountains over thirty miles all the way to the sea. I began quickly to put out of mind Mussolini, his mountain road-building, Asmara and all else. It was hot on that desert, infernally hot.

I had started from Asmara in my blue uniform, even wearing my overcoat for a while, for it was cold there and I had no desire to risk a recurrence of the Eritrean version of "Gyppy tummy" from which I was still weak. Part way down the mountains I had shed my overcoat but my blues had still felt comfortable. Now it was so hot, they were insufferable.

I had my aviation kit bag with me in the back seat of the car. A little cramped for space but not minding that, with the desert shooting by at seventy miles an hour, I stripped off my blues and slid into a pair of shorts and a khaki shirt, which last I left unbuttoned from waist to throat. At least I should get some ventilation from the hurricane of hot air streaming down the car sides.

How hot it was in that Army sedan, I never knew. The sun, high overhead, was playing directly on us. From both sides and the road underneath, radiant heat from the baked sands was darting at us. The blast of hot air shooting by gave no relief.

In a few minutes I was completely soaked in perspiration, as well as burning with the heat. Neither in Khartoum nor in Port Sudan had I been so uncomfortable. I began to get an inkling of why Massawa was unique on earth—it combined in *one* spot the highest temperatures and the highest humidities known anywhere as did no other place in the tropics.

Khartoum and Port Sudan were probably as hot, but they were dry—Khartoum because it was in the desert far from the sea; Port Sudan because the desert winds blew with a free sweep across it toward the sea, giving it a desert dryness. And that dryness, evaporating swiftly all perspiration, gave the body a chance to cool itself off and regulate its internal temperature.

I could see now why Massawa was different. Those high mountains I had just descended literally put Massawa and its narrow coastal desert in a bowl, shutting off any land breezes having a tendency to dry things out. And the scorching sun, working on the hot Red Sea before Massawa, sucked up from it vast quantities of vapor. Cut off from blowing away by those same mountains, this vapor hung in the bowl, giving Massawa the highest humidity all year round of any place on the globe.

So that was it. First the heat scorched you, making you perspire profusely in the body's attempt to hold its temperature down; then the terrific humidity prevented any evaporation, leaving you to stew in your own sweat, and there you were.

We raced into Massawa itself, swung left past the vast salt pans onto the Abd-El-Kader Peninsula where lay the old Italian naval base which was my destination, then in the screeching of brakes came to a sudden stop. Seared by the heat, basted in perspiration, I stepped out of the car.

What I had been told was correct. The next stop beyond Massawa *was* Hades.

CHAPTER

17

THE ARMY CAR IN WHICH I HAD come from Asmara turned about and hastily started back there. Its driver presumably had no wish to remain an unnecessary moment in Massawa.

With my bags at my feet and my thoroughly useless overcoat over them, I put on my sun helmet and my sun glasses to protect myself from the burning sun and looked about.

I had been deposited in front of the former Italian naval headquarters building. It stood empty, a sizable two-storied office building with massive masonry walls, stuccoed over and finished in the drab yellow which covered everything, apparently to match the dust blowing in from the desert. There was no glass in the windows, only heavy slatted shutters intended to keep out the sun and let in the air, while further to forward the same purpose, a wide veranda ran round the building and the eaves had an enormous overhang to shade the walls. The Italians had done everything they knew with that building (and all the others thereabout) to fight the sun.

Behind the headquarters buildings were many others much larger and covering considerable ground, but all shuttered and with locked doors. These I judged were the naval base shops, deserted, full of sabotaged machinery, locked now to avoid having the wreckage stolen for junk. That, I supposed, was also the purpose of the few Sudanese sentries posted here and there, the sole signs of life around me.

Everything near by was abandoned, but toward the end of the peninsula and beyond a flat open space baking in the sun was another group of buildings, some two-storied stucco, some one-storied wood, which seemed to be occupied. Above them on a high flag pole floated the White Ensign, so I judged that there, evidently in what had been the Italian officers' quarters and the barracks for the naval base, the Royal Navy in Massawa had already installed itself.

I swung around to face the sea. Before me and a little lower down lay the naval harbor, the north harbor of Massawa. It was a considerable body of water, beautifully landlocked, a mile across and of somewhat greater length. Stretching out on the water front close by was a heavy masonry pier paralleling the shore with three concreted roadways carried to it on piles. Here was the first visible evidence of war and sabotage—the R.A.F. had bombed Massawa heavily before its surrender and they had hit that pier three times, leaving three sizable gaps in it; while to complete the job, the electric cranes on it, which the Italians themselves had sabotaged before surrender, leaned drunkenly over the water in various crazy attitudes.

Farther out in the lifeless harbor lay more striking evidence of Italian sabotage—across the entrance to the harbor from the sea lay a string of scuttled ships. Two which had capsized in going down, lay on the near edge of the entrance with the waves breaking over their now horizontal sides which stretched away, vast flat rusty steel islands a few feet above the water, to form a resting place for innumerable gulls fishing from these convenient newly man-made reefs. Farther away lay several more large wrecks, these erect, with only their masts and smokestacks and the tops of their bridges showing above the surface.

Inside the naval harbor itself, not much showed. Well over toward the far shore, the roiled water and a few tiny nondescript objects looking like awash rafts indicated that there probably the floating dry docks had been scuttled—what looked like rafts might be the tops of their deckhouses showing a little above water.

I turned from the sea with a sigh. The commercial harbor and the south harbor where I knew most of the wrecks lay, were invisible to me from the naval base, but I had already seen enough to occupy far larger forces than I should ever have.

It was no use trying to enter the abandoned Italian headquarters building which would later be my base for work—first it was locked and second it was probably depressing in its emptiness, even should I force my way in. Instead, indicating in pantomime to the nearest Sudanese sentry that he should also guard my bags and overcoat, I trudged off on foot for the point marked by that British flag to make my presence known and pay my respects to NOIC, the British Naval Officer in Charge.

[114]

It was a hot walk under the near noonday sun, made more disagreeable by the fine yellow dust (disintegrated coral, I afterwards learned, from the coral formations of which the whole seacoast was composed) which rose in clouds with every step. There were no trees and no shade; it rarely rained on that coast at any time of the year.

I was a somewhat bedraggled figure between perspiration, dust, and low spirits, when, with my khaki shirt now buttoned up part but not all the way to my throat as my sole concession to naval propriety, a British seaman doing sentry duty ushered me toward the office of Captain Colin Lucas, Royal Navy, commanding His Majesty's naval forces in Massawa. The office lay, as I had surmised, in the low, wide verandaed wooden building immediately adjacent to the White Ensign floating high over everything.

It was a very formal entry I made, hardly in keeping with my non-reg appearance. The bluejacket presented arms, an aide announced, "Commander Ellsberg of the American Navy, sir!" and I stepped in.

Captain Lucas, who had had two fans blowing directly on him as he sat at his desk, and consequently looked much cooler than I, rose to greet me. Hastily I sized up the man with whom I should have most contact in Massawa, and I received an immediate surprise. In spite of what had been said in Cairo about age for duty in Massawa, the British were clearly not taking their own medicine. Captain Lucas was plainly much closer to sixty than he was to fifty, and showed it in every way—his florid face, his bulging waistline, his thinning gray hair. He had been in Massawa almost since its capture, some eight months anyway. One look at Captain Lucas and I already felt better—if he could stand it in Massawa, I was sure I could.

We shook hands, Captain Lucas welcomed me to Massawa, and motioned me to a chair, which he thoughtfully hauled into the line of action of one of his fans. We both sat down.

I told the captain (which he already knew) that I had come to take command of what was to be the U.S. Naval Repair Base, Massawa, the ex-Italian Naval Base, and, of course, also to command the salvage operations. While at the moment I had no men at all for either purpose, shortly there should be some, together with three salvage ships, one of which was certainly already on the way via the Cape of Good Hope.

On his part, Captain Lucas acquainted me with the British situation in Massawa. His responsibilities in Massawa were mainly two—

first, to maintain communications with the outside world, chiefly by naval radio, handling all confidential dispatches and coding and decoding them; and, second, to maintain a naval guard over the ex-Italian base to prevent the natives, the Arabs, and the Italians themselves from making away with even the cement blocks of which the base was built—all were bloody thieves and there was an excellent black market in Eritrea for everything they could steal. While he had a moderate staff, both of officers and enlisted men of the Royal Navy for these two purposes, still he found himself in straitened circumstances covering even these two tasks adequately and he regretted that he would be unable to lend me any assistance in my tasks. However, if I thought there was any way he might aid, he hoped I should always feel free to ask. He'd do the best he could to help the common effort.

Ah, yes, come to think of it, there was one other thing the Royal Navy was doing to help me. A new liaison officer was being ordered, to be always at my disposal. Where the blighter might be, though, he couldn't imagine, for while he'd had a wireless a week before from Cairo saying the new officer was starting immediately, he hadn't shown up yet in Massawa.

I smiled grimly at that.

"I think I can throw some light on that, Captain," I said. As noncommittally as I could, since I had no desire to cause any trouble in the Royal Navy, I explained briefly where the liaison officer was, and conveyed his request to be quartered in the hills, not in Massawa.

Captain Lucas stiffened instantly.

"The insufferable ass! Does he think he's a duke or something? He'll stick it in Massawa the same as all the rest of us! Lieutenant Maton!" he shouted towards an adjoining office.

At that imperious call, Lieutenant Maton of the British Navy, apparently the communications officer, came running with a message pad.

"Lieutenant," ordered the flushed captain, his wide nostrils practically breathing flame he was so angry, "priority dispatch to Commander—whatever's his name—you know, that new liaison fellow from Cairo—only send it to Asmara, that's where the malingering blighter is now, 'Report immediately in Massawa or face court-martial.' That's all, Maton; get it right off!"

I rose. Inwardly, I thought, "Good for you, old boy! We'll get along fine!" But what I said was,

"Sorry, Captain, to have caused you all this trouble. I advised him not to do it, but he insisted."

Captain Lucas rose also, still fuming.

"The idea of an officer in the Royal Navy doing that! A commander, too! The man must be crazy!"

"That's what I thought, Captain," I agreed. "Well, I'll get over now and take a look at that cottage they told me in Cairo'd been assigned me as my quarters. I'll see you later."

"Ah, yes, Commander; it's off that way, a bit to the left about a hundred yards from here." He escorted me to the door, pointed out the direction. "And I say, Ellsberg, you can't possibly be settled by tonight, so come and have dinner with me. I should have invited you before if that blithering idiot in Asmara hadn't driven it out of my mind."

"Thanks, Captain. I'll accept with pleasure." I put on my sun helmet, saluted, and stepped out. The bluejacket presented arms, I saluted him also in return, and walked off in the dust.

It turned out I had a very busy afternoon. I found the cottage without trouble, a very good cottage, too, airy, built with the usual widely overhanging roof for sun protection, and with some tropical flowers and shrubs about it, undoubtedly kept alive by profuse artificial watering. But—the cottage was occupied, very fully so, in spite of the fact that I had been told at Cairo headquarters that it had been assigned solely for my occupancy.

It appeared that another American naval officer, Commander Dickeman of the Civil Engineer Corps, who had come out to the Middle East via Hawaii and Singapore before war broke out in the Pacific, was in Massawa on a business visit. He had several engineering surveys of African facilities to make for the Navy Department before going back to Washington, and had arrived a week or two earlier in Massawa to check the machinery needs of that spot. There being no other place for him to live, he had naturally enough moved into the single house reserved for U.S. Navy use.

Then, the week before, Colonel Claterbos from Asmara had sent down a Major Knapp of the Army Engineers to take charge of the Army construction work and transportation in the commercial port of Massawa. Knapp could find no place at all to live in Massawa and Commander Dickeman had generously invited him to share the cottage at the Naval Base some miles away till the Army could do something about it.

So there were my quarters completely occupied, for the cottage was small and had only two single beds.

Dickeman would be in Massawa at most only a couple of weeks more; there could be no question in the circumstances of his staying where he was. Major Knapp, very embarrassed, offered to move out immediately to make room for me.

"But where will you go, Major?" I asked.

"Damned if I know," said the major. "There isn't a vacant room in the whole blessed town. I've looked already. There's a closed building, The Bank of Italy, facing the commercial docks that we're using for Army offices right now; I was figuring on converting the second floor of that for living quarters, but it'll take some time yet. You'll find the British Army's got every hotel in the town of Massawa, every Italian club, and every Italian government building, as well as part of this naval base, full of their own men. And Commander Dickeman can tell you the British Navy's got every other usable building on the naval base, except this cottage, assigned to theirs."

"Yes, that's so," agreed Dickeman. "Maybe they haven't got personnel enough to run this base, but anyway they've got enough to fill up all the livable quarters. All except one building," and he pointed out a very fine two-storied stucco building facing the sea a quarter of a mile off. "You see that? That was the main quarter building for Italian naval officers. It's fine inside—I've been there—terrazo floors, big rooms, some with private baths, wide terraces outside roofed over, batteries of shower baths, and, best of all, it's close to the water. If there's a sea breeze, you get it there. And what do you think they've done with it? They've given it to a private English company, Cable and Wireless, Limited, for their quarters, when, if and as they ever need any. Right now Cable and Wireless is strictly limited around here. They haven't got a cable and the Lord knows when they will have; they'll probably never have a wireless here; and all they've got in that big building which'll hold two dozen officers in comfort is two Cable and Wireless managers who've got nothing at all to do for months yet! So they're putting in their time figuring on fixing up one whole floor into suites for themselves right now and saving the other floor for maybe three or four cable operators

[118]

in the sweet by and by. And where are all our men to run the naval base going to live? Those two limeys from Cable and Wireless say it was promised to them in London and they're keeping it. If we need quarters, we can go and build a new building—as if you could do that by waving a wand around *here*, of all places!"

Commander Dickeman, who felt warmly on the subject of quarters, and apparently with much reason, paused a moment, looked me over, then in pity at my perspiration-soaked state, suggested,

"It's too hot to talk. Let's have a drink; you look as if you need it. I've got some ice and I've got some cans of pineapple juice I wangled off a ship here. Just a minute."

That cold pineapple juice with ice tinkling in the glass was a life-saver. I was both extraordinarily thirsty and hot, and it helped both ways. I guzzled a huge tumbler full. When it was gone, I sat back, feeling a little better.

"Well, boys, I tell you what. Don't you move out of here, Major; you might find yourself sleeping in the gutter, if they've got any gutters around here. But the British Navy is bound to take care of me. Now I've got a dinner date tonight with NOIC. I'm going over to take a look first at that building you say Cable and Wireless have got, and tonight I'll see if Captain Lucas can't fix it so I can have one of those rooms with a bath in it, and use some of the rest of it for the other officers Colonel Claterbos promised me. Tonight I'll sleep on this settee I'm sitting on. I've done worse. And talking of baths, can you lend me a towel, Dickeman? I want to get into your tub right now!"

"Certainly," said Dickeman. "And I've got a tub of water cooling right now. Help yourself. Meanwhile, Major Knapp and I are driving over to Massawa for lunch. Don't you want to come? You can have a bath afterwards."

"No, thanks. First things first with me; right now a bath comes first. Lunch can go hang."

They stepped out to Major Knapp's waiting car, and I promptly turned to in stripping off my soaked clothes.

I jumped into the well-filled tub, looking cool and inviting before me. It wasn't; it was uncomfortably hot. Evidently Dickeman had run in too much hot water. I looked for the cold water faucet to cool the tub more, but there was only one faucet there and it wasn't marked anything. I turned that on a moment to experiment, then hastily shut it off again. The water coming out was even hotter than what was already in the bath.

I began to catch the significance of Commander Dickeman's casual remark, which before I had ignored—"a tub of water cooling right now." I had wondered why the tub happened to be full when I wanted a bath, now I saw it. There was evidently only one kind of water on tap in Massawa—hot. If you didn't want a hot bath—and who did?—you filled the tub in the morning and let it stand all day before your evening bath, trusting to evaporation from its surface to cool it a little. Perhaps it worked, but the tubful I was in hadn't stood long enough. It was too hot for my purposes. I jumped out and began to swab myself with the towel.

I got back into my wet clothes; that didn't make any difference for I realized that if I had any dry ones at hand, they would be just as wet in a few moments. Then I called the houseboy, who seemed to know a little English, and sent him down to the water front to retrieve my bags from the custody of the Sudanese sentry.

CHAPTER

18

Next morning found me moving into Building 108, the one assigned to Cable and Wireless, Limited. Captain Lucas, with some difficulty, had arranged for my occupancy and that of such other officers as I might bring, but only, he regretted to inform me, on a temporary basis till Cable and Wireless said they required it all for themselves. Beyond that, the matter was out of his hands. London had turned it over to Cable and Wireless and unless I could persuade them to relinquish or London to change its assignment, nothing more could be done.

For the moment, I wasn't concerned. Not for months did it seem Cable and Wireless could colorably say they needed the building except at most for the four rooms their two managers were already using; long before then, I was sure they would see our need was greater than theirs, and agree to relinquish it or at least to split its use. So I forgot the question and moved. All the first floor and most of the second was empty. I chose a corner room on the second floor facing the sea, which gave me a cross-draft as well as a private shower (no tub, this time).

Meanwhile, I had acquired a few other things—first of all, a houseboy of my own, brought round by a friend of his serving as houseboy to Commander Callwell, R.N., executive officer at the Royal Naval Base. Commander Callwell's houseboy recommended him highly, so I hired him. His name, I was assured, was Ahmed Hussein.

That was the only thing of which I was ever assured regarding Ahmed. He was a very black young Sudanese (not to be confounded with American Negroes who were all West African), barefooted, of course, draped in a white robe topped off by a turban which he spent most of his time winding. Ahmed and I completely didn't understand each other, since he talked only Arabic and I didn't. However,

I was fairly good at pantomime by now and I had hopes Ahmed might pick up some English.

Ahmed's job was to make my bed, take care of my room, send out the laundry, and get it back (this last no minor trick). What wasn't his job, but what turned out to be the only thing Ahmed ever took the slightest interest in, was to shine up my automobile.

For I now had a car. Major Knapp had taken out the afternoon before from under the wraps in which it had been stored in the Army warehouse, awaiting my arrival, the car assigned to me as Commanding Officer of the Naval Repair Base—a brand-new 1942 Chevrolet sedan, complete with driver. The driver was, as usual, an Italian, an ex-enlisted man now a P.O.W., but wearing civilian clothes as they all did. He had quite a rig which made him look like a movie director—leather puttees, riding breeches, an Army wool shirt, and no hat at all. How he ever survived in that costume I could never figure out, but perhaps his luxuriant hair, of which he was very proud, helped. At least he could talk fair English.

My Chevrolet was the only U.S. military car in Eritrea that was *not* painted in the Army khaki color. When I got it, it was still its original glossy black, and I concluded that as I was not in the Army, I should be different and leave it that way, black.

That suited Ahmed right down to the ground. He could get a shine on that black enamel that would have been absurd to attempt on the flat Army field paint that covered all other cars, and whenever I wanted Ahmed, I could always find him shining away on that car, regardless of what else he should have been doing.

I paid Ahmed (in Italian lira) thirty cents a day, plus his board. He wasn't worth it.

With my clothes unpacked and stowed either in the closet or the bureau, most of which I did myself to show Ahmed what was expected of him, I shoved off to inspect the town of Massawa and its two remaining harbors. We drove slowly off the Abd-El-Kader Peninsula so I might have a better chance to observe what I had missed before on my racing entry into the naval base establishment.

There was more to it than I had thought. Beyond the deserted naval shops was a huge barracks building, stuccoed masonry as usual. This I now saw was housing Indian troops. Behind that building was a maze of one-storied wooden barracks, portable apparently, which were full of Sudanese soldiers. Further along was another stuccoed masonry building, two floors, looking very much like the building in which I was now quartered, except that this building, alone of all those I had seen, was surrounded by barbed wire, entanglement style, with only a narrow gate through it, also of barbed wire, which was closed.

Apparently this was a specially important building, converted perhaps either to an ammunition magazine or to the decoding chambers to warrant all that protection. I indicated it to my driver, asked what it was.

"Brothel," he responded briefly.

"A brothel?" I repeated, astonished.

"*Si, signor Commandante*. Army brothel. Black girls for Sudanese, Indians."

I shut up. A beautiful building to be wasted on an Army brothel! I wondered whether the barbed wire entanglements were to keep the black girls in or to keep the colonial troops out, but I didn't ask. All the same, I made a mental note to see at some future date about acquiring that building for possible use as quarters for ourselves.

We drove off the peninsula and that ended the naval base area. On the mainland, we were shortly passing the salt pans, vast shallow rectangular diked-in ponds, into which the Red Sea waters were pumped. There under the blazing sun, the water soon evaporated, leaving the salt .

This, I learned, was the only major natural industry of Massawa, which before the war exported salt in huge quantities, especially to Japan. Massawa was an ideal spot for it, as the Red Sea water is the saltiest of any of the oceans and the sun obligingly provided a superabundance of no cost heat for the evaporation process.

Beyond the salt pan area we passed through the native Eritrean quarter—terrible-looking hovels with signs at frequent intervals,

OUT OF BOUNDS TO ALL TROOPS,

and frequent sentries to see that the order was enforced. Apparently the brothel, probably for medical reasons, had an officially enforced monopoly of the oldest trade in the world.

At the end of the native city, we made a sharp left turn onto a long causeway leading to ancient Massawa itself, which stands really on an island, not on the mainland. And now I began to see wrecks in

Stretching across the south harbor lay seven large vessels.

profusion on both sides of me as we crossed the causeway.

To my right was the south harbor, where perhaps most of them lay, though that was hard to say. In a long string stretching across the south harbor lay seven large vessels—some erect with only masts and stacks visible, some on their sides, some apparently bottom up. One, on its starboard side in the middle of that sad-looking string, was a huge passenger liner, apparently as large as anything under the American flag, with a large hole blown in its exposed port bilge and what damage below water only divers could tell. Scattered at random outside that line of scuttled ships were masts and stacks all over the place—one set of masts far off on the horizon.

To my left in the commercial harbor, I could see one large ship on its side right at the entrance. Inside the commercial harbor were others right side up, marked as usual by stacks and masts protruding sickeningly from invisible hulls. As a variation, alongside one of the main quays, the massive steel work of a gigantic floating crane rose from the water, looking like a distorted Eiffel Tower with nothing to support it. Somewhere below lay the hull of that crane, no longer floating. And elsewhere in that harbor were the invisible hulks of smaller ships, some alongside the quays, others most anywhere.

Here certainly was a salvage man's paradise, with all kinds of salvage jobs to suit all tastes—wrecks laid out in neat rows, wrecks sunk individually, wrecks on their sides, wrecks right side up, wrecks upside down, wrecks wholly submerged, wrecks partly awash, large wrecks, small wrecks, medium-sized wrecks, wrecks of merchant ships, wrecks of warships, wrecks of docks—wrecks everywhere, enough to make a wreck of any man contemplating all that wreckage, knowing how scant would be his equipment, how few would be his men, how terrible would be his working conditions.

A little sick at heart, wishing more than ever that I had chosen Iceland, I ordered the driver to turn about and go back to the naval base.

CHAPTER

19

I HAD LUNCH AT THE BRITISH NAVAL
Officers' Mess (which I had joined) in the building which had served
the same purpose under the Italian flag. It was located as well as
might be for the purpose, right on the edge of the open Red Sea,
with a very wide veranda actually out over the water. There was no
beach there—the rugged coral formations formed a miniature cliff
against which the waves broke beneath the veranda in music pleasing
to any sailor's ear.

There I met the British naval officers on Captain Lucas' staff, some
ten of them altogether—Commander Callwell, Executive Officer, a
slight, mild person; Lieutenant Hibble, the Base Engineer Officer,
tall and what was unusual for an Englishman, garrulous; Lieutenant
Fairbairn, officially the pilot for the port, about my own size, which
meant he wasn't very large, who was exceedingly serious in looks
and in speech; Lieutenant Maton, whom I had seen before as Communications Officer but whose main task turned out to be Intelligence Officer; and half a dozen others, including the naval surgeon,
with none of whom did it turn out I ever had much to do.

All wore the universal costume for Massawa, khaki shorts, khaki
shirts open at the neck, sun helmets (which temporarily lay on a
table near the inevitable bar), and all had gold-striped shoulder
marks attached to their shirts (not an American naval custom) to
denote their rank. In distinction to them, in accordance with American regulations, I wore pinned to my shirt collar on each side, a tiny
silver oak leaf designating my rank, which designation I shortly discovered meant nothing to either Italians or natives in Massawa
where the American Navy and its symbols were both equally unknown

The major-domo at this officers' mess was an Italian (so also was
the bartender) who had evidently run the place in Fascist days; the

servants were all turbaned Arabs. The food was both scant and poor —partly obtained as rations from the British Army commissary, partly purchased in the open market which had little to offer that was safe to eat. Very clearly my British shipmates were used to an austere diet since I heard no complaints from any of them, and naturally I made no criticisms. If this was the best war conditions in Eritrea permitted them, I could stand it as well as they. I may add here, that in my long stay with that mess, the only decent meals we ever got was when we had fish, of which the Red Sea furnished an abounding variety. The drawback to having more fish was that the Arab and Eritrean fishermen were shy on boats and very scary of risking themselves and what few boats they still had in fishing, since the waters outside the harbors were thickly sowed with Italian mines—one could never tell when a net or a line might set one off.

Lieutenant Fairbairn, on being introduced to me as the new American salvage officer for Massawa, looked me over with much gravity, then said sympathetically,

"My best wishes, Commander. I hope you manage to live longer than the first salvage officer we had here."

"The first salvage officer?" I asked, puzzled. "I didn't know there'd been one here before. I understood my predecessor was stopped at Pearl Harbor and never got here at all."

"Oh, yes, there was one," affirmed Fairbairn. "A Royal Navy Commander, tophole chap in salvage, best we had in England, with a fine salvage ship, too. He spent some time in Massawa last summer after the surrender making a diving survey here, those sunken dry docks particularly. He was going to do this job—that is, what could be done. I was on his ship when we went out to lend assistance to some British ship that had beached herself around the Daklak Islands—they fringe Massawa some forty miles out. There are a lot of Italian wrecks around Daklak but we weren't bothering with them that day. You haven't seen those wrecks yet, Commander?"

I had to confess I hadn't seen the wrecks on the Daklak Islands yet, only those in Massawa harbor itself.

"You simply must see them, Commander; they're a fine lot of wrecks—six big ships or more scuttled in the harbors in those islands," Fairbairn assured me gravely, as if he feared I might run short of wrecks to keep me occupied. "Well, to get along with it, we pulled the ship off the beach, she wasn't on hard, but by the time she was all clear in deep water and on her way again bound for Aden, it was dark. There weren't any lighthouses going out there and the charts are none too reliable, either, so we were in a hurry to get clear ourselves and back to Massawa before it got too black. The commander took her into what looked like a wide channel between two low islands, and then we hit an Italian mine. Ever hit a mine in a salvage ship, Commander?" he asked.

I had to admit I hadn't—yet.

"It's wicked, when you're on such a small vessel. Tore her all to pieces. Killed the commander on the bridge. Most of the rest of the crew, too. Terrible explosion. All I know is there I was in the water, wondering why I was alive. No sign of our ship any more—just four or five other chaps like me, bobbing about, trying to keep afloat. We did, too, all night long, managing to stay together for company, while we shed what little clothes we had on to make the swimming easier.

"In the morning, we spotted land a mile or so off, one of those low, uninhabited Daklak Islands. We swam toward it. Tough swim, but the tide helped us, fortunately. As we got closer, we saw we were in luck. There on what we'd supposed was a deserted island were a lot of Arabs, white robes, white turbans, squatting on the beach, watching us. That gave us heart—only half a dozen cables' lengths or so more and we'd have no more worries—we'd get help.

"When we were perhaps only a cable's length from the beach, all those Arabs lazily took wing and flew away—they were just a flock of big white pelicans! Devilish feeling it gave us. We made the island, all right, but before we got through with it, I give you my word, Commander, we wished we'd all been blown to hell in a hurry like our shipmates. There wasn't a drop of water on that island. It was small, flat, only a few feet above sea level, all coral sand, with not a palm tree, not a shrub, not a sign of shade anywhere, and we had no clothes to speak of—a few undershirts among the lot of us. We were on that island three days—I won't weary you with the details—three days with no water and no shade. The sun was horrible—I'll never see the like of it again this side of hell. The fourth day, an Arab dhow bound from Yemen to Massawa saw us waving, sheered in, and took us off."

Fairbairn rose from the lunch table.

"I've got a ship to shift berth this afternoon, so I must leave. Better luck to you in salvage than the first commander had." He picked up his sun helmet and walked out.

"Good man, Fairbairn," commented Lieutenant Hibble, as the pilot disappeared. "Takes things too seriously, though, for his own good. You should see him piloting a ship in or out of the commercial harbor among all those wrecks. He takes it so gravely you'd think he was the Archbishop of Canterbury trying to get the crown front side to at the Coronation."

I had nothing to say. Fairbairn was evidently grave by nature, but certainly his experiences had given him no reason for levity. Nor me either. It was news to me, but not pleasant, that the British Navy had undertaken itself the salvage task till that Italian mine had put a period to their efforts. I wondered casually how many mines were left about to send me to join my Royal Navy predecessor.

Lieutenant Hibble and I left the mess table together. As Base Engineer Officer, he had the keys to all the locked-up Italian naval base shops, and was to accompany me on a tour of inspection of those shops.

We saw them all, in each under the watchful eye of some Sudanese sentry with bayonet fixed who had orders to see that nothing was stolen and meant to insure that no one, uniformed or not, violated his orders. Those Sudanese (there was no talking with them, they understood only Arabic) descendants of the fuzzy-wuzzies who had hurled themselves regardless on the murderous machine guns of Kitchener's squares at Khartoum, were intensely proud of the British uniforms they wore now and made fine soldiers. Long before I was through with Massawa, I was willing to add my "Amen" to Kipling's verse:

So 'ere's *to* you, Fuzzy-Wuzzy, at your 'ome in the Soudan;
You're a pore benighted 'eathen but a first-class fightin' man;
An' 'ere's *to* you, Fuzzy-Wuzzy, with your 'ayrick 'ead of 'air—
You big black boundin' beggar—for you broke a British square!

The condition inside the shops was about as I'd been told. In every one, the electric driving motors of every piece of machinery had been smashed by Italians swinging sledge hammers with fiendish glee, judging by the results. In addition, driving gears here and there were broken, and others were missing, apparently tossed into the Red Sea. All machinery was rendered useless, both by destruction of driving power and destruction of essential parts.

That was the condition in the machine shop, the carpenter shop, the electric shop, the boat shop, the shipfitter's shop, the pipe shop, and the foundry, except that in the foundry there were also the shattered fragments of its indispensable and irreplaceable graphite crucibles.

Other than the destruction, I noted the complete absence of any sign of small hand tools like hammers, saws, or chisels. The insides of those naval shops thoroughly warranted the bitter comment which the first Royal Navy Board to survey Massawa made of them:

"The whole of the machinery of the Depot and workshops, all cranes, portable plant and tools and equipment were firstly effectively sabotaged by the Italians; secondly, thoroughly looted by the Free French and remaining Italians; thirdly, anything portable of value left has been appropriated by the Army."

There was sufficient cause for the statement which had come to us in Washington that a complete outfit of new machinery must be furnished Massawa to make it operative again as a naval base.

Our tour of the naval shops took some hours. As we left each shop, it was carefully relocked and the sentry posted there resumed his vigil outside. But why it was necessary was not very clear—unless one wanted to steal something for scrap iron, what was there inside to steal?

About three in the blistering afternoon, Lieutenant Hibble and I concluded our inspection tour and drove back to the British naval headquarters. There I had my first experience with the Eritrean telephone system—all Italian equipment and Italian operators, save for the British seaman running the small telephone board at the naval base itself. I gave him the call. It took him about an hour, going through the main Italian boards in Massawa and Asmara and the various villages between, to get me Colonel Claterbos in Asmara, seventy miles away. What that seaman went through with the Italian operators in both cities and villages in getting the connection, I could easily judge by listening near by. If he had not been English, I'm sure he would have gone raving mad before finally he looked up at me in triumph and announced,

"You're through, sir."

I picked up the Italian hand phone, a gingerbready affair with the Italian coat-of-arms in colors decorating it, and to my delight I found

I actually had Colonel Claterbos!

However, I might well have saved myself my enthusiasm. Before I got through with that conversation, fifty minutes had passed, the connection had been broken somewhere at least seven times, and seven times in the midst of a sentence I found myself suddenly listening to or talking to some unknown Italian, Englishman, or American somewhere else in Eritrea. Each time my English sailor came stoically to my rescue and re-established the connection or the conversation with Colonel Claterbos would have foundered ingloriously. As it was, I finally managed to convey piecemeal to Colonel Claterbos that I had quarters arranged, both for the military assistants promised and the civilian supervisors, and had heard enough in driblets from him to assure me that next morning they would be sent to join me in Massawa.

With that hard-won understanding established, I hung up the phone at my end, feeling as if I had been through a major engagement, saved only from annihilation by the traditional tenacity of the Royal Navy in doggedly reinforcing me at crucial moments.

" 'Ard going, sir, with all them bloomin' Eyties on the line," sympathetically observed my seaman as I swabbed my brow, "specially in all this 'eat. But we 'as 'opes, sir, as 'ow the Signal Corps will take over soon."

It couldn't be too soon for me, fervently I assured the long-suffering sailor as I thanked him and departed for my new quarters, determined to stand under my shower till dinner time. For the water in my new domicile, I'd found, wasn't so hot—only somewhere around 90° to 100° F. Apparently it was brought down to lukewarm proportions by being exposed to evaporation to cool it in a vast open wooden tank sheltered by a well-ventilated adjacent building intended only for that purpose.

I had a bad night.

My room, as good a one as Building 108 afforded and probably as well located as any for comfort, had two large windows looking directly eastward over the Red Sea and two others facing south. In addition, it had a large door opening to the corridor on the west side. Since all these openings were without glass, shielded only by heavily built slatted shutters, the room was as exposed to cross ventilation as it was possible to make it, and in addition there was a large overhead ceiling fan to stir up the air. The fan, I may say, was never stopped. It ran night and day.

There were, however, no screens over any opening, possibly on the theory that screens shut out the air. At any rate, flies, mosquitoes, and gnats had free access also, but they were to be taken care of otherwise. Before I turned in, Ahmed sprayed the room thoroughly with a Flit gun to take care of uninvited insects, and I had a complete fine mesh mosquito net over my bed, which as a bed was not much, being an Italian affair slightly better than a folding army cot.

Lying in the bed, I carefully sprayed the inside of my net-enclosed area to finish off any mosquitoes which might have gained access there, then shoved the Flit gun down on the floor and hurriedly re-secured the netting on that side under the mattress. Thus protected, I hauled my sheet over my pajama-clad form and rolled over. Ahmed, meanwhile, stretched himself out on the floor in the corridor outside the door, ready at hand in case he should be called (which he never was).

I didn't go to sleep. Very swiftly I came to the conclusion that a sheet over me was unnecessary and I shoved it off, wapsing it up at the foot of the bed. Once more I tried to doze off, but found it impossible. I was too hot and too wet. It was clear I didn't need or want the pajamas which were already soaked in sweat. Off they came, to join the unused sheet at my feet. Completely naked now, I lay only on the bottom sheet, quite well exposed to what air there might be moving under the impetus of that ceiling fan or a night sea breeze.

If any air was stirring, I couldn't feel it inside my mosquito net, and with no outside screens, I did not dare to push aside the net. Restlessly I tossed from side to side all night through, simmering gently in the heat, while the sheet and mattress beneath me got wetter and wetter from sweat dripping off my body, which didn't get any wetter only because it was completely wet to start with. If I slept at all, I was unaware of it. Fully awake, at long last I watched the sun rise over the Red Sea, a burnished ball of fire from the instant its upper limb appeared above the distant sea horizon.

Wearily I pushed aside the mosquito netting, dragged myself into the bathroom and turned on the shower. After a long stay there, I came back into my room to stand directly beneath the fan while I tried to dry myself. I took a look at my bed. The lower sheet and the mattress were so soaked they looked as if a set of month-old, un-diapered quintuplets had occupied that bed since birth. I glanced at my khaki clothes which I had hung over a chair beneath the fan to dry. They were as wet as I had left them the night before.

I reflected. This was only April 1. It couldn't possibly get any more humid, but it could get much hotter. Still there were limits to the amount of suffering one could consciously appreciate—beyond a certain point the body couldn't differentiate any longer. That was comforting. I started to dress.

About the middle of the morning, the first contingent from Asmara arrived to join me, having made an early start from there. Had I had the slightest spark of brotherliness, I should have met them waving a yellow quarantine flag, warning them to turn about and flee back to Asmara while yet they were well and hearty. But instead, feeling inwardly like a fiend, I stood silently by and let them toss their luggage out of their cars.

Under the chilling gaze of the two Cable and Wireless men, who looked on this new Yankee invasion with frigid disapproval, the newcomers hastily took over the remaining vacant rooms on the second floor, and part of those below.

I found I had drawn one officer assistant—Captain David Plummer of the Medical Corps as surgeon for the Naval Base. In addition, Patrick Murphy had come down as Construction Superintendent for the contractor, together with several civilian supervisors.

With the one officer given me, and some of the civilians, the United States Naval Repair Base at Massawa was put in commission.

I started the job of recruiting a Naval Base working force—Italians, Eritreans, Arabs, anybody I could hire except Americans, of whom there would be none available for us. All the American mechanics who had come over with me were earmarked for the contractor's various construction projects in Eritrea. Unfortunately for my purposes, these were the air base at Gura on the plateau first, housing at the mountain village of Ghinda and elsewhere second, and construction at Massawa (housing again, mainly) a poor last, since no machinery for Massawa was expected for a long time.

I had also the job of getting the shops going without waiting for the machinery from America. My inspection of the Italian shops had convinced me that no matter how thorough a job the Italians thought they had done, as saboteurs they had committed a terrible blunder which left the door open to us for a quick rehabilitation of all the smashed machinery. I meant to take advantage of it.

Helping on this I had six of the contractor's civilian supervisors whom the contractor was glad to lend me temporarily at least, since in his construction projects in Massawa he had as yet no equipment for them to work with. These six men—Austin Byrne, master machinist; James Lang, electrical superintendent; Herman Weinberg, sheet-metal foreman; Pierre Willermet, pipe foreman; Paul Taylor, electrical foreman; and Fred Schlachter, carpenter foreman—worked like Trojans for me; with their help I managed to give the Axis its first shock in sabotaged Massawa.

For I had observed that while there wasn't an unsmashed electric driving motor on any machine, the smashing had not been symmetrically done. On some motors they had smashed one end, on others the opposite end, on still others the main frame. There were hundreds of motors involved of different sizes, but of each size there were dozens at least.

That situation was the key to our solution. If only we could disassemble all the broken motors, out of some dozens of broken motors of a given size, I was sure we could find enough undamaged parts of every kind needed to reassemble a few complete motors at least.

Aided by the local British military and naval authorities, I started to hire workmen. Eritreans were not hard to get—there were hundreds available as laborers. A few dozen Italian workmen were obtained, some of them ex-mechanics of the naval base, some P.O.W.s eager to exchange the meager fare of the concentration camps for square meals at the American Naval Base, plus real wages, more than they had ever earned in Italy or Eritrea, either as soldiers or civilians.

Then in the beginning we got some Arabs also—carpenters, all of them, for apparently none of the Arabs had ever had a chance at machinery. But they were good carpenters, and Fred Schlachter, foreman in that shop, hailed them with glee.

Now I ran into other troubles—I had a plan, I had some workmen, but we had no hand tools for them to work with, even on the simple tasks which must come first. Unbelievable as it may seem, we found ourselves practically in the position of primitive man; the commonest hand tools—saws, hammers, screwdrivers, monkey wrenches—which all of our lives we had taken as a matter of course, we didn't have and we couldn't get in Massawa. The American solution, going around to the nearest hardware store and buying any tool wanted, was as remote as America, 13,000 miles away from us. There were no hardware stores, there were no tools for sale in Massawa.

That was a problem that had to be solved immediately. I took Fred Schlachter in my car and we started for Asmara. Surely there must be some tools there. And at the same time, I sent off all the other foremen I had in Army cars to scour the hinterland of Eritrea— the shut-down Italian gold mines, the cement mills, the little village repair shops over which the tide of war and looting had not swept. They were to commandeer for the United States whatever in the way of tools they could find, and pay the owners whatever was demanded.

Up and down again over that seventy-mile mountain drive to Asmara I went myself, more slowly this time, since I had some real control over the driver. In Asmara, after appealing to the British and the American army quartermasters and going through several Italian plants taken over by the occupying forces, we acquired a few tools—two saws, four hammers, a few screwdrivers, files, and chisels, and one wrench. Had I been given the British crown jewels, I could not have been more jealous of them as we stowed these few precious tools beneath the back seat cushion for our return trip, held down by Schlachter and me, sitting on them to make sure they did not mysteriously disappear before we got them to Massawa.

Coming back from Asmara, I had a better chance to scan the scenery than on my first ride. It was magnificent—vast precipices, sheer mountainsides, long vistas, opening continuously, as cautiously we swung around the mountain switchbacks. Now and then we passed a laden camel train or a solitary burro, almost hidden by a huge load several times bigger than himself.

But what struck me most was neither the scenery nor the primitive transport bearing produce to Asmara—it was the decorations with which the Fascisti had lined that mountain road. Every hundred yards at least on some prominent rock or cliffside, where it could not escape attention, was carefully and professionally painted in large letters,

"W il Duce!"

which my driver assured me meant *"Viva il Duce."*

Very carefully spaced, one to every ten "W il Duces," was

"W il Re!"

and again, roughly in the ratio of one to every hundred "W il Duces," was

"W il Duca de Aosta!"

From all this it was apparent that Mussolini had had little intention of letting any Italian in Eritrea forget him, or forget who was boss, he or the King of Italy, whom evidently he rated as worth only ten per cent of regimented Fascist *vivas*. As for the Duke of Aosta, cousin of the King, Commander of the Italian East African Army, and Governor of Eritrea, one per cent of the painted cheers would do for him.

None of these "spontaneous" cheers for il Duce had been painted out or defaced by the British, even though they had been in occupation for nearly a year. Nothing, I thought, so showed British contempt for Mussolini and all he might yet attempt as those uneffaced self-testimonials. No Italian in Eritrea could travel that road now without blushing. No American or Britisher could travel it without laughing at that clown, Mussolini.

We got back to Massawa in the late afternoon, feeling twice as uncomfortable as when we had left, for the few brief hours in cool Asmara made the hot coast seem even more intolerable. I resolved to go to Asmara as little as I could—the flames of hell are not made more bearable by short vacations in heaven.

Soon my other foragers were all back—some with fair luck, some with none. But when we inventoried our acquisitions, it looked as if we had enough hand tools to get perhaps two dozen mechanics going.

Next morning we got under way. In every shop, a few Italians were turned to, unbolting smashed motors from machine beds. Crews of Eritreans carried them to the electric shop, where other Italians started to disassemble them, making heaps of all similar parts that were still good. Still other Eritreans were set to work on the huge scrap and junk piles behind the foundry, instructed to sort out every undamaged gear, every piece of anything in an undamaged condition that looked like a piece of machinery.

Meanwhile, Austin Byrne, master mechanic, started a careful piece by piece scrutiny of every machine in every shop. Each machine had, aside from the smashing of its driving motor, been rendered unserviceable by smashing some vital gear, sometimes more than one, or removing some vital part; but not every gear on every machine had been either smashed or removed.

Byrne's task resolved itself into a gigantic jigsaw puzzle—it was his job in the wide assortment of still undamaged gears and parts to see if he could find somewhere in cannibalizing that damaged collection of machinery, enough unbroken gears and parts to assemble at least one good lathe and one good milling machine—more, of course, if possible.

It worked out marvelously. By the second day, Lang and Taylor in the electrical shop had reassembled completely half a dozen three- and five-horsepower electric motors from what had once been parts of some twenty-five other damaged motors. Within the same time, Byrne had refitted completely the driving trains on an eighteen-inch lathe and on a milling machine. Two of our first batch of reassembled electric motors were bolted to those two machines, belted up, power thrown on the lines, and we were ready to go. It was a happy moment for all hands when Byrne pressed the button and our first lathe began to spin perfectly.

Oddly enough, no American there seemed any happier than the delighted Italian machinist who had been assigned to that lathe—one of the very Italians who the year before had helped swing the sledges which had destroyed everything. Now he positively beamed on the ingenious Americans who had given him that smashed machine in working order again.

From then on, the rehabilitation literally snowballed up. On the junk piles we had found three discarded graphite crucibles from the foundry. They were old and thin and cracked about the rims, but they were whole, and with delicate handling, usable. Literally I thanked God when we found those crucibles, saved miraculously from being smashed by having been tossed out previously as junk too worn for use. Nowhere in all the Middle East (for I had contacted every Allied warehouse and shop) were there any crucibles available to us —without them the foundry was useless.

But with those heaven-sent crucibles in our hands, we went to town. Using broken gears as patterns (or where there were none, then patterns carved by hand by Schlachter and his Arabs) we cast what new gears we needed to complete the next machine. We didn't try to cast in iron or steel—we weren't ready for that—but only in brass or aluminum, which were easier both to cast in the foundry and to machine afterwards.

Hardly was the first gear casting cool enough to break out of the molding sand when it was rushed to the machine shop, where on our one lathe it was turned true, faced, and bored, and then shifted over

[137]

to our solitary miller to have its teeth cut. That large gear and another smaller one, when finished, went immediately into place to give us a third machine in working order—a boring mill.

Each machine, as it went back into service, increased our capacity to make new parts for others—vital parts we couldn't find. Soon we were casting in aluminum or brass and machining parts to replace broken parts of electric motors that we needed and couldn't find in our heaps of disassembled parts—end bells mainly.

Each new motor made another machine serviceable; each new machine widened perceptibly our ability to make parts for other motors and other machines. The enthusiasm in the shops among our heterogeneous collection of workmen as, one after another, they saw additional machines starting to turn over and produce, rose feverishly —it was amazing to watch the Italians especially, jabbering delightedly to each other as, one by one, in ever shortening periods those smashed machines came to life again.

The rehabilitation had another unexpected effect. After a few days it became obvious to every Italian that the few energetic Americans bossing them had neither any intention of locking Massawa up till autumn cooled it off a bit nor of waiting till new machinery arrived from America—in spite of heat and in spite of destruction, those Americans were going to have everything sabotaged going again and that before long. Such being the case, what was the value to the Italians in holding out information they had till it was worthless to them, since its lack was doing us no great hurt?

Evidently they saw no value in it any more. Privately, so that none of their co-workers saw them, one after another of our Italian mechanics sought out his own foreman, Austin Byrne, or me, always with the same story. He knew where this or that missing gear or part had been secreted against the return of the Fascisti. But now he was himself sure the Fascisti were not coming back. Perhaps we should like to know where that part was? Maybe we might pay a little something for the information? But we would be willing to keep it a secret for fear of Fascist reprisals on his family in Italy?

Always the answer was the same—we should be happy to know, we should be glad to pay, our secrecy could be relied on. The policy brought gratifying results. Missing parts by the dozen miraculously reappeared, for which we paid up to 1000 Italian lira (about ten dollars) apiece, and in a few cases, considerably more.

[138]

The net effect of our efforts in heat too intolerable for work was to produce the first Massawa miracle. One American officer and six American supervisors, using nothing—labor or materials or tools— that was not on hand in Massawa or thereabouts when we arrived, in only one month after my arrival had every sabotaged Italian shop in the naval base working at at least the full capacity intended by the Italians themselves; in some cases more. The United States Naval Repair Base at Massawa was fully ready for business the first week in May, 1942, and yet not one of the new outfit of shop machines ordered in America to make it serviceable had as yet been loaded for shipment out of New York!

Our naval base went right to work, not a week too soon either, for in Libya, Rommel was crashing eastward and soon was to be knocking at the gateway to Egypt.

CHAPTER

20

F<small>ROM THE SECOND DAY OF MY AR-</small>
rival in Massawa, I had another pressing problem literally staring
me in the face each time I looked out the windows of my room at
the Red Sea. Lying in the open roadstead outside the naval harbor,
swinging to one anchor only, was what looked like a sizable white
elephant which had been the immediate cause of the crack-up of the
first British liaison officer sent to Massawa.

It seems that the year before, both Axis partners had been urgently
concerned in stirring up revolt in Iran and Irak against British influence, hoping immediately to shut off oil to Britain and later to
acquire it themselves. Meanwhile, also, in Iran they would shut the
back door for supplying Russia. The Iranian government, very partial
to Axis ideas, had co-operated enthusiastically, so also had elements
in Irak. Fighting broke out. But Britain had reacted energetically.
With tanks and planes and infantry, her Middle East forces had
swiftly flattened out the Axis co-operators and in Persia particularly,
a new government more favorably disposed toward Great Britain
had hastily taken over.

Looking over now quiescent Persia with access to its archives in
Teheran, British officials discovered an interesting situation. Lying in
the Persian Gulf, practically never used because of a sad miscalcula-
tion in the depth of water available for its operation, was a medium-
sized floating steel dry dock. On the face of things, this dry dock had
been purchased some six years before by the then Persian government from Italy, where it was built to order, but an inspection of the
treasury archives in Teheran indicated that not one cent had yet
been paid the Italian builders for the dock.

In British eyes, this situation had promising possibilities which
she promptly proceeded to turn into realities. From captured Mas-

sawa was a report from her own salvage expert (later killed) based on his diving survey, that the salvage of the two scuttled Italian docks there was impossible. Britain badly needed a dry dock, any kind of a dock, if Massawa were ever to function at all. Here in the Persian Gulf was a dry dock the Persians couldn't use anyway for lack of water, and which they didn't own either, since they had never paid for it, even partly. Ownership under those conditions lay with the unpaid builders who were Italians (and presumably the Italian government which for reasons not too obscure, had never pressed for payment). The Italians were enemies who had treacherously declared war on Britain; Italian property anywhere within reach was subject to seizure, and certainly that dry dock was now within reach of Britain's Navy.

Given all these facts, there was only one conclusion to be drawn and the British drew it. The Royal Navy seized the dry dock as an Italian prize of war. All I had to do was to gaze out of my window in Massawa to see it swinging to one anchor in the outer roadstead, where it had arrived after a 2000-mile tow several weeks before I had.

If that floating dry dock had been a useless white elephant and a problem to the Persians, it was still quite as useless a white elephant and just as much a problem to the British in Massawa, though for different reasons.

Temporarily it was anchored in the open roadstead where the ocean-going tugs which had brought it had dropped it and promptly fled from Massawa. It could neither be used where it was nor left there, no matter how many moorings were put down to hold it. In that exposed location the first heavy blow, either from the sea or the desert, was bound to take that high, flat-sided dry dock and pile it up on the coral-fringed shore, a total loss.

The logical answer, of course, was immediately to tow it into the sheltered naval harbor, which was the only spot the dry dock could be operated, and moor it permanently there for use. But there were obstacles to logic. Two sunken Italian docks already occupied the only logical spots for floating dry docks, even though they were no longer floating. Whether a third spot existed inside that harbor with water enough and a usable approach for ships being docked, was an unanswered question. Then part of the mooring chains for the dry dock had been lost on the long tow—she no longer had chain enough for a safe mooring job anywhere.

Finally, there was the actual problem of towing the new dry dock through into the sheltered naval harbor, now too sheltered, unfortunately, with five ships scuttled across it to block the entrance.

My first British liaison officer, faced in my absence with all these problems, had earnestly striven to find the answers before the first severe storm came along and added the wreck of the Persian dry dock to all the Italian and German wrecks with which Massawa waters were already too liberally bestrewn. He tried to obtain mooring cables from the British Naval Base in Alexandria. He received, instead of chain cable, the stereotyped Middle East answer to everything which I very soon learned by heart,

"There is none available."

In desperation he then sought to figure out a way of taking the dry dock into the harbor between the scuttled wrecks, of finding some place inside the sheltered harbor at least to anchor her. He got nowhere. Between the Massawa heat, the demoralizing sight of all the wrecks roundabout, and the vision haunting him night and day of that valuable dock gone to join the existing wrecks, he cracked up. A nervous wreck himself, he was shipped off to the hospital in the hills shortly before my arrival. Now I had the problem of that dry dock, along with all my other Massawa problems. Since the U.S. Naval Base was now in commission, the Royal Navy had turned over the Persian dry dock to me as part of it.

How long did I have to find an answer? No one could tell me. Even though it was early April, it was not too late for occasional heavy blows from the Red Sea. After early May, quite as severe sandstorms could be expected off the desert. Something must be done immediately, or I should now be responsible for the loss of the dock.

So while I was in the midst of my hectic start in getting the rehabilitation of the sabotaged shops under way, I had also to undertake to save that dry dock. Accompanied by Lieutenant Fairbairn of the Royal Navy, I went out in the ex-Italian launch which served him as a pilot boat to survey the wrecks which lay across the channel entrance to the naval harbor.

Looked at from the sea, from left to right the wrecks were those of the *Acerbi, Impero, Oliva, XXIII Marzo,* and *Moncalieri.* It was immediately apparent that while these vessels had been stretched out before scuttling in a string across the channel, bow to stern, to block it, the Italians had not succeeded too well in their intentions. Evidently in going down, the *Oliva* had rolled over on its side and in so doing had swung its stern away from the bow of the *XXIII Marzo*.

At any rate, a clear channel, certainly wide enough to pass an ordinary ship, existed between the hulks of the *Oliva* and the *XXIII Marzo*, provided the entering ship was brought in at an angle to the line of wrecks. Was the clearance great enough also to pass the dry dock, which was far wider in the beam than any ordinary vessel, as well as being far more unwieldy since it was box-shaped, had no rudder and no power, and in a tow was likely to sheer about unpredictably, particularly at low speed?

By careful measuring with a sounding line, Fairbairn and I determined the passage between the two wrecks gave us a few fathoms clearance for the beam of the dock between the bow of the *XXIII Marzo* and the stern of the *Oliva*—if only we could bring the dock in at the proper angle and hold her steady on that angle till her entire length, about 400 feet, had passed both wrecks. There was not clearance enough to allow passage with a tug secured to one side (let alone both sides) to help hold the dock steady—our unwieldly dock with all the grace and maneuverability of an overgrown rectangular cracker box would have to be handled by tugs secured to her only by lines ahead and astern.

To me, bringing the dock through looked possible. But Fairbairn, shaking his head dubiously, pointed out the dangers. He was in a bad way for tugs to handle even an ordinary tow, let alone one requiring the very highest degree of tugboat skill. All he had to work with was two tugs, when the job obviously required at least four, and six would be better.

Then, of the two tugs he did have to lean on, one he could only regard as a broken reed, and the other as at best a somewhat flexible one. His first tug, a Royal Navy craft sent down from Port Sudan, was manned by a set of officers wholly incompetent for tugboat work —they were big ship sailors, tossed against their will onto a tug which they despised with no wish at all to acquire the skill they lacked, and intent only on escaping Massawa at the earliest moment.

"When those chaps are secured to the end of a towline, Commander, I nearly always have heart failure wondering what they'll do with it the minute my back's turned," confided Fairbairn. "They've already crumpled the bow of their own tug, ramming a ship they

[143]

should have been backing away on. Only the Lord knows what they'll do next time."

The other tug he had more faith in, but even about that one he was none too sure.

"You see, Commander, she's a Chinese tug, manned completely by Chinamen, excepting only her skipper, who's English and quite a decent chap. She belongs in Hong Kong; when the Japs assaulted that last December and it surrendered, that Chinese tug, the *Hsin Rocket*, was the only thing that managed to escape the harbor—quite a smart performance considering all the warships the Japs had blockading the port. Why she ended up in Massawa, of all the places she might have gone, I can't explain. Now the *Hsin Rocket's* a good tug and her Chinese crew know their business, but I'm always a little afraid that in a tight spot her skipper may lose some precious seconds in translating my orders into Chinese for his crew, and land me in a jam."

Fairbairn went on to point out to me, as he previously had to the first Royal Navy liaison officer, that due to insufficient tugs, to the possible inept handling of the two tugs he had, to the unpredictable action of that box-shaped dock coming in across the tidal current due to the oblique course he must steer, and worst of all, to a possible sudden slew of the high-sided dock if a gust of cross wind hit her, there was grave danger of ramming one wreck or the other coming through with the possibility of the dock being sunk in the only opening now existing in that line of wrecks, blocking off the naval harbor completely.

From Lieutenant Fairbairn's launch, I scanned what showed above water of the capsized *Oliva* and the upright *XXIII Marzo,* the Scylla and Charybdis between which the Persian dock must pass if it were to be saved. I made up my mind. If ever I went to join that first liaison officer in the hospital as another nervous wreck, it was going to be as a result of doing something, not of doing nothing.

"I'm responsible now, Lieutenant," I told Fairbairn. "I'll take the risk. Whatever happens, the fault will be mine. I'll survey the inner harbor this afternoon for the best anchorage, and tomorrow you get your tugs and take her through at slack tide. I know you can do it," and I meant that, too, for by now I was beginning to acquire a great deal of respect for sober-faced Lieutenant Fairbairn.

"Aye, aye, sir," he responded, unemotional as always. "I'll have the tugs round from the commercial harbor and we'll move at eleven tomorrow morning. That will give me an hour to get her straightened away outside so we can hit the entrance right at high water slack. But mind you, Commander," he warned me earnestly, "not if it's blowing tomorrow. I won't touch her in any wind. And I want a flag marker buoy with no slack planted exactly on the sunken bow of the *XXIII Marzo* and the sunken stern of the *Oliva* to mark the clearance for me."

I spent the afternoon in a broad-beamed heavy launch, which in contradiction to her scowlike lines, was elegantly named the *Lord Grey*. The *Lord Grey*, manned now by an Italian crew, had been brought from Alexandria and was the only power boat that went with my newly acquired Naval Base.

From the Italian chart of the harbor, there was a spot with six fathoms of water at low tide just to the northeast of where the two Italian docks were scuttled. This offered the only remaining area in which the Persian dock could possibly be operated, though even there, when flooded down at low tide to take a ship, the dock would probably touch bottom. To make matters worse, the approach was bad. A ship coming in to be docked, would first, of course, have to sidle through between the wrecks at the entrance. After that, it would have to dodge a three-fathom shoal spot on its port side while it made a sharp 90° turn to starboard to line up for going onto the dock. All this was going to be very tricky seamanship in handling each ship for docking and undocking, but there was no help for it. It was that one spot for the Persian dock, or nothing.

It remained to be seen whether in that solitary available spot showing six fathoms on the Italian chart, there really were six fathoms of water and, more important, to discover whether in the area the dry dock would cover, there were any high spots which might pierce the bottom of our dry dock when it was flooded down to take a ship.

With a British quartermaster and half a dozen British seamen to do the work, I put in a very hot afternoon while the *Lord Grey* cruised slowly back and forth and circled about over the proposed site and the British naval ratings sounded, dragged grappling hooks, and swept drags in circles over the entire area. Finally, I was willing to call it a day. The chart soundings were correct; our drags had caught on nothing that indicated any coral pinnacles below.

I visited the dry dock swinging at its anchor off the seaward face of the Abd-El-Kader Peninsula. It was a fair-sized dock, capable of lifting a dead weight of 6ooo tons, enough to take the average merchantman if it came in light—that is, with no cargo aboard to speak of. I met the dock crew, and my eyebrows lifted as I learned that the range of nationalities to be employed at the U.S. Naval Repair Base was widening out. The supervisors recently provided by the British with the dock, were English—Mr. Spanner, dockmaster; Mr. Reed, assistant dockmaster; and Mr. Hudson, engineer. But the operating crew of the dock were its original Persian complement—nine Persians, only two of whom spoke any English, plus about a dozen Hindoos who spoke no English at all.

This took me somewhat aback, as docking ships, particularly in floating dry docks, is a delicate business, not unlike in many ways the problem of safely delivering an infant. How in heaven's name, I wondered, was I going to make these men understand in a pinch what was wanted? Already I had Arabs, Chinese, Eritreans, Italians, Somalis, Maltese, and Sudanese to deal with. Now Persians and Hindoos! But I pushed that worry away for the moment. The present problem was a tow for the dock and mooring her inside. Docking ships would have to await its turn in my string of pressing problems.

There was also temporarily aboard the dry dock the Master Rigger from the Royal Naval Base at Alexandria, sent down from there to moor the dry dock if ever she got inside the harbor and provided also he ever found gear enough to moor her with. My discussion was mainly with him.

The towing problem was first gone into. I must arrange to borrow from Captain Lucas every one of his seamen not actually on watch, twenty at least, to handle lines and later to help handle the anchor cables. I will not go into the details, they were many, but that English Master Rigger knew his business and we got along beautifully on the towing arrangements and the preliminary anchoring once we got the dock inside (if we ever did).

What bothered the Master Rigger was how to moor the dock permanently in place. She required eight heavy anchors with three-inch thick chain cables to hold her; she now had only five since three of her cables had been lost while being used as towing bridles on the long tow from the Persian Gulf. Where, this side of Portsmouth Dockyard on the English Channel, was he going to get those three missing cables?

I told him not to worry, the Bible gave the answer: "Seek and ye shall find." While on my surveying party in the *Lord Grey* that afternoon on the far side of the harbor from the Naval Base, my eye had lighted on a solitary Italian building standing on the deserted far shore. Very evidently that building, from all the huge concrete mooring blocks lying in front of it, had been the Italian mooring and submarine defense net depot. I had taken the *Lord Grey* over for a closer look. Stretched out, half buried in the sand near that building were heavy chain cables in great variety, apparently undamaged. The Italians had neither been able to sabotage that massive chain nor to dispose of it—all that under the hot Massawa sun would have been too much work for the saboteurs. We need no longer search—the Lord (in co-operation with the Italians) had provided for all our needs.

Leaving to the Master Rigger the task of planting the marker buoys on the wrecks and the additional marker buoys on the site I had indicated on the chart for the dock, I went ashore, inordinately thirsty and, as usual, completely soaked in sweat. My car was waiting at the Naval Base dock, and I made a bee line for the shower before tackling anything else.

After that and dinner, I went to see Captain Lucas about borrowing his seamen for the work in shifting the dock. He was very willing to help and there was no difficulty on that score, but obviously he was much embarrassed over something. Finally he blurted out,

"I am ashamed to have to say so, Ellsberg, but that liaison chap in Asmara has outmaneuvered me. He isn't coming to Massawa. The moment he got my message, instead of starting here as ordered, he reported in at our military hospital in Asmara. And would you believe it, the Army surgeons there admitted him as a patient! Remarkable case of triumph of mind over matter—you know—the kind of thing that puts so many blighters that have never even been under fire in the hospitals with shell shock. I wouldn't have believed it of a commander in the Royal Navy! Bloody fool he's made of me! I had to wireless the Commander-in-Chief in Alex that the second liaison fellow had cracked up before he even got here; to send another one posthaste. A reply came this morning—they're ordering a third commander; he should be here day after tomorrow. I trust he lasts longer than the others. My apologies, Ellsberg; the Royal Navy makes a better go of things usually than it's done on this."

I had to laugh. Captain Lucas stared at me nonplused—he could see nothing humorous in the tribulations of His Majesty's Navy.

Next day, as scheduled, we went out to move the Persian dry dock. Lieutenant Fairbairn had quite a time deciding which arrangement of his two tugs involved the least danger. Finally he concluded to let the *Hsin Rocket,* the Chinese tug, tow ahead, supplying the power for the tow and its direction, while the British tug dragged astern where it could cause the least amount of trouble, to help as best it might in steering.

The tugs picked up their respective towing bridles at bow and stern, we weighed anchor on the dry dock, and hauled away from the coral-fringed shore toward the open sea. Fairbairn rode on the dry dock; so also did I, with naval signalmen posted on the dock and on both tugs for communication, though Fairbairn depended most on a very shrill whistle, always clenched between his teeth, for his signals.

We made a very wide swing out into the open sea, so that Fairbairn might have a good opportunity to get well lined up on his approach course and settled down on it before we got into close waters where every inch of clearance might count.

Nobody said anything. Ahead, the *Hsin Rocket* puffed valiantly at its load, churning up a vast wake which eddied and broke erratically against the square flat bow of the slowly moving dry dock. Astern, the second tug dragged along on its line to our stern bridle, keeping everything taut so that at least it might attempt to help sheer us one way or the other when required. Occasionally semaphore flags waved or the whistle in Fairbairn's teeth shrilled out, as he directed the tugs in our wide circle.

Two miles out we finished our circle and came about on our final course, 239° or SW by W¼W (true), pointed for the narrow gap between the wrecks which both Fairbairn and I were watching through binoculars.

Weather conditions were perfect for our attempt. There was only a slight sea and a gentle breeze from seaward, practically astern of us; according to our tidal data, it would be slack water at the entrance in half an hour when we got to the wrecks again, so we should have no crosscurrents to bother us.

The thirty minutes following passed very slowly and in complete silence on the dry dock as the *Hsin Rocket,* holding straight as an arrow herself, bore down from seaward on the narrow pass with the dry dock yawing gently as it followed. We went slowly by the sunken *Moncalieri* on our starboard hand, clearing her side parallel to us, by hardly twenty feet. That was good; about correct to give us the slightly less clearance we wanted in passing through the gap when abreast the next wreck.

Fairbairn glanced ahead at the two wrecks forming the gate, then astern at the tug there. She was still dragging along, holding the stern line taut. Once more his eyes came back to the *Hsin Rocket* churning up the sea ahead; she was now in the gap marked by the two flag buoys on the wrecks, and exactly in the center of that gap.

Fairbairn, for the first time, released the grip of his teeth on his whistle, let it drop from his mouth to dangle on the lanyard round his neck. A cool pilot, Fairbairn, I reflected, watching him. When nothing could be done, he had no intention of balling up the situation by shrieking orders. And nothing could be done now that would make any further difference—the unwieldy tow must proceed as it was, come what might.

Another couple of minutes and the square bow of the dry dock was entering the gap between the side of the *XXIII Marzo* and the stern of the *Oliva,* both submerged, of course. Looking down from the high port side of the dry dock, almost forty feet above the sea, both wrecks could be seen through the clear water, the upright *XXIII Marzo* to starboard parallel to us, and the capsized *Oliva* to port, at about a 45° angle. Apparently we were beautifully splitting the gap between them. It would take two minutes for the long length of the dry dock to pass clear; if we didn't swing either way now, we should be all right.

Keeping pace with the slow speed of the tow, I walked aft along the top of the port side wall of the dry dock, holding myself abeam of the *Oliva's* stern as the dry dock slid ahead under my feet, my eyes glued on the few feet of eddying water between our steel side and the flag buoy exactly on the submerged stern of the wreck. If that distance either opened out or narrowed down we should be in trouble instantly with one wreck or the other—if Scylla didn't get us, Charybdis would, and one more bottleneck impeding the war effort would be solidly plugged, to impede it even more effectively.

The inertia of our massive dry dock held her steady against what little wind or current there may have been—foot by foot we went through with no appreciable change in our clearance! On the stern of the dock at last (which brought my walk aft to an abrupt halt) I watched the submerged stern of the *Oliva* draw slowly away from us; in another moment we were clear also of the bow of the *XXIII Marzo,* safely inside the naval harbor with our precious dock.

From far forward on the bow of the dock, I heard Fairbairn's whistle shrilling out orders again to the tugs. He was starting his sharp 90° turn to starboard to clear the shoal and the two sunken Italian dry docks which lay ahead a little on the starboard bow. I wiped the streams of sweat from my face and breathed a deep sigh of relief. The 6000-ton load of the Persian dry dock was off my shoulders. I could safely entrust the placing of it in its permanent berth to Lieutenant Fairbairn, and the permanent mooring of it there (about a ten days' job) to the British Master Rigger, now that I had shown him where he could find the mooring cables he was short of.

CHAPTER

21

ONCE THE PERSIAN DRY DOCK WAS inside the harbor, all my attention for the next few weeks was concentrated on the restoring to service of the Naval Base shops and on gathering together for it a sufficient operating personnel.

We went through all the records available to the British as to what had happened to the former Italian personnel; a few dozen we were able to retrieve from P.O.W. and concentration camps and from other occupations into which they had drifted. Some other Italians with mechanical skills we were able to get from the P.O.W.s who had never worked in Massawa; but on the whole, the results were disappointing; we got no more than half as many as we needed.

We swiftly learned we were up against too much competition for skilled labor. The Army's contractor at Asmara was hiring all the Italians he could for his construction programs at Gura, at Asmara, at Ghinda, and at other places on the plateau or in the mountains. Massawa's reputation hung like a millstone round our necks—why should any Italian, P.O.W. or not, voluntarily go to work in Massawa when he could get just as good a job with the American contractor in comfort 3000 to 8000 feet up in the cool mountains? The climate bonus of 20 per cent which we were authorized to pay in Massawa over other areas in Eritrea, never proved attractive enough. We paid the Italians fifty lira (fifty cents) a day. Highly skilled mechanics received seventy-five.

With native Eritreans, we were more fortunate; we could hire them by the hundreds. Those who belonged in Massawa neither knew nor cared about the rest of the world. For thousands of years they had lived on that arid coast, and they looked it. Not for two thousand years at least did it seem that any coastal Eritrean had had a square meal. For these people, akin to the Ethiopians and with clear-cut features intelligent in appearance, lived in what has aptly been called, "One of the world's less promising deserts."

All were reasonably tall, but I doubt if the average adult Eritrean weighed 100 pounds. They were so generally emaciated, I never saw one whose skinny calf or bicep I could not have encompassed in one hand. This condition, a combined result of countless generations facing starvation rations and that steaming heat, made the ordinary Eritrean a very poor workman—he simply had not the strength to do very much. I have seen one American easily move a pump that six adult Eritrean laborers were struggling vainly to budge.

We hired the Eritreans, who worked on the ancient tribal system, in tribes. The deal was always made with the sheikh of the tribe, who was above working himself, but bossed the rest of his tribe, received all orders about the tasks required, and, of course, collected the wages due. In fairness to the sheikhs, however, who were generally quite patriarchal, I have every reason to believe the money was fairly divided, and that every member of the tribe, even though too ill or too old to work, received a share of what the tribe earned. The stand-ard wage for Eritreans was twenty-five lira (twenty-five cents) a day.

Next above the Eritreans in the scale of laborers, came the Sudan-ese. They were big, strapping fellows, excellent as laborers, and we hired all we could, but as they were foreigners in Eritrea, there were few available. Naturally, in view of their much greater strength, they were paid more than the Eritreans, about thirty-five lira a day, which was a source of continuous irritation to the Eritreans who objected to other blacks getting more than they in their own country. However, except to get the entry of further Sudanese laborers barred by the British, they were unable to get anything done to equalize the wage scale.

Next came the Arabs. There were no Arab laborers in Massawa—all were either merchants, sailors, or artisans. The Arab merchants didn't interest me; I had no need for Arab sailors (who were sailors in the strict sense of that word, being acquainted only with sail, not with engines); but we hired all the Arab artisans we could get and our carpenter and boat shops had no other workmen—just Arabs. Fine carpenters they were, too, fully sensitive to the dignity of their ancient trade even working on modern power-driven machines. They were paid the same as the Italian mechanics.

By American standards, all Italian and native labor was very low paid, but the wage standards were all set by the British Military Government; we abided by their rules.

While we were rounding up a working force and putting them to work on our ever growing number of repaired machines, I struggled with the problem of some office help. If I were going to run a Naval Base on any basis other than that of growing chaos, I simply had to have a secretary who could type a letter and handle the office files.

As usual, there was none available. The contractor would not part with any of his civilian clerks, the Army could not part with any of their few enlisted clerks, and as for my getting a navy yeoman from far-off Washington, that was hopeless.

In this dilemma, the Royal Navy saved the situation, though indirectly. Lieutenant Maton, the Intelligence Officer for the British Naval Forces, had his wife with him in Massawa. This odd situation (for there were no white wives in Eritrea save those of Italians) had come about before the war when Mrs. Maton had left England to join her husband on the then peaceful Mediterranean Station. Stranded in Malta by the outbreak of hostilities, she had been moved for safety to Egypt, and later, when he was ordered to Massawa, she had been permitted to join him there, where now she was housekeeping in the cottage next the one I had been assigned but had never occupied.

Mrs. Maton, tired perhaps of housekeeping as her only diversion in a spot where servants were plentiful, volunteered to serve as secretary to the new American Naval Base. She could type, she said (and she could), and thought she might make a fair clerk. So, being neither an enemy alien nor a native, she was hired at the going rate for an American typist in the Middle East and promptly began to draw more pay than her husband received as a lieutenant in the Royal Navy. Whether this ever caused her any trouble at home, I don't know, but as the Matons were a very devoted couple, I doubt it.

Mrs. Maton (in her early twenties, slight, brunette, and reserved) turned out to be a very efficient secretary, whom, for every reason but one, I was always glad to have. That one reason was that her husband was Intelligence Officer for the Royal Navy. We never had any secrets from the British, for whose benefit our Naval Base was being operated, but occasionally American affairs with respect to our relations with the contractor's supervisory personnel in Asmara went none too smoothly. I should have preferred to have had all knowledge of these family squabbles kept strictly in the family, maintaining the fiction before our British friends that all Americans were 100 per cent engaged in forwarding the joint war effort in all ways. However, with the British Intelligence Officer's wife right in my office, handling my telephone, handling all my correspondence, I'm afraid the Royal Navy soon learned some Americans, even in the war zone, had other interests which came first.

The first half of April passed along with the heat increasing daily. Bathed all the time in perspiration, out in the sun a great part of each day, trudging from shop to shop or on the dry dock where the mooring work was progressing, I began to lose weight rapidly; so did my few American associates who were struggling fiercely along with me to get things going. As regards the Naval Base, I threw all the Massawa legends and traditions to the winds—the Middle East situation was getting more serious each day as Rommel fought his way further eastward across the Libyan sands, increasing the threat to Alexandria. It was that summer or never, if Massawa was going to have any influence on the war.

So I cast into the discard the hoary belief that the white man can't stand the tropics—in Massawa, the hottest spot on earth, he was going to have to, or shortly land in a Nazi concentration camp.

The first Massawa custom to go by the board was that of working only three hours in the morning and two in the early evening—instead, a ten-hour working day was instituted for the Naval Base, commencing at 7:00 A.M. and ending at 6:00 P.M., with an hour only out at noon for lunch. I had a theory (which I still believe to be correct) that giving a man six hours off in the middle of the day, from 10:00 A.M. to 4:00 P.M., resulted only in his putting in six more hours sopping up all the liquor or beer he could lay hands on in his free time, ostensibly at least trying to quench his thirst in the torrid heat. After six extra hours a day spent that way, it needed no proof to demonstrate that the white man can't stand the tropics. He went to pieces in a hurry.

Now there could be no argument about the reality of the thirst— somehow the loss of body liquids apparent in the profuse perspiration had to be made good, or a man would shortly be a bleached-out mummy, especially if he were engaged in active outdoor work. But as long as a man was kept on the job, he could be made to drink water and nothing else to quench his abnormal thirst.

As to prostration from the extraordinary heat, a common cause of collapse in Massawa previously, we had a preventative for that also, administered under the supervision of Captain Plummer, our Army medical officer. This had been fairly well proved out in American industrial practice. In blast furnaces and steel mills, where the workers were exposed to unusual heat from molten iron, salt tablets had greatly reduced cases of heat collapse. The theory of this was that excessive perspiration, no matter how well replaced by copious water drinking, shortly leached out from the body all its mineral salts, leaving the body in condition unable to maintain normal resistance to fatigue or the sun's heat. The answer was to replace the lost salts constantly by taking a salt tablet (looking very much like an aspirin tablet) with every few drinks of water.

In Massawa, at any rate, it worked out fairly well. We drank huge quantities of water, swallowed salt tablets by the dozens, dripped perspiration constantly day and night, wiped the crust of salt exuding from our pores off our hides whenever it became a nuisance, and worked ten hours a day constantly, including Sundays, sometimes more.

By the middle of April, the eight moorings on our Persian dry dock had all been laid out and the dock permanently secured in working position. The Persian crew, superintended by Mr. Hudson, the English dock engineer, began to get the long-disused pumping and other machinery of the dry dock back into operating condition. On shore, the sabotaged naval shops were assuming such shape that I could hope in a few weeks to commence actual operations on docking and repairing ships to lift some of the load off Alexandria.

I finally had also a liaison officer, Commander W. E. C. Davy, Royal Navy, the third British candidate for that post in a month. Commander Davy had been Engineer Officer of the battered battleship *Queen Elizabeth,* which for some weeks past had been, and for some months yet to come was to be, the occupant of the large naval dry dock in Alexandria while that vast hole blown in her bottom was being repaired. Since under those conditions the immobilized *Queen Elizabeth* had little need for an engineer officer, Commander Davy, who had distinguished himself in keeping her from going down when she was mined, was seized on by the British Commander-in-Chief as being both available and most likely to stand the gaff in Massawa. I hoped with him, the merry-go-round of British liaison officers through Massawa would come to a stop.

Commander Davy impressed me favorably for the task. He was an engineer officer in the Royal Navy, good training for Massawa, since battleship engine rooms are always hot and usually sticky. Then physically he was well fitted also; he was tall and thin and unemotional, little given to complaints about anything. Later I learned (but not from him) that he was a descendant of Sir Humphry Davy, most famous of British chemists of over a century before. Long before I was through with Massawa I had no cause to regret the chain of circumstances that had brought Commander Davy to Massawa.

Davy's first job as liaison officer was to arrange with the naval authorities in Alexandria for the initial ships to be sent to Massawa for us to work on. I considered that by the first few days in May, we should be ready to turn to.

But hardly had he started on this matter than we received a heartbreaking setback. When I started for the Officers' Mess for dinner on the evening of April 17, it was raining, not very hard, but unquestionably it was raining. A little skeptical over this phenomenon, fearing another mirage effect, I waited a moment before emerging, for I had been assured that rain in Massawa was most unusual. All the dry river beds I had seen on the hot coastal desert between Massawa and the mountains supported that belief—the whole area gave sound backing to the saying that when you fell into a river in Eritrea, you got up and dusted yourself off.

Now undoubtedly here was rain, it was no mirage. As I had just put on a dry shirt and some dry khaki shorts, hoping to enjoy a brief period of dryness while I dined, I went back for my raincoat before setting out. Dinner, as usual, was served on the open veranda out over the water, and started off wonderfully with a real breeze fresh off the Red Sea to cool things down, the first time I had felt comfortable in Massawa.

But shortly the breeze became so fresh it began first to blow rain in on us, which we didn't mind much, and then to blow everything off the table, which was a nuisance. Dinner had to be suspended while the Arab servants cleared the outside tables, reset everything on tables inside the building, and hurriedly closed all the window shutters.

This turned out to be useless. Before the inside tables could even be set, the wind had risen to gale proportions and the rain had turned into a downpour. In spite of closed shutters on the sea side, rain was driving in through the slatted shutters, soaking everything. Then the lights went out. The electrical effects accompanying the storm were evidently too much for our power system. Using flashlights, the native servants attempted to carry on, but this was quickly seen to be an idle gesture. Even if they could get the tables reset, there was not going to be anything to eat. The kitchen for the mess was in a latticed basement directly below us, with a flight of concrete steps ten feet wide leading down to it. Down those steps a real Niagara was pouring, a torrent of water eight inches deep at least, completely obliterating all vestiges of the stairs in a roaring cascade.

We gave up all thought of dining. The wind swiftly increased to hurricane force till it was blowing at least 100 miles an hour and our masonry building quivered as if it might blow away. A terrific electrical display, with lightning flashing all about and the deafening roar of thunder, added to the tumult of the wind. In spite of my raincoat, which I had hastily donned inside the room, I was soon drenched through, for the rain, driven by hurricane winds now, came through the shutters with such force it drove horizontally completely across the forty-foot interior of the building, attacking from an angle which made a raincoat practically useless and flooding everything inside.

Huddled silently inside the room, momentarily expecting that stout building to collapse about our ears or the next bolt of the vivid lightning striking all around us to get a direct hit on our mess building, we waited, while outside the tables literally took off in the wind to crash ominously somewhere in the dark. From farther away, between the ear-splitting thunderbolts, we heard the dull thud of one roof after another, torn free of its building, collapsing somewhere in the open.

I could not keep my mind off that Persian dry dock. Had it remained swinging to one anchor in the Red Sea before our building, where previously it had been, we should long since have had it practically in our laps, pounding itself to pieces on the coral cliffs fringing the Officers' Mess as the waves broke fiercely over them. How was it faring now, even enclosed in the harbor with the surrounding shores and the artificial breakwater made of wrecks to shelter it from the force of the seas? For its high, flat sides, rising far above the low coast, had no shelter from the roaring winds; would those eight heavy moorings we had just completed hold it safely, or had it perhaps already torn adrift to be wrecked even inside the harbor? From where

I was, I had no view of the naval harbor—despite the lightning flashes illuminating everything, I could not see the answer.

Sick at heart over the mounting disaster outside, I huddled in my raincoat, bracing my legs for support against the wind. That hurricane was making a wreck of Massawa ashore, perhaps had already made a wreck of our precious Persian dock. And there was nothing anyone could do to mitigate damage. There was not available to us even the slight personal solace of tobacco—all my cigarettes were thoroughly water-soaked; so were all those of the British naval officers about me.

And then, *mirabile mirabilis*, it started to hail! In hot Massawa, which had never known snow or ice in any form, huge hailstones began to beat down, hailstones large enough to have killed a man had any been fool enough to remain exposed in that storm! But fortunately, this phase lasted only a few minutes.

Soon after the hail ceased, there came a sudden lull in the wind, which had been blowing from the east. It was of short duration. In a brief space of time, the wind was shrieking past us again, strong as ever, this time from the west, threatening now to tear our building off its foundations and toss it into the Red Sea. The rain came down in bucketfuls as before, isolating us on the land side in a vast lake which poured down our basement steps and flooded in an unbroken sheet over the cliff tops each side of us.

The storm lasted two hours. By 10:00 P.M. the worst was over and the wind gradually died away. It took another hour for the lake outside to drain away sufficiently so the servants might dare the cascade and re-establish contact with our kitchen. By that time everything was hopeless, for the galley ranges had long since been drowned out. What food had not been washed away was uneatable. There would be no dinner for anyone that night.

Guided by my flashlight, I stepped out of the Officers' Mess and waded back to my quarters, dodging as well as I could the debris strewn everywhere. Wires were down all over, the darkness was complete, it was useless to try anything that night. Clearance would have to wait for dawn.

Daybreak disclosed a dismal scene. Not a road on the Abd-El-Kader Peninsula was passable to any vehicle—the wreckage of roofs covered everything on the ground. The roof on the seaward side of our newly established office building was gone, my office and all its papers were completely waterlogged. Buildings which had come unscathed through a dozen R.A.F. bombing raids on Massawa now looked as if direct hits had been scored on all their roofs—the destruction was beyond belief. Nothing all the British bombing had done to Massawa approached one per cent of the damage that hurricane left in its wake.

But my precious Persian dry dock, toward which my eyes had first turned when the earliest rays of the sun lighted up the horizon, was still safe. There it lay in the naval harbor, moored as before in place, apparently undamaged. Our heavy moorings had held and saved it; my speed in getting it inside and secured with all the cables it required, had got that task done none too soon. A later check with instruments showed that it had dragged even with all its moorings some fifty feet out of position before its anchors dug in deeply enough to stop further motion, but that endangered nothing.

Work on the rehabilitation of all sabotaged machinery stopped abruptly, of course. All hands, American, Italian, and native, turned to on the task of opening up the roads again, clearing away debris, restringing broken electric power wires, and repairing our many roofless buildings, using any and all materials we could get—tile, transite sheets, asphalt sheathing, and finally, even corrugated iron, which normally we would have shied away from as from the devil, since it transmitted the heat of the sun without resistance.

A week went by before our shops were again under shelter comparable to what we had had the night the hurricane hit us, and power and light had been restored to all of them. Not till then were we able to resume rectifying the man-made damage inside the shops. And it took about that long also to get the soggy mass of papers that had once been my plans and office records dry enough to refile.

Inquiry among the native sheikhs disclosed that not for thirty years at least had any hurricane at all comparable to this struck Massawa. That was comforting. As I went about the task of restoring order, it was pleasant to reflect that it was unlikely I should have such a chore every month or two. Long before the conclusion of the thirty-year cycle which might bring the next hurricane, I was sure I should have lost all interest in whatever might strike Massawa.

CHAPTER

22

On MAY 8, 1942, FIVE AND ONE-HALF weeks after my arrival in Massawa, the United States Naval Repair Base, Massawa, commenced operations. The only thing naval about it was its Commanding Officer. The only things American about it were, in addition to the Commanding Officer, one Army officer as assistant and six civilian supervisors on loan. We had none of the new American machinery, we had no American mechanics, either military or civilian. We had only the refitted Italian equipment and the Persian dry dock seized from Italy, with the Naval Base working force composed now of a few Englishmen, a fair number of Italians, hundreds of Eritreans, and a conglomeration of Sudanese, Arabs, Maltese, Persians, Somalis, Chinese, Greeks, and Hindoos.

With nothing but equipment seized from the enemy and with our skilled working force made up mostly of enemy prisoners of war, we turned to under the American flag (except that I had then not even an American flag we could hoist over our Base) to do our bit in Massawa to stop the Axis.

The British Commander-in-Chief in the Mediterranean, Admiral Sir Henry Harwood, K.C.B., O.B.E., Royal Navy (victor over the Nazi *Graf Spee* in the battle off the River Plate), gave us our orders. He was struggling to supply Tobruk, 400 miles west of Alexandria, and the British Eighth Army in the desert to the westward of Tobruk. His only means of supplying them was a fleet of armed freighters plying between Alexandria and Tobruk, always under Axis air attack, often under submarine attack. Not for over two years had a single one of these supply ships been dry-docked or overhauled; now in the warm waters of the Mediterranean their bottoms were so fouled with barnacles and grass as to cut their speed in half. Too many ships were being lost due to their slow speed—maneuvering to avoid bombs

was impossible to them; they were so slow now even a submerged submarine could easily overhaul any of them. In addition, the carrying
capacity of the fleet was sadly reduced; it took each ship an ungodly
length of time for a round trip to Tobruk, even if it escaped attack.

Alexandria had its large dry dock tied up with the *Valiant* and the
Queen Elizabeth from the previous December to some unforeseeable
date in the late summer. Its smaller dry dock was as a consequence
continuously occupied by British cruisers, destroyers, and submarines,
undergoing imperative cleaning and repairs of war damages to maintain their fighting efficiency—it could not be spared even for a moment for any of the supply ships, no matter how desperate the need.
And with Durban in South Africa, 5000 miles from Alexandria, the
nearest spot where war conditions permitted docking merchantmen,
it had been out of the question to send any of the supply ships on
that 10,000-mile voyage to be docked—the mere journey to Durban
and back would take two months and waste a terrific amount of
precious coal.

So the first task assigned Massawa by Admiral Harwood was restoring the Mediterranean supply train to some degree of efficiency.
Later, depending on how the war developed, we should get a chance
at destroyers, which were the largest warships the Persian dry dock
would take, and perhaps a chance to overhaul cruisers where dry-
docking was not involved.

We were ready. Beneath my feet, the Persian dry dock was flooded
well down—only a few feet of its side walls on either side showed
above the sea. Just coming through the gap in the line of wrecks at
the harbor mouth, towed by the *Hsin Rocket* and steadied astern by
the other tug, was our first customer, the *S.S. Koritza,* an armed Greek
steamer which had arrived the night before from Alexandria. Lieutenant Fairbairn was on her bridge, piloting her through.

On the dock, we prepared to receive her. Spanner, the English
dockmaster, posted his Persian and Hindoo operators at the winches.
Hudson, the English engineer, stood by with his Persian staff to operate the machinery. Along the top of each dock wall was a large squad
of Eritreans to help handle lines to the ship while she was being
warped into the dock.

The dry-docking went smoothly enough. Fairbairn made a sharp
turn to starboard with the *Koritza,* dodged the shoal spot inside, and
lined her up for the dry dock with her bow only a few hundred feet

away. At this point, the pilot boat ran out the head line, a six-inch hawser, the *Koritza* picked it up, the *Hsin Rocket* let go and steamed clear, and we began to wind the *Koritza* into the dock. I acted as docking officer.

I found that the Persians, and particularly the head Persian who spoke English, knew their business. In their hands, heaving lines flew smartly through the air to the *Koritza* and the steadying lines rapidly followed. The head Persian moved back and forth, shouting orders in languages I didn't understand but the results were standard—Persians, Hindoos, and Eritreans dashed up the dock as the bow of the *Koritza* came slowly forward, shifting the steadying lines from bitt to bitt, holding her centered.

In less than half an hour, we had the *Koritza* in proper position inside the dry dock, secured there by bow and quarter lines, and the dock slowly pumped up till she touched the keel blocks fore and aft. Then the side spur shores (massive square timbers which on this dock were mechanically operated) were run in to brace her against heeling as the dock was lifted further. When she was solidly on the keel blocks, the sliding bilge blocks were hauled in under her bilges and Hudson was given the word to pump up the dock full speed. Water started to go overboard from the dock pumps at over a hundred tons a minute; the dry dock and the ship in it commenced a steady rise. In about another hour, we had the *Koritza* lifted completely out of the water, ready to begin operations on her bottom.

By then I had learned a great deal. I could rely on Hudson; he was a stolid, slow-spoken, steady-going Englishman who evidently was a good engineer. Hudson gave few orders to his Persian assistants, but when he did, they were obeyed with alacrity. As for the Persians themselves, they were all first-class, intelligent men who knew their jobs; so also were the Hindoos. Reed, the assistant dockmaster, had not had much to do but at least he had had little to say while doing it.

But Spanner, the dockmaster, I would have sold then and there for two cents if there had been any market. Theoretically, he might know all about docks and his trade as a shipwright, but practically he didn't belong on an operating dry dock. He was rather slight, with sharp, birdlike features which reminded me of a sparrow, and his manner was exactly that as he hopped about excitedly when there was no cause. I was sure he would blow up in a crisis, of which there are many in docking and undocking, instead of acting as a steadying in-

S.S. Koritza in the Persian dry dock.

fluence when things were going wrong.

Still, all of that remained for the future. Right now, the *Koritza* was high and dry on the dock, her superstructure and hull towering far above even its high sides, and her foul bottom needed immediate attention.

I had hired two hundred Eritreans and their sheikhs for work on ships in the dry dock, a special deal handled through an English shipping agency in Massawa harbor in order not to cause a crisis in the supply of longshoremen in the port. Now the Eritreans were swarming aboard the floor of the dry dock from the Arab dhows which had brought them out. Swiftly they were divided up into groups, each under its own sheikh, and distributed starboard and port from bow to stern of the *Koritza* to scrape its bottom.

The bottom of the *Koritza*, when exposed, was a terrible sight. Barnacles covered it to a depth of several inches, the older layers hardened practically into limestone by their years of growth; long streamers of marine grasses hung like moss from her plates. With a bottom like that, it was plainly evident why she could make no more than the five or six knots which was now her top speed.

Armed with steel scrapers, most of which had been forged out for the job in our new blacksmith shop, the Eritreans turned to. The scrapers were of all lengths—short ones for the men working under her flat bottom where no one could stand erect, medium ones for work around the curved bilges, and long-handled ones on wood poles for scraping high up the sides till we could get staging rigged.

The work of scraping went disappointingly slowly. The grasses came off easily enough, but when it came to scraping off barnacles, the Eritreans just weren't there. I knew they were weak—that was why I had hired twice as many as the job really required—but even for weaklings they were getting little done.

I went to the superintendent who had been provided to boss the Eritreans by the British shipping agency, through whom I had hired them. He was a large, beefy, very red-faced Englishman in white shorts, equal in weight to about three Eritreans. He had spent years in the Middle East and was well acquainted with native labor. I objected to what was going on.

"See here," I pointed out to him while both of us stood on the floor of the dry dock, adjacent to the barnacled bilges of the *Koritza*, "these men aren't working. You've got to get some punch into them."

He shrugged his shoulders.

"What can you expect of Eritreans?" he countered. "Now if I had a gang of Sudanese or even of Gyppos, I'd get cracking."

I refused to take that for an answer. He knew as well as I that Sudanese or Egyptian laborers were for us in Massawa unrealizable dreams; we should have to get along with Eritreans.

"Get after those sheikhs," I ordered. "Make them get their men's backs behind those scrapers. We're just wasting time this way."

Dubiously he set off to gather the sheikhs together and talk to them. I walked aft along the floor of the steaming dock to its stern, where I boarded the *Lord Grey* to go ashore, leaving him an uninterfered-with chance to get some action.

Ashore, I gave Commander Davy a message to be wirelessed to the Commander-in-Chief in Alexandria:

"S.S. *Koritza* successfully dry-docked at Massawa at 0900. Expected time on dock three days. S.S. *Athos* to follow," for we had word that the second supply ship, also a Greek freighter, had sailed from Alexandria and would arrive at Massawa that evening, ready to go on the dock the minute the *Koritza* came off, with no idle time between.

There was some repair work also the *Koritza* wanted—some sea chests, which could only be opened in dry dock, to have the valves reseated, and some pump rods and cylinders to be turned true so she might quit wasting steam. Austin Byrne, master mechanic, went off in the *Lord Grey* with a dozen Italian machinists to dismantle the valves and pumps and bring the parts ashore for the new machine shop to work on that night.

Also there was another matter. The Greek captain of the *Koritza*, happy over his brief respite from the nerve-racking run to Tobruk and proud of being chosen as the vessel to inaugurate service at the first American Naval Base in the East, wanted to bother us as little as possible. Still he had a number of leaky rivets in his hull from near miss bombs. Could we caulk them up for him?

I had no ironworkers among the Italian mechanics I had picked up; some welders, yes. As a last resort, I was willing to try welding, using a worn-out Italian portable welding machine we had patched up, but I preferred caulking (or redriving rivets, if necessary) to get a solid watertight job on underwater rivets.

I went to see Pat Murphy, who was superintending the contractor's construction projects in Massawa. Could he lend me an ironworker who could caulk, and if necessary, drive rivets, for a day? I could provide Italians as helpers and holders-on.

"Got any air?" asked Pat skeptically.

I assured him the Persian dry dock had a small air compressor as part of its diesel engine starting equipment, and some air banks. It could furnish enough air.

"Got a gun?" he asked next.

I reassured him on that score also. We had found both an Italian pneumatic riveting hammer and a caulking hammer previously hidden in a warehouse; they were useless when found, due to missing parts, but our machine shop and forge shop had already made good the missing parts. They would work.

"Well," said Murphy, "in that case I could lend you Cunningham for a day. I'm using him for a rigger over in the commercial port just now, but he's an ironworker. Remember Bill Cunningham? He's not much good."

I remembered Bill Cunningham, all right. I was sorry to hear Murphy didn't think much of him; I had hoped Cunningham would make out well in Massawa. But I accepted the offer; anybody who knew rivets at all could do the job on the *Koritza*.

"He'll do, Pat. Have him on the wharf in the morning for the seven-o'clock trip of the *Lord Grey*. I'll see everything he needs is there in the boat for him."

Next morning, I shoved off at 7:00 A.M. on the *Lord Grey* for the first trip to the *Koritza* to see how the work was progressing. The *Lord Grey*, for all her forty-foot length and broad beam, was jammed, mostly with Eritreans she was taking out, partly with Italian mechanics. I noted that a complete riveting and caulking outfit was in the stern-sheets; air hammers, chisels, hoses, forge, rivets, and even coke for the forge. Crouched over his equipment was Cunningham, apparently guarding it from any itching fingers in the mob surrounding him.

I squeezed into the boat alongside the Italian coxswain and we shoved off for the mile-long trip over the harbor to the dock. Once we were under way, I greeted Cunningham, attired only in shorts and a sun helmet, whom I had not seen since the day we made Lagos in the *Pig's Knuckle*.

"How are you making out, Cunningham?" I asked.

"Not so hot, Commander," he replied mildly in that oddly soft voice of his which I so well remembered. "Nothing much for me in my trade in the kind of wood and masonry building they're doing round here. They got me rigging now; I don't care a lot for it. Glad to take on this riveting job for you today. It'll be a relief to get a gun in my hands again."

"Having any trouble?" I persisted, wondering what lay behind Pat Murphy's lack of enthusiasm for him.

"No, nothing to speak of, Commander. Too many limey M.P.s around the town at night, but they haven't bothered me—much," he concluded lamely but honestly enough.

· I wondered how much he had bothered the British M.P.s. I had been so busy at the Naval Base peninsula, I had not yet once been in the town of Massawa in the evening, so I knew little of what went on there, though I could guess from the glimpses of the Italian cafés I had seen on my few daylight visits.

I pressed the discussion no farther. After all, Cunningham was not my responsibility now—he was working for the contractor, not for the Naval Base. As for today, he looked perfectly sober and I had no qualms over his cleaning up all the leaky rivets on the *Koritza* long before evening.

The *Lord Grey* rounded to alongside the seaward end of the dry dock, with the stern of the *Koritza* towering high above us. All hands scrambled out on the floor of the dock. Already it was covered with workmen, for the Arab dhows had delivered their cargoes of native laborers.

I walked forward along the dock floor close by the line of keel blocks, stooped low to get in under the bottom of the *Koritza* near her stern, then went slowly toward her bow on the starboard side, back under her on the port side, and ended with a walk around her hull in the narrow gap between her high sides and the side walls of the dry dock. Dirty water, barnacles, and sea grass dripped on me; underfoot, barnacle shells crunched beneath my water-soaked shoes; and all through my inspection trip my nostrils were assailed by the stench rising from dead and dying barnacles rapidly decaying, now they were exposed to the air and the fierce Massawa heat. Altogether, the inside of that dry dock, beneath and around the *Koritza*, was a most unpleasant place.

I finished my inspection trip in dismay. Not a third of the work necessary to scrape clean the underwater hull of the *Koritza* had been completed in the first day. At that rate, far from concluding the scraping and painting of the *Koritza* in the three days allowed us for it, we should be lucky to finish the job in a week. And the next ship to be docked was already anchored off Massawa, waiting to go on; a third vessel should be starting from Alexandria that day, to follow her. We should shortly have the roadstead off Massawa crowded with idle ships waiting to be docked, while in the desert the Eighth Army would be looking in vain for the ammunition and the supplies those ships should be carrying to Tobruk. What was the matter?

I stepped back against the side wall of the dry dock and watched the Eritreans manning the scrapers. Naked, except for breechcloths and turbans, covered with the mess of decaying barnacles that spattered their black skins as they scraped, they were an unlovely sight. But so was I. They were puny, too, there was no questioning that. But what drove me nearly to distraction was the deliberation of their movements. For all the world like a movie illustrating something in slow motion, their arms moved back and forth with the scrapers so leisurely as to require watching for some time to make sure they were moving at all.

In despair, I sought out the English superintendent again. I must have more speed. Men, Englishmen, his countrymen, our Allies, were dying in the Libyan Desert, facing Rommel's superior forces, when some of them might live, I told him, if only we could get the empty ship above our heads, her empty sister swinging at anchor outside, other empty ships bound for Massawa for docking, back to Tobruk in a hurry, loaded with desperately needed equipment for the British Army.

"You get me better men, Commander, and I'll get you more speed. I've already spoken to the sheikhs. That's everything I can do. You can't expect any better of Eritreans," was his reply.

"But they're not even trying!" I protested. "I know they're weak, but anybody could go faster than that. For God's sake, get some life into 'em!"

"When you've been out in the East as long as I have, you'll know better, Commander," he advised me. "All natives are poor laborers; these Eritreans are the worst of the lot. I can't do any better with them, especially in this heat, but if you think you can, you're welcome to try. What do you want?"

"Call the sheikhs together again," I answered. "I'll talk to them, you interpret."

He gathered up the sheikhs, about a dozen all told. Unlike their tribesmen, they were fully clad in long white robes. Clustered beneath the overhanging stern of the *Koritza* for shade from the blistering sun, they listened gravely while my reasons for more speed were expounded to them.

Then all together in Arabic they opened up on my interpreter. Though I understood not a word, I got the gist of what they were saying from their gestures and their expressions. I did not need the confirmation I shortly received from their English superintendent—in the eyes of the sheikhs, their men were doing the best they could, nothing more could be expected.

Silently I turned away and the sheikhs went back to their various tribes. Their superintendent clambered up the ladder to the top of the port side wall of the dock, where beneath an awning it was a little less stifling than below in the stagnant air of the dock.

From beneath the motionless propeller of the *Koritza*, I watched the Eritreans again. It was nearly 8:00 A.M. now. I had cherished the delusion that we might scrape and paint the *Koritza* with the larger force I had brought to her in two days instead of the three allowed us, and perhaps undock her that evening, or at worst, in the morning. Now I should be lucky if I got her off the dry dock in seven days instead of three, and then I should have to explain to the Commander-in-Chief that with the poor labor I had, it was the best Massawa could do.

Dejectedly my eyes followed the hardly perceptible motions of the Eritreans scraping under the starboard bilges before me. It just couldn't be possible—no human being, no matter how skinny he was, could move that slowly because of weakness. Perhaps they needed an example of what might be done. I went up to the near-by group, seized a scraper from the closest Eritrean, who gazed at me in astonishment that a white man and particularly the Ras commanding the Naval Base should so soil his hands, and motioning the sheikh and his other satellites to watch, went vigorously to work scraping a patch about one yard square of the *Koritza's* bottom plating. In about a tenth of the time the Eritreans were doing it, I had all the barnacles off down to the metal plate.

With that, I handed the scraper back to its owner, inviting him and his fellows by a wave of my arm to go and do likewise. With an oxlike expression, he took his scraper back and proceeded to scrape. My heart sank. His slow motion pace had not accelerated one iota; neither had that of any others of his tribe who had watched.

I went farther forward. Perhaps I had chosen a poor group for my demonstration, perhaps my technique was wrong. Amidships I got hold of one of the sheikhs and in pantomime showed him what I wanted. He shook his head in disagreement.

Persuasion and example were useless. Perhaps chastisement would help. I went still farther forward. Up near the stem, I selected an Eritrean scraper whose lifelessness was even more marked, if that were possible, than that of his fellows, and indicated to him that he should scrape faster. When he failed to respond, I seized him by both bare shoulders and shook him so hard I shook his breechcloth off. Then I dropped him, completely naked, motioned him to pick up the scraper he had lost, and get busy. He looked at me with sad eyes, picked up his scraper, and resumed his ultra-slow-motion scraping.

I retired, baffled. But still nothing could make me believe that these Eritreans weren't doing any more because physically they were unable to—it must be because they lacked proper incentive to produce. But what more could I do to incite them? I couldn't talk to them; any third-hand appeals I might make through an interpreter and their sheikhs would lose whatever persuasiveness my arguments had in filtering through to them. And shaking them and showing them had proved equally futile.

Long ago as an ensign, before World War I, I had listened to Admiral Sims expounding how to get results out of a gun crew—"Don't waste your breath on appeals to patriotism or duty. The fear of punishment and the hope of reward are the only two forces that move most men." Admiral Sims' method was to dangle the hope of reward, in money, mainly; the fear of punishment he held in the background. With that lever, he accomplished wonders in gunnery improvement.

His precept came back to my mind in that hot dry dock, far away from the cold North Atlantic where I had heard Admiral Sims expounding it.

Somehow I *had* to move these Eritreans to action and that right away. The hope of reward, money reward, was my last chance of moving them. But my hands were tied by law—the wages of all Eri trean natives were rigidly fixed at twenty-five lira a day, and my laborers were getting that—I couldn't change it. The week before I had tried to raise the wage of one Eritrean laborer who showed skill in running a small Italian diesel, from twenty-five to thirty lira a day, an increase for him of five cents a day. I was blocked—nothing could be done till two weeks hence a board of a dozen government bureaucrats in Asmara considered the special case of this Eritrean and argued pro and con over the propriety of my giving him an extra nickel!

My mind raced over various ways of paying these men an incentive wage to produce, law or no law. Could I claim that all these Eritreans were really Sudanese and pay them the thirty-five lira allowed to Sudanese, provided they jumped the output of their scrapers? I doubted I could get away with it. I could never explain the sudden increase of two hundred in the limited Sudanese population of Massawa. Besides that, any suspicious official looking at the skinny arms and legs of my laborers would recognize them instantly for Eritreans, and my incentive pay plan would promptly come to an inglorious end, with no one could tell what repercussions on my labor situation.

There was another possibility of incentive pay, over the legal technicalities of which I felt I was prepared to argue with the most red-tape-minded bureaucrats. At any rate, as an evasion of the wage scales, it wasn't so obvious and was little likely ever to get me up to Asmara to explain myself. I made up my mind to that scheme in a hurry. It was already 8:30 A.M. and no more time was to be lost. I sang out from the bottom of the dock to the British superintendent sprawled out in a deck chair under the awning near the control house, to get down into the dock with me once more.

"Get all the sheikhs back here under the stern again," I ordered him. "I want to have another talk with them."

In a few minutes all the sheikhs were gathered about in their patriarchal robes, looking silently at me. I decided to parade the fear of punishment first; the hope of reward I would save for the end.

"Tell them," I said to the interpreter, "that the time I allow for scraping and painting a ship on this dry dock is only three days, no more. Explain that to them."

He did. There was no comment from any of the sheikhs; they were indifferent to American theories of how long a job should take. In the East, time stretched out limitlessly—the past was long, so also was the future.

[171]

"Now tell them that if the scraping and painting of this ship are not finished by tomorrow night, three days, they are all discharged, sheikhs and everybody. I'll finish the job with what Italians I can get, no matter how long it takes, and they can never work for the Americans again. I mean it; this is no idle threat."

The Englishman looked at me incredulously, but my last words convinced him I was in earnest.

He began to translate again. This time, long before he had concluded, some of the sheikhs began to argue; by the time he had finished, they were all talking—to each other and to him. My threat had struck some sparks, that was evident. When finally all the sheikhs had had their say, he turned to me.

"They say it can't be done. They say they will regret being discharged in disgrace, especially to be replaced by the Italians, whom they hate. They beg that the American Commandant, to whom they wish long life and many sons, will change his mind. Allah himself, they say, could not do it in three days."

I nodded that I understood, then continued. Having set forth the punishment, I would now offer the reward.

"Now tell them this. I am going to pay three days' pay to them for cleaning and painting this ship and every ship that follows her. There will always be plenty of work. If the *Koritza* is not done by tomorrow night, they get three days' pay and they are all discharged. If the ship is finished by tomorrow night, they get three days' pay and they can stay. If the ship is finished by tomorrow morning, they get three days' pay. If the ship is finished by tonight, in two days, they still get three days' pay. If they ever finish a ship in less than two days, they still get three days' pay. The Eritreans are envious of the Sudanese, who get thirty-five lira a day while they get only twenty-five. Let them show that they are better than the Sudanese by finishing this ship and every ship in two days or less, and they will earn more each day than the Sudanese, who will then have cause to envy them. Tell them I promise it shall be so."

This time an animated open forum broke out under the propeller of the *Koritza* long before the interpreter was half through. Questions in Arabic interrupted him, the sheikhs argued with each other over the meaning, he had to repeat several times. At last he finished and the sheikhs gathered in a knot for a family discussion. Without doubt, my proposition had made an impression.

The discussion among the sheikhs was quite brief. In a minute or two, they turned to the superintendent; one of them spoke for all. When the speaker had concluded, the Englishman turned to me.

"They pray that the blessing of Allah may fall on your head. They say that they will do what they can with their followers."

I nodded that I understood. Nothing further was said. The sheikhs dispersed to their various tribes scattered from bow to stern of the *Koritza,* and called their tribesmen about them for discussion. For perhaps five or ten minutes all work on the bottom of the ship ceased. Nothing was heard except the clatter of an air hammer as Cunningham caulked rivets up forward, and a confused chatter, muffling somewhat the rattle of that pneumatic hammer, as two hundred Eritreans jabbered simultaneously over my proposals.

Then the Eritreans went back to *work.* Had I waved a magic wand over those Eritreans to transform them, the results could not have been more miraculous. I never heard Cunningham and his air hammer again that day. A fierce jungle chant, drowning out all else, rose from all over the dry dock and never ceased; to its barbaric rhythm, there were those puny, previously lifeless Eristreans dancing wildly beneath the hull of the *Koritza,* while they slashed savagely away overhead with their scrapers at the barnacles! All I had to do was to imagine those scrapers replaced with spears, and I had before me a scene from the fantastic legends of Darkest Africa—the embattled tribes in a frenzied war dance, preparing to attack their enemies.

By noon the bottom of the *Koritza* was scraped clean. Paint brushes and pots of paint supplanted the scrapers in the hands of the Eritreans. Still chanting furiously, they danced now in their bare feet on layers of sharp barnacles inches deep covering the floor of the dry dock, while they slapped on the paint. Soon every Eritrean was more yellow and red than black as paint slobbering from his brush while he danced barbarically beneath that ship spattered him and his swaying fellow tribesmen.

But no one cared. On went the paint, the quick-drying anti-corrosive yellow undercoat on the steel plates first, to be followed later by the red anti-fouling paint as a finish. By two in the afternoon, it was clear that the task was going to be finished far ahead of schedule. I sent the *Lord Grey* ashore with two urgent messages. One was to Lieutenant Fairbairn to have his tugs and himself at the dock by 6:00 P.M. to undock the *Koritza.* The other was to Austin Byrne, master mechanic. He must get the valve and pump parts the machine shop had worked on all through the night, together with himself and enough mechanics, back aboard the *Koritza* by four o'clock to permit reinstalling all the sea chest parts at least by five o'clock or he would be responsible for delaying the undocking.

Then I went in search of Cunningham to make sure he would be no cause of delay. No longer could I locate him by the ear-splitting rattle of his pneumatic hammer; in all the din in the dock, a mere riveting gun banging away on steel was lost. I had to use my eyes instead. I found I need have no fears of Cunningham. He had already cut out and redriven afresh the only two rivets so loose as to require it; the other slack rivets he was hardening up and recaulking and he was certain he would get them all before the dock went down and the rising water flooded him out. As an ironworker, Cunningham was both willing and good.

Satisfied, I went aft to watch proceedings. The Eritreans were keeping up their fierce pace. A dozen were kept busy doing nothing but rush about refilling empty paint pots from the drums of paint near the stern; all the others were putting paint on so fast it was unbelievable; the sheikhs were anxiously peering about under the ship to make sure no holidays were left in the painted surface which might give an excuse to refuse payment on the ground of poor work.

But any thought of refusing payment on any ground was farthest from my mind, in view of the miracle I was watching. I had hoped for and expected a better performance than that of the first day—never should I have believed those emaciated Eritreans capable of what actually they were now doing. If ever I had had any doubts as to the value of incentive pay in getting production, they vanished that day in that steaming, stinking dry dock in Massawa. That valiant seaman, Admiral Sims, long since dead, would have looked on with interest at the verification of his principle, could he only have been present to see how his words of long ago to a young ensign had borne fruit.

At 4:30 in the afternoon, the last brushful of the final coat of paint went on the hull of the *Koritza*. Their skins covered almost in a camouflage pattern of paint, but their eyes shining with a light of triumph, not the least factor in which I am sure was the feeling that they had proved themselves better than the rival Sudanese, the Eritrean blacks and their sheikhs trooped off the barnacle-covered dock floor to board the waiting Arab dhows, where they were paid off by their English superintendent.

At 5:00 P.M., with all the staging stowed and lashed down, we began flooding down the dry dock. In a few minutes, the sea was surging in over the dock floor, to swirl over the mass of barnacles and sea grass and wash part of it at least away. Steadily the dock went down and the sea rose about the shining coat of fresh red paint now enshrouding the clean hull of the *Koritza*. At a quarter of six, the *Koritza* lifted off the keel blocks and floated free.

At 6:00 P.M., we had the *Koritza* out of the dry dock, steaming up, and, towed by the *Hsin Rocket* and her sister tug, in Lieutenant Fairbairn's hands on her way out of the naval harbor through the line of wrecks to her anchorage for the night in the outer roadstead. In the morning, when daylight made it safe for her to dodge any mines which might be drifting even in the swept channel, she would start back for Alexandria, less than forty-eight hours after she had first gone on the Massawa dry dock. Only now with a clean bottom, she would go back with her speed doubled, making her normal eleven knots instead of the five to six knots which was her maximum when she came to Massawa.

That evening Commander Davy started another wireless message on its way to Alexandria:

Undocked *Koritza* 1800 today at Massawa. *Athos* follows 0700 tomorrow. Expected time on dock two days. What ship follows?

By midnight we had our answer from the Commander-in-Chief, Mediterranean Fleet.

Well done, Massawa. Schedule for next ten days will be communicated tomorrow.

I read that message as, naked as usual, I lay stretched out on my bed bathed in perspiration inside the mosquito net in my darkened room, while just outside the netting the British seaman who had brought it to me from the decoding room held a flashlight shining through the net so I could read.

Weary though I was that Saturday night with over five weeks' continuous effort in getting Massawa under way, topped off by that sweltering day down in the dry dock, I smiled in contentment over that dispatch. Massawa had won its first accolade. Tomorrow I should see that those few Americans who had struggled with me to win it, saw that message also. They badly needed a little lift just then.

Next morning, the *Athos* followed the *Koritza* on the dry dock. She also was finished in two days and departed. I had feared that the emaciated Eritreans could not keep up their fierce pace, especially as the weather was getting hotter. But I could have spared my fears. Over the next few weeks, one ship followed another at slightly less than two-day intervals over the keel blocks of that dry dock; twelve in the next twenty days. My only real concern turned out to be the naval staff in Alexandria controlling ship movements. Caught between the needs of ship movements to Tobruk and of furnishing empty ships for docking at Massawa, I have no doubt we nearly drove them to distraction by our urgent messages calling for ships lest the dry dock in Massawa remain idle a few hours.

Once they had their teeth in the job after the first few weeks, the Eritreans speeded up instead of slowing down. In the hundred and twenty days allotted to docking merchant ships that season, including the worst summer months, we pushed eighty vessels across the keel blocks of that dry dock—a final average of a ship every day and a half. Soon Lieutenant Fairbairn had to have another British officer assigned as Assistant Pilot, and another tug also, lest he delay the job by the loss of time of transferring pilot and tugs from the outgoing vessel to the newcomer waiting at anchor in the outer roadstead. After that, the vessel to be docked passed the outgoing ship regularly just beyond the line of wrecks; the load of one ship was hardly off the keel blocks before the weight of her successor was compressing them again.

No dry dock in the world in war or peace has, I believe, ever equaled the record made that year by that one dock in Massawa in taking full-sized ships. We not only ran the whole Mediterranean fleet of supply ships over that dry dock, doubling their speed at sea, but some of the faster ones we took again after a few months to keep them up to topnotch efficiency. And all of it was done by the worst labor in the world under the worst conditions anywhere in the world. The Eritreans in Massawa did their bit to win the war—it should not be forgotten when some day around some table the United Nations delegates meet to decide the future of Eritrea.

The worst labor in the world? I often wondered how true that was as month after month in the Massawa heat I watched those puny

Eritreans slashing away with scrapers, fiercely swinging paint brushes while all the time they danced and swayed to their barbaric chants. There is no worst labor in the world. Touch the proper chords— pride, incentive to produce, whatever fits the situation—and men will be found men, whatever their color, whatever their physique.

CHAPTER

23

Meanwhile, trouble in another direction, which had been simmering some weeks, began to boil.

We now had on the payroll of the Naval Base several hundred men, not counting the two hundred Eritreans on the dry dock whom, fortunately, I was hiring for the time being through a British company, by whom they were being paid daily.

For several weeks there had been growing signs of dissatisfaction among our assorted workmen in the Naval Base shops. They had not been paid. The payroll for the Naval Base was being handled in Asmara by the civilian contractor there, along with the payroll for the hundreds of employees he had in Massawa on his various construction projects. To keep the time records and handle the accounts, the contractor had sent to Massawa one of his supervisors, a Mr. McDonald, together with several clerks, who were installed in an office on the ground floor of our office building.

Our labor force, starting early in April, was small, cost accounting for it was simple. However, when the first pay day rolled around (the men were supposed to be paid weekly), there was no pay for anybody. The excuse from Asmara was that the time sheets were not yet worked out; they would be soon.

Our labor force was growing rapidly. When the second pay day came around on April 18, and a sizable mob of natives and Italians gathered round the pay office for their wages, there was still no pay either for the overdue first week or for the current week. The men started to grumble now in strange tongues; understandably enough they wanted their money. I went to see McDonald about it. He shrugged his shoulders. The payroll was made up in Asmara from his time sheets; it hadn't come down; he couldn't pay off.

I got the contractor's office in Asmara over the telephone, with the usual exasperating delays in getting a connection and the usual trials in keeping it. Yes, they were working up the pay accounts there; next week they would surely be ready; I could assure all the workmen that next week they would be paid.

I went out to assure the sheikhs for the natives, and the Italians and the other assorted races separately that next week they would certainly be paid. They looked a little dubiously at me, but they accepted the assurance and dispersed, muttering, I suppose, over how I expected them to pay the groceryman.

Next week, April 25, came around and still no pay for anybody, not a lira. By now I was exasperated—it goes without saying what the unpaid workmen felt. McDonald blamed the office in Asmara; I got the Asmara manager and he blamed McDonald for lack of proper time sheets. I informed the contractor that the situation was getting both scandalous and dangerous; the men must be paid immediately, proper time sheets or not. All I got was a run-around; Asmara would handle the matter; by the following Saturday, May 2, they would pay off for the whole month of April; meanwhile, I should quit worrying them about it.

I hung up the telephone in disgust with the contractor and all his works. Asmara was overrun with his highly paid executives (who rarely visited Massawa) and his large head office staff—so large an American civilian force they had taken over completely the biggest hotel in Asmara just to house these men. And yet with all that in the cool comfort of Asmara, they had not yet made up the payroll! How could I face again the growing mob of trusting natives outside the pay office and tell them that the wealthy and the efficient United States was not able yet to pay them their long overdue wages?

To mitigate the blow, I sent an officer posthaste in my car to the town of Massawa to draw out in small bills and silver all the money I personally had on deposit in Barclays Bank there. It wasn't much, £200, but in lira it sounded like a lot more, about 20,000 lira, approximately the payroll for one day for all the men we then had employed at the Naval Base.

With that money at hand, ashamed of myself and enraged at the contractor for having put me in that position, I made the announcement—there would be no pay-off today; it would surely be taken care of the following week. Doubt, suspicion, and distrust showed in the mass of black and white faces before me when the statement was

[179]

translated. Was the wealthy United States worse than the Fascist regime they knew—was it trying to deceive them with fair words while it swindled them out of their pay—a petty swindle, besides, since none of them was being paid more than a few cents a day?

I did what I could to ease the situation and restore confidence with my own 20,000 lira. I advised the sheikhs and the other workers, not Eritreans, that I would personally lend any man who badly needed money up to 100 lira to help him out; I could not afford to go higher than that in order to try to cover as many cases as possible with the money I had. All that was required was to ask; I would trust them to repay me when finally they were paid themselves.

In fifty-lira notes and in East African shillings, the money rapidly went out. I believe everyone who wanted help got at least fifty lira. Sick at heart over the whole spectacle, ashamed of some of my fellow Americans in responsible positions, I watched the unpaid laborers, their faith in the United States badly shaken, slowly disperse.

Another week went by, another pay day, May 2, came round. Once more there was no pay-off, but this time, distrustful myself of the contractor's promises, I had learned the bad news in advance by inquiring of McDonald some hours before quitting time. No, no money and no payroll had come down from Asmara; none was on the way.

I got hold, by telephone, of Colonel Claterbos in Asmara, to learn from him that the situation in Massawa was being more or less repeated all over Eritrea. The contractor, claiming lack of help, was so enmeshed in the complications of his own accounting systems that pay to natives everywhere was in arrears. Colonel Claterbos was as much disturbed over the situation as I; in fact, disagreement with the contractor over that and other matters was literally making him sick and had already put him in the hands of the doctors; but the civilian contractor was a law unto himself, he could not force him to pay off.

Getting this information from Claterbos over the Italian telephone system from Asmara was practically equal to a day's work in itself. When, after many interruptions on the line, I finally hung up, I was thoroughly washed out. Claterbos, I supposed, had stood it better; at least he could telephone from a cool room—not from the super-heated Turkish bath atmosphere of my office.

The time for paying off, with the final blow to American prestige and good faith when words instead of cash would be all that could be offered our long unpaid workmen, was only a few hours away. I told Mrs. Maton to get hold, by telephone, in Asmara, of the top executive present in the contractor's office there. After a while, she succeeded and handed me the telephone.

"McDonald tells me no pay day today. Is that right?" I asked after the usual salutations.

"Yes, Commander, that's so. We're still working on the payroll."

"Well, quit working on the payroll!" I burst out in exasperation. "You've been doing that for a month now! Send down some money! All the Eritreans and a lot of the Italians can't buy anything to eat any more! They'll quit on us and tie this Naval Base up in a hard knot just when we're getting under way. Never mind the payroll; put enough cash for two weeks' pay for everybody in a car and start it down here four bells! That'll leave you a margin for safety when you get your accounts worked out, and it'll save our hides down here till you finally pay off. Quit figuring! Send us some cash!"

"Now, Commander," I heard in a soothing voice from the other end, "we can't do that. We're short of help, but we'll get it figured out by next week—"

"Next week!" I exploded. "Don't you know these natives can't be told that again? You've already made a liar out of me with that story! To hell with next week! You pay these men something *now!*"

"Calm yourself, Commander. We'll take care of it. Keep cool, you're getting hysterical—"

"Hysterical?" I roared. "You're damned right I'm getting hysterical! Damn your hide, *you* come down to Massawa a while and you'll get hysterical, too! Don't you tell me from Asmara how to keep cool in Massawa! Quit talking and get busy! SEND DOWN SOME MONEY!" and I hung up the telephone with a bang that nearly smashed that fragile Italian instrument.

But no money came down and there was no pay day that Saturday. Nor the following one either. The foremen were continually besieged by sheikhs, by individual Italians, begging for their pay, asking why the Americans were breaking their promises. Even the Fascisti had done better than that. Wild rumors, all discreditable to the United States, flew about among the workmen, none of whom believed the real reason, that the contractor, his executives, and his employees were so inefficient they couldn't work out the payroll.

For myself, I kept away from my office and the naval shops as much as I could to avoid entreaties. I no longer had any faith in the contractor. I was making no more promises as to when the men would be paid. I warned the foremen to make none either. And I had no more money of my own in Eritrea to help anybody out.

After May 2, a sullen air fell over all the naval shops to replace the enthusiasm with which the men had worked the first month. Men started to absent themselves, production began to fall off. It was evident an explosion was coming soon. I wondered what form it would take—more sabotage, a walkout, violence?

The faith and honor of the United States with the Eritreans, the Italians, the Arabs, and all the other assorted races in Massawa stood infinitely lower than that of Mussolini. How the ardent Fascists, still unweeded out amongst our Italians, went to work behind our backs in hot Massawa!

And all the while, 7500 feet up in comfortable Asmara, coolly, calmly, unhysterically, the contractor's executives and his accounting force worked, short-handedly they claimed, on the payroll sheets. I never saw any evidence then or later that any one of them from the top down, lost any weight trying to make up for short-handedness in their office, or in trying to solve the problem any other way.

CHAPTER

24

T͟IED UP AS I WAS ALL DAY LONG OF Saturday, May 9, 1942, with the completion and undocking of the *Koritza,* I was unaware until evening that that day at last I had received some reinforcements, opening up another field.

In the late afternoon, invisible to me down in the dry dock, the *S.S. President Buchanan,* which had sailed March 21 from New York bound for Suez, had paused briefly in the roadstead outside Massawa harbor and had landed via a tender my first contingent of salvage men.

At the same time, another small group, landed at Port Sudan by a different vessel, had arrived from there via Asmara by plane and car.

I heard of all this only when I had come in from the dry dock after the departure of the *Koritza.* I hastened to greet the newcomers, though the added information that another week was ending with still no pay day in sight, somewhat dampened my enthusiasm for anything.

I found I had received two supervisors and thirteen men altogether; not a very large contingent to tackle the huge salvage job before us. Heading the party was one of the two Salvage Masters hired on the West Coast, Captain William Reed. With him were five divers: Melvin Barry, Jesse Enos, Ervin Johnson, George Kimble, and Alvin Watson. Accompanying the divers were Lloyd Williams, Salvage Master Mechanic, with eight salvage mechanics and tenders—James Buzbee, Jay Smith, James Riemer, Lew Whitaker, "Buck" Schott, Charley Hoffman, "Tex" Powell, and "Whitey" Broderick.

Bill Reed I had first met seventeen years before, when as a civilian diver he was making a preliminary underwater survey of the sunken submarine, *S-51,* just before the Navy undertook the task of lifting her itself and I was ordered to the job as her Salvage Officer. Reed, still a civilian, and a number of years older than I, was too old for much diving now. As a matter of fact, he was too old for Massawa also and should have folded up there in a hurry, but as he was blind in one eye in addition, perhaps his failure to see that clearly and fold up swiftly, as most of the older men and many of the younger men soon did, must be excused.

I greeted Reed, and Lloyd Williams whom I had with difficulty persuaded in New York to take the job as Salvage Master Mechanic, with great joy. None of the others I knew anything about. The divers, except Ervin Johnson whom I had engaged in New York, were the men I had hired in Hollywood. So were part of the salvage mechanics and tenders. How a salvage crew accustomed to the artificial atmosphere of movie studios would make out in the face of real wrecks, I was dubious of.

I stowed Captain Reed and Lloyd Williams in one of the vacant rooms in Building 108 with me, to the intense disgust of the two Cable and Wireless men who looked with horror at the increasing number of Americans invading the sacred precincts of Building 108. Then I found quarters for the others in one of the ex-Italian wooden barracks along with Cunningham and the other American mechanics employed by the contractor. I told them all to take Sunday to get themselves settled and get acquainted with Massawa and the Naval Base; on Monday morning, salvage operations were going to commence in Massawa.

That Saturday night as I tossed about on my soaked bedsheet, for once I didn't regret my inability to get a decent night's rest. Even the wireless message at midnight from the Commander-in-Chief about the *Koritza* swiftly vanished from my thoughts.

Weeks before, I had decided on which salvage job I should tackle first when my first salvage ship, its crew, and its equipment arrived. Now I was determined to tackle that same job, even though I had no salvage ship and next to no equipment, for nothing in the way of salvage gear had been shipped with Reed's little party on the *President Buchanan,* except only two diving rigs and a small air compressor, which were Reed's personal property and which he had brought with him on his own initiative.

But I was itching to get to work on salvage. Now I had two supervisors, five divers, eight mechanics, and two diving suits—all my own. Nobody could tell me how I must use these thirteen American workmen, the first Americans I did not have to beg for as a loan. With them, I intended to tackle immediately the hardest job of all first, the task which officially had been rated impossible—the lifting of the large Italian dry dock. Impossible to raise though it was considered to be, that dry dock was by far the most valuable prize of war of anything scuttled in Massawa. The Italians knew that, too—that was why eight large bombs had been placed in it as against only one quarter that number placed to sink the ordinary ships.

The week after my arrival in Massawa, Captain Lucas had shown me an inquiry from the British Admiralty in London:

"Request you have American salvage experts examine scuttled Italian dry docks and obtain their opinion as to possibility of salvage."

I smiled inwardly when I read that inquiry. So London, in spite of all the expert opinion it had received regarding the hopelessness of that task, was still cherishing the faint hope that something might yet be done to recover the richest prizes in all Africa.

I had already cruised slowly many times over and around the two sunken Italian dry docks, the larger one particularly, in the *Lord Grey*, peering down through the quiet sea-green waters of Massawa harbor at what I might see of those two hulks from the surface. It had not been much; I could see down into the water on the smoothest days only some five to ten feet.

I had also studied the report of the first British salvage officer (later killed off the Daklak Islands) on his diving survey of the docks and the terrific damage he had found—seven huge holes had been blasted in the cellular horizontal main hull structure of the large dock, tearing out the bottom, the floor of the dock overhead, the intermediate bulkheads. The damage was described in considerable detail—the Italians had intended to make an end of that dock forever to prevent it from serving their enemies. In their eyes, in his eyes, in the eyes of every salvage expert in Africa and in England who had studied that report, all of them with wide experience on scores of war-torn ships, the Italians had succeeded.

But not in mine. A study of that report had convinced me I could raise that dry dock; what little I could see of the dock, leaning over the gunwale of the *Lord Grey* had confirmed me in my belief.

But sure as I might be in my own mind over what could be done, when I was shown that inquiry from London, I was still an expert without any of the tools of my profession to make the examination requested on which my opinion was to be based. So at the time I had simply told Captain Lucas he might report to the Admiralty,

Commanding Officer American Salvage Forces considers salvage possible. An attempt will be made when men and salvage equipment arrive.

Now that some men but no equipment to speak of had finally arrived, the time had come to make the attempt. As I tossed about naked on my soaked sheet inside my mosquito net and oozed perspiration all through that Saturday night, I laid my plans. There was underwater work enough on the blasted hull of the large Italian dry dock to keep fifty divers, several hundred surface mechanics, and several well-equipped salvage ships working a year or more to patch up the damage so the dock could be pumped out and lifted—as it was put in one British report,

Upon consideration of all reports received, the Admiralty have abandoned all idea of salvage. The salvage work would be long, difficult, and probably unsuccessful.

That statement was correct. There was bomb damage enough to that one dry dock to have sunk swiftly seven large ships.

But even while I was looking over the sunken dry dock, I knew I should never have anything like fifty divers to work with, nor the hundreds of skilled men and well-equipped ships needed to back them up. At most, I could count on only seven divers all told, two trifling tugboats, and an ill-equipped base ship, if everything arrived safely.

Now I didn't have even the two tugs, the base ship, nor what equipment they carried. But I did have fifteen men to command at last, two of whom at least, Reed and Williams, I knew were good; the others I hoped were. Before they all cracked up in the increasing Massawa heat, waiting for ships and equipment to arrive which might be sunk on the way, I intended to lift that dry dock. With our bare hands, with such mechanical help as my Naval Base shops could render, and with only such equipment as had been lying around Massawa for months or years, available to anybody, we would tackle it.

For from all the surveys made of that sunken dock and its damage,

I saw a way of raising it that had never entered the minds of the Italians who had scuttled it, nor of all the salvage experts all the way from Massawa through Alexandria to London who had knitted their brows over the problem. Instead of a task which had to be abandoned because it "would be long, difficult, and probably unsuccessful," I intended to make it short, easy, and certain. I had to. I had no means to do it the hard way, even if I had wanted to, as some salvage jobs have been done for the publicity value and the profit of the salvors.

I was little concerned over the opinions of all the experts who had rated it impossible. I was, as a matter of fact, somewhat irritated by seeing myself denominated an "American expert" in the Admiralty inquiry. For I didn't consider myself an "expert" in anything and besides I had a very low opinion of "experts" anyway. "Experts" are people who know so much about how things have been done in the past that they are usually blind to how they can be done in the future.

C H A P T E R

25

O<small>N</small> SUNDAY, WHILE REED, WILLIAMS, and their men were learning firsthand for themselves what Massawa was and getting themselves unpacked and settled, I docked the *Athos* in the morning and put in the rest of the day with my foremen. I outlined for them the materials and the men I wanted them to gather up round the Naval Base for the salvage job—plenty of drinking water and lots of ice first of all; then a thousand feet of Italian steel pipe together with connecting fittings; some lumber; a few thousand feet of electric wire and several dozen light sockets; about a dozen Italian mechanics, pipefitters mainly, with a few electricians; half a dozen Arab carpenters; and about thirty Eritreans for laborers. In addition, five Maltese we had, who had been exiled from the Alexandria Naval Base in disgrace and sent to Massawa as a punishment, whom I had observed to be good riggers, were to be sent out for handling weights and materials. They set out on their tasks.

A floating dry dock resembles, looked at end on, a huge capital U. The horizontal part at the bottom may be likened to a tremendous hollow rectangular raft, fifteen feet deep, a hundred feet wide, six hundred feet long. It is watertight, of course, strongly braced with steel girders inside to carry the weight of a ship lifted out of the water and resting on wood keel blocks along the fore and aft center-line of the floor of the dock. The buoyancy of this bottom section is tremendous, sufficient to float the weight of the dry dock itself as well as that of the ship it has lifted clear of the water.

The vertical parts of the U are the two dry dock side walls. These run fore and aft on each side of the dry dock for its entire length. They are massive hollow steel walls, fifteen feet thick, thirty-five feet high above the floor of the dry dock. Their major purpose is to give the dry dock stability and hold it vertical and upright, so that while the horizontal raft section is completely submerged in order first to take aboard the ship to be docked and later to lift it up out of the water, the dry dock will not tilt or capsize and spill the rising ship off the keel blocks.

In the normal operation of a floating dry dock, the upper few feet of the side walls always remain above water; the dock is so built, in fact, that it cannot be flooded down far enough to submerge the side walls completely (unless damaged).

By their very nature, harbors are not usually very deep. A harbor with a clear depth of water of fifty feet is fortunate. The usual trouble with using a floating dry dock is to find a spot in the harbor with water deep enough to sink the dry dock far enough down to take on a laden or damaged ship. Massawa harbor happened to have one fifty-foot deep clear spot; that was the spot chosen by the Italians for mooring their large dry dock and that spot naturally when they blasted it with bombs, was where it sank till it touched bottom in some eight fathoms of water.

As it rested on the bottom, the tops of both side walls at the stern of the dry dock were awash at high tide; from there forward, the tops of the side walls were a few inches clear of the water all the way to the bow. At low tide (the average tide in Massawa ran only from one to two feet in range with a maximum range of three feet) the entire top decks of the side walls from bow to stern were a little exposed, giving us something to stand on while we worked, which was fortunate, as we had no salvage ships to work from.

On Monday morning, May 11, the salvage job on the large Italian dry dock began. I took Bill Reed, Lloyd Williams, and their little party, thirteen all told, out to the dry dock in the *Lord Grey*, together with Reed's diving gear. We clambered aboard the exposed port side wall of the dock and sent the boat back to the Naval Base wharf to bring out what materials had already been procured.

With the waves lapping round our feet, I sat down on a box on deck the dock, stripped off my khaki but prudently kept on my sun helmet, and the tenders began to dress me in one of Reed's two suits —I would make the first dive myself to examine the dock and start the job off.

While I stood dressed only in a pair of light cotton drawers, two tenders commenced sliding me inside a stiff canvas-covered rubber diving dress. For once, I looked forward to a dive with some pleasure.

The water in the Red Sea was very warm—about 95° F. I had done most of my salvage diving in cold water, in the practically freezing water of the cold North Atlantic off the New England coast in wintertime. There the major problem had always been to keep the diver from freezing to death in the ice water surrounding him. Three suits of heavy woolen North Woods underwear pulled on one over another, two pairs of thick woolen socks, and a pair of heavy woolen mittens were the standard clothing one put on, before the diving dress with watertight gloves went on over them. Even so I had always come up after a dive numbed and stiff from the cold, requiring a powerful "submarine cocktail," a pint of hot coffee and whisky, mixed half-and-half, to help thaw me out.

Now all of that was past—no more cumbersome woolen underwear, no more hands so encased in woolen mitts and stiff rubber diving gloves as to be practically worthless as hands, no more freezing. Massawa had one good point: the Red Sea, the hottest ocean on earth, was so warm a man could dive in it in comfort, with his bare hands exposed outside his rubber watertight cuffs so he could use them.

On went the bulky diving dress, the copper breastplate, the massive lead-weighted diving belt, the heavy lead-soled shoes, expertly draped over my perspiring body by Al Watson and Melvin Barry, acting as tenders. Meanwhile, Captain Reed poured gasoline into the tank of his little diving air compressor, started it up, and laid out the diving hose and a manila lifeline, ready for use. There was no diving telephone set; all communication would have to be by signaling on the lifeline or air hose.

The helmet with the diving hose attached was next tested out; compressed air was coming through. On went the helmet; Al Watson gave it a vigorous quarter turn to lock it in place to the breastplate, while Melvin Barry braced my shoulders to prevent my being twisted into a knot during the helmet-locking operation. I tested out my air inlet valve and my exhaust valve; everything appeared to be in working order.

Held up by Watson and Barry, for now I was draped with 200 pounds of lead and copper, I dragged myself laboriously to the inboard edge of the port side wall and the two tenders lowered me over the side into the water inside the dock. Once the sea rose over my helmet and I was fully submerged, they ceased lowering a moment and held me, hanging on my lifeline, while once more I checked all my valves to insure their operation, and adjusted both inlet and exhaust air valves so to inflate my diving dress as to make me only slightly negative in weight. That settled satisfactorily, I signaled to lower away, and swiftly down I went through the Red Sea.

It was about six fathoms down to the floor of the dry dock; not a bad water pressure to work in. In considerably less than a minute I was on the floor of the dock, peering out through my faceplates into the sea. The visibility was none too good. The light, six fathoms down, was fair, but the sea was peopled by myriads of amoebae, giving the water a somewhat milky translucent effect which prevented seeing clearly more than a few fathoms. To make matters worse, the moment I started to walk, my lead-soled shoes stirred up the thick mud with which the floor of the dock was covered, leaving it to rise in lazy clouds floating in the sea above the dock floor, obscuring that from my sight.

Still keeping close to the vertical port side wall of the dock towering above me in the water, I walked aft slowly through the sea, my head tilted back so I could look up through the upper faceplate of my clumsy helmet. For the method I intended to use in raising that dry dock, the condition of the steel floor and of the steel bottom of the dry dock and the holes blasted in them were of no great moment to me; but the condition of those steel side walls was all important. Were they also damaged, or had they, as I imagined and the lack of contrary evidence in the previous surveys indicated, been left untouched as of no importance by the Italians in their orgy of destruction?

With each step as I plodded laboriously along through the sea, straining my eyes upward, I felt better. I could see farther looking up towards the surface than in any other direction and what I saw was decidedly cheering. The side wall of the dry dock alongside me was heavily covered by mussels and barnacles, growing in a solid mass all over it; I couldn't actually see the steel plates themselves, but I could see that wall rising straight toward the surface with not a sign anywhere of an explosion—no torn steel or bulging plates or vast holes blasted in that vertical wall such as bombs or torpedoes always leave in their wake.

Satisfied that my theory of raising the dock would work out, I left the port side wall, and started walking inboard toward the centerline of the broad dock floor to see for myself what the Fascisti *had* done to the dry dock. A few steps inboard and that vast outside wall faded from my sight altogether in the murky water. From then on, I had great difficulty in maintaining any sense of direction and my course, as indicated on the surface by the stream of air bubbles floating upward from my helmet, must have seemed that of a drunkard zigzagging homeward under grave difficulties.

To make matters worse, I began to stumble over unseen obstacles in my erratic path. Close inspection, mostly by feel, for not much could be seen in the muddy water, indicated they were massive blocks of wood, five or six feet long, over a foot square. Undoubtedly these were the oaken keel blocks of the dry dock, tossed by the explosions helter-skelter over the floor of the dock, where they had remained, too heavy and too waterlogged to float away.

Somewhat further inboard, I approached something looking vaguely like the crater of a volcano. Here one of the bombs must have exploded beneath the floor. Ragged steel plates, twisted steel girders, all barnacle-encrusted, rose from the mud-covered dock floor in fantastic shapes, curled back like tissue paper. Beyond the fringe of broken and bent plating I could dimly make out an irregular black spot some fathoms across in the otherwise gray-green water—the hole in the dock floor that explosion had made.

I didn't investigate that hole any further—it was big enough to have driven a huge truck through and it was garnished round its rim with sufficient torn steel to make any diver wary about cutting open his rubber suit on its jagged edges. Besides, that hole in the sunken dry dock floor made little difference to me; I had no intention of bothering with it or of doing any of the terrific amount of diving work required to patch it up on the bottom before we raised the dry dock. That vast hole and its six mates, the sight of which had left aghast the original salvage officer and all who had seen his report since, was a matter of no moment to me in salvaging the dock.

I turned aft with the thought of taking a look at the floor of the dock near the stern. The dock floor was built of eight separate watertight steel sections. Seven of them, from the bow aft, had been blasted open by bombs; the eighth section at the stern was reported undamaged. Apparently the bomb which must have been placed there had failed to explode when the other seven forward of it had gone off. I thought I might see some signs of that unexploded bomb, so we could remove it before it blew up in our faces while we worked. And at any rate, I was desirous of checking for myself that the stern end section *was* the undamaged one—that made some difference, though not a vital one, to my plans.

Keeping a little to port of the line of keel blocks, I started aft through the water. By now, I was no longer so sure of the advantages of diving in the Red Sea; I began to long for the icy waters of the North Atlantic where I could freeze to death, or at least into numbness, in comfort. The inside of my diving suit was nearly intolerable. The water outside was practically at body temperature; it was doing nothing to cool me off. I was nearly drowned in perspiration, for the hot air coming down to me from the compressor, thoroughly saturated already with moisture when it started down, was not only not doing anything to evaporate the sweat from my body but was adding profusely to it. I was practically blinded also by sweat running off my forehead into my eyes; with my head totally enclosed in that diving helmet, there was no way I could get my hands or anything else to my eyes to wipe them clear. And as a final torture, hot as I was, I saw that I had made a serious blunder in not putting on a complete suit of woolen diving underwear. The stiff canvas folds of my diving dress, pressed in against my body by the weight of the sea which had me in its grasp, worked like a rasp on my skin each time I moved, removing cuticle by the square inch. Over these raw spots in my hide, salt sweat was percolating downward continuously, irritating me frightfully. In hot water or not, neither I nor anyone else was going to make another dive in the Red Sea except encased in a full suit of woolen underwear for skin protection.

Cursing volubly inside my helmet as the only means of relieving my distress, I plodded aft over the dock floor, hardly able to see anything any more. Then on the flat muddy floor before me, a darker strip than usual loomed dimly up through the water. Before I could stop and appraise the significance of that, I had stepped off into nothingness and felt myself going down, engulfed instantly in blackness. With my lead boots still feeling nothing beneath them, I was brought to in that Stygian darkness by a sharp jerk as the slack in my lifeline took up suddenly and left me dangling on it somewhere in the bowels of that dock.

Where the devil was I now, I wondered? What sort of mantrap had I stepped into? I had not walked off the stern of the dock; before I went down, I could still see the floor of the dock stretching away before me in the water. And I had surely not walked unexpectedly into one of those craters blasted in the floor of the dock by exploding bombs—they were certainly all surrounded like a fence with torn steel turned upward like the one I had just seen.

But wherever I was, I was certainly in a hole and an inky black one at that. There was no profit in staying there while I investigated the inside of that cavern; something unpleasant might happen to me in the process.

There were several ways for a diver to escape that hole, but climbing out was not one of them, since my fingers, clawing about in the dark water, felt nothing within reach. The simplest way out was to be pulled out. Since my lifeline was taut, I couldn't be sure any signal on it would be felt above. Instead I reached for my slack air hose, seized it, and jerked sharply three times, the signal to haul me up.

In a moment both my lines came taut and I felt myself rising through the water. In another moment, I was up in the light again, clear of that hole, but I did not signal to 'vast heaving. I had already learned enough on that dive; I felt too chafed all over for any eagerness to lengthen it out further. I was quite willing to call it a dive and come up.

So as I came clear I did nothing and the continuing pull on my lines floated me obliquely like a hooked fish on a line through the water towards the side wall till the lines were up and down; after that, I rose vertically towards the surface. For a depth of six fathoms of water, no stops on the way up for decompression to avoid "the bends" were necessary. In another couple of minutes, everybody on the topside who could get a hand on my rig was helping to lift my heavily weighted figure over the gunwale of the dock onto its upper deck, where I promptly sagged down exhausted on the box thrust under my knees.

My helmet was twisted off. I gasped with relief at my first breath of open air, hot though it was, and instantly my wet hands rose to wipe clear of sweat my still wetter eyes.

After I had been undressed and was being rubbed by a towel in the hands of a tender, futilely endeavoring to dry me off, I gathered all the diving party round me for a report.

"It's the way I thought. The bottom's torn wide open. The side walls look undamaged, the port side wall anyway. The next man can examine the starboard side wall to make sure. We'll go ahead on the scheme I laid out, to raise her as a diving bell; the holes in the bottom won't make any difference. Let's go."

In brief, my idea was to convert that blasted dry dock into the equivalent of a huge diving bell, open at the bottom, and raise her solely with compressed air pumped into the side walls which had only to be made airtight on the top and sides. The openings in the bottom made no difference; the compressed air pumped into the tops of both side walls would force the water down steadily and out through those holes in the bottom till enough water had been expelled to make the dock slightly buoyant. After that, it should start to float up, buoyed by the air-filled side walls. The more compressed air we pumped into the side walls, the farther up the dock would rise. It was very simple. All we had to do was to make the undamaged side walls airtight by plugging all openings in them, both top and sides, either in or out of water, and then leave the rest to the big air compressors (which I didn't have yet).

I dressed again in khaki shorts, put on my sun helmet and dark glasses, and still smarting from the raw spots on my skin, turned to. In a minute or so, everything I had on was completely soaked in sweat.

The next diver was being dressed (against his violent protests, wearing a suit of woolen diving underwear) to examine the starboard side wall and the stern which I had not seen. After he had been warned to beware of unexpected pitfalls in the floor of the dock, everybody else except Bill Reed and two tenders went to work on deck.

The *Lord Grey* had returned, loaded down with two-inch Italian steel pipe, lumber, and native workmen. All hands started to unload her, part of her cargo going on top the port side wall, the rest to the other side of the dock atop the starboard side wall.

To make my scheme work, a great deal of labor was required, though fortunately most of it could be done above water where labor conditions were normal, if any conditions in Massawa could ever be called that. I should have to lay a compressed air main along the top of each side wall, connect each one of the eight watertight sections in each side wall to that air main, interconnect the port and the starboard air mains across the eighty-foot gap of sea between what little showed on the surface of the side walls, provide air gauges

[195]

The scuttled large Italian dry dock on the bottom.

to check the pressure built up in each of sixteen side compartments as the compressed air went in, plug up or seal off every opening of any nature in the tops and sides of both side walls to make them airtight, and finally provide enough big air compressors to expel thousands of tons of water from the dry dock through those holes in its bottom.

There were innumerable small tasks that had to be done also to make the scheme work. The above were the major ones, for which divers were required only for plugging such normal openings, airports, scuppers, and drains, now submerged, as existed in the side walls. Everything else could be done on the surface by ordinary mechanics.

Drinking water service was our first imperative. Arab carpenters hastily knocked together a large wood box to make an impromptu icebox. Into that immediately went several hundred pounds of ice brought out on the *Lord Grey* and at least two hundred quart bottles of water. A little awning was rigged over the box to protect it from the direct rays of the sun. Three Eritreans were appointed as water boys to rush promptly a bottle of cold water to anyone singing out, "Mai!" (Water!) Each man was provided with his own quota of salt tablets. Those black water boys were always kept on the run.

With the water problem thus disposed of, I went over with Lloyd Williams what else was required of him. I indicated where I wanted the 500-foot long air mains run on each side, where to interconnect them from port to starboard across the water, how he was to run a branch line from the mains to each one of the sixteen dock compartments. I picked out where we would locate the big air compressors (when I got some), and laid out some other work required which I figured would keep Williams and all the men he had, both American and otherwise, busy the rest of that day.

After some further instructions to Bill Reed (who now had his first diver down inspecting the starboard side wall) about locating underwater openings in the side walls with succeeding divers, I piled into the *Lord Grey* myself to go ashore and get that which was the *sine qua non* of the whole plan—some big air compressors.

I had no fears about the physical lack of the necessary air compressors in Massawa—there are always air compressors of some kind in every place on earth where there is any machinery at all, or where there has been any road-building. While the Naval Base itself had not a single air compressor, there were, I knew, in Massawa the very air compressors I needed—in fact, the mates to the air compressors I had ordered in America for my salvage work but which had not yet arrived.

For a strange situation existed in Massawa in connection with salvage, which I had learned immediately after my arrival—the British themselves already had a substantial salvage undertaking under way months before I saw the place. It was another one of those "Alice in Wonderland" situations which have to be seen to be believed.

Lying near the docks in the town of Massawa was a huge warehouse stuffed with salvage equipment of all kinds—more salvage gear than I had ever before in my life seen collected in one spot, all of it the property of the British Admiralty. Lying in the commercial harbor of Massawa was a beautiful Danish salvage ship and its Danish salvage crew, a finer ship by far for salvage than any I should ever have, under charter to the British Admiralty. Controlling all this salvage equipment and this Danish salvage ship was a private British company which had a contract (and what a contract!) from the Admiralty for the salvage on a commercial basis of the wrecks inside the commercial harbor only of Massawa, the center harbor of the three at Massawa.

The British company (a firm of shipping agents) which held that salvage contract had never been in the salvage business before; neither had they any equipment for the job, so the Admiralty had generously furnished them with sufficient British equipment at no cost to make any salvage man's mouth water, and in addition had given them control of its chartered Danish salvage ship and crew.

In explanation of the course of the Admiralty in this case, it must be said that every British concern with salvage experience already had its hands full around the British Isles; I can think of no other reason for giving a salvage contract to a concern with neither salvage nor engineering experience.

The British company had sent out to Massawa as its Salvage Officer to run this operation, a Captain McCance, presumably a merchant service captain (if one at all), for he certainly was not in the Royal Navy. If anything further was needed to give an *opéra bouffe* touch to the whole situation, Captain McCance gave it. He knew no more about salvage than the company employing him, and to top off all, he was the very embodiment of the low comedy Englishman, and the butt for the caustic humor of every Royal Navy officer in Massawa. He wore a monocle, the only one in Eritrea. Exceedingly affected in his manner and his speech, he signed all his letters (written always in a bizarre green ink) "Younger Brother of Trinity House," which dubious claim to distinction never failed to draw a raucous laugh from the British naval staff in the port. Had he been put on any American stage just as he was as a burlesque Englishman, the dramatic critics would have denounced him as a caricature too grotesque for belief.

As little like a seaman as can be imagined, he was never dressed other than in perfectly laundered whites—white shoes, white socks, white shorts, white shirt, white sun helmet—that rig on a salvage officer, especially when topped off with a monocle, was enough to make any real salvage man accustomed to work in the muck and filth of wrecks, doubt the evidence of his own eyes. Most of his time, probably six days out of seven on the average, he spent in Asmara where it was cool, seventy miles away from and 7500 feet above the wrecks in hot Massawa that he was supposed to be salvaging. The seventh day, very careful not to soil his lovely white clothes, he came to Massawa to examine languidly through his monocle the progress on the wrecks his men were working on—that the progress was negligible went, of course, without saying.

To make matters worse, he refused to use on either of the two wrecks he was engaged on, the solitary capable group he had, the Danish salvage ship and her crew, leaving her lie idle month after month in the harbor, useless to anybody, useless to the war effort, while her men ate their hearts out in bitterness, looking at all the wrecks about them. I swore every time I thought of that idle ship, till finally some months later, the Admiralty sent her elsewhere.

The two jobs McCance had his men on, the huge floating crane sunk alongside the main Massawa wharf and the Italian combination passenger ship and freighter, the *Gera*, scuttled in the middle of the commercial harbor, they had been busy with since the previous December, when it was reported to London they were making excellent progress. It was now May, but neither of his two wrecks showed any signs yet of coming up. In about six months, McCance and his men (quite a sizable civilian force) had raised exactly nothing. I judged that in his incompetent ignorance, he was botching both jobs, at the expense of the British Admiralty which was standing all the costs.

[199]

I sensed immediately after my arrival in Massawa that I was not welcome on board either of McCance's salvage jobs. I learned from some of his men whom on the quay in Massawa I had asked a casual question as to how they were getting along with the sunken crane, that they had all been warned to give me no information. So since that moment, Captain McCance and I had gone separate ways—not a difficult matter since most of his time was being spent in Asmara.

Now I had observed, on one of my few inspection jaunts about the town of Massawa, through the open doors of his warehouse all the unused salvage gear the British Admiralty had placed at Captain McCance's disposal—in particular two large Ingersoll-Rand air compressors which were just what I needed for the salvage job on the large Italian dry dock. I had not entered the warehouse—I had no desire to give McCance the opportunity of accusing me of trespassing on his domain—but even from the doors I couldn't miss a good view of those two big air compressors, shining in glossy paint, apparently new and unused. I had never mentioned those heaven-sent compressors or my need of them to anyone before; I preferred to wait till my own inspection of the sunken dry dock showed the job could be done the way I had hoped. But now I knew.

Immediately I had disembarked from the *Lord Grey,* I went to my near-by office. Austin Byrne, my master mechanic, and Commander Davy, liaison officer, looking out over the naval harbor, were scanning through binoculars the motley crew of men now swarming over the top of the sunken dock. Both of them turned questioning eyes on me the moment I entered. I tossed aside my sun helmet and my sun glasses and, looking very much like a beachcomber, sank wearily into my chair. Mrs. Maton looked me over sharply, then went immediately for a glass of ice water. I swallowed a salt tablet, guzzled the ice water, and thanked her heartily. Mrs. Maton went to the cooler to refill the glass.

"Commander," I said to Davy while I swabbed the sweat off my grimy face, "you can send a wireless to the C.-in-C., Alex, with a copy to the Admiralty in London, reporting that this day salvage operations on the large Italian dry dock have commenced." I paused, seized the second glass of water, and gulped that also. Mrs. Maton went for a third one, and Commander Davy, thinking that was all, with a respectful, "Aye, aye, sir," started for the door.

"Wait a minute, Davy," I sang out after him, "there's lots more."

He came back, regarded me quizzically. "Look, Commander, now's your chance to do some real liaison work. I need a couple of big Ingersoll-Rand air compressors for that salvage job. Now your Royal Navy owns a pair right in this town, some big 210 cubic feet a minute air compressors, just what I need, only they are in the hands of Captain McCance in his salvage warehouse over in Massawa. He's not using them at present, it's doubtful if he ever will, but you know McCance. He's like some other—" I paused suddenly, considering the rest of my intended remark undiplomatic, for I had meant to say "Englishmen around here," meaning the Cable and Wireless outfit who were clinging like grim death to title to Building 108. "He's, you know, a regular dog-in-the-manger over everything he gets his hands on," I concluded instead.

"Now, Commander, let's see how good a liaison officer you are. Maybe you can fix it through Captain Lucas, but if you can't, keep going right on up the line to the First Lord of the Admiralty himself in London, if necessary. I want those two big Ingersoll-Rand babies out of McCance's warehouse for as long as I need them on this salvage job, and I want them loaded aboard that Danish salvage ship he's got lying around doing nothing, so she can steam over and land those compressors with her salvage boom on top of our sunken dry dock just where I want them. And I want them landed there by Tuesday morning, that's tomorrow, at the very latest. That *is* all, Davy. You get me those two compressors and you'll have done more for your country than you've had a chance to do since you kept the *Queen Elizabeth* from sinking when the Eyties mined her."

Commander Davy blushed a bit at this reference to his heroism (for which King George had decorated him) but all he said was a very serious "Aye, aye, sir," and departed on his tasks.

I turned to my master mechanic.

"Byrne," I informed him, "all the air compressors we can get won't be any too many for this job—that dry dock is going to take lots of air before she comes up. You get on the telephone to Asmara and see what you can do with Colonel Claterbos in getting me all the air compressors the Army can lay its hands on in Eritrea. There ought to be some Eytie compressors around this country the Army can commandeer. I want them in Massawa tonight so they can go out on that Danish salvage ship tomorrow morning along with those two Ingersoll-Rands Davy is going to finesse for us from McCance."

"Aye, aye, skipper; leave it to me," replied Byrne. "If they're in Eritrea, you'll have 'em." He seized the telephone and went to work to get Asmara; a harder task, I felt, than getting the air compressors. By now I was firmly convinced the best way to solve the long distance telephone communication problem in Eritrea was to shoot half the Italian operators out of hand, put the other half in a concentration camp, and then take an automobile for Asmara whenever a discussion was necessary.

"You can tell anyone who comes in, Mrs. Maton, that I've gone to my quarters for a shower. After that, I'm going to see Dr. Plummer for some ointment for my hide—I feel as if I'd been flayed. I'll be back here in about an hour," and I went out to collect my Italian chauffeur for the ride to Building 108.

When I got back an hour later, feeling a little better for the shower bath and the skin lotions which had been liberally applied all over me, Byrne, his soaked shirt clinging tightly to his back, was expostulating with some Italian somewhere in Eritrea to whom he didn't wish to speak but with whom he had suddenly found himself talking nevertheless. He started jiggling the telephone switch.

"I just lost Colonel Claterbos again," he muttered grimly, "but I'll get him once more if it's the last thing I do on earth. If I ever get back where I can use American Tel. and Tel. again, I'm going to kiss everybody in the company from the President down, on both cheeks, I'll be that glad to— Hello, Colonel Claterbos? Thank God! When did you say you would load those compressors, Colonel?"

I didn't laugh. There wasn't anything about the situation that was funny; having to communicate with anyone in Asmara over the Imperial Italian Telephone lines was the last straw necessary to break completely the spirit of the sweltering talker in blazing Massawa and make him a ready candidate for Mai Habar hospital up in the hills.

Byrne listened for a moment, and then hung up the telephone. His eyes gleaming in triumph a little more than usual, he swung about and faced me.

"Those Eyties nearly threw me for a loss," he announced, "but I made it anyway, even with seven Eytie operators pulling plugs all over Eritrea trying to stop me." He went over to the water cooler, and in quick succession, swallowed a salt tablet and four glasses of water to make up for the sweat he had oozed during his hour's torture on the telephone.

"Now, here's the dope, Commander," he continued when at last he could hold no more water. "Colonel Claterbos says they've got two Eytie air compressors that Colonel Clark of the Ordnance Corps has just finished overhauling in an ordnance repair shop he's fixed up in Asmara. They're nothing to brag about—two 150 cubic feet a minute Eytie jobs, old as the hills, semi-diesel drives—but at least Colonel Clark claims they'll run now he's overhauled them. That's all there is till Colonel Clark and his ordnance men turn out some more, so I grabbed 'em. Colonel Claterbos says he'll have 'em loaded on a big Eytie truck late this afternoon and started down, so you'll have 'em tonight if the truck makes all the curves coming down that mountain road. Where do you want 'em unloaded at this end—if they get here?"

I told him to arrange that with Davy; to have the truck routed into the commercial harbor to the point on the quay most convenient for the Danish salvage tug to swing the Italian compressors with its salvage boom directly from the truck onto its own deck, after it had taken aboard the two Ingersoll-Rands Davy was to procure.

Byrne nodded, then asked,

"Can I borrow your car, Commander? I think I'd better get over to the Royal Naval Base and see how Davy's making out with Captain Lucas."

"Certainly, I won't be using it a while. I'm going out in the *Lord Grey* again to see how they're making out on the Persian dock with that second Greek ship. She's supposed to be undocked tonight. After that I'll stop off on the way back to see how my salvage gang is coming along."

That gave Byrne, who was about to depart, a thought. He paused in the doorway to remark,

"By the way, speaking of salvage, if you want to get anything done on your sunken dry dock, skipper, you'd better get cracking, as our limey friends say. This Naval Base is going to turn into a good imitation of The Deserted Village any day now. 'No pay, no eat, no work.' I've learned enough dago and Arabic to make out that's how the Eyties and the natives around here feel about it. And who can blame them?" Byrne vanished.

I groaned, but I saw no answer to my master mechanic's parting question. To the contractor in Asmara, busy with big schemes, whether a lot of assorted dagos and niggers in Massawa got paid now or next year was too trifling a matter to cause him to cut the Gordian knot of his accounting complexities. And I could do nothing about it save wait for the blow to fall; everything I could possibly say had already been said to everybody involved, directly or indirectly. Thank God, the crew of Eritreans I had on the Persian dry dock had neither been hired nor were they being paid through our American contractor in Asmara. The British contractor with whom I had that deal, with only one Mohammedan clerk on the dock to handle all the lack of paper work and absence of complex accounting, was paying off daily, as was the Eritrean custom with the poverty-stricken natives. What a black eye to the idol of American efficiency!

I dared not venture near the naval shops to see myself how matters stood for fear of being besieged by a mob of hungry natives begging for their pay. Instead, as I followed Austin Byrne out of the office door, I said briefly to Mrs. Maton,

"I'll be out on the water the rest of the day, till after the *Athos* is undocked. Signal me out there if you need me for anything."

CHAPTER

26

OUT ON THE SUNKEN DRY DOCK,
things were moving fast. My new American workmen, less inhibited
than I, who had spent a good part of Sunday in the Torino Bar over
in the old town of Massawa, where they had mingled with British
soldiers and sailors, McCance's salvage crew, various Italians, and
other Americans who had preceded them to Massawa, had picked up
a great deal of fact and fiction about the scuttled wrecks. The wrecks
were all booby-trapped for divers—close an innocent-looking submerged valve anywhere and you'd blow yourself to bits. The wrecks
(but not the dry docks) were loaded with alluring treasures—gold,
cases of champagne, cases of whisky, cases of beer—whatever you were
most interested in. And, of course, they had learned all about the
impossibility of raising the dry dock they were to work on. Some of
them, with firm faith in themselves and their salvage officers, had
made some bets on that with pessimistic Englishmen who had more
faith in British reports than in American ingenuity.

I laughed as I listened to their tales while all of us munched sandwiches and guzzled bottled water during our brief pause for lunch.
Booby-traps in the dry dock? Ridiculous! The idea could never have
entered the minds of the Fascisti, who would have considered them
completely unnecessary. As for the fabulous cargoes in the sunken
ships, that was all moonshine, too. Those ships had all been in
blockaded Massawa harbor a year or more before they were scuttled;
their cargoes, especially cased liquors, must all have been removed
for use ashore long before they were sunk.

As for the impossibility of raising the dry dock, they had it under
their feet now; two of them, Barry and Doc Kimble, had already
been down after me and had seen it for themselves. They all knew
the damage and they knew my plan for the dock. Only one question

was asked regarding the dock's raising. Bill Reed asked it.

"Can you get any air compressors, skipper?"

"Four of 'em, Bill! Two big new Ingersoll-Rands and two old Eytie compressors, total air capacity 700 cubic feet a minute, will be on deck this dock tomorrow," I replied confidently. "They'll push the water out from inside this dock ten tons a minute, excepting always air leaks."

"It's in the bag then, boys," said Reed gleefully. "We'll make monkeys out of them limeys over in the Torino Bar who're betting we can't raise it."

Lunch didn't take long. In a few minutes everyone was working again and in spite of no shelter at all from the burning midday sun, all hands, stripped to the waist for ventilation, were hard at work. By late afternoon, when I had to go over to the Persian dock to undock the *Athos,* both of the long air mains had been strung and the pipe coupled up, running the complete length of the dry dock on each side. In addition, most of the small branch lines to feed air to the sixteen separate side wall compartments were piped up, tapped into blank steel flanges which I had had made in the machine shop to go in place of the six-inch mushroom vents atop each of those compartments. These blank flanges killed two birds with one stone— they sealed off the air vents from the side wall tanks, and at the same time gave us an easy connection for pushing compressed air down into the tops of those tanks.

Laying the cross-connection air main from the starboard to the port side of the dock across the eighty feet of water between, was harder, but even that was finished also by evening. To carry it, Whitey Broderick and the Maltese riggers had strung two half-inch wire cables, supported on each side high above the side wall decks, across the water. From these cables they had hung a wooden foot walk across the water, giving us both a suspension bridge to get from one side to the other without a boat, and a support for our athwartship air main. It wasn't long before some wag draped a sign on the side of the foot walk marked,

"George Washington Bridge. New York, 13,000 miles," with an arrow beneath it pointing westward.

Meanwhile, the divers had closed all the airports in the upper part of the submerged hull and plugged all of the other openings they could find in the side walls, scupper holes mostly. Into such openings they sledged home tapered wood plugs, mostly six-inch-diameter ones, that Fred Schlachter had turned up for us on a lathe in his carpenter shop. We made no investigation as to the purpose of any hole we found in the submerged side walls; so long as the hole was round and the diver could get a plug to fit it, a sledge hammer promptly drove it in hard after he had cleaned away the barnacles from inside the hole so the tapered plug would seat tightly enough to hold air.

I undocked the *Athos* at 6:00 P.M. and then went back again to the sunken dock, to which all the American salvage crew returned also after an hour off for supper ashore. Our electrician, Charley Hoffman, had salvaged from the electric shop ashore a small gasoline-driven generator which he hooked up to the electric light wires and the lights which he and the Italian electricians had strung on impromptu poles erected by Buck Schott and the Arab carpenters. When we got back from supper, the little generator set was already chugging away and our crudely hung lights were already on. We needed them, for in the tropics the twilight is brief and night falls early.

We worked till 10:00 P.M., putting in a fifteen-hour day, with all hands soaking up drinking water like sponges and exuding it from their pores like sieves. I drank twelve bottles of water, three whole gallons, myself. When finally we all knocked off, all the piping was completed, ready to connect up the air compressors; and all the openings the divers could find, several dozen, were plugged. There would be plenty more holes discovered, I felt sure, and innumerable leaks, but they could wait until the compressed air hit them. After that, they would make their locations plain immediately by the streams of air bubbles rising through the water.

It was a very hot and a very weary crew of salvage men that embarked with me on the last trip ashore for their last night ashore in some time, but a very satisfied one. Every man felt he knew that dry dock now and that it belonged to him, but he also knew that once he compressors started, the salvage job was going to be an around-he-clock performance for every one of them.

We turned to again at 7:00 A.M., but I had to dock the third vessel on the Persian dock before I could join the salvage crew. By that ime, the Danish salvage ship was feeling its way cautiously alongide the nearly submerged port side wall of the sunken dock to avoid vhat we knew must be a hidden menace to navigation close aboard there. For in scuttling the dry dock, the Italians had also capsized overboard the two large traveling cranes which ran on tracks atop each side wall of the dock. We could tell where they had gone over the sides—there were two huge gaps in the pipe railings guarding the upper decks. One gap was a little forward of amidships on the port side outboard; there the port crane had been flipped over into the sea, and looking down in the water, a vague shape ten or fifteen feet down could be seen near the dock, probably the top of the steel crane boom. The salvage ship coming in had to avoid that or it would tear its bottom out.

The starboard crane, from the evidence of the broken railing on that side, had been tipped inboard into the dry dock itself, where completely invisible in the water, it lay with its boom broken, on the floor of the dock, constituting no present danger to anybody except the divers who might get fouled up in it.

That Danish vessel had its quarterdeck completely covered with air compressors—there were the two shining Ingersoll-Rands and two somewhat dilapidated-looking (by contrast) Italian Fiats. Commander Davy had evidently functioned 100 per cent as a liaison officer—he had got both the desired compressors and the ship to transport them —no simple task I perfectly well knew. I learned later he had persuaded Captain Lucas to order McCance to turn them over to us, not allowing him any option as to whether he wanted to or not. Captain Lucas had personally guaranteed that the compressors would immediately be returned should McCance have need of them. Over that guarantee, I never worried. I felt sure I should long since be finished with them before McCance, at the pace he was going, could possibly have any need of those compressors, more especially as it was evident McCance showed no signs of knowing the value of compressed air in salvage work; he was wholly relying on pumps in what he was attempting in the commercial harbor.

Under my directions, the Dane backed slowly in, stern first against the port side wall, while we on the dock handled lines for him. Shortly his salvage boom was swinging aboard us one after another, two compressors weighing several tons each—nasty objects to have to handle aboard had we not had his husky boom to do it for us. After landing the two compressors, one Ingersoll-Rand and one Italian Fiat alongside our new air main compressor connections, he cast loose and steamed slowly around to the starboard side of the dock, where he likewise deposited the other two.

That completed, the only bit of salvage work in months his fine ship had been permitted to do, her Danish captain gave us a friendly parting wave. From his wistful expression he would have given his right leg for a chance to remain and help. Then in English which surprised me, he sang out,

"Good luck to the Americans!" as he steamed clear of us and headed back through the wrecks to his berth inside the commercial harbor and more enforced idleness.

It didn't take long to couple up the air compressors—we used no pipe, only lengths of two-inch rubber air hose to give us flexible connections so the vibrations of the pounding compressors wouldn't shake our rigid air mains to pieces. In less than an hour after they had been landed, we had fresh water in their radiators, fuel in their tanks, lubricating oil in their crank cases, and both Ingersoll-Rand machines running, throbbing rhythmically as they pounded compressed air into our mains and then into the tops of the side dock compartments.

I breathed a deep sigh of satisfaction—the full-throated bass of those massive Ingersoll-Rands hammering compressed air into the sunken dock beneath my feet was heavenly music to my ears—I wouldn't have traded it for any symphony on earth!

Getting the two Italian compressors going was another matter—they were a primitive semi-diesel drive type requiring the insertion of a slow-burning chemical cartridge into the tops of some of the engine cylinders to start combustion while somebody cranked them over by hand. I had never seen anything like that before, neither had any of my salvage crew, and we should have wasted hours figuring out how to start them had not one of our Italian mechanics who was watching our strong man, Buck Schott, in his futile efforts at cranking, come to our rescue.

Tony, which was the only name I ever knew him by, though I doubt that was really his name, knew no English at all, but he knew all about those Italian compressors and indicated by signs that he would be happy to show us. He looked into the compressor tool box and found there a package of small square sheets of paper, apparently impregnated with some chemical. Rolling one of these into a tight tube, he unscrewed a cap from on top an engine cylinder, inserted one end of his newly made cartridge into a recess inside the cap, lighted the other end. It didn't burn, it merely glowed dully like a piece of Chinese punk. Tony screwed the cap, glowing fuse and all, back into the cylinder top and then started to crank furiously.

It was lucky Tony had a stout right arm, a stout heart, and oceans of determination, for he used up half a dozen cartridges, all his Italian cuss-words, and most of his strength on the crank before finally that semi-diesel gave in, coughed sporadically and then decided to keep on rolling over. Tony, naked to the waist and a limp wet rag by then, stepped back proudly.

"*Bono*, Tony!" I exclaimed (that and "*no bono*" being all the Italian I knew) as I patted him enthusiastically on his dripping back. "I'll put you in charge of these compressors! Now you go over there," and I pointed across the suspension bridge to the starboard side where alongside the quivering Ingersoll-Rand the other Italian compressor stood idle, "and you start that one, too."

Tony smiled cheerfully at me and nodded that he understood what was wanted.

"*Si, signor Commandante!*" he beamed as he started across the swaying footpath. "*Immediamente!*"

I had no doubt Tony meant immediately, and certainly his intentions and his will were of the best, but Tony was in for a battle. Before the other compressor also was running, he had used up practically all the chemical cartridges that had come with both compressors and Tony was a wreck, hanging gasping over the rail.

"Huh," I remarked to Lloyd Williams, who also was in bad shape having spelled Tony on the crank of the second machine, "let's hope these damned Eytie compressors never stall! It's a day's work for a man just to start one of 'em. Now you see Tony gets promoted right away to foreman for this and find someone who can tell him that in Italian. That'll give him seventy-five lira a day instead of fifty—if he ever gets anything. He's worth all of that and lots more to us out here. And, Lloyd," I concluded, "send someone ashore to rustle up a lot more of those chemical cartridge sheets. We're going to need 'em by the dozens."

Hour after hour under the hot sun, the laboring compressor pounded away, pushing in the compressed air. It was going to take a whole skyful of air, rammed down into that dry dock, before we could push out enough water from inside it to make any impression. My major concern was whether the smoking compressors would stand up long enough under the terrible operating conditions to do the job. With the only air available for cooling them the hot blast atmosphere of Massawa far over 100° F., how effective would their radiators be in keeping the engines and the compressors cool enough to avoid overheating and seizing of the pistons?

They weren't any too effective, we swiftly found out, when all the radiators shortly started to boil. After that, we learned that those radiators gulped down more water than we did, and it had to be fresh water, too, all brought from shore. Shortly we had to provide a 1000-gallon tank to store fresh water on the dock for radiator re-filling, and the refilling job kept the four Italians whom I gave Tony to help him, busy all the time. Aside from that, and replenishing frequently the crank-case oil (for the hot engines also used that up at a terrific rate), we had at first no great trouble—the Ingersoll-Rands ran beautifully. The Italian Fiats, however, as befitted their age and antiquated design, vibrated very badly; so badly they would shortly have waltzed themselves off the dock into the sea had we not chocked them solidly beneath their wheels and then lashed them securely down to the deck.

Our real troubles soon began. Before enough air pressure had even built up inside the dock compartments to register anything on the pressure gauges I had installed atop each compartment, we began to find air leaks in the upper decks above water. They weren't hard to find—the air could be heard hissing gently as it escaped back to the atmosphere, under practically no pressure at all.

My respect for the craftsmanship of Mussolini's shipbuilders back in Italy where that dry dock had been built hardly six years before, went sharply down. Seams in the steel plates forming the top decks and connecting seams between the decks and the side walls, all of which should have been tightly caulked in any ship structure, were either caulked in slovenly fashion, or in some spots difficult to reach, had never been caulked at all. The Fascist inspectors on the construc-tion of that dry dock should all have been shot for allowing such leaky steelwork to be palmed off on il Duce, but there it was and now it was my headache, not Mussolini's. The top decks of the dock were leaking like sieves—no air was being contained inside and none could be till we had stopped those leaks.

All hands, divers, electricians, carpenters, pipefitters, were knocked off their normal tasks and turned to caulking seams in the steel plates. Ordinarily this was ironworkers' work, but I had none such in my own crew. So every mechanic, regardless of his trade, so long as he was a mechanic and had any skill at all with tools, was put on the task. Armed with hammers, such chisels as we had aboard, and more that I had hastily sent out from shore, they all began caulking steel plates—not a pleasant job, for those steel plates, under the vertical rays of the Eritrean sun beating mercilessly down on them, were soaking up so much radiant heat they were too hot to touch with the bare hand.

Even the Eritrean natives, accustomed to going barefooted all their lives on the desert sands and with soles to their feet tough as elephants' hoofs, couldn't stand those sizzling steel plates. I noticed they were binding their bare feet in burlap or old canvas, and frequently soaking them in the sea as added protection, before they walked the hot grill of the deck plates of that dock.

But hot steel or not, we had to caulk. So seated on improvised pads of wet canvas or wet burlap, anything at all at hand available to prevent burning our sternsheets as we sat on deck, we all caulked. Seams which were not too badly open were sealed in the usual way, by forcing the steel edge of one plate down tightly on the plate beneath with hammer and chisel. Some spots where the plates were so badly fitted (especially at the forward corners of the dock) as to make that impracticable with the primitive hand tools at our disposal, we sealed up as best we could by caulking soft lead strips into the open joints and then hammering the steel hard down on the lead with sledges.

We gained on the leaks. By early afternoon we had stopped enough of the worst ones on deck so that the dock commenced to hold some air and slight indications of pressure began to register on the gauges. As the afternoon wore on, by ounces almost, the needles on the pressure gauges drew away from the zero marks; each ounce of pressure meant the water inside the dock had been forced down about two inches.

I had no plans of that Italian dry dock at all—of its construction, its design, its weight, or of its size. I had to judge everything by what little of it I could see on the surface and by such crude measurements of it as divers could take of it as it lay on the bottom. Nothing of this gave me any very accurate data as to how much it weighed how much air I should have to pump, or how far down I should have to force the water in the side walls before the dock became buoyant enough to break free of the bottom and commence to float up. There was a great deal of guesswork in the problem—all I really knew at the moment was that at last I was starting to push some water out.

At 6:00 P.M., except for Tony who wouldn't leave his compressors, and me, and three Americans who stayed aboard also to keep an eye on matters and to help service the compressors, all hands went ashore in the *Lord Grey*. The Italians and the natives were through for the day. The salvage men, after they had procured their suppers, were coming back with cots, mattresses, and mosquito nets for all of us and some food for those remaining aboard, prepared thereafter to live on the dock.

The sun went down, darkness quickly fell, our electric lights twinkled on, glowing cheerfully on the quiet waters of Massawa harbor. It didn't cool off perceptibly; the air stayed just as hot as during the day, but at least now we could lay aside our sweat-soaked sun helmets, spared for a few hours the fierce rays of the sun boring in on us like drills. And caulking on the steel plates, which all of us continued after supper, was no longer quite such an ordeal; with the sun gone, the steel soon changed from sizzling to merely hot.

At 10:00 P.M., we quit, except for the watch set to service our quivering air compressors all through the night. All the air leaks in the decks we could detect, even with soap and water, had been practically sealed except for very minor pinholes. That more leaks would develop when the air pressure inside the dock built up substantially, I very well knew, but for the present at least the surface leaks were licked. What underwater leaks there were, we should learn when the water inside the dock was lowered appreciably.

Lloyd Williams and two men took the first night watch. The rest of us, roasted to a medium rareness where we had been sitting while caulking, and well seared elsewhere all over our hides, sprawled out on mattresses or cots spread at random on deck; we would sleep under the stars till our turns came to service the compressors.

I picked out a spot forward on top the starboard side wall, where if we had any breeze off the water a few inches away, I might get it. There, as far away from our hot compressors as I could get and still remain on the dock, I set up an iron cot, spread out my mattress, rigged my mosquito net, and crawled in, soaked as I was, not even removing my waterlogged shoes.

It wasn't bad there. Overhead, I could look directly up at the marvelous display of tropic stars, the constellations burning in unearthly splendor against the blackness of the night. I loved the stars and never tired of admiring them. Now to my aching body they were a solace from on high as slowly the heavens above revolved, lifting yet new stars into sight—a spectacle to raise the spirits of the most distressed. To salvage men (who have more need of faith than any shepherds ever had) as well as to shepherds do

> "The heavens declare the glory of God."

Then to add to the glory of that scene, there was a symphony of sounds about, blending together harmoniously—the gentle lapping of the sea against the steel walls of that dry dock both sides of me, the deep bass of the Ingersoll-Rands, the higher-pitched pulsing of the Fiats, all throbbing rhythmically away in the night.

Soothed by sight and sound, but not comforted any by the sweltering air inside my net, I rested somewhat but I didn't sleep any better than in my room—there was too much of uncertainty wound up in the problems of that dock for my mind to relax. How many days would the compressors hold out? How bad would the underwater leaks prove? How long could my new men, not so accustomed to the Massawa heat as I now was, last before they cracked up on me? What else, completely unexpected, as always happens on any big salvage job, was going to smack us before we got that dock up?

At 1:00 A.M., I rolled out from under my mosquito netting, and with Al Watson, diver, and Jay Smith, carpenter, to help, relieved Lloyd Williams and his two companions on the compressor watch.

"All the compressors have just been serviced, Commander," Williams told me. "Once an hour is enough to check on oil and fuel, but watch those radiators! If the water gets below the top hose connections, it'll all boil out like a geyser before you can get to it with a water can! Keep 'em well filled up! And the ice in that wooden oven we've got for a refrigerator is all gone; all you'll have to drink till tomorrow is going to be nice warm water. There's a few dozen bottles of that we left you."

"O.K., Lloyd, and pleasant dreams. We'll take care of it," I assured him. "And thanks for leaving us anything to drink. We'll try to do as much for Bill Reed when he comes on."

Al Watson and Jay Smith, very different personalities, I learned on that watch, were both exceptionally able and willing men, keeping a sharp eye on the compressors and their needs and leaving me little to do except roam the tops of the side walls, crossing our swaying footbridge from time to time, while I studied with a flashlight the pressures showing on my collection of sixteen air gauges. They were, of course, scattered, each gauge directly on top its own compartment, so that by the time I had made one round only over the dock to inspect them all, I found I had walked more than one-third of a mile in the process.

The sight of those gauges was, however, heartening. The pressures were building up; we had shoved the water down inside the dock perhaps two feet. So far, the salvage wasn't going badly.

In my rounds, I paused a while each time to talk to Al Watson, since it was important to know my divers, their powers of observation and judgment, and how much confidence I might place in what they said they saw and did on the bottom. Al Watson I found a very keen person, inquisitive, and observant, crisp in his speech, which was unusual for a diver, and as salty in his expressions as any of them. He wasn't big, a hundred and fifty pounds perhaps, but he had a splendid athletic figure which showed off well in his scant costume— smooth, hard muscles and a streamlined pair of shoulders and hips that made me think he must have been an expert swimmer. I later learned he actually was—the finest in Massawa. Before that watch was over, I felt sure I had a good diver in Al Watson which soon he proved himself to be—one of the best I ever saw. Meanwhile, he was tending the two compressors in his care with all the attention a fond mother might bestow feeding her infants.

Jay Smith, carpenter, tending compressors on the other side of the bridge, was different. Tall and thin, quiet and slow in speech, much older than Watson, he took everything more phlegmatically. He somehow didn't seem to fit the picture amidst a lot of smoking machinery, but he was tending it carefully nevertheless, learning, I suppose, that a salvage man has to do everything required from painting to pipefitting.

So my three-hour watch on the lonely dock dragged along as I plodded endlessly the one-third mile course round the decks, armed always with two things—in my left hand a bottle of warm water from which occasionally I drank from the neck, and a flashlight in my right to avoid the mass of obstacles littering the decks of that sunken dock and particularly the naked bodies of the salvage crew sprawled aimlessly out on their mattresses, sleeping restlessly in the hot night.

Bill Reed, with cadaverous-looking Jess Enos, diver, and big Buck Schott, carpenter, to help, relieved us at 4:00 A.M. Everything was going well (too well, I thought to myself, for a salvage job). I warned them about the radiator water and sympathetically informed them they would have only warm water to drink themselves—we had left them still a few bottles in the iceless icebox. And with that I tumbled back under my mosquito net, where flat on my back, I could once again regard the stars—almost a new-looking set which a three hours' revolution of the heavens had brought upon the scene.

Uneasily I tossed about on my damp mattress, wondering a little about myself and my own chances of standing Massawa much longer. I had lost twenty pounds since my arrival six weeks before; I couldn't afford to lose any more. Neither could I afford to take things any easier. My assistants were willing enough but they were neither seamen nor salvage men, and if I slowed down, everything ashore and afloat around the Naval Base would slow down also. With everything just getting under way, this was no time for a slow-down—not with the war situation what it was in Libya. But several little things had impressed on my mind what Massawa was doing to us—first my leather belt, stiffened and rotted by the salt sweat soaking it all the time, had disintegrated completely several weeks back, leaving me dependent at the moment on a piece of halyard to hold up my shorts, which more than ever needed holding up: since I had shrunk so much about the waist, my khaki shorts were far too loose. Then my leather wrist watch strap (the second one in six weeks and the last one I had) had cracked in half that afternoon, all the life rotted out of the leather from the same cause—salt. I had been lucky enough to have caught the watch as it dropped, or it would have gone overboard to make yet another salvage job for me; now it reposed in my pocket. I puzzled vaguely where in Eritrea I could get another strap for I badly needed the free use of that watch.

Then there were my shoes—not the ones I was wearing, those were so salt- and water-soaked and cracked as to be a disgrace to any hobo —my better ones stowed in my closet in my room in Building 108. The day before I had had to warn Ahmed not to keep them in that closet any more—they were all covered with green mold from the never-ceasing humidity. Perhaps if they were exposed daily to the sun and then kept under the bed, they might do better.

And all my undershirts were going fast. When I wore one, which was rarely now, it usually came off in handfuls when I tried to get the sticking garment off my wet back—the rotted materials could no longer stand any strain.

Finally, there was my knife—to a sailor, especially one wound up in salvage, a most important article. It was of good steel but not stainless; I hadn't been able to get a stainless steel knife before I left New York. My knife was always rusty now, the blades corroding so fast I had practically worn them away trying to keep them sharpened up, so when I had to cut a line in a hurry, I could cut it. It wouldn't last much longer. Where in Eritrea was I going to get another knife to replace it?

These little things were all symptoms only, but worth regarding. Leather, cotton, steel, and flesh—Massawa was fast rotting away everything I had; would I last myself, I wondered, till I had finished the task I came for? There were many Army officers already in the Middle East, but General Maxwell had not a single naval officer under his command to send to take my place should I crack, or to spell me a while so I shouldn't.

Wound up in these musings, but finally lulled by the soothing lapping of the waves and the throbbing of the compressors, I dozed off.

Seven A.M. brought the usual flotilla of Arab dhows sailing before a slight early morning breeze to the Persian dock, loaded with half-naked Eritreans to begin their day's scraping and painting. But it didn't bring the usual boatload of Eritreans and Italians to the sunken dry dock to begin the day's salvage work there.

Not till it was an hour late did the *Lord Grey* arrive alongside, and then it was empty except for the two Maltese riggers who formed its night crew. While the engineer held it in with a boathook, the coxswain clambered aboard with a note which he had for me.

It was from my master mechanic and was very brief.

> Come ashore immediately. There's trouble.
> BYRNE.

I sprang into the boat, singing out to Captain Reed,

"Take charge, Bill! Keep those compressors going. I may be ashore quite a while!"

"Aye, aye, Commander! Leave 'em to me!"

The coxswain was back in the boat also.

"Shove off!" I ordered sharply. "Ashore!"

The engineer pushed the heavy boat clear, and the coxswain gave him the ahead bell. We started over the glassy surface of the harbor, for now with the sun well up, the early morning breeze had died away completely.

"What's the matter?" I asked the Maltese coxswain, who spoke good English, once we were well under way. "Where's the day crew of this boat? Where're all the workmen?"

The coxswain shrugged his shoulders.

"No Italianos came to relieve us, so we stayed on. All night on this boat and no breakfast yet. I'm hungry. Then no natives came to the quay to bring out, so we waited for them till Mr. Byrne gave me that message to bring out. That's all I know, Commander. When do we get relieved so we can eat?"

"I don't know, either," I confessed. "Stay in the boat when we get ashore and I'll see you get some breakfast sent down. I'll get you relieved as soon as I can find out what's wrong with the regular day crew."

Byrne was waiting for me on the wharf with my car which apparently he must have driven himself since there was no sign of a chauffeur. He wasted no time.

"It's come, Commander. No workmen. Not an Eytie, not a native in the Base this morning. Everything's dead. They've all gone on strike! What do you want done about it?"

We drove up to the Naval Base from the water front, Byrne at the wheel, and stopped in front of the machine shop building, our busiest shop always. I got out and looked in. It was completely deserted. Austin Byrne, master mechanic, gloomily surveyed all his idle machines. Not an Italian machinist was in sight.

Next door was the carpenter shop, normally manned by Arabs with Sudanese for laborers. Fred Schlachter, foreman, was standing in the open doorway; I glanced past him. The Arabs and the Sudanese had acted no differently than the Italians—not a machine was going, not a native was in sight.

"It's the same all over the Base, Commander," said Byrne. "Nobody came to work. And it's the same with the contractor's building operations, too. None of his gang showed up either, except his Americans, so he's still going after a fashion."

So the strike had come at last! Seeing that neither natives nor Italians had any organization, and the natives were of many diverse races, it was amazing in its completeness. But on second thought, perhaps it wasn't so amazing. There is nothing like completely empty bellies to compel unity of thought; it required next to no organization under those circumstances to get spontaneous action to force some pay, at least. Our men hadn't been paid since they started, many of them over a month before.

I trudged through the dust with Byrne back to our office building. Except for the usual Sudanese sentries about, I saw nobody. The Naval Base was as silent, as dead, as deserted, and as useless as that day I first arrived in Massawa and was dumped out on the front steps of that same office building.

Inside the door on the first floor was Pat Murphy, construction superintendent for the contractor, and a group of his American foremen, of whom he had plenty, discussing the strike.

"Well, Commander," said Murphy, who I believe had previously protested the pay situation to his employers in Asmara as strongly as I, "now we've got a strike. Got any ideas on the subject?"

Before I could answer, I started to get profane advice from some of his foremen, demanding action which apparently they had been pressing on Murphy. The gist of it seemed to be that I should get the British to give us soldiers to break the strike. They had two regiments in Massawa—one of Sudanese, one of Bengalis and Sikhs, both fine fighting regiments. With those we could easily force the Italians at least, many of whom were prisoners of war and the rest enemy aliens subject to concentration camps, none of whom had any ordinary civil rights, to go back to work at the point of a bayonet. That should terrify the Eritreans sufficiently so they would return also.

I shook my head.

"I'm doing nothing, Pat, except report this to Colonel Claterbos in Asmara for his action on your company. That's the only spot bayonets may do some good. I'm *not* asking the British here for troops; I'll get out of Massawa myself first. I want work out of these men in Massawa, not sabotage, and sabotage is all we'll get with bayonets in this case."

I continued up the stairs. So far as I could judge from his expression, Pat Murphy was of the same mind.

In my office, I found Mrs. Maton. Byrne looked very glum as he stared out the rear windows at his deserted shops.

"See if you can get Colonel Claterbos in Asmara, Mrs. Maton," I said to her, then turned to Byrne. "Any of your workmen been to see you about this before this walkout?" I asked.

"No, Commander," he said, "nothing but the usual breaking off of some Eytie or some Eritrean whenever I passed through a shop, to beg me for some pay. It wasn't any worse yesterday than any day. When quitting time came last night there wasn't anything different, no demonstrations at all. They all jammed into the trucks for the ride back to the native village, Edaga Berai, and Massawa. Only this morning when the trucks with the night crews of drivers went to meet them at Edaga Berai causeway, there just wasn't anybody to meet, and nobody's shown up round here since. You just can't help sympathizing with these skinny natives—when they say they're hungry, it means they're starving. I don't blame 'em for staying home to scratch round for something to eat," Byrne concluded, and returned to gazing morosely at his idle shops.

I looked out southward towards the Royal Naval Base; there were no shops there but Captain Lucas always had a considerable force of natives working on ground maintenance. Apparently everything was normal with him; there were all the usual signs of activity around the British buildings, with the usual natives working on the grounds at their usual pace. Only the Americans were the object of the strike.

"Colonel Claterbos, Commander Ellsberg," said Mrs. Maton. She had succeeded in getting him in jig time, for once.

"Hello, Colonel, this is Ellsberg," I said. "We've—"

"You've got a strike down there, I hear," he broke in on me. So the news must have traveled fast to Asmara.

"Yes, just what I expected," I replied. "Complete tie-up, every shop's dead. Queer strike, though—no delegates, no ultimatums, no demands, no nothing—just no workmen. The U.S. will get a hell of a black eye out of this all over the Middle East. The news will be in Yemen just as fast as the first Arab dhow can sail across the Red Sea, and then God knows what the Axis propagandists will do with it on the radio from Rome and Berlin! Starving Mohammedans strike because those friends of democracy, the Americans, gyp them out of their pay! Italian prisoners of war risk death to quit working for pluto-democracy rather than be swindled! You know how Goebbels will dress it up! It's a natural for him and this is one time he won't have to lie! What can you do about it, Colonel?"

"Only get after the contractor," replied Claterbos grimly. "And I will! He's got to settle this."

"There's only one way to settle it," I advised. "Make him quit talking about payrolls and start paying! It doesn't have to be everything; a couple of weeks' pay now and an honest promise to pay the rest in a few days or so and then no more delays in paying off, will get them back. Only do something quick! I've got a salvage job on the fire, and ships to repair on the dry dock and no shops to do anything with! Put the screws on 'em; let 'em know there's a war on!"

"I will," said Claterbos. "I've sent for the contractor already. That all?"

[221]

"That's all!"

I hung up the telephone with relief, surprised to have finished my first Asmara telephone call without a broken connection. I wondered how Colonel Claterbos would make out; back in the United States the contractor would long since have been in bankruptcy for failure to pay off on any pretext at all, the way he was doing here.

I sat back and thought. There was a great deal of work for everybody in Eritrea in all the shops—for the British, for the local Massawa authorities, for the contractor, for the ship in dry dock. Everything would have to wait now till the strike was settled, though it would be awkward explaining, especially to the British forces. But that ship in dry dock couldn't be delayed—she was due to come off that night. I wondered what we had for her.

"Come on," I said to Byrne, "let's get over to the machine shop. I've got to find out what you've got in way of work for that ship on the dock. We can't hold her up."

Austin Byrne, thin, gray, and eagle-eyed, reminding me every time I saw him of what I thought one of the old Roman senators must have looked like, led the way to a battery of lathes. Some partly turned valve disks were held in the chucks.

"I've got only some valve parts left now," he said, "some disks and some seats for two sea chests. They were to have been trued up this morning, so they could go back by noon."

"What can you do about it, Byrne?" I asked. "I can't flood the dock down without those valves and she's got to go off. Another ship's here already from Alex to go on tomorrow."

"Finish 'em myself, I guess," said Byrne. "Have you got any machinists to reinstall 'em?"

"There's only Hudson, that English engineer on the dry dock. He's a good machinist; he could do it, with his Persians to help him. That crowd's on a different payroll; they haven't quit."

"Good enough, Commander. I'll have these valve parts down on the pier by one o'clock; I'll stay right with it till the job's done." Byrne quit talking, started up the nearest lathe, and went right to work facing off the worn valve disk held in the lathe. I went back alone to the office.

"Mrs. Maton," I said, "there're two Maltese manning the *Lord Grey* haven't had any breakfast yet. Can you get over to the employees' mess hall, get some coffee and something for 'em to eat, and then get

[222]

back here with it? I'm going out again immediately, but I can't let 'em go out hungry. They've been on all night and now they're going to have to stay on a long while yet. The *Lord Grey's* the only boat we've got. I can't tie her up without a crew."

"Yes, Commander," answered Mrs. Maton. "I'll be right back with something, if I have to cook it myself."

Just then the telephone rang. Mrs. Maton lifted the receiver, then said,

"Captain Lucas, Commander Ellsberg."

I took the instrument, while Mrs. Maton departed.

"This is Lucas, Ellsberg. Commander Davy's here and he has just informed me all your Eytie workmen and the natives have left you flat. Sorry to hear it, old chap. Is there anything I may do to help?"

"No, Captain. It's just as you've heard it; we're all tied up in the Naval Base, but I'm all right out on the water. We'll keep the dry dock going and hold up no ships for Alex. Thanks for your offer, but whatever's to be done to settle this has to be done in Asmara. Colonel Claterbos is handling it there. Oh, come to think of it, there is something you can do. Will you fix it with Davy while he's there to furnish a British naval crew for the *Lord Grey* right away? I'm in a bad way for seamen for her while this lasts."

"It will be a pleasure, Ellsberg. And if there's anything else, let me know."

I hung up the receiver and mopped my brow. The *Lord Grey,* our only harbor transportation, would not much longer be one of my worries.

Mrs. Maton, loaded down with a bag of sandwiches and a can full of hot coffee, was soon back. I went out to the dry dock in the *Lord Grey.* While I steered, the crew fell ravenously on their belated breakfast. I couldn't leave the sunken dock for long, and what few excursions I might make from it would mostly be to the other dry dock to see that our program there did not slack down, strike or no strike ashore. I could do nothing ashore—there was one way only of settling the strike—payment in part (or in full, if possible) immediately and no more delays in regular pay days in the future.

Only when the contractor was actually ready to pay off was it necessary to get in any of the Naval Base employees, natives or Italians, to parley with them; neither the Naval Base nor any of its officers could take part in any discussions with the workmen on any other basis.

I imagined that with a disgraceful strike with international implications tying up an American Naval Base on his hands, our civilian contractor might not now be so unhysterical and calm as previously in ironing out the pay accounts; he would find some way of hastening matters.

I disembarked alongside the sunken dock, with a final order to the coxswain to see Davy immediately on his return and get the promised relief crew for the Maltese. The boat shoved clear for the return trip.

Bill Reed and Lloyd Williams, both very curious over my sudden departure, were at the rail to meet me as I clambered back aboard. I told them the sad news—for some time, we should have no laborers at all to assist us; the thirteen men in the salvage party, plus the three of us, would have to carry on by ourselves.

"Well, for Christ's sake, anyway call back that boat!" exclaimed Reed. "Don't you know we've run out of ice and the drinking water's all gone, too? We can get along without those strikers but not without ice water! Not on this job!"

I came to with a jolt. This was really serious.

"Boat ahoy!" I sang out at the top of my lungs to the *Lord Grey*, already a hundred yards off. "Come back here!"

The startled coxswain put his helm over sharply, started to circle back. When the boat was close enough, I shouted to him,

"Don't come alongside! When you get ashore, strike or no strike, get half a ton of ice and at least a couple of hundred bottles of water down on the wharf and send them out, four bells and a jingle! We've got nothing to drink here! Never mind how you do it! Get us that ice and water right away!"

"Aye, aye, sir!" he acknowledged. Without slacking its speed, the boat finished its circle and kept on for the shore, while I swabbed my brow and looked apologetically at Reed. "I'm damned if I see how I ever forgot about the water, Bill, even with a strike shoved in my lap. Can't we drink some of that water for the compressor radiators till some more drinking water comes out?"

"Naw," said Reed, "we've tried that already. The Eytie tank it's in is snafu. That water stinks! I guess we keep on going dry. And I'm dying of thirst already! God, how I wish I had a can of nice cold beer!" He looked at me reproachfully with his one good eye. "And I was telling Lloyd here when you came back, you'd certainly bring us a boatload of ice and water; you knew it was all gone. What kind of a salvage officer are you, anyway? I thought that was what you were going for when you shoved off in such a sweat! A strike! Hell, what's that against some water on this job?"

I had nothing to say in rebuttal. Reed was right; I was thirsty already myself and I had been inside a building most of the time with several drinks while I was gone. How must my men feel who had been out in the sun half the morning with no water at all? I'd be lucky if they didn't want to heave me overboard.

I looked around. Only three of the compressors were running. One of the Eytie compressors, the Fiat on the port side, had stopped. In front of it, Tony and Buck Schott were taking turns cranking, trying to get it started again.

Buck, who was the most powerful man we had, was a giant, not in height exactly, but at least in circumference. Naked to the waist, his protruding stomach stood out magnificently; he resembled that way the carved images of Buddha, or perhaps more precisely those massive Oriental wrestlers who are tremendous in their girth. He had powerful arms also; his biceps were in proportion to his waistline. Alternately, first with his right, then with his left, he spun the crank of that Fiat each time a new chemical fuse was screwed into its head by Tony; his whole body, covered with sweat, positively glistened in the sun as he labored.

But he had no luck. The recalcitrant Fiat refused to start. With a bang that nearly bounced it overboard, Buck angrily flung the crank down on the deck, and flopped heavily back against the rail, gasping for breath. He was through.

Tony, whom I was surprised to see on the dock at all since he must have known his countrymen were going on strike and he might have gone with them the night before or at least have left with me in the boat that morning, picked up the crank. Tony, no weakling, had neither Buck's avoirdupois nor his strength, but he did have more finesse. Alternately he inserted burning fuses and then cranked madly, but there was no start in that Fiat. Finally Tony, in a frenzy himself, smacked the crank to the deck, and with both fists shaking menacingly, danced up and down, cursing the compressor. Then he retrieved the crank and once more went at it. All to no avail. At last, too exhausted even to curse, he let go the crank and sagged back alongside Buck.

"I shouldn't wonder that machine's so worn the compression's bad,"

I muttered to Williams. "Don't let anybody else bother with it till night, Lloyd. Maybe when it's cooled a bit, we can get it going again. And when his tongue has quit hanging out, you try to make Tony understand he can go ashore in the next boat. I don't want to take advantage of him just because we've still got him aboard. He can quit with all the other strikers. Make sure he knows I won't hold it against him."

Williams nodded, and I passed along to make a tour round the dry dock to read all the pressure gauges. They were the first encouraging news I'd had that morning; the pressures were rising steadily all over the dock; already we had reached two pounds on every tank. That meant the water inside the dock was continuing to go out; now it must be down four feet below the level of the sea outside. In spite of leaks, in spite of the loss of one compressor, we were gaining.

By the time my inspection was finished and I had returned to the port side, I found all hands, including Tony, clustered beneath the awning over the empty icebox, trying to escape the sun. No work was going on; the thirsty men were all past doing anything further till some water came aboard.

Lloyd Williams indicated Tony.

"We had a long conversation, mostly with our hands," said Lloyd. "Tony knew all about the strike, but he's not striking; anyway not while this dock is on the bottom. He wants to stay and watch it come up—you haven't got a stronger fan in the world on this job, Commander, than Tony. He says you let him stay and he takes care of the compressors, night and day, all by himself—he doesn't want any help. That's how Tony feels about, leaving. I told him you'd let him know."

I twisted round and looked at Tony. He knew he was the subject of the discussion and was eagerly watching me.

"*Bono,* Tony. You stay," I nodded at him.

Tony smiled gratefully as if I were doing him a great favor in letting him stay to kill himself over those sizzling compressors, and wan as he was, picked up the watering can by his side and sidled out from under the awning into the broiling sun to water the compressor radiators. He might be ready to collapse from thirst himself, but his pets were not going to go without a needed drink.

In an hour the *Lord Grey* was back in charge of three British sailors, who landed it most expertly alongside, not a surprising feat since it was a Royal Navy boat. But it was the cargo, not the crew, which interested us—there were six huge cakes of ice and stacks of bottled water rising to the gunwales. Never was a boat unloaded any faster than that one nor water greeted more eagerly. Hastily the ice went into our box, but nobody waited to cool any of the water; warm as it was, off came the cap the instant each man got his hands on a bottle and down his parched throat went the water.

After a free-for-all lunch of cold canned willie, topped off with more water, everybody went looking for leaks again, but except for the forward corners on both sides of the dock, nobody found anything serious. But those corners, where the deck plate, the side plate, and the end plate met were bad. We had already caulked all the lead we could get into the seams, but the results were far from perfect. I put Jay Smith on one side of the dock and Buck Schott on the other to keep hammering away at the joints with caulking chisels, trying to make them tighter.

In the early afternoon, the *Lord Grey* came by again with the sea chest parts for the ship in the Persian dock. I boarded her and went over with them to that dock to tell Hudson he'd have to install them.

Hudson, a short, stocky, broad-faced Englishman with a thick accent I had difficulty always in understanding, was much surprised at the request, but very willing to undertake the job. Everybody on the Persian dock knew of the strike; they had consequently not expected to see those essential valves for days yet and had given up any hopes of undocking on schedule, though the Eritrean painting crew had not slacked down. Hudson started talking to his head Persian. In a few minutes the newly machined valve parts were on their way down into the vessel's engine room, and I had Hudson's promise that by late afternoon everything would be installed and the ship ready to go off.

"No more repair jobs on this dock till the strike's over ashore, Hudson," I warned him as I left, "only cleaning and painting. You tell the skipper of the next ship we take that if he opens up anything on his hull, he'll have to put it together himself before we're ready to flood down, unless he wants the sea coming in on him. I can't count on getting any more work done ashore."

"Aye, Commander, I'll see to that," Hudson assured me. After telling the dockmaster, Spanner, that he was to start flooding down as soon as both Hudson and the painters were through, I left. This was

May 13, the sixth day since the dock had started operating, and we would be finishing our third ship. We were doing all right. As the *Lord Grey* pulled away, I looked down the length of the dock at the horde of Eritreans beneath the partly painted hull, chanting and dancing as they painted. They had not slowed down any yet; there was still all the savage madness of the jungle in their chant. I wondered if I could get half a dozen tom-toms somewhere to help the illusion.

Back on the sunken dry dock, I watched the gauges as the afternoon dragged along, and only the pounding of the compressors and the metallic ring of steel on steel, as Smith and Schott banged away at the leaks, broke the silence. No diver was dressed; no air leaks had shown up in the water yet, requiring attention.

Except for Tony and Lloyd Williams, watching the compressors, the two men working on leaks, and Hoffman, the electrician, rigging additional lights, everyone else was in what scant shade he could find, resting after two strenuous days and nights. I congratulated myself that I had pushed the job so hard the first two days while we had plenty of help. All the tasks requiring mule-hauling we had managed to get done while still we had all the laborers; now, I imagined, the little salvage crew left could handle what more troubles turned up while we pushed down compressed air and waited for results.

At 5:00 P.M., Spanner started to flood down the other dock and I went over to watch, intending to let him handle the undocking. Nothing unusual happened. The ship floated smoothly off the blocks as the dock went down. Spanner, more excitable in action than I liked to see any dockmaster, handled her out and clear with nothing going wrong, however. From there, Lieutenant Fairbairn, already on the ship's bridge, took over and with the *Hsin Rocket* and the *Pauline Moller* as usual towing, piloted her out of the harbor to the outer roadstead from where she would sail for Alexandria in the morning. Altogether, docking was getting to be a completely routine operation now for all hands.

When I got back on the sunken dry dock, it was getting dark and supper was in progress. We had rigged up an informal galley just forward of our port side air compressors; Hoffman had wired it for electric percolators and a small grill. There was no cook; everybody was welcome to cook for himself or to use a can opener as he preferred, so far as our stock of canned goods and other provisions from on shore permitted. The menu was far inferior to what was served in the contractor's messhall ashore for American employees, but so far as I was concerned, it beat what I usually got at the Royal Naval Officers' Mess. And I shouldn't wonder that Tony, who was also invited to help himself, found it considerably better than his accustomed Italian fare.

Darkness fell, our scattered lights came on, and we started our second night on the sunken dock. An unearthly silence enveloped both the harbor and the Abd-El-Kader Peninsula, broken only by the throbbing of our three air compressors. The gleam of our quivering lights was the only illumination visible anywhere over the dark waters of the harbor. The heat was as oppressive as ever; now that the sun was gone, not a breath of air stirred anywhere. Gripped in the heat, the silence, and the darkness, I moved cautiously about the wrecked decks, unable to escape the eerie feeling of being part of a scene wholly out of this world.

A little later, we made another attempt to restart the stalled Fiat compressor, but it was futile, in spite of cranking by half a dozen volunteers. Rather than wear everyone out, I called off the attempt, determined to wait now till the strike was over and I could get some Italian diesel expert out from the machine shop. At any rate, I doubted we were losing much; probably the Ingersoll-Rands were pushing down practically all the air that was being compressed.

By 8:00 P.M., the pressure in our compartments had risen to over four pounds and here and there the deck plating could be seen to be bulging slightly from the air pressing up below. Reed eyed these evidences of weakness dubiously, then asked,

"How much pressure do you figure you need to start her up, Commander?"

"There's no telling exactly, Bill. I don't know the weight of this dock, and I can't even guess how much it will take to tear loose if she's stuck in the mud. But I figure that around six pounds should give her buoyancy enough to start lifting. She probably won't start with any less; how much more it may take, nobody knows."

"Well," said Reed, "if she's bulging on four pounds pressure, I'm damned if I know how she'll act with six. We ought to start shoring those weak spots down right now, but there's nothing we can shore against up here except the sky. What are you going to do?"

"Let her bulge," I suggested. "We can't do anything else. I've looked

at those spots; there are only a few of them where the stiffeners be
low decks are wide spaced. That flat plating can bulge quite a bi
yet without anything letting go. I'm not concerned."

We set the same compressor watches as the night before. Tony in
sisted he would stay up alone all night and tend the compressors, bu
I refused to let him. He was, however, permitted to take Jay Smith'
place on the mid-watch, since Smith, worn out from his efforts in th
fierce heat at caulking leaks, looked all in.

Most of the men turned in early that night to try to catch up o
lost sleep. Since I slept very little anyway, I continued on my round
reading the air gauges till nearly 11:00 P.M., by which time the pres
sures had risen to about five pounds all around and everything wa
still holding together.

At 11:00 P.M., leaving the watch to Lloyd Williams, I crawled un
der my mosquito netting, to rest at least, if not to sleep, for I had lot
on my mind. What progress, I wondered, had been made that day ir
Asmara on ending the strike? If it lasted very long, with Rommel al
the while getting closer to Egypt to encourage them, we would giv
the Fascisti still at large among our workmen excellent ammunitior
for a campaign of sabotage and disaffection that could hamstring th
Naval Base very effectively. Our success so far had rested in grea
degree on the co-operation of our Italian mechanics; if I lost that
was at least badly waterlogged if not wholly sunk, for I had no Ameri
can mechanics at all in the naval shops.

But the throbbing of the air compressors brought my strayin
thoughts back to matters closer to my cot. I thought I could detec
an erratic note in the pulsations of our sole remaining Fiat. Yes, i
was so—that laboring semi-diesel was beginning to miss fire—it prob
ably wouldn't last much longer. Perhaps if it stalled, Tony might hav
more luck in restarting it than he'd had with its mate. I hoped so.

Once again as I tossed uneasily about in the stifling heat, I dreamil
watched the stars. Being close to the Equator, practically the whol
panorama of the heavens was unfolded above me as the earth slowl
revolved—the southern constellations as well as the northern ones t
which I was more accustomed. The southern stars, I thought, wer
overrated; there was more beauty in the constellations always visibl
in the northern hemisphere. I speculated idly on why God had seer
fit to bestow most of His blessings north of the Equator—in the skie
as well as on earth. But I saw no answer.

[230]

One A.M. finally rolled round, and armed again with my bottle of water and my flashlight, I rolled out to begin again my night watch. This time I was backed up by Melvin Barry, diver, and Tony when I relieved Williams, who pointed out to me the erratic firing of the last Fiat before he turned in.

"She'll probably fold up soon," commented Lloyd. "I guess she needs another overhaul after two days' running."

I indicated to Tony that he should pay special attention to that machine, but there was no need. Already he was fiddling with the fuel injection, trying to get smoother firing.

I started my initial tour of the pressure gauges, going aft on the port side first. The gauges were cheering; the needles were hovering around the six-pound marks on the dials. We had done a fair job, evidently, on caulking leaks. I judged we must be retaining inside the dock to push out water through those vast holes in her bottom at least half the compressed air we were pushing in at the top.

When I went forward on the port side wall to check the gauges there, I was surprised to find Bill Reed huddled on deck in the darkness, intently looking over the side at the water. Reed heard me coming, and glanced up at me as I turned my flashlight on him.

"Commander," whispered Reed, as if afraid a louder tone might upset matters, "look! See that big mussel shell just above the water line on that vertical guide roller? Half an hour ago it was just in the water; now it's an inch out. The dock's starting to come up!"

I looked where Reed pointed. There was an unusually large mussel clinging to the guard roller at the dock entrance which Reed evidently was using as a marker. It was undoubtedly wet, though it was now a little clear of the surface and out of water.

"It doesn't mean anything, Bill," I replied after sighting it. "The tide's probably fallen a little and uncovered it; you know while there's not much tide here, there's still a little—maybe a foot or so rise and fall."

"Tide, hell!" whispered Reed emphatically. "She's coming up, I tell you! It was high tide when you undocked that last ship; then it fell till midnight when it was low. I've been watching here ever since you turned in. At midnight the tide turned and she was rising a little on them oysters till half an hour ago when the water quit rising on them and started to drop! She's rising!"

I sat down on the hot deck plates alongside Reed and carefully sighted his impromptu marker, that large mussel shell dimly visible in the glow of our electric lights on the water. I swung my flashlight on it to illuminate it more sharply. Reed was right about the tide, I remembered. Such as it was, it should now be running flood, not ebbing. In a few minutes my heart began to pound. That mussel shell was slowly but without question increasing its distance from the glassy surface of the lake of water between the two dock walls. The impossible was happening before our eyes! My scheme was working; only two and a half days after we had begun operations, that "long, difficult, and probably unsuccessful" operation on which "all idea of salvage had been abandoned," was showing success. The terribly blasted large Italian dry dock *was* coming up!

CHAPTER

28

By MORNING, THE SCENERY IN THE naval harbor of Massawa had changed appreciably. Anybody looking out over the water could see (and even without looking, could smell) the difference. The Italian dry dock already protruded several feet above the water, a very prominent object, and was steadily rising fore and aft.

On board the dock, my salvage men were practically delirious with looking at their handiwork—no very beautiful object, crusted with a heavy layer of barnacles and mussels which began to stink horribly when the sun hit them—but beautiful beyond any words in the eyes of those few who had struggled to make the sight possible.

There is no need to go into the details of the intensive salvage work necessary around the clock over the next few days to keep the dock rising; they would interest only salvage men. A few only will be mentioned.

The second Italian Fiat compressor folded up in the heat and quit on us that morning. Tony broke his arm trying to start it again when the crank suddenly snapped back and struck him. But he refused to quit; after a brief journey ashore where Captain Plummer reset the broken bones, splinted his arm, and then bandaged it up for him, Tony was back on the rising dry dock with his arm in a sling, tending the two panting Ingersoll-Rands which nobody could drive him from. They were his children; with his one good arm, he patted them affectionately. On their continued hammering down of air rested now the continued rise of the dock; Tony, sure no one else could do it as well as he, would not from then on, night or day, let anyone else service those two all-important machines. His brief periods of rest he snatched by flopping on the hot deck alongside his charges. And every time I came by him, Tony pointed out excitedly to me the new inches the

[233]

dock had risen since my last round, fearful lest I should not have observed them.

The strike ashore lasted till next day, when it was ended by the contractor sending down a heavily guarded car from Asmara loaded with money, something that could as well have been done weeks before. I didn't see it; Byrne told me there was nearly a riot trying to keep the hundreds of assorted natives and Italians lined up in some order so they might be checked off as they were paid. Most of them (not all) went back to work, once they had their money.

The ending of the strike had now a special and a new interest for me. If we on the dock were not all to be asphyxiated by the stench rising from mussels rotting beneath an incandescent sun, the foul sides of the dry dock had to be scraped continuously as it floated up. If ever those huge dock walls, high as four-storied buildings, long as two city blocks end to end, covered all over with barnacles and mussels, were exposed, unscraped, all at once to the sun, the decaying mussels would shortly drive all hands from the dock.

I had to have a big gang of natives to scrape off barnacles as the dock, day by day, rose further. With the strike over, I could get them Soon all other noises on the dock, including the compressors, were drowned out by the cries of Eritreans, working all around the dock walls from floats, scraping away for dear life.

There would, of course, have been an end to the further rising of that dry dock after a couple of days, once the compressed air was forced so far down inside the side walls as to reach the level of the holes in the blasted floor of the dock where it could escape freely into the water still covering the whole floor—except for one thing. That one thing I knew of from the beginning and had counted on to finish the lifting for me. The eighth and last bottom compartment forming the floor of the dock at the stern was undamaged. The bomb placed there had failed to explode, so the British had reported on their survey, and so I had found in our own diving.

There were over 1200 tons of buoyancy in that one undamaged but still wholly submerged bottom compartment, fortunately for me located at the very stern. When the buoyant side walls had lifted the dry dock off the bottom as far as they could and began to blow compressed air out in geysers through the bomb holes in the seven damaged bottom compartments, I went to work on that undamaged stern compartment. It was first isolated from all the other compartment by closing off the valves connecting it to the common piping systems of the dry dock. Then we expelled practically all the water from inside it by putting more air pressure on it than on any of its mates to force the water out through its still open sea valves.

That did the trick for us—the buoyancy in that stern compartment not only lifted the dock floor at the stern completely out of water, but pulled the two compartments forward of it up far enough for work on their floors also without diving.

From then on, everything was certain. Working in the open, where a man can do ten times as much effective work as he can in a diving rig, all hands went to town. With my salvage mechanics, with my divers, with all the Arab carpenters and Italian mechanics I could drag out of the reopened naval shops, we patched temporarily with wood and canvas the exposed hole in the floor of the dock compartment next forward of the stern so it would hold a moderate air pressure on top. Putting more air pressure in that compartment pushed out enough more water through the open hole in its bottom to lift the dock still farther, exposing more of the damaged floor forward, where the process was repeated on such compartments (not all of them) as we needed to lift the dock.

In that way, we walked ourselves forward along the dock floor, patching temporarily one huge hole after another while the bow of the dock steadily lifted further.

Meanwhile, there was the problem of the unexploded bomb in the stern compartment. Once we had the stern well exposed, I went back to the manhole in the floor of that compartment. Before the dock came up, the divers had found that manhole cover off, lying near the opening. We had replaced it and held it down by a few nuts to make the stern compartment watertight on top during the lifting operation. Now that manhole (too small for a diver in his bulky rig to get through) was again exposed to the air.

Cautiously I opened up our air main connections to that stern compartment to let the air pressure inside it vent down to atmospheric so we could enter it. There was a vast quantity of compressed air in that compartment; it took quite a while to whistle out. But when at last all signs of inside air pressure were gone, we unbolted the manhole cover in the floor and looked down inside.

There, some fifteen feet below, resting on the bottom plates of the dry dock, was the unexploded bomb. Jess Enos and I, neither of us very big in girth, both stripped naked and went down through the opened manhole into the hold on the dock to remove the bomb.

Once I was standing in the few inches of muddy water still covering the bottom plates of the stern compartment, without touching it I examined that unexploded bomb with great respect. It was a vertical steel cylinder several feet high, with the biggest diameter that would go through the manhole, and it was still standing on its end. In its head, masked a little by slime covering everything, I could see where the detonator charge and the primer had been screwed in, and from that primer still hung some ten or fifteen feet of waterproof detonating fuse.

What had caused that bomb, alone of all eight the Fascisti had placed in the dock, to misfire, I never knew then or ever. All Jess Enos and I were concerned about at the moment, however, was that we should do nothing to cause that armed bomb, 200 pounds of TNT, to explode right under our noses.

It was obviously too heavy for us to lift, even together, and push up through the manhole fifteen feet above. So very gingerly, while Jess tilted the bomb a bit so I could get under it, I slung it in a manila bridle kept well clear of the firing mechanism in its head, and looped the slack fuse in a small coil on top of the detonator to get it out of harm's way.

Then while half a dozen men heaved slowly from the topside, Jess and I, down in the hold, carefully guided it upward and out through the manhole, with our lives staked on our care in seeing that in that lift we kept both fuse and whatever type of firing mechanism the Italians had installed in that bomb, clear of any contact that might detonate it.

We got it safely out of the hold, through the manhole, and into the *Lord Grey*, where it went immediately ashore to be turned over to the Royal Navy's torpedo specialists. They took it some five miles inland into the desert, where from a respectful distance they fired it. In spite of having been submerged over thirteen months, it went off with a roar that shook distant Massawa so badly as to cause all the natives and Italians to rush for air-raid shelters, thinking Massawa was being bombed again from the air, this time by Rommel's planes.

We worked in the muck and the slime covering the floor of the dock. In diving rigs when it was necessary to get inside some of the still-flooded hold compartments to plug bomb-damaged bulkhead but mostly half naked when we could work out of the water, divers and salvage crew struggled night and day to make the dock bottom watertight enough so it could float without the continuous running of the air compressors to hold it up.

We built a number of moderate-sized wooden cofferdams which we slid under the bottom of the dry dock to seal off temporarily the holes blown in the steel bottom of the dock. This turned out to be not as hard a job as I had anticipated, for invariably we found that the holes in the bottom plating of the dock, while large, were still smaller than the holes torn in the steel floor overhead. To help us even further, we ran into the odd situation that in every case, the bottom plating, instead of being blown down as might have been expected from an internal explosion, was blown *up* and into the dry dock. This freak of explosive effect was a godsend. It left no protruding steel below the smooth bottom of the dock to interfere with the quick installation underneath the dock of our wooden cofferdams—a very great blessing. I had in Massawa then none of my underwater cutting torches needed to burn away the interfering steel had there been any.

And so we came to the end of our salvage job on the evening of May 19, nine days since we had started.

In nine days the large Italian dry dock was fully and safely afloat from end to end, all salvage work concluded. As salvagers, we were through with it. One American officer, two American supervisors, and thirteen other American divers and mechanics, with only two old diving rigs and nothing else brought from America, had lifted that impossible to salvage dry dock in nine days. To have lifted it in nine months would have been considered a remarkable performance by any salvage officer. With only such equipment as had been lying round Massawa for long months, available to anyone who had the vision to try, that "long, difficult, and probably unsuccessful" operation was ended in nine days, the shortest salvage job I had ever tackled.

It proved to be a nine days' wonder in the Middle East (and in some other places).

CHAPTER

29

MAY 20, THE DAY FOLLOWING THE
completion of our salvage job on the large Italian dry dock, turned
out to be a red letter day for us in Massawa in many ways, not all
of them pleasant.

I had spent the previous night ashore in my own bed, the first night
since May 11. When I turned out on the morning of the twentieth,
the two Cable and Wireless managers seized the opportunity (the
first they had had to get hold of me in over a week) to serve an evic
tion notice on me. I and all the other Americans must get out of
Building 108 by June 1. Where we went, or whether there was any
where we could go, was none of their concern; on June 1, Cable and
Wireless wanted the whole of Building 108, though it had no more
men in Massawa than it had had seven weeks before when I had first
moved in.

I went to see Captain Lucas of the Royal Navy about that imme
diately; there wasn't a place in Massawa available to us as quarters
Captain Lucas knew of the situation, I found; he was terribly dis
tressed over it and had objected on his own. But the Cable and Wire
less men had insisted; the building had been promised them, they
wanted it June 1 to start rearranging it into suites for themselves.

All Captain Lucas could do, he said, was to recommend strongly
and immediately to his superiors that the building be given to the
Americans, with some other provision made for the two Cable and
Wireless men there and such others as might ever come later
What would happen, he didn't know. But I knew by then that Cable
and Wireless was a powerful British corporation with excellent gov
ernment connections in London; I feared the worst in spite of Cap
tain Lucas' recommendations.

Somewhat down in the mouth over this scandalous reward for our fforts, I rode from the Royal Navy headquarters to my own office. Mrs. Maton greeted me there with news of a different nature. She had just had a telephone call from up in the hills. Major General Russell Maxwell, commanding all American forces in the Middle East, was in Asmara. About 11:00 A.M., accompanied by various high ranking officers of the British Army, by Colonel Chickering, his Chief of Staff, and by Colonel Claterbos, he would visit Massawa for his first inspection of the Naval Base.

Immediately on hearing that, I looked out the windows over the Abd-El-Kader Peninsula and the array of ex-Italian buildings covering it. The scenery didn't suit me; it never had since first I had seen the place. To the south, floating high above everything, was a British White Ensign, the only flag in sight; there wasn't an American flag anywhere.

I had tried previously to rectify that situation by getting a large American flag suitable for flagpole use, from the Army with the usual Middle East results—there was none available. I had refused to hoist as a flag over our Base, one of the little handkerchiefs I could get. Within sight of that large British ensign, it would only serve to make the United States look ridiculous in the eyes of both Eritreans and Italians.

Now something had to be done; I couldn't let General Maxwell on his first visit to one of his posts gaze on a situation where that British flag seemed to be covering everything in sight.

There happened that morning to be an American freighter, the S.S. Oregon, unloading in the commercial harbor; one of the first to reach Massawa. I seized on Herman Weinberg, sheetmetal foreman, a very forceful person, ordered him posthaste to Massawa in my car to present my compliments to the captain of that freighter and beg him, as a patriotic favor to us orphaned Americans, to lend us for that day only the largest American flag he had on his ship.

Then I got hold of Austin Byrne, told him to gather up my Maltese riggers, and erect immediately on top of the highest building we had (the three-storied end of the electric shop) the longest pole or substitute thereof he could find in the Naval Base. He was to approximate in height above the ground that flagpole, ex-Italian, which the British were using. I warned him he had only a few hours in which to get results. Meanwhile, once he had that job started, he was to canvass the multitude of American workmen the contractor had on his construction work and see if he could find anybody who knew how to blow a bugle. I would borrow the bugle from the Royal Naval Base, on which errand Commander Davy immediately departed.

In less than an hour Weinberg was back with the flag—a large ensign, fine for my purpose, which Weinberg told me was not a loan. The merchant ship's captain had insisted on making me a gift of it; he had another for ship's use.

In less than two hours, Byrne had the flagpole up—a real flagpole which he had found in the dust alongside the carpenter shop. It wasn't so long in itself (which was fortunate when it came to securing it in place) but on top of the building, it stood about as high as the British pole a quarter of a mile off. And he had a bugler, a young American, not so long before a Boy Scout, whom I sent into a closed room to do some practicing on the British bugle till I wanted him

At 10:00 A.M., I shut down all the naval shops briefly and mustered all hands I had ashore—Americans, Eritreans, Arabs, Somalis, Sudanese, Maltese, Italians, and all the diverse races we had—on the hot baked plain in front of our highest building.

There with the few American and British officers present at "Salute," and all the others in such attitudes of respect as their various customs dictated, our American flag was first unfurled to the Massawa breezes. As the bugler feelingly sounded "Colors," it was swiftly run up to the masthead. It floated out beautifully—to those Americans who had struggled along with me in torrid Massawa to make a naval base of the sabotaged junk we had found beneath where that lovely flag now streamed out, a thrilling sight. It was the first American flag to fly over an American naval station in Africa; perhaps the first to fly over an American naval base on former enemy territory anywhere in the world in this war.

As the last note of "Colors" faded away into silence and our hands came down from "Salute," we felt very proud of it. Our American Naval Base now looked American, ready for its Commanding General's inspection.

About 11:00 A.M., four dusty Army cars bearing General Maxwell and his party from Asmara hauled up at the Naval Base. As we had neither any guard, any band, nor any means of firing a salute, the military formalities of receiving him and the two British Major Generals accompanying him had to be reduced to hand salutes on the part of myself and Captain Plummer.

But General Maxwell was little interested in military formalities. He and Colonel Claterbos, together with his British guests, Major General B. O. Hutchinson, commanding His Majesty's Forces in the Sudan; a South African Major General, representing Field Marshal Jan Smuts, Premier of the Union of South Africa; Brigadier Stephen Longrigg, who had just taken over as British Military Governor of Eritrea; and their staffs were interested only in seeing what was going on in Massawa which might be of use in helping to stop Rommel.

Before lunch, I escorted them through all the naval shops, every one of them humming with activity with all the lately sabotaged Italian machines busily engaged on war materials with which to smash the Axis. (I thanked Heaven our strike had ended some days before or I shouldn't have had a machine running.) In each shop as we entered it, I introduced General Maxwell and the accompanying British generals to its American shop foreman.

I couldn't help laughing inwardly as in shop after shop, that group of generals raised their eyebrows in puzzled astonishment over the heterogeneous collection of P.O.W.s and assorted natives that they saw running the machines. At last they asked me where were all the Americans they had heard of who had rehabilitated that Naval Base? I had to tell them there might be plenty of Americans elsewhere in Eritrea, but they had already seen all the Americans who had ever had anything to do with making good the sabotage in Massawa; you could count the lot of them on the fingers of two hands and have some fingers left over. Austin Byrne, James Lang, Paul Taylor, Herman Weinberg, Pierre Willermet, Fred Schlachter, and myself—that was the whole story.

We had lunch, served in a sweltering atmosphere that I knew even General Hutchinson from the Sudan was not accustomed to, and which nearly melted away the others acclimated only to the Egyptian and Libyan Deserts, and even cooler spots in Africa. After lunch, I packed everybody into the *Lord Grey,* by no stretch of the imagination any admiral's barge, and took them out on the water to cool them off a bit as well as to show them what was going on afloat.

The major object of interest, of course, was the salvaged Italian dry dock, salvaged only the day before. Its vast bulk, standing out low above the harbor waters like the Great Pyramid over the desert, completely dwarfed the Persian dry dock on its starboard side. General Maxwell insisted on boarding the newly raised dock, undeterred by the barnacles, the mud, and the miscellaneous wreckage littering the dock floor, and the British generals went with him. There were some startled gasps as they saw the huge holes, twenty feet across some patched with wood, some still unpatched, which gaped in the floor of that dock, now a major repair job in any shipyard. Gingerly they skirted the keel blocks scattered about the dock, ducked under the traveling crane lying a barnacle-crusted wreck in the middle of the dock where the Italian saboteurs had dumped it from the starboard side wall above, and finally threaded their way to the bow of the dock.

To save them the very messy journey back over 200 yards of still muddy deck, I had the *Lord Grey* run around the dock to the bow end to pick them up.

I had to admit they weren't as good-looking a set of generals when they left the dock as when they had boarded it, but they certainly seemed impressed. That dry dock, still considerably festooned with barnacles and covered with mud, with startling evidences of violent explosions all over its floor, looked like a mountain which had suddenly been spewed up from the ocean floor by an eruption. It was enough to impress anybody.

From the salvaged Italian dock, we moved over to the Persian dock, where one of Admiral Harwood's Mediterranean armed supply ships, a British vessel for a change, was lifted out of the water, the seventh ship we had taken on that dock in thirteen days. Here our visitors were more than impressed; they were incredulous. That good salvage man could have lifted that Italian dock in a hurry they were willing to believe, having seen it; that anybody could get Eritrean natives to work the way those Eritreans before them were working was more than anyone who knew Eritreans could believe even when he thought he was seeing it. Brigadier Longrigg and General Hutchinson, who knew Eritreans best, opened their eyes wide in astonishment at those dancing natives, and wanted to know what I had done to them. But I was non-committal. Longrigg, as Military Governor of Eritrea, was the last word on native wage scales. I had no desire at all to do other than let that sleeping dog, my incentive wage plan, keep on sleeping. I laughed it off with the statement that it was so damnably hot in the dry dock, they were just trying to stir up a breeze under the ship, and we all moved on. It *was* hot in the dry dock.

We got back into the *Lord Grey* and ran out of the harbor to give everybody a good look at the wrecks lying at the entrance of the naval harbor, in the commercial harbor, and in the south harbor. As we left the south harbor on our way back, having seen them all, the South African Major General, with what I thought was at least no overstatement, observed,

"Messy lot of wrecks the bloody Eyties left you, old chap. Likely to keep you hopping a while yet, eh, what?"

It was a long ride back in the slow *Lord Grey* from the south harbor. The Major General from South Africa, ruminating on what he had seen, again commented after a while,

"Blessed lot of work here yet. Any way I might help you, Commander?"

"General," I assured him earnestly, "there are lots of ways. But what I need worst now is men, mechanics; and when it comes to mechanics, what I need worst is some ironworkers. I haven't got a damned one! You saw the wreck of that dry dock; she's salvaged now, but if I'm ever going to repair her, I need ironworkers. Where I'm going to get any, God knows!"

"Ironworkers, eh? Well, I'm on my way to our army in Libya; when I get there, I'll see what I can do about it." He relapsed into silence. I promptly forgot it; Libya was a long way from South Africa where alone he could get workmen. A very polite gesture on his part, but what good could a general on his way to join the fierce fighting west of Tobruk, do me?

The *Lord Grey*, once more manned by her regular Italian crew, lumbered along on her journey over the Red Sea. I was having a rest, anyway; it was the first day in seven weeks I was not wrestling, afloat or ashore, with some part of the work in my dual command. We rounded Sheikh Said Island. Then in the open sea again we were shortly passing on our port side the entrance to the commercial harbor. Standing prominently out in the narrow entrance was the wreck of the *S.S. Crefeld*, a German steamer, lying on her side where in an attempt to plug the bottleneck entrance, she had been scuttled. Fortunately the Nazis and the Fascisti between them had bungled the task; she had swung round enough in capsizing to leave a narrow but workable channel into the commercial harbor for even the largest ships entering.

The wreck of the *Crefeld* drew all eyes as we passed. The conversation in that boatload of Army officers became quite animated, the topic, naturally enough, being the sabotaged condition in which the Fascisti had left all Massawa on the surrender. Major General Hutchinson, of the Sudan forces, whose Sudanese troops had helped to take it, remembered well its depressing state when first they had entered Massawa to find everything apparently an irretrievable wreck. He better than anyone else present was in a position to judge what had happened since. Leaning aft toward me on the thwart on which he sat, he said, "Commander, I know of no one who is doing as much to help win the war as you."

That, I thought, was laying it on a bit thick, but it was a pleasant compliment anyway. That General Hutchinson really meant it, however, I soon found out, for in an official letter which he sent to General Maxwell that night, he repeated his statement in practically the identical words.

Soon we were back at the Naval Base pier with the afternoon nearly gone and all hands disembarked. It was time for the inspection party to start back for Asmara if they were not to traverse that hazardous mountain road in the darkness.

General Maxwell, who had had very little to say all day long apparently too busily engaged in observing everything to talk much now drew me aside for the first discussion I had had alone with him since he arrived.

"Commander," he said crisply, "there's too much required here for any one man to handle alone without breaking down. You need naval help. Tell me what officers you need and I'll have them ordered here from Washington."

"Thanks, General," I replied, "I agree with you, but there's no use asking Washington. I was told in the Navy Department when I was ordered here that I was the only officer who was going to be sent; wasn't going to get any assistants. They said they had no officers to send; I wasn't to expect any later. No use your bothering over it; I do the best I can alone."

"Ridiculous!" countered General Maxwell. "I can't leave you here this way! Tell me what you need, not what the Navy won't give you. Getting them for you will be up to the War Department."

"Aye, aye, sir, but I'm not hopeful. What I need for Massawa seven naval officers: one lieutenant commander as general assistant two lieutenants for engineering assistants, two lieutenants as h assistants, one lieutenant as docking officer, and one lieutenant as supply officer and paymaster. That's the least I need to run this Base; it's not much. Captain Lucas over at the Royal Naval Base next door has ten British naval officers from commander down to lieutenant to help him, and he's got no ships, no shops, no docks, and no salvage to look after—just, piloting, communications, intelligence, and guard duties. That's the story."

General Maxwell noted down my list.

"I'll get on this the moment I get back to Cairo," he said. "No question you need them badly."

I stood at "Salute" as General Maxwell and the others climbed into their cars. In a moment, with friendly farewell waves from my visitors, the four Army cars shot out of Massawa, bound for the cool mountain plateau.

I wondered as I watched them go, if anyone had noticed the flag. No one, British or American, had commented on its presence. I was sure, however, I should have heard comments enough had there been none. But comments or no comments, it gave me a lift as I looked up at those beautiful stripes and that starred blue field waving over my Naval Base. Even in God-forsaken Massawa, it made us still a part of far-away America.

CHAPTER

30

Not the most important but at least the most pressing problem I had on my mind was where my few Army officers and myself and all the American supervisors, both for the Naval Base and for the contractor, were going to sleep shortly. (The little cottage, once assigned to me as quarters, had long since been reassigned to Commander Davy, liaison officer, as his quarters.) For in a few days, in spite of Captain Lucas' recommendations and their approval by Admiral Harwood, the British C.-in-C. in Alex, the answer on the housing problem came back negative from London. We must all get out of Building 108, the promise to Cable and Wireless was to be kept, the building given to them exclusively unless they voluntarily agreed to some other arrangement, which in Massawa their representatives refused to do.

Where could we go? There was no building in any condition for occupancy, least of all any intended as quarters. Of the other abandoned Italian buildings, I picked out Building 35 as the least objectionable—a two-storied masonry building used once by the Italians as an engineering office building. It was vastly inferior in location, ventilation, and coolness to Building 108.

It had no water supply, no plumbing, and especially no shower baths, without which life in Massawa was intolerable. (Normally, when ashore, I took from three to five shower baths a day to keep myself going.) It stood as far from the sea as was possible on the Abd-El-Kader Peninsula, in the middle of a dusty plain where no sea breeze ever penetrated, but plenty of fine dust always did. Still, it was that or nothing. I arranged with Pat Murphy, construction superintendent for the contractor, to take some of his men, particularly pipefitters, off building construction elsewhere and do what he could to pipe up that dilapidated Eytie office building with showers and toilets and cut it up inside into rooms.

Pat estimated that at best the job would take him three weeks. The sole concession I could get out of the Cable and Wireless nabobs in Massawa was to defer our eviction date from June 1 to June 14. Murphy dragged some men off the job of building a badly needed new and larger shipfitter shop for me at the Naval Base and turned them to on the conversion job on Building 35.

To add to my distresses, now that June was approaching and the already unbelievably hot weather was getting still hotter, we who were working outdoors began to suffer from a tropical affliction. It wasn't any of the dread diseases we had all been inoculated against— typhus, yellow fever, typhoid, tetanus, cholera, smallpox, or even malaria, against which there was no inoculation. It was none of these; it was something peculiar apparently to Massawa—prickly heat. I had always laughingly regarded prickly heat as something you dusted a baby's delicate skin with talcum powder for, against minor skin irritations in the summertime.

In Massawa, we found prickly heat was no laughing matter, to be eased by talcum powder. There was no easing at all of the Massawa variety. Bathed all day and all night in perspiration, a raw irritation burst out all over us and stayed there, giving our skins the appearance of a coarse grade of Scotch pebble-grained leather. Talcum powder was no palliative for the terrible itching—the sweat washed it away immediately. Lotions and salves did no good either against the salt sweat exuding continuously from every swollen pore.

There was no help for any man working in the open except to grin and bear it if he could, or to bear it without grinning if he couldn't. But for everyone working on salvage, especially the divers, the situation was even worse. The mud, the filth, the decaying barnacles, infected the prickly heat eruptions, causing major boils at random on the body, nearly driving the victim wild. Captain Plummer did all he could, lancing boils, bandaging where possible, but that afforded negligible relief. All my salvage men suffered continuously the tortures of the damned.

I was lucky even to conclude the swift salvage of the dry dock before my divers began to crack. Long, lanky Jess Enos went first. With his whole body a mass of unbelievable sores, his arms swollen to twice normal size, Jess was carted off to Mai Habar Hospital up in the mountains, a sad case. He never came back to us. Months later, with his original skin all gone and what had taken its place from beneath looking like something run through a hot-calendering machine, he was shipped back to the United States.

Next went Melvin Barry. Between the prickly heat and the heat in general, aggravated by the terrible diving conditions, his blood pressure shot sky-high and his heart showed signs of trouble. He went to join Jess at Mai Habar; soon he also was on the way home. My first salvage job had cost me two out of the only five divers I had; that wasn't all. "Tex" Powell, carpenter, gashed his leg badly, slipping on a float in the half-raised dock. The deep gash landed him also in Mai Habar. A month later, however, when he came out of the hospital, he had had enough of Massawa and never came back to us either. Instead, while convalescing, he got himself assigned temporarily as paymaster in Asmara where he could wear a gun while traveling in the contractor's pay car. That gun simply fascinated "Tex" and he refused ever to come back to work in Massawa. "Whitey" Broderick, rigger, quickly had enough, too; he was transferred to a job ashore where life was not so exacting.

So in about two weeks I had lost permanently four of my little salvage crew of thirteen; quite a casualty rate. The others, together with most of the men I had or ever got, afloat or ashore, spent approximately 25 per cent of their time from then on in the hospital being treated for aggravated prickly heat. We had a rough time with it.

Meanwhile, the older men began to crack up. Colonel Claterbos had informed me, while on his visit to Massawa with General Maxwell, that he also was through, that he was being shipped back to the United States as soon as transportation was available. I looked at Claterbos incredulously when he told me that—no American in all Africa could match his magnificent physique. But it was so, he assured me—his heart was going bad, the doctors wouldn't let him stay. A little later, when I visited Mai Habar to see my own men, there was the huge colonel, himself a patient in a wheel chair, hospitalized till departure. I commiserated with the colonel over what Eritrea had so swiftly done to him, but he corrected me.

It wasn't Eritrea, he assured me bitterly, that had broken him down; it was the interminable bickering with the American contractors (of whom, I could thank God, I had only one to deal with; he had several) which had done the trick. Eritrea was merely the climatic background which had made it impossible for him to stand up physically under the strain. I was sorry. I had worked with Claterbos back in New York on Mission plans before either of us had come to Africa; since then, he had done everything he could to lend me a hand.

Then shortly Pat Murphy vanished from the Massawa scene, also to take a bed in Mai Habar, never to return except in the fall on brief inspections. Murphy, rather elderly, had been knocked out by the Massawa heat. That also was a calamity to me, I felt; Pat Murphy had worked hard from the beginning on the Massawa construction projects, always strictly on the job. His successor as construction superintendent, sent down by the contractor, was a much younger man.

But there were a few things on the brighter side over the last weeks of May and the early part of June.

A few days after the inspection visit to Massawa, I received a letter from Colonel Chickering, General Maxwell's Chief of Staff. In it was a copy of Major General Hutchinson's letter to our Commanding General. As General Officer, Commanding His Majesty's Troops in Sudan, General Hutchinson took occasion officially to repeat to General Maxwell what he had said to me in the *Lord Grey*.

But that was not all. In the same envelope was a pink routing slip of the North African Mission, bearing in Colonel Chickering's handwriting a note,

General Maxwell desired that this copy of radiogram be furnished you. We all join in the chorus.

W. E. C.

Attached to the routing slip was a green carbon copy of a very long radiogram from General Maxwell to the War Department in Washington. The gist of the radiogram was that the War Department request the Navy Department to promote me to Captain in the Navy without delay for "most outstanding service with this Mission." The bulk of the radiogram was given over to General Maxwell's relation of the outstanding services (apparently while he had said very little on his inspection trip, there wasn't much he had missed); the rest of it to his reasons for prompt action.

In remarkably few days, considering the difficulties of communication between the Middle East and Washington and the normal interminable routine of any inter-departmental actions in Washington itself, a wire was received in reply. The rising of that dry dock must have stirred up more commotion in Washington than it had done in the waters of Massawa harbor, so to have short-circuited all usual delays. By direction of the President, I was promoted immediately to the rank of Captain in the Navy. Six months before, I had entered the Navy from civil life as a Lieutenant Commander. Now, almost as rapidly promoted as if I had joined the Air Corps instead, I was a Captain. For the Navy, that was something.

I hastened to get an Arab tailor over in Massawa to change the gold stripes on my shoulder marks from three to four. Those shoulder marks (which I now always wore on my shirt like the British so the Sudanese sentries about the Base might recognize me in the dark as a naval officer and not shoot me) were the only insignia of my rank that needed changing. It was folly to bother about changing the sleeve stripes on my solitary blue uniform which in Massawa would never be worn. In fact, to get the extra gold stripes for the shoulder marks, I had the Arab tailor strip a stripe off my unused blue uniform, the only available source of gold lace in Massawa.

So now I was a Captain; that had its advantages. No longer would I have to salute every colonel, American or British, who rolled through Massawa. Better yet, in the eyes of all the natives and all the Italians, the commanding officer of the American Naval Base was the equal in rank of the commander of the Royal Naval Base near by. In the East, that counted for something.

But other than those imponderables, my promotion made little difference. It didn't affect my pay except negligibly. If financial reward had been a factor, I might have bettered myself considerably more by resigning my commission altogether and taking a job with the contractor as a civilian mechanic. There was hardly an American workman I had whose pay didn't exceed mine. As for the contractor's major executives, luxuriously ensconced in the best hotel in cool Asmara, who were the bane of my Massawa existence, my salary as a naval captain (subject to American income tax which heavy war tax they wholly escaped in Eritrea) was simply not to be mentioned in the same breath with theirs.

But I felt very proud of my promotion nevertheless. I had received it as a reward "for outstanding service," not as a merely routine matter after having managed to live the required number of years without being court-martialed, until some vacancies occurred to which someone had to be promoted. And the greatest thrill I got from it came not from receiving the congratulations of all the senior British officers, Army and Navy, in Massawa, cordial though they were, but when I lifted the telephone in my office to make my first call the morning the news came through. Before I could say more than the number I wanted, the British seaman (whom I knew only as a voice) manning the switchboard on the naval peninsula, before he started to get the number paused to say,

"My 'earty congratulations, Cap'n Ellsberg. All us lads 'ere at the Royal Naval Base are 'appier at seeing you promoted Cap'n 'n if we'd all been rated up ourselves!"

The same day I got another surprise, quite as welcome as my promotion. A British military transport plane landed on the seldom-used ex-Italian airport on the fringe of Massawa. Out of it, still in full battle equipment—tin hats, rifles, bayonets, cartridge belts, and mess kits—piled ten South African soldiers, fresh from the Libyan battle front just west of Tobruk, all in charge of a sergeant with orders to report to me! I could hardly believe it. That South African Major General had made good on what I had taken only as a polite but meaningless gesture! He had combed a South African regiment immediately on his arrival in Libya, picked out ten men who were ironworkers before they became soldiers, piled them all into the first transport plane he could lay hands on, and started them off for Massawa to help someone he felt badly needed help.

There was a man! If ever he should see this, he will know I have never forgotten him, even though our solitary meeting was so casual I have no record of his name. But there is one American at least who will always cherish in his heart a warm spot for South Africa for what her soldier son and the men he sent did to help the U.S. Naval Repair Base at Massawa when it terribly needed help.

That was much more than our own America did for us. A few days later General Maxwell received a reply to his other radiogram asking for the seven American naval officers badly wanted for the Massawa Naval Base. The answer was no; no more American naval officers would be sent to Massawa. I wasn't particularly disappointed; I had expected no help. But General Maxwell, shocked, couldn't believe it and again pressed for help. However, in spite of all his efforts, he came out exactly where he went in. To the end of my tour in Massawa, no other American naval officer was ever detailed there to help me. I might have four gold stripes now, but in spite of all the dignity that might go with my new rank, I was left just as free to crack up in hot Massawa without assistance as when I had only three.

CHAPTER

31

Early in June, pushing up a huge
bow wave that resulted in a report from the British naval lookout
station that a destroyer was coming in full speed, my salvage tug, the
Intent, arrived safely in Massawa. Three months on the way from
Port Arthur, Texas, she had circumnavigated Africa, sailing 13,000
miles with her General Motors diesel pushing her steadily along.
Always a mere lone speck on the face of the ocean, now with all the
1200 horsepower of her diesel electric machinery driving her, she
came at full speed, eleven knots, into Massawa, her tiny hull invisible behind the foaming bow wave her stubby stem pushed up.

Edison Brown, skipper and salvage master, H. M. Keith, chief engineer, and their little crew of twelve men had done a fine job in
bringing their trifling cockle-shell of a harbor tug half the distance
round the world, mixing their seasons scandalously on the way. They
had left Port Arthur in late winter, arrived in Capetown in mid-
autumn, and reached Massawa in early summer. I welcomed them
enthusiastically as they maneuvered slowly in against the pier at the
Naval Base, both for their voyage and for this reinforcement to my
sadly depleted salvage gang. In addition, I looked with pleasure on
the two .50 caliber anti-aircraft guns I had ordered mounted on top
the *Intent's* bridge; now if we had an air raid on Massawa, I should
at least have something to shoot back with at the bombers.

The next few days, so far as the *Intent* was concerned, were spent
first in arranging quarters ashore in wooden barracks for her crew,
since her stuffy little forecastle was uninhabitable beneath the Massawa sun and in taking her captain and engineer into Building 108
with me; and second in breaking out from the storeroom under her
fantail, the salvage gear she was carrying. Naturally, being very small,
she wasn't carrying much—one small air compressor for diving use,

a small electric generator lighting set, her diving rigs, four small salvage pumps, and some miscellaneous tools—enough to work with.

I had a salvage job already picked out for her. Two days after her arrival I took her over to the south harbor and introduced Captain Brown, Keith, her Chief Engineer, and their twelve shipmates to their first task, the scuttled *S.S. Liebenfels,* a large German freighter sunk at the south end of the line of seven wrecks strung out in a line there.

The *Liebenfels,* sunk to block the approach to the oiling pier for the large oil tank storage in the desert near by, had gone down as intended as a block ship. Her hull was well submerged; only her superstructure amidships and a little of her forecastle and poop showed above water, three little islands rising from the sea. Ahead of her lay the *S.S. Colombo,* capsized, and five more wrecks.

The British diving survey indicated that the *Liebenfels* had one large hole blasted in her hull on the port side forward. From the damage and the way she looked on the surface, I sized up the *Liebenfels* as a routine salvage job—not easy, but one on which normal salvage methods together with hard work should assure results.

Brown had three divers. "Buck" Scougale, a small, wiry individual, was the only one rated a first class diver (which he swiftly proved he was). Wiard, a husky, athletic young man, and Dorcy, tall, fairly heavy, and rather studious in appearance, were the other two. They were rated divers, second class, and so they were, though Dorcy, at least, gave all he had to the task. Wiard, after his first wreck, decided he had had enough of diving in Massawa.

Buck Scougale made the first dive to inspect the hole torn in the *Liebenfels,* and finally came up from his initial dive bathed in sweat to describe to me in crisp, incisive phrases what he had seen. The bomb had evidently been placed in the port forward bilges of the number two cargo hold, all the way outboard of the double bottom, and against the after side of the heavy steel bulkhead separating the number two hold from the number one hold just forward of it.

The Nazis had chosen with great care the most damaging point possible for their heavy bomb. In the explosion, they had blown a huge hole in the ship's side about twenty feet long, laying wide open the side in both the number one and the number two holds. They had destroyed the lower outboard corner of the vertical bulkhead inside between the two holds; they had blown out the bottom of the ship in that vicinity; they had torn wide open the double bottom compartments near the point of explosion in both holds. Roughly two-thirds of all the damage was in hold number two (the largest hold on the ship); hold number one (smaller because the ship started there to narrow down towards the bow) was laid open only half as much as number two.

While the two remaining divers in succession went over the side of the *Intent* to make sure there were no holes blown in the *Liebenfels* elsewhere, I discussed with Brown as salvage master, what I wanted him to do. We would make no attempt at all to seal up the big hole in the number two hold. A rough calculation indicated to me that if we sealed up the hole in number one hold, which was easier, and closed off all the sea chests on the ship which had undoubtedly been opened to help scuttle her, and then pumped out all holds except number two hold, we should have buoyancy enough, with a fair margin for contingencies, to float up the *Liebenfels*. That was work in plenty for his three divers and the slight crew he had to assist. I was sure we could lift the ship with the biggest cargo hold in her still flooded and wide open to the sea; we would attempt no more under Massawa conditions than would permit me to raise the *Liebenfels* in water-logged condition and immediately put her in dry dock for repairs.

On that plan, Brown proceeded. Early each morning, the *Intent* sailed out of the naval harbor for her station alongside the *Lieben-fels;* late each evening she came back so her crew might have ashore in the barracks, while not so good, at least the best chance for sleep Massawa afforded.

To seal up the hole in the number one hold we had to install a huge cement patch, a cement filling, so to speak, containing over thirty tons of concrete, all of which had to be placed under water by divers.

In addition to patching the hole, there were about a dozen sea chest openings in the way of the boiler room and the engine room which had to be made watertight. A cursory inspection in the engine room of the one sea chest valve Buck Scougale in a diving suit could at great risk to himself even get to amidst the mass of machinery there, showed the Nazis had sabotaged the valve by removing its insides and cover, leaving that open sea connection impossible to close. Undoubtedly they had done the same to all the sea chest valves in the crowded bilges to which we couldn't get a diver close enough to inspect, even by feel. No doubt the Nazis figured even trained eels, once cased in cumbersome diving suits, could never get to those dismantled valves to seal them against the sea.

But we easily beat them at that. While Buck, by far the best diver, was working on the hole forward aided by Dorcy, Wiard was given the simple task of sealing off the sea chests from *outside* the ship, not from the inside, where even the best diver could not get at them. All Wiard had to do was to locate in the shell plating down near the bilges just above where the *Liebenfels* rested in the mud, the perforated grating in the outer shell covering each sea chest connection. Then on a thin wood batten which he carried down with him into the sea, he marked with a diving knife the height and the width of that grating, and if there was any curvature to the shell in that vicinity, he carved one side of the thin batten to a shape to fit that curvature.

Up on deck, under the direction of Scotty McLay, the *Intent's* energetic first mate, the ship's carpenter swiftly knocked together a heavy canvas-covered wood frame to dimensions slightly exceeding those of the perforated grating, and chiseled the edges of the frame to suit its curvature. The four edges of the frame, which were to go against the side of the ship, were covered with canvas stuffed with oakum to make a somewhat flexible soft pad which would seat tightly against the steel plating of the ship all around the sea chest grating.

A couple of long iron hook bolts, made by Keith, the engineer, completed the assembly. These had hooked ends inside, small enough to pass through the perforations in the sea chest gratings and catch inside them. On the outside, these hook bolts were threaded, with a washer and a nut where they passed through the canvas-covered frame.

When the first frame, about two feet wide and three feet high and slightly curved, was done, it was weighted so it would just sink and was lowered down the side to Wiard. Far below us in the water, he was standing on a little diving stage hung against the side of the wreck just below the main sea injection for the condenser, which that frame was to seal off.

The installation went swiftly. In less than half an hour Wiard had got the frame over the grating, hooked the two bolts into the grating, and set up the two nuts tightly against the canvas-covered frame so that its oakum pudding was bearing hard against the steel shell plates, completely sealing off the opening from the sea to the largest valve inside the ship. We had no need for any further worry about that sabotaged valve inside; no great amount of water would ever leak by that seal outside when we started pumping.

In that manner, every sea chest opening in both sides of the ship was plugged off; most of them took smaller frames than the one just described.

There was one other diving task that had to be done, a very difficult one. Each cargo hold on the ship had to be separated as watertight as possible from all others, especially forward, where number two hold was to remain waterlogged. To do this required closing the drainage manifold valves, difficult of access but reachable, which stood on the floorplates of the submerged engine room. Buck, who if any diver could get in, could do it. He wormed his way down the maze of steep ladders to the engine room floorplates. There by feel in that black water he closed all the drainage valves he could find, driving tapered wood plugs hard into the seats of all the valves whose bonnets were missing so they couldn't be closed. With that I figured, the inter-connecting piping systems were fairly well sealed off.

We had one further major job, as well as a number of minor ones. There were five large cargo hatches to the holds of the ship, all but one of which hatches lay wide open to the sea in the well-submerged decks. (The fifth hatch was out of water in the superstructure amidships.) We couldn't start to pump out the three holds, one forward and two aft, which we had to dry out (together with the amidships hold, the engine room, and the boiler room) while those three huge cargo hatches lay open beneath the sea. To take care of that problem, we had to build three heavy rectangular vertical wood cofferdams (large vertical trunks, open at both ends) to go over each of the three submerged hatches. Each of these vertical cofferdams, anchored watertight to the hatch coaming below, rose some ten feet through the sea to just above the high tide line, to form a watertight shaft from the tops of the holds below to the open air above.

Each of these cofferdams was of the size of the cargo hatch below it, about twenty feet athwartships and eighteen feet fore and aft. Made of tongue and grooved planks two inches thick, their construction and installation, partly with divers, partly from the surface, was a slow and laborious task.

On these installations, both amidst the wreckage and the mud down on the ocean floor and the blazing heat up on the surface, Brown and his crew, only fourteen men all told, labored day after day, no time out for Sundays or anything else, that stifling June for three weeks.

Meanwhile, as the *Intent's* little crew was getting along all right, I was with them only part of the time in the south harbor, having considerable in other directions to attend to, but at least I received now some officers to help me with it.

General Maxwell, since he could get no aid for me from the Navy, decided to do as well as possible with Army officers. So he seized on two young officers, one of whom had been sent out to the Libyan Desert as an observer on tank warfare and the other as an engineer, and ordered them to Massawa to report to me—Captain Paul Morrill of the Infantry and First Lieutenant David Woods of the Corps of Engineers.

Promptly I assigned Morrill as my Executive Officer and Woods as Shop Superintendent. I found I had been lucky in the two officers given me, both young men, of course. Morrill was a stocky, bull-dog-jawed pugnacious individual of excellent organizing ability; Woods, a slightly-built, slow-spoken, phlegmatic young engineer (a Southerner, I think, from his drawl, though I was never sure). Neither of them know nor pretended to know anything about ships. But they both had what was most important—enthusiasm, ability and a desire for action. That was all I needed, and I turned them both to at once, where they relieved me of most of the shore load.

Afloat, I had the problem of repairs to the salvaged Italian dry dock. On that, which I considered the most important repair job of all confronting the Naval Base, I put Lloyd Williams, salvage master mechanic, in charge. I gave him the remnants of Reed's original salvage crew, three divers, and the six American mechanics he still had left himself, plus the ten South African ironworkers who had just arrived, together with a few Italian mechanics from our shore base and a large gang of Eritreans for laborers.

I suspended all further salvage by Captain Reed's crew for the present, feeling it more important to use him and his divers to help the repair gang on repairs under the dock floor where only divers could get at the bottom. Normally such a repair job as that Italian dry dock presented would have been solved by dry-docking her in an even larger dry dock; for Massawa that was impossible. There was no larger dry dock in Africa or elsewhere which could be taken for the job, even if she could be towed there. The *Queen Elizabeth* was tying up the only dock in Alexandria which could take her; her sister, the *Valiant,* was tying up in Durban in South Africa the only other Allied dry dock big enough for the task.

So it was up to us to repair our salvaged dry dock as she lay afloat in Massawa harbor, a devilish job under the circumstances, which Lloyd Williams uncomplainingly took over. But there were complications even in Massawa to that procedure. We needed several hundred skilled mechanics; we had only a couple of dozen, mainly South Africans. We needed a great deal of steel; there was only a trifling amount in Massawa. I radioed America to ship several hundred tons of steel for the job and at least fifty shipbuilding mechanics. Very promptly I received an answer—no. America was too busy on its own shipbuilding program requiring some ten million tons of steel a year to spare any men or a few hundred tons of steel for us. We were in "an area of British responsibility"—Britain must furnish us both the steel and any men needed.

By what process of logic anyone in Washington could reconcile the sending of our Mission to the Middle East to help hard-pressed Britain, with the statement to us that we must look to Britain for help in materials and men, I couldn't figure out. Who was to help whom was another "Alice in Wonderland" problem. But so it was. In Washington, we weren't even step-nephews of Uncle Sam; apparently we were completely orphans.

I had Commander Davy go to work on the British C.-in-C. in Alex to get us some steel and some more men, seeing America had washed its hands of us. Very soon we had an answer—the C.-in-C. would be glad to help but every ton of ship steel in Africa, which wasn't very much, was already being swallowed up in repairing the vast holes in the battleships *Queen Elizabeth* and the *Valiant,* on the dry docks in Alex and Durban, respectively. All the shipbuilding mechanics in Africa were similarly tied up; none were available to us. Steel for us would be ordered in England, overwhelmed already with demands for steel, but God alone knew when we might get it. Then the delivery would take three months, even after some were pinched from England's meager stocks. However, we were informed there might be a few stray steel plates and beams in Port Sudan.

Commander Davy promptly flew to Port Sudan to find out. He came back, having arranged for the shipment from there of what he

[259]

could find—fifty tons all told perhaps. That cleaned out Port Sudan. I started an intensive search of Massawa itself. We found a little in some unexpected places which I had explored. The Fascisti had taken all the steel ship plates and steel channel bars there were in Massawa and used them to construct the roofs of underground air-raid shelters. Buried beneath tons of overlying coral rock, I found what ship steel Massawa had possessed. With bulldozers borrowed from the contractor, we tore all the air-raid shelters on the Abd-El-Kader Peninsula to pieces to recover that precious steel—perhaps fifty tons more—leaving us naked under heaven should we be raided ourselves. We should have nothing save tin hats (if only we could get some tin hats) for protection against bombs or air strafing should it come—now no very remote possibility as events swiftly proved.

But so great was our need for steel I have no doubt I should still have demolished those shelters for it even under a rain of bombs. Out from beneath the coral overlay it came, to be turned over to Lloyd Williams. With that immediately at hand, and the little which arrived in a week from Port Sudan, he started his repair job. We should need vastly more to finish. Where it might come from, only a crystal gazer might foretell.

But for the moment, I had everything going. On the Persian dry dock, we were running merchant ships over the keel blocks at a pace averaging now a ship every day and a half—the jungle ballet of my Eritrean natives wielding scrapers and paint brushes was dizzying to behold. On the Italian dry dock, Lloyd Williams and his assorted crew (the South Africans having laid aside their bayonets) were busy with acetylene torches cutting away blasted steel. In the Naval Base shops, all hands were busy on repairs for the ships in dry dock, fabricating materials for Williams' job on the Italian dock, salvage materials for the *Liebenfels*, and on miscellaneous orders from all over Eritrea.

Meanwhile, it was getting hotter; now was the time when the Italians had always locked up Massawa and retreated to the high hills for the summer. I had been curious about the Massawa heat and humidity ever since my arrival, but having nothing with which to measure them, I had written my wife to procure a hygrometer, and a thermometer reading up to 150° F., and mail them to me. The first week of June, they arrived—a wet and dry bulb hygrometer and the special thermometer. The hygrometer I saw at once would be of no use to me in the daytime, at least; its two thermometers read only up to 110° F. As regards the thermometer, Mrs. Ellsberg wrote in a note contained in the first class package, that she had been unable to get a 150° F. thermometer; they either stopped at 110° F. or else ran very much higher. The one she was enclosing, a technical thermometer, read up to 220° F., made for testing boiling water; it was the best she could do.

I took the thermometer the day it arrived, June 6, out to where the men were working on the floor of the Italian dry dock, and as un-ostentatiously as possible, held it a few minutes at the level of the keel blocks in the center of the dock, about head high. In spite of my precaution, in a moment there were gathered round me half a dozen American and South African workmen, attracted irresistibly the instant they saw the thermometer; they were curious, too, about the temperature.

When I swung the thermometer round and took off my sun glasses to scan the reading, I tried to keep it a secret but it was no use; everybody grabbed at the thermometer to read it. It read 149° F.!

That, of course, was in the sun, but so also were all the workmen.

Retrieving my thermometer from alien hands, I then laid the thermometer on the steel plates of the dry dock floor. When I took it up from there, it read 163° F.! That steel, I knew before was far too hot to touch without heavy gloves or for the natives to go barefooted on; now I knew why.

This was only early in June. It kept getting hotter as June dragged along into July and August but I never again dared drag out my thermometer to check what the July and August temperatures had risen to. My little experiment immediately cost me several hours' work on the part of all Americans and South Africans; 149° in the air; 163° on the steel floor! Everyone instantly began to swab himself and look for some shaded spot, feeling twice as hot as he had been a moment before. How was any white man expected to live, let alone work, in temperatures like that, they asked me?

I really didn't know; all I knew was that there was a war on and that we had to. But I didn't argue with any of the poor, half-naked devils before me suffering with prickly heat; I let them loaf in the shade, shouting for the water boys and some ice water till finally after guzzling a few bottles apiece, they recovered enough from the shock to go back to work. But that thermometer never saw the Massawa sun again. We were close enough to the temperature of hell already to suit me; if I ever actually *knew* that it was any hotter, I doubted that I could stand up myself under the knowledge.

CHAPTER

32

On June 14, we were evicted from Building 108. Our substitute quarters, Building 35, were not completely ready, but were at least habitable and we all went, but not without the bitterest hard feeling, especially on the part of the civilian supervisors. They did not hesitate profanely to say what they thought about being thrown out, over a dozen of them, from the only half decent quarters in Massawa so the same space might some day be used by three or four of Cable and Wireless' British mechanics.

Actually I was confronted for a while with their flat refusal to move at all—if Cable and Wireless wanted them out, let it try throwing them out by force and see what happened. Short of bayonets, and perhaps even in spite of them, they were perfectly willing to wait and see who possessed Building 108 when the fight was over—themselves or Cable and Wireless.

But I was undesirous of having what would undoubtedly have been a bloody riot between British and Americans furnished to Goebbels' propaganda mill. There were troubles enough for the Allies that month, especially in the Middle East where the British were in hasty retreat to El Alamein with the siege of Tobruk by Rommel just beginning. Still all my arguments to move out peaceably would have gone for nought had not a vessel arrived in Massawa the day before moving day with a consignment of portable room air conditioners for us. With these we might make our new rooms in Building 35 livable when we could get them installed there; it was worth a try. So finally, muttering threats and curses, all hands packed their few belongings into bags and the houseboys carted them down to a waiting truck for the move. Nevertheless, I had to warn the two Cable and Wireless managers to keep themselves well away from Building 108 and not show themselves again till everyone was completely out or I would not answer for their personal safety. They prudently disappeared completely on moving day.

In Building 35, my new room contained only a desk for me to work on, a chair, a flimsy wooden wardrobe, and an even flimsier apology for a narrow wooden bed, either of which I could have kicked to pieces with ease. Bare as a prison cell, there were no curtains, no carpets, no pictures; there never was anything else except the air conditioner which was later installed. Being far from the sea, it was hotter than hell and as dusty as the desert. It did have a shower in one corner and a tiny alcove for my bags.

I promptly stripped and got under the shower, then twice as promptly got out again—the water from the solitary valve to the shower head came out steaming—scalding hot!

With my skin blistered where the spray had struck it, I looked in dumb amazement into that shower. What was the matter? There couldn't be any heater on the water line; there never was anywhere in Massawa, but that water seemed practically boiling to me. I knew a completely new water supply system had been installed for the building, but something must be wrong with it. I hastily drew on a bathrobe and some slippers and went out on the veranda to locate the trouble.

The trouble showed up plain as day. To provide the pressure in that forsaken locality to force water for Building 35 up to the second floor where I was, the pipefitters had installed a vertical steel pressure tank three feet in diameter and eight feet high, together with an old Italian automatic pressure pump to force more water into the tank when the level got low. There out in the sun on the hot coral fifty feet from Building 35, stood the bare steel water tank, soaking up heat from the sun like a boiler exposed to a fire!

I pulled on a few clothes, my sun helmet and my sun glasses and went to sick bay to see what Captain Plummer could do for the blisters overlaying my prickly heat. On the way back, coated with salve, I stopped in at the pipefitter shop to tell the foreman, "Frenchy" Willermet, that he should have known better than to expose a water tank in Massawa. But he protested there wasn't any place else he could have put it and still provide for it the suction he needed and the required accessibility for servicing of its ancient Italian automatic pumping equipment. In that, after some reflection, I concluded he was right.

Still, something had to be done or our water system was useless. No one could use steaming water for a shower bath, and even for flushing a toilet, it had drawbacks. A solution was finally reached by coating the entire steel tank with a three-inch-thick insulating jacket of magnesia block and asbestos cement—a paradox if there ever was one. We had heavily to insulate a water supply tank, not to keep the heat in as in all civilized climates, but to keep the heat out!

After the insulation went on, things weren't so bad. The water thereafter ran merely very warm in the showers, instead of scalding hot, except on the frequent occasions when the decrepit Italian pumping mechanism broke down, when there wasn't any water at all. That usually happened when I came back in the evening before dinner after a terrible afternoon in the sun, feeling that unless I had a shower immediately, I couldn't live another minute. At that time, it ordinarily took an hour or more to locate a pipefitter (all of whom by then had quit for the day) to get the damned contraption going again.

All this, borne by my fellow occupants of Building 35 as poorly as by me, did little to alleviate the bitterness caused by our eviction from Building 108, which for months thereafter remained mostly unoccupied. To the end of my stay in Massawa, there never were one quarter as many British occupants as when we Americans had lived in it. Never could I pass Building 108 without cursing.

CHAPTER

33

IT TOOK NO VERY KEEN OBSERVER from the middle of June onward to note a marked change in the attitude of our P.O.W.s and other Italian workmen. The British Eighth Army under Ritchie, outmaneuvered and defeated west of Tobruk, was in headlong retreat toward Egypt. All Libya was swiftly reconquered by Rommel and his Afrika Korps; only in vital Tobruk was a British garrison left to deny to Rommel the use of that harbor as a supply port for his army. Making no attempt at a stand before Tobruk itself to stop Rommel there, Ritchie and his battered troops not only evacuated Libya but also most of western Egypt, not pausing in their flight for anything till finally they came to El Alamein, only forty-five miles from Alexandria and not much further from Cairo.

With this retreat, gloom descended everywhere in the Middle East, lightened only by the fact that instead of continuing in hot pursuit of Ritchie's beaten Eighth Army, Rommel had paused before Tobruk with his whole force to besiege it. Instead of by-passing Tobruk as he easily might have done, and continuing eastward to give Ritchie the *coup de grâce* before the shattered Eighth Army could pause for any effective stand in defense of Egypt, Rommel had elected to break off the pursuit while he took Tobruk.

All hands breathed a little more freely at that. Tobruk was left well defended; its British garrison was now the largest in Tobruk's war history. With lesser forces, Tobruk had held successfully the year before against an Axis siege for nine months till relieved by a British advance. Even though Rommel himself was now its besieger, it was confidently expected it would hold a long time, if not indefinitely. That was the sole gleam of hope amid spreading disaster.

This depressing situation was reflected by my Italian working force as by a barometer. Never a reticent crowd, where before in the shops

I used to hear denunciations of Mussolini and his Fascisti and praise of American democracy, now those I had suspected of Fascist sympathies were openly exultant; the remainder were keeping their mouths shut lest they be soon the victims of reprisals from their triumphant Fascist associates. And the events leading up to the strike of the month before were trumps in the Fascist hands—if the vaunted Americans couldn't even manage a payroll, why should anyone ever fear they could win a war?

I got further light on the probable future from my new South Africans, only recently arrived from the desert west of Tobruk. I didn't have to ask them for information; I received it involuntarily. One after another, all ten of those South African ironworkers came individually to see me, pleading to be permitted to rejoin for the last battle their comrades, now in desperate straits in their flight past Tobruk into Egypt. I refused each man's request; I needed him too badly as an ironworker where he was to let anyone go. But in their urgent entreaties, I learned a great deal. Every man of them, having fought back and forth in the Libyan Desert for two years, had great respect for Rommel—he was smart. Of the men of his Afrika Korps they had no fear; they were as good soldiers themselves as any Nazis. The trouble lay in the generalship so they felt; neither Auchinleck, top commander, nor Ritchie, field commander, could compare with Rommel—he outsmarted them every time. But all the same, outsmarted generals or not, each man entreated me to let him go back—he felt like a coward who had deserted his comrades in their most desperate hour. He just had to get back into the fight. For God's sake, wouldn't I release him?

I wouldn't, but while we were talking about the desert war, how about Tobruk? How long could it hold out? I got varied opinions, none optimistic. Some thought a month or so; some only a few weeks. I got my most decided answer from the youngest of them, a fair-haired boy of twenty from Johannesburg who had been in the Libyan fighting since he was eighteen.

"Rommel's only playing with Tobruk a few days yet; he hasn't attacked it. When Rommel hits Tobruk, Captain, he'll knock it over in a few hours. You wait and see."

I didn't have long to wait. On the morning of June 21, 1942, Rommel opened a heavy artillery and air bombardment on the rings of concrete pillboxes, wire entanglements, and vast fields of defensive land mines encircling Tobruk. In the early afternoon he moved his tank columns up for the actual assault. Through the narrow lanes, which under cover of his artillery fire, his low flying fighter planes with light bombs to avoid cratering had plowed in the mine fields, went the tanks—a very smart trick. Passing down those safe lanes, within four hours his tanks had broken through, Tobruk and its entire garrison of 25,000 men had surrendered, and the British vessels, naval and merchant, trying to escape from the harbor, found themselves under the pointblank fire of armored tanks enfilading them from the quays as they fled the port!

Complete gloom instantly fell on all Allied hopes in the Middle East at this disaster. If Tobruk, a naturally defensible and heavily defended fortress, could not last a day against Rommel and his triumphant Afrika Korps, what hope now for stopping him anywhere? Headlong for Suez on came Rommel, in swift succession by June 29 occupying Sollum, Sidi Barrani, Mersa Matruh, to bring up finally against El Alamein where the Eighth Army had at last paused in flight, thanking God for the week the too-smart Rommel had given it to dig itself in there unmolested while he paused to prepare his brilliant assault on Tobruk.

Once more Rommel halted to organize his assault on the British position, not so good naturally this time as that of Tobruk, but the last possible point short of Suez where any defense at all could be attempted. General Auchinleck, British Commander-in-Chief of the land forces, relieved Ritchie, his field commander, to take personal charge himself. But the situation looked hopeless; already short-range Stuka bombers flying hardly twenty minutes from fields in Rommel's rear, were dropping bombs on the British Naval Base at Alexandria making it untenable.

Auchinleck sent word to Alex and to Cairo that when the assault came (which might be any day now) he could promise to hold only for twenty-four hours. What happened after that was in the laps of the gods. If Rommel then broke through, in two hours his tanks would be in the streets both of Cairo and Alexandria—El Alamein was that close.

A wild exodus, inelegantly termed "the flap," of all Americans and British started from both cities, by air, by truck, by sea. By nightfall Asmara airfield in Eritrea was swamped by the American personnel civil and military, of the North African Mission and of our Egyptian

Ambassador's staff. Nobody but General Maxwell himself, Ambassador Kirk, and a handful of their staffs remained in Cairo.

The British evacuation situation was worse. The Naval Base at Alexandria was hastily shut down, all vessels there, naval and merchant, hurriedly got under way for Suez jammed with British refugees, men, women, and children. But Admiral Harwood, aside from that, had a terrible problem on his hands. On the large dry dock still lay the battleship *Queen Elizabeth,* her bottom amidships a vast open hole with repairs to it uncompleted. For weeks the frantic British had been trying to get some haste out of their Egyptian workmen and Egyptian contractors ashore so they could get the *Queen Elizabeth* plated up and away before the worst happened.

But why should the Axis-minded Egyptians hurry? It wasn't their battleship; shortly Rommel in person would be welcomed by their king to thank them for not hurrying. They didn't; the hole in her bottom remained wide open.

Admiral Harwood made a desperate decision. Hole or no hole in her bottom, the *Queen Elizabeth* must go immediately if she were not soon to be sunk by bombs from the planes day and night now attacking her. Her bottom was a wreck, but there was nothing the matter with her guns. Spouting fire like a volcano, the *Queen Elizabeth* had so far successfully fought off all air attacks, but would her luck long hold out? Still, even if by some miracle she continued to avoid destruction from the air, nothing could prevent her falling a welcome prize into Rommel's hands when he entered Alex.

So on the *Queen Elizabeth,* all watertight doors and hatches to the boiler rooms beneath which that hole gaped, were once again tightly closed. The floating dry dock was flooded down, with the sea once more freely entering the stricken battleship amidships. Waterlogged, heavily convoyed, the wounded *Queen Elizabeth* moved slowly out of abandoned Alexandria towards Port Said on her long voyage (with a stop at Durban to finish patching that hole) to America where she was finally to be repaired. With her departure, the last British Naval Base in the eastern Mediterranean shut down and resigned itself to awaiting imminent occupation by the Nazis. In the deserted base, only Admiral Harwood and his staff remained, prepared to demolish everything when they had to.

It was against that situation in the Middle East that events in Massawa now moved. I had the only remaining Naval Base and dry dock in the Middle East; I kept it busy. But we were sitting on a powder keg. What might our Italian workmen, ex-soldiers, most of them, do to force the issue now that their Axis forces were on the verge of breaking through and flooding all the Middle East?

There were scant British troops left in Eritrea, only a few battalions. East or west, most of the Indians and Sudanese had been drawn off to the battle fronts. Orders came down from the Army headquarters in Asmara to organize all the American civilian workmen who cared to volunteer into militia companies, arm them with rifles, drill them. Many men joined; Captain Morrill and another Army lieutenant sent from Asmara started to drill them.

For the first time also, another order came down from Asmara permitting officers to wear side arms, loaded .45 Colt automatics. The Colts were issued, but as the order was not mandatory, I never wore any. I had no intention of indicating to the Fascisti in Massawa that the Commanding Officer of the Naval Base was any more afraid of them now that Rommel was at the gates of Egypt than I had been when he was on the other side of the Libyan Desert west of Benghaz.

But there was no use blinking my eyes to the seriousness of our situation. If the El Alamein line cracked, Eritrea would be swiftly overrun, with Rommel's planes, operating from Jibuti in the hands of his satellites, the Vichy French, available to him at once as a base blocking to all ships the narrow exit from the Red Sea. There would be no place for anyone in Massawa to go to escape immediate capture except southward into Ethiopia. I took a look at the moldy pair of heavy leather mountain boots I had brought from New York and wondered whether they would last me over that 500-mile trek to Addis Ababa.

CHAPTER

34

JUNE 30, THE DAY AFTER ROMMEL came up to the El Alamein position and paused to gather his forces for the final assault which was to overwhelm the Middle East and bring the war everywhere to a swift conclusion, my salvage crew on the *Intent* completed all the underwater work on the scuttled *Liebenfels* and we were ready to start raising her. What salvage pumps the *Intent* had, four four-inch pumps and one six-inch pump, were rigged on platforms over the amidships and after water-filled holds and cofferdams. In addition, I had two British-made six-inch pumps (much heavier and clumsier than our American pump of the same size) which Captain Lucas to help us out had obtained for me from McCance's stock of British salvage equipment. These two pumps were rigged over the number one hold forward to give us maximum pumping capacity from that damaged compartment, sealed off now with a heavy concrete filling where it had once been blasted open.

As all the pumps, American and British, were driven by gasoline engines, I had a dozen fifty-gallon drums of gasoline standing by for refueling. Those seven pumps, running night and day, would eat up huge quantities of gasoline. With all of them running, we could expel 6000 gallons (22 tons) of water a minute from the *Liebenfels'* holds. On the estimate that the weight of the empty *Liebenfels* was 5000 tons, it would take from four to five hours to start the ship up, assuming no leakage into her, which assumption was, of course, ridiculous. There would be plenty of leakage, both through our crude concrete patch and nearly everything else on the ship till we got her main deck above water, and even after that still a considerable amount.

The pumps, all started by hand cranking with magneto ignition to fire their engines, were put in operation early in the morning. The

American pumps, all new Jaeger self-priming machines, started easily and immediately began shooting beautiful streams of water overboard from the *Liebenfels'* holds. We had more trouble getting the British engines to fire and still greater difficulty in getting their complicated self-priming pump mechanisms to pick up a suction, but finally we achieved both objects and the British pumps also began ejecting water at a great rate.

Watching those streams of water flowing overboard made me forget the battle line at El Alamein and everything else from then on. My job, everybody's job on the *Intent* from that moment on, was getting water overboard from the *Liebenfels.* Hoping for the best, we left the war, both on land and sea, to General Auchinleck and Admiral Harwood till the *Liebenfels* was up. To keep those pumps running and get that scuttled Nazi ship off the bottom and back into Allied service was for the time being our war job.

All our pumps ran smoothly enough, and from bow to stern what little of the *Liebenfels* showed above the sea looked like an enormous fountain, gushing water in glistening streams at seven points. Rainbows, lovely in their iridescence, glittered in gorgeous arcs over every pump as the sun shined through the clouds of spray, and in ever widening circles little trains of ripples chased away over the calm Red Sea from the foaming vortex where each stream cascaded into the ocean.

Tended by the deck force of the *Intent,* mainly by thin Holli Miller, stocky Terry Engdal, and even stockier Herald Bertolott ("Muzzy," short for "Mussolini" to his shipmates) who made regular rounds to replenish oil, gasoline, and radiator water, the pumps ran on steadily. I was happy to note that inside each of our wooden cofferdams to the submerged deck hatches, the water level was steadily falling. So also was it going down inside the steel hatchways rising to the superstructure from the engine room, the boiler room, and the midships hold (number three) where we needed no cofferdams. It wasn't falling very fast, for there was a sizable area in every hatchway or cofferdam, but it was certainly going down all over.

All day long, with the tiny *Intent* lying alongside the scuttled *Liebenfels,* we pumped. The sun rose high in the sky, beating mercilessly down on the sweating seamen scrambling with cans of oil, water, or gasoline along the flimsy staging rigged to give access to the pumps each perched on a little island of its own rising from the sea.

[272]

I was aided in one thing by a new assistant recently arrived, young Robert Steele, a naval architect about a year out of college, whom I had hired in New York to help in lifting from my shoulders the burden of all the complicated mathematics involved in the buoyancy and stability of the wrecks to be lifted. He had come just in time to assist on the *Liebenfels*. Together we made the rounds of all the holds, measuring how far down the water had gone in each. Then Steele figured how much of the 6000 tons minimum of buoyancy we needed to start the *Liebenfels* up, we had gained. Plenty more buoyancy was still required.

The day dragged along, we fried under the burning sun, drank water constantly to keep from being completely dehydrated, swallowed salt tablets, and endlessly watched our smoking engines and their steaming radiators. We soon found we could improve them. Each gasoline engine had a thermostatic control valve inside its discharge line from the engine block to the radiator. The thermostat was intended, as in any automobile engine, automatically to choke down the circulation of cooling water in cold weather as required to prevent the engine from being cooled too much. Of course, in Massawa no choking was ever required; the thermostat valves were all automatically wide open in a futile endeavor to circulate water enough to prevent boiling. But the mere presence of the thermostatic control valve inside the discharge line was of itself a choke, even when wide open. So one by one, we shortly shut down every pump. Without waiting for it to cool, we dismantled the engine discharge casting holding the thermostats, threw the thermostats bodily into the Red Sea, reassembled the engine connections, and restarted the pump. We found that helped; nothing could stop the radiators from boiling, but at least they boiled less vigorously after that.

The afternoon wore on, evening came to relieve us of the radiant heat of the sun, though the air temperature dropped very little, and the humidity not at all. To light the job as darkness fell, the *Intent* switched on her searchlight and trained it to rake the sea over the *Liebenfels*. In addition, the little portable electric generator set, a 5-kilowatt machine, which the *Intent* carried had already been set up on the superstructure of the *Liebenfels* exposed above the waves. It was connected up to electric wires suspended precariously from the masts and from whatever else fore and aft on the scuttled ship that showed above water. Now the generator set was started up, to add the racket of its exhaust and the humming of its electric generator to the chorus of the seven pump engine exhausts and the roar of falling water already playing the prelude to the rising of the *Liebenfels*.

As the water levels inside the holds dropped, and the pumps had a greater and greater lift to overcome to suck the water up into them, the volume of water discharged from each pump decreased. Hour since, the water levels had dropped completely out of the ship's hatches and the wooden cofferdams we had built to trunk the sub merged deck hatches off from the sea. Now we were pumping water out of the ship's holds and the machinery spaces themselves, but we had to suck it just the same all the way up to the levels where the pumps stood, a very considerable suction lift. With no tremendous gain in buoyancy resulting from it, we had unavoidably set up a situa tion where the laboring pumps were no longer gaining very much against the inevitable leakage into the ship.

There was no help for this situation except to lower the pump themselves down inside the hatches and the cofferdams to bring thei suctions close again to the water. (A practically perfect pump will not work with the water over twenty-eight feet below it; a salvage pump does well to keep going when the water is down about twenty four feet and even then loses considerably in volume.)

Long before midnight, we were forced to start lowering away ou pumps, a terrible job at any time, a worse one in the darkness. Ther was no sleep for anyone on the *Intent* that night. All hands turne to, first to rig new pump platforms some fifteen or twenty feet dow inside the slimy, dripping hatchways we had freed of water, wel below the level of the sea outside. When that was done, each pum in succession, shut down temporarily but still scorching hot, a mas of smoking metal weighing from half a ton to well over a ton for th larger British pumps, had to be lowered away with such improvise blocks and tackles as we could rig up from the masts of the *Liebenfe* protruding above the sea.

That task, in the weird semi-darkness of the deep hatchways i spite of the best light we could provide, took real men. Everythin was wet, slimy, and excessively slippery. On the frail planking abov and on the flimsy improvised platforms below in the trunks, hal naked men streaming with perspiration fought for a footing, heave on the tackles, cursed as the heavy pumps, smoking all over, swaye drunkenly as they came down, threatening to crush any unwary se

nan below against the sides of the hatchway if he were not agile as a
at in side-stepping on what little slippery planking he had to ma-
euver on.

There were seven pumps to lower; there were only fifteen men, in-
luding officers, on the *Intent* to do the job. One by one, we got the
umps down, lengthened out their discharge hoses so they would dis-
harge the water over the tops of the cofferdams into the sea, re-
:arted them. Not till the flaming dawn broke over the Red Sea and
ie sun, an intolerable ball of fire from the moment it rose above the
istant horizon to the eastward of us, was up, did we finish that task.
*nly by then did we get the last pump (and one of the two heaviest)
)wered far down the cofferdam over number one hold, and with
reat difficulty restarted and pumping again, to begin our second
ay on the salvage of the *Liebenfels*.

In brief shifts, the weary salvage crew had breakfast, some jammed
a the hot combined galley and messroom of the *Intent* to eat, while
ie others serviced salvage pumps. After breakfast, all hands, with still
) sleep for anybody, turned to on servicing our pumps, for now the
.sk had suddenly more than doubled in difficulty and far more
ian doubled in danger. No longer could any man get to a pump
eading a horizontal scaffolding set above the sea. Now the pumps
ere all down wells twenty feet or more deep, to be reached only by
inging with one hand to a can of water, of oil, or of gasoline, while
ith the other as best one might, one clutched the greasy, wet, slip-
:ry rungs of a vertical wood ladder on the descent.

But at least, close to the water again, our pumps were doing better.
ill the water levels went down only slowly, for now in each hold the
ater was being drawn from over the whole area of the hold, a vast
vernous space dimly to be seen beneath the dripping steel beams
 the *Liebenfels'* decks overhead—an area about sixty feet fore and
t, and of about the same width athwartships.

We struggled on during the morning, servicing pumps endlessly,
uring unbelievable quantities of fresh water into the radiators to
ep the pump engines cool enough to avoid (God save the word in
 that heat) freezing the pistons in the cylinders.

Towards noon, the water in all the holds, but especially in the
lds aft, had gone down far enough below the level of the sea out-
le to give me reason to believe something should soon happen. I
ed up two marks on the poop of the *Liebenfels,* exposed a little

above the sea, with a mark on the concrete oiling pier on shore astern of her. Thereafter every half hour I sighted along it.

In the early afternoon, with the slight Red Sea tide flooding in to help us a little in buoyancy, I noted that my line of sight on my shore marker had shifted a bit, not only upwards but also a little to port. The stern of the *Liebenfels* was beginning to rise at last! And to put the matter beyond doubt, she had certainly swung in her bed in the mud a trifle to the westward!

That news cheered the worn seamen of the *Intent* tremendously. They needed cheering for, utterly exhausted from lack of sleep and the interminable climbing of steep ladders, they were all staggering unsteadily as they made their rounds.

In another hour the lift of the stern was easily visible without the need of any markers; by mid-afternoon, the bow of the *Liebenfels* also came clear of the mud, and the whole ship drifted a little to port till she brought up on her anchor cable which was already down forward, and on a steel hawser we ran out from her stern to the oiling pier abaft her.

By late afternoon, the main deck of the *Liebenfels* came awash and soon, thickly crusted with barnacles, it was above water. Once again from bow to stern, a sailor could walk the decks of the scuttled *Liebenfels,* provided he had on a stout pair of shoes to prevent his feet from being cut to pieces.

Now our wreck began to look like a ship once more, though counter-balance that she began to stink like a charnel-house. But nobody minded that. In the eyes of any salvage man nothing on earth is so beautiful as his first sight coming up above the sea of the wreck to which he has given his heart's blood, which is probably fortunate for that is the only real reward the deluded fool ever gets for his sufferings.

The wreck continued to rise from the sea, more and more of her steel sides showed above the water. But we began to have trouble. One after another, without apparent cause, the pumps quit running. Immediately that happened, some seaman of the *Intent's* crew scrambled down the ladder, checked the oil, the gasoline, and the radiator water to make sure everything was all right, retarded the ignition so the engine would not backfire and break his arm, and started cranking furiously. After a while, the engine would fire again and commence pumping, but the trouble necessary to restart a pump increased appreciably; the task was killing the already exhausted men.

After that had happened on five pumps, I went down the number four hatch with Keith, the *Intent's* engineer, when it happened the sixth time to the pump there, our six-inch American Jaeger. Keith looked the engine over. Everything seemed in running order; it shouldn't have stopped but it had. While I cranked the engine, Keith gingerly tested the spark on one of the plugs with a screwdriver. There wasn't any spark; some more cranking (tough work in that hot, steaming hold) showed not a spark on any of the four cylinders.

"Magneto must be grounded," announced Keith laconically. He examined the magneto; it looked all right but it was damp, evidently grounded by moisture.

It had a right to be. The interior of that cargo hold was saturated with water vapor. Below, the hold was over half full of very warm water; from every deck beam and the steel plating overhead moisture dripped constantly. The humidity in that hold was certainly 100 per cent; everything electrical in that high tension magneto was bathed in the hot vapor-saturated air. No wonder it had quit furnishing any spark. No machinery was ever designed to work under the conditions in that hold. Nor men either.

Keith laboriously climbed up on deck and got a pyrene hand fire extinguisher off the *Intent*. With that, when he came back he sprayed the magneto, the distributor, the spark plugs, and all the ignition wiring with carbon tetrachloride to dry them out. Then he retarded the timer, threw on the ignition switch, and I cranked once more. The engine started up, the pump again started to throw water.

There was no question of the trouble; moisture-grounded magnetos in those steaming holds were stopping the pumps.

It was getting on towards evening. We had a second night's work and no sleep facing us, and the little crew of the *Intent* was already badly knocked out. The pumps had to be kept going though, or the holds would refill from leakage, submerge all our pumps now well down inside those holds, and the *Liebenfels* would sink again, this time taking our precious salvage pumps down with her.

I got hold of Bob Steele, put him in the *Lord Grey* which had come alongside with more gasoline for us, and sent him back from the south harbor to the Naval Base to round up Bill Reed, Lloyd Williams, and the nine men they had in their salvage party and bring them all back to the *Liebenfels* immediately, prepared to work all night.

It was dusk when Steele shoved off; it was completely dark three hours later when he came back with Reed and the relief salvage party. They took over none too soon. The sleepless, fagged-out crew of the *Intent* now could hardly drag their weary bodies up and down the ladders to the pumps.

Reed, Williams, and their nine men had all worked already all day long themselves on repairs to the hot dry dock. They were no fresh and rested reliefs, but they knew salvage and its troubles and they took over with no grumbling. Brown's drowsy and over-fatigued men dropped in their tracks in the darkness all over the *Intent's* deck to snatch some rest.

The second night began, a repetition of the first night, only worse. Once more new pump stages had to be rigged still lower down in the holds, and the pumps lowered again to keep their suctions. The pump working in the engine room was worst of all. The water level there had gone down so far the *Liebenfels'* huge reciprocating steam engine was wholly exposed as well as most of her auxiliary machinery. Because of the engine room gratings and the interfering machinery, we could no longer lower the four-inch pump we had in the engine room hatch with a block and fall; it had to be taken down the narrow steep steel ladders going from one grating level to the next below. Those ladders, four of them altogether, sloping steeply, wet with the sea just receded from them, slippery beyond description from oil and grease coating them, only dimly lighted from far above, were terrible traps to send a half-ton gasoline engine and pump down, handled only by men to mule haul it about.

But the pump went down, with men beneath it holding it back, men above it slacking it away, men struggling each side to guide it, all sweat-soaked, their muscles straining in the half light and the eerie shadows of that engine room, looking like demons of the nether world struggling in some unearthly task. The pump never slipped from their greasy hands, no one was crushed in the lowering of it. That seemed unbelievable.

Down on the engine room floor plates at last (for in the engine room the water had been pushed down that far) the pump suction hose was led to the waterlogged bilges below the floor plates, a long discharge hose was coupled up to lead to the open deck far above, and once again the engine cranked up. We had another problem now; the exhaust from the gasoline engine had also to be piped all the way up to the open air or we should shortly have filled that engine room so full of poisonous carbon monoxide gas from the engine exhaust as to kill anyone who came down the engine room ladders to service the pump.

Servicing pumps became more of a trial than ever; getting to most of them meant going down and up thirty to forty feet of vertical ladder—a man-killing job each trip. The stopping of any pump was now a calamity for us, but still they stopped. Each time, some salvage man had to descend to the pump, spray its magneto with carbon tetrachloride, even then nearly kill himself in the heat and the steaming air cranking it over till at last it fired again.

I was up all through the second night with Reed's crew, for now as the water went far down and the lightened *Liebenfels* rose well out of the sea, stability problems started to enter. With her number two hold completely flooded and in free communication with the ocean through the huge hole there, and a free water surface still existing in every other hold (none of which were yet pumped dry) the stability of the top-heavy *Liebenfels* was negligible and she started to list to port.

Ordinarily this would not have been serious; we would soon have dried out some of the nearly emptied holds and made the *Liebenfels* quite stable, able to float erect.

But I swiftly found out salvage in Massawa had nothing ordinary about it. Under the terrific humidity conditions to which all pumps were now exposed far down in the holds, they kept stalling with grounded magnetos before we could get a single hold completely dried out. Then while we struggled to restart a stalled pump, water leaked back into that hold, the unstable ship listed more to port, all the loose water in all the holds ran to that side, increasing the list so greatly we suddenly had thrust upon us the need of abandoning all else to concentrate on lashing all our pumps securely to their platforms lest they slide off into the water below them.

Under such conditions, struggling to keep enough pumps running all at once to prevent too much of a port list, I got no sleep at all the second night either.

The sun rose again, the third day on the lifting of the *Liebenfels* commenced. The crew of the *Intent* with some sleep to recuperate on, took over once more. Reed's salvage gang, worn by twenty-four hours straight of back-breaking labor, sprawled out beneath whatever shelter they could find from the sun, to sleep themselves.

Somewhat haggard myself, I turned to with Brown's crew on the problem of straightening up the lightened *Liebenfels* so we could tow her away and put her on the dry dock, thus ending our struggles.

Under any normal conditions, anywhere else in the world, salvage on the *Liebenfels* was already completed. We had the ship well afloat, high out of water, drawing twenty-four feet, considerably less than her ordinary loaded draft of twenty-eight feet. Ordinarily under those conditions, we should simply have towed her into the nearest shipyard, which could easily have docked her, and washed our hands of further concern over the *Liebenfels*.

But not in Massawa. The only dry dock I had operating was the Persian dock, not a large dry dock. It could lift only 6000 tons, and could not take any vessel coming in drawing more than nineteen feet for strictly routine dock operation, or perhaps twenty feet if I were willing to take a chance with the dock and sink it farther than it was designed to go down safely.

That situation left me with two incompatible conditions to meet with the *Liebenfels*. To get her on the dry dock, I had to lighten her up to twenty feet draft or less. But with free water in all her holds and one big hold (number two) completely flooded, getting her that high out of water made her excessively top-heavy and unstable, likely to capsize on me. Still both things had to be done, or the *Liebenfels* could not be saved, even though we had already lifted her. There was nowhere else in the world we could tow her; it was Massawa or nothing.

So I started the third day with that insoluble problem on my hands to solve. There could be no sleep for me till I had the answer.

There was only one hope. I must get the boiler room, the engine room, and the number three hold absolutely dry so as to give the ship sufficient stability to stay right side up at all. To control her listing, I would juggle water in the two after holds, numbers four and five, across the shaft alley.

The shaft alley, a long horizontal tunnel from the engine room to the propeller, passed through those two cargo holds to divide the lower eight feet of each hold, along its fore and aft centerline, into separated starboard and port compartments. Back and forth across the top of that shaft alley, I must pump water as necessary from the low to the high side to balance the ship. It would be a neat trick if I could do it, somewhat akin to keeping a pencil balanced on its point.

All day long, the crew of the *Intent* struggled to keep enough pumps going together to do what I had to do. It was the story of Tantalus all over again. Occasionally we approached dryness in the midships hold and the machinery spaces, with the water far enough down in the forward hold to approach the light draft we needed. Then most of the pumps would stall, water would begin gaining on us, increasing the draft again, and the ship would begin again to take a bad list, sometimes to starboard, sometimes to port, depending only to which side she happened to be listed when the pumps quit.

Over and over again we fought to restart our pumps, to settle the matter. Each time we gained something permanently in lightening her up, but that resulted only in decreasing her stability as the ship rose higher from the sea. When next several pumps quit and some water returned, all pouring over to the low side, the ship listed even worse than the time before, beginning to assume really dangerous angles to one side or the other.

All day long in the blistering heat and the intolerable humidity far down in the holds of the *Liebenfels,* we fought that battle, with the *Liebenfels* mostly heeled so badly as to make climbing up or down the vertical ladders to the pumps an acrobatic feat on top of a fatiguing one. Night came. We had not won. Brown's knocked-out crew went off, Reed and his men again took up the struggle. I could no longer keep my eyes open or drag myself about. I lay down on the superstructure of the *Intent* for a little rest. Two hours later I was up again, making the rounds of the holds to encourage the weary salvage men to keep the pumps running till we had her straightened up, now seemingly a hopeless task.

Dawn came again, the fourth day. Still our ship wasn't light enough. Brown and his tired men took over; all hands were beginning to get discouraged. This was like no salvage task they had ever worked on before; they were nearly dead on their feet on a ship which by all the rules was already successfully salvaged. But even so, if only all those pumps would keep on pumping, as anywhere else on earth they would have, everything would soon be over and they could rest.

The fourth day was worse than all its predecessors. The *Liebenfels* was higher out of water and lighter than ever (though not yet light enough) and more top-heavy and unstable than at any time before. It took less loose water to give her a bigger list. She was never near erectness any more. When I tried to straighten her up somewhat to make work on the broken-down pumps, walking on deck, and climbing up and down those alarming ladders less arduous, by trimming water in the after holds from the low side to the high side across the top of the shaft alley, it resulted only in heart-breaking failure. The ship would gradually straighten up to within 5° of vertical, then for no cause at all would suddenly flop over to take a big list to the opposite side, in which sudden roll no one could help wondering as she went whether she was ever going to stop. Each time it seemed for certain that she was going to keep on and capsize, to go down on her side like the *Colombo* lying just ahead of her in that line of wrecks in the south harbor.

I gave up trying to get the *Liebenfels* erect while we lightened her further; keeping her listed 10° to port, a bad list to work with, satisfied me. Walking the decks under those conditions was difficult. My shoes, waterlogged, soaked in salt, cracked and stiff whenever a few minutes on deck gave the scorching sun and the hot steel a chance to harden up the leather, were killing me, they had shrunk so much. To make matters worse, because of the list, when walking fore and aft along the deck my shoes were at a bad angle to my ankles and the stiff leather rubbing hard against them swiftly wore through the skin and into the raw flesh—between the sweat, the salt water, and the muck I had continually to walk through, those raw spots on both sides of both my ankles made walking a torture.

The day wore on. We gained on lightening up, we lost on stability, for we could never keep the pumps working long enough together to get our midships holds completely dry and hold them that way. Keeping pumps going and restarting them when they stalled, got more and more of a murderous job—apparently the moisture was working deeper into the magneto coils and each time it was harder to remove the grounds by spraying the magneto with carbon tetrachloride, our only cure.

I had cleared the Persian dry dock, ordering no other ships to be docked on it from that morning on, so that the moment we got the *Liebenfels* both light enough and erect enough, we could tow her directly from where we had raised her around to the naval harbor, seven miles away, and put her on the dry dock immediately, whether by night or day.

By early afternoon, it began to appear as if we were getting through. The *Liebenfels* was nearly light enough to go on the dock; I felt sure I could juggle trimming water in the after holds fast enough to keep her reasonably erect while we docked her. So I sent word to Lieutenant Fairbairn to get over to the south harbor with his tugs, prepared to pilot us round for docking. By the time Fairbairn and the tugs arrived I felt that we would be in condition to go.

Then disaster struck us. One after another the pumps began to stop and the half-dead seamen were unable to restart a single one. As the pumps quit the ship started to make water slowly, to increase her previously light draft, and worst of all to increase her list to port. Gradually she heeled more and more—from 10° port to 11°; then to 12°. Standing on the sloping decks became difficult. Below, all the men I had, both in Reed's crew and in Brown's, were fighting to get the pumps going again, to stop that increasing list. Finally the last pump of all, the one on the engine room floor plates, quit also. Silence fell on the *Liebenfels,* broken only by the imprecations of agonized sailors far down in the sweating holds, cranking away on moisture-saturated pump engines, cursing the day they ever saw her.

The list of the *Liebenfels,* bad already, got worse. At that unpropitious moment, Lieutenant Fairbairn and his two tugs entered the south harbor to tow us away. Fairbairn didn't even come near us. It took no very experienced navigator to see that no ship with that heavy list on her, with her tall masts lying far over to port in evident distress, was going to be towed away, still less to be docked. The pilot took only one look, then turned his tugs about, and steamed back to the commercial harbor.

Down the greasy ladders of the *Liebenfels'* engine room I shot, followed by Keith, the *Intent's* engineer, when the last pump coughed uncertainly a few seconds and then quit, leaving us helpless to prevent the ship's capsizing. To preserve some remnants of stability, that engine room pump was the most important of any on the ship—it had to be restarted, regardless of the others.

Keith sprayed the magneto. I tried cranking, Keith tried cranking, one of his huskiest machinists tried cranking. We couldn't get the engine to fire; not even a solitary sputter did we get from its exhaust.

"That magneto's completely grounded now. She'll never spark,"

Keith finally announced glumly.

"She's got to start, Chief!" I countered. "If she doesn't, the ship's lost after we've all but killed ourselves to save her! There must be something you can do to get this engine running again!"

"Nothing'll do it but taking off that grounded magneto and putting on a new one, Captain. I've got a spare magneto in my storeroom. But it'll take over an hour to make the shift. Will this leaking bucket last that long before she capsizes?" Keith asked me gloomily, looking questioningly up at the huge main engine of the *Liebenfels,* already leaning crazily to port over our heads.

"I don't know. We'll have to gamble on it. You try, Keith."

"Aye, aye, sir." Keith sent his mechanic up on deck to board the *Intent* and get the spare magneto, the only spare he had. Then Keith turned to himself with a wrench to remove the grounded magneto from the engine, no very simple job on a badly tilted gasoline engine resting on the greasy, slippery floor plates, with little room to get at the bolts he had to loosen.

"I'll be back in a minute, Chief," I told him once he had started. "I want to check on where we stand on the list."

Whether Keith thought he was being deserted at the bottom of that mantrap of an engine room while I prudently retired to a safer spot on the open deck, I don't know. But he said nothing while I left, only clenching his teeth involuntarily while he strained to get at those hard to reach bolts.

I climbed the slippery, winding steel ladders up from the floor plates, a tortuous climb under any conditions, a dangerous, terrifying one with every ladder slanted dizzily to port. There was scant room to pass; all about was the crowding machinery of the *Liebenfels,* so badly tilted now as to look as if any moment the massive main engine and its auxiliaries would tear loose their holding down bolts and go crashing downward into the port bilges, capsizing the ship instantly. It was a climb equal in height to that from the basement to the roof of a four-story building; nobody down on the floor plates could ever possibly make it when the ship started finally to capsize.

Panting for breath, I came out at last in the ship's superstructure to the only side escape door in the engine room hatch, and cautiously made my way forward. Walking along the frightfully heeled over deck was next to impossible except by grasping one thing after another protruding from near-by bulkheads to avoid sliding headlong into the port scuppers and probably overboard.

Toward the forward end of the superstructure, in what had once been one of the cabins for the ship's officers, I had several days before rigged up a crude inclinometer against a vertical athwartship wooden bulkhead. It was simply a steel bolt suspended on a string from a nail in the bulkhead; nearly six feet long, that improvised pendulum swept over an arc carefully marked out in degrees with a pencil on the bulkhead. For measuring the ship's heel, it was accurate enough, even if it had no pretensions to the beauty or to the machined finish of a regular inclinometer.

With great difficulty, I made that cabin. Inside it I found my youthful assistant, Bob Steele, busily engaged with a slide rule and a pencil in figuring out the rate of our heel to port. Already my pendulum had reached 15° port heel; 10° more to port and the pendulum would be off my scale.

Without stopping, Steele glanced up momentarily at me as I came in, then continued on his figuring.

"Don't bother to figure much beyond 20°, Bob," I advised him. "After that we probably won't care."

"I've been watching this pendulum and logging its rate," he advised me. "She's heeling down steadily to port; no intermissions, Captain."

"How fast is she going over?" I asked anxiously, wondering how much time Keith had for shifting the magneto.

Steele looked at his log, did a little mental arithmetic.

"On the average, about a degree every seven or eight minutes, though I'm not sure but that it's a little faster than that right now. I'll try to check the next degree," and he took out his watch, then carefully read both the pendulum scale and the time. "Shall I let you know, Captain?" he added as he saw I was about to leave.

"No, never mind. It won't help me any." She ought to stand five degrees more list. That might give us thirty-five or forty minutes yet, I thought, to shift the magneto and get the pump going again before the end. I must get back with Keith; I started out of the cabin into the deck passage to port.

"When will she roll over, Captain?" asked Steele with professional curiosity evident on his face as he followed me out of the tilted cabin. "I figure that when the gunwale goes under, that's her limit."

I clung to the rail while I looked down the port side of the *Lieben-*

fels at the Red Sea alongside us. Even on the superstructure we weren't very far from the water, being on the low side of the ship; but the port main deck edge, one deck down from us, was very close to the sea. I estimated roughly the distance from the main deck gunwale to the water. The gunwale was only out of water a few feet now, instead of the twenty feet of freeboard that on the normally erect light ship should have been showing there.

"You're right, Bob. Keep your eye on that port gunwale," I indicated, pointing to the listed main deck below us. "As long as that gunwale shows above the sea, she's safe. But the minute the water rises above that gunwale onto the main deck, she'll go over on her side and down like a rock. We've got maybe two or three feet to go yet before the sea washes over that gunwale and ends it. I've got to get back to the engine room. Never mind that pendulum any more. You stay out here and watch that gunwale. When the sea is within two or three inches of it, you sing out down the engine room hatch and down the holds for everybody to get out. That'll give us maybe a few minutes to get clear. Then you'd better go overboard yourself and start swimming away."

I started on my return journey to the bottom of the engine room. Clinging tightly to anything I could get my hands on, getting back over the steep deck and down that dizzying maze of insanely tilted ladders, fast as I dared go, took me five minutes.

Keith's mechanic was already back with the spare magneto, still left wrapped in its waxed paper cover to protect it as long as possible from the surrounding moisture bathing us as in a Turkish bath. Kneeling on the greasy steel plates alongside Keith, he was holding a flashlight to help light the job. Keith himself, the bolts of the old magneto just freed, was cautiously working it off its foundation, careful not to rotate its shaft and so destroy all knowledge of the position of its rotor with respect to the driving shaft on the engine. If he lost that position, the ignition timing would be wrong; even with a good magneto the engine wouldn't fire. It might take hours to retime the new magneto to the engine. We would never have the hours.

Holding his breath tensely as if his life depended on it (as indeed it did if he stuck with the job), Keith delicately worked the magneto free of its pedestal and out onto the floor plates. Then with a deep sigh of relief, he set it tenderly against the base of the near-by ship's condenser so it wouldn't slide away from him, while he wiped his eyes clear of the sweat pouring down his forehead.

"Thirty minutes yet, Keith, I think," I said to him. "You're doing fine!"

Keith paused only long enough to look up to note I had rejoined him, then with his eyes dried enough so he could see, he picked up the old magneto again and studied its coupling to note the position of the timing marks punched on it.

I took the flashlight while the mechanic tore away the waxed wrappings of the spare magneto. Keith seized it and hurriedly but carefully set its rotor to match exactly in position the marks on the grounded magneto he had removed.

After that, down on his stomach on the sloping engine room floor, he started to install the replacement magneto while I held the flashlight for him and the mechanic passed him the little open-ended wrenches he required. It was a watchmaker's job to get the coupling re-engaged correctly under any conditions. In the semi-darkness of that terrifying engine room far below the level of the sea with the minutes ticking away and the ship perceptibly increasing its awesome heel, that Keith's fingers got the new magneto back in place instead of having it slip from him into the bilge water inexorably rising to port of us over the floor plates, was a miracle.

Steadily, methodically, Keith held the magneto in place with one hand while with the other, he began to set up its holding down bolts. Directing the flashlight a little this way and that, so to light the nut he was attempting to reach with the little S-wrenches, I still could not keep my eyes from wandering a bit to observe what lay about us. Over our heads hung the tilted main engine, dismayingly inclined, apparently defying all the laws of gravitation, for it looked as if long since it should have toppled over to crush us. All about us was other machinery, bulkheads, gratings, all at nightmarish angles, so that one might almost as easily have walked on what had once been a vertical bulkhead as on what was supposedly serving us as a deck.

Would Keith get it done in time, I wondered? It was a fussy job. No use trying to hurry him, that would only ball it up. Keith's fingers, heartbreakingly slow as they seemed while he nursed his little wrenches round the nuts, were nevertheless going as fast as prudently they could without losing in the bilges the slippery wrenches. If we lost the ship, and with it probably the three of us down there, it wasn't going to be Keith's fault.

[287]

I watched in agony as endlessly it seemed he tightened nuts and the *Liebenfels* leaned over more and more till it appeared she couldn't possibly delay another second the sickening sudden roll that would bring the sea cascading down the open engine room hatch above us, our only escape, and spell the end for us and all our troubles with the salvaged *Liebenfels*.

Keith finished tightening the final nut, fingered the magneto coupling a moment to satisfy himself as to its free alignment, then painfully dragged himself up off his stomach.

"O.K., Captain," he announced soberly. Hastily I threw on the ignition switch, retarded the timer. The mechanic sprang for the crank, fumbled about a moment for something to brace his feet against, then cranked madly.

Thank God, the engine fired!

In another moment, the pump picked up a suction (an easy matter since the water level in the flooding bilges was close to its base) and the laboring engine slowed a bit as it started to push water from the bilges far overhead to the open air to throw it over the side into the sea.

Engulfed as we three were far down in the bowels of the *Liebenfels*, we could still hear cheers from all over her as the salvage crew, down in the other holds or on the topside, caught the roar of that engine exhaust and the music of that heavy stream of water splashing overboard.

I swung the flashlight upward toward the first steel ladder.

"Come on, boys!" I sang out. "It's time we got the hell out of here!"

CHAPTER

35

T HE "LIEBENFELS" WITH HER MASTS
and stack lying over at a horrifying angle, had heeled down to 21°
port I found when I got to the topside again. Only a little freeboard
remained before the port gunwale went awash, when suddenly the
heavenly music of water cascading overboard again had ended everybody's agonies.

The heeling of the *Liebenfels* stopped, then very gradually, she began to right herself.

In the hours that followed, by baking out the grounded magneto
in the galley oven to remove the grounds, and then interchanging
it continuously with the other magnetos to be similarly baked out,
we finally got most of the other pumps running again.

Night came, the fourth night. All during the dark hours we worked
endlessly beneath the tropic moon, all hands shifting magnetos and
servicing pumps, but at least we were spared the need of lowering
pumps any further. At odd hours during that night, I managed to
snatch three more hours of sleep, a total for me of five hours' sleep in
four nights and days.

By late morning we had the *Liebenfels* light enough to go on the
dry dock and listing only 13° to port—to all of us now, a mere trifle
of a list, though once I should have considered it very bad.

Once again I sent Steele in the *Lord Grey* for the pilot and the
tugs. About an hour later the tugs came into the south harbor, and
Lieutenant Fairbairn boarded us from his pilot boat. Dubiously he
looked up at the masts of the *Liebenfels*—13° port heel was nothing
to be laughed off.

"This is unsafe for towing, Captain," Fairbairn gravely advised me.
"I'd rather not assume the risk. And you can't dock her at all with
any such list, so why bother to move her?"

I didn't have to look at the masts to estimate the list—my aching feet told me all I wanted to know. I could stand now on deck without having to hold on to anything; to me any such list was negligible. Besides I was dead on my feet; I couldn't possibly spend any more time working on the *Liebenfels* without collapsing; neither could my knocked-out salvage crews.

"You tow her, Fairbairn," I ordered, "and leave the docking of her to me. It'll be my funeral, not yours. Get her under way!"

Fairbairn, having warned me, like a good sailor objected no further. He started whistling signals to his two tugs to come close in and pass us the tow lines.

That didn't take long. Meanwhile, we on the *Liebenfels* unshackled the heavy anchor cables on her forecastle, ready to let slip the chains, for we had no means of weighing the two ponderous anchors the ship had down forward. Similarly we stood by to slip our stern hawser when the tugs had hold.

In thirty minutes we were ready, with the panting tugs straining on their tow lines, hauling the high out of water and stinking *Lieben-fels* well up to the eastward, clear of the line of wrecks where she had so long rested on the bottom. Fairbarne nodded to me he was ready to go.

From the bridge of the salvaged ship, I waved to Brown on the forecastle and Reed aft on the poop.

Instantly sledge hammers came down on the pelican hooks to knock them free, releasing the preventer gear, and with a terrific banging the freed ends of the two anchor chains flew out the hawse-pipes. At the same moment, the stern hawser was slipped and the *Liebenfels* was under way again at last.

Simultaneously, with the halyard aft manned by Bob Steele, amid the feeble cheers of the men who had salvaged her, up to the peak of the mainmast went her colors, the Stars and Stripes floating proudly out above the Nazi swastika under which the *Liebenfels* had always sailed before.

And with those two flags, one above the other, streaming out over our salvaged wreck, we slowly towed the *Liebenfels* out of the south harbor into the Red Sea past Massawa. There everybody, British, native, and Italian, turned out to watch the procession—the light but listing *Liebenfels* with her flags flying high above her barnacle-covered decks and sides, the tiny *Intent* which had raised her steaming alongside like a duckling trying to convoy a swan, and the two tugs towing.

Slowly we all steamed around Massawa and through the entrance gate between the wrecks into the naval harbor. There I boarded the Persian dry dock, flooded it far down, and (against Spanner's violent protests) heeled it over to a marked port list, almost causing the port side of the dock to disappear beneath the sea. But I had got to the point where, if a few inches of anything showed above the water, it was safely afloat so far as I was concerned.

Then back again I went to the *Liebenfels* which I carefully brought up to only a few degrees port list, to match the list I had given the dry dock. Hurriedly I dragged my ship onto the drydock, landed her on the inclined keel blocks before she could flop over to starboard, and started to pump up the dry dock, a very tricky docking which left the timid Spanner aghast that I should try such a thing.

It happened to be the Fourth of July when we came in with our prize of war. That parade at sea with the American flag flying in triumph over Hitler's on the once scuttled *Liebenfels* was our Fourth of July celebration. I never had a happier one.

Once the *Liebenfels* was safely landed on the keel blocks in the dry dock and well started on her way up and out of the water so nothing further could happen, I left her to the dockmaster and the Eritreans. I went ashore, covered with the grime and sweat of four nights and five days' constant labor, to tumble wearily into bed, with Ahmed ordered to guard the door and see that I was not called for anything till next morning.

I needed a rest.

CHAPTER

36

Nᴇxᴛ ᴍᴏʀɴɪɴɢ, ɪ ᴛᴜʀɴᴇᴅ ᴏᴜᴛ ᴀꜱ usual at 5:00 ᴀ.ᴍ. My first concern was for my salvage crews. They badly required a vacation from Massawa after those last five days and four nights on the *Liebenfels.* So I locked up the *Intent,* put a Sudanese sentry aboard to guard her, and sent Edison Brown and his entire crew, together with Bill Reed and all his salvage men, up in the hills to Asmara for five days to recuperate.

My next concern was what had happened at El Alamein, for I had been completely out of the world for nearly a week. To my intense relief, I learned that Auchinleck and the Eighth Army were doggedly holding their positions; Rommel had failed to achieve a breakthrough on his first assault. For the moment at least, the Middle East was safe. No one was particularly optimistic over the future, however, for since Tobruk, Rommel was a name to conjure with. But I felt better; if the British Eighth Army had pulled itself together enough to withstand the first shock, they would hold at El Alamein. No soldiers in the world could excel the British in a pure slugging match, and El Alamein was a position naturally guarded on both flanks (by the sea to the north, by the Quattaro Depression to the south) which could be taken only by a frontal assault—all strategy was out, the best slugger would win.

Rommel, with all his tricks, had been too smart. He had thrown away his golden opportunity to win the war immediately, by giving the Eighth Army a chance to dig itself in at El Alamein while he took relatively unimportant Tobruk in a grandstand play. For that feat, Hitler had instantly made Rommel a Field Marshal; if Hitler had had any real military sense, he would have ordered Rommel shot instead for letting the main objective slip while he grasped at baubles. But Rommel, likely to renew his assault at his own moment, still hung like a threatening cloud over Egypt. Alexandria remained shut down under the rain of bombs from his Stukas. The "flap" from Egypt was slacking down only because hardly any Allied personnel were left to flee. In Cairo, the Egyptians confidently awaited the coming of the Axis, and Rommel, grandstanding as always, was radioing *en clair* to the manager of Shepheard's Hotel in Cairo to reserve the whole hotel for himself and his staff; they would arrive shortly.

Once I had learned that Rommel had not broken through at El Alamein, my mind came back to my own job at Massawa. I had been away from the shore base five days; it urgently needed attention and I turned to at once, mainly on repair matters afloat. With all my salvage forces gone to the hills, I couldn't undertake more salvage for a while even if I had wished to.

First there was the matter of the damaged *Liebenfels*, now high and dry on the Persian dry dock, tying it up. It was imperative that I repair that bomb hole in her port side and get her off the dry dock as swiftly as possible; two supply ships already were waiting outside the harbor to go on that dock; more would be coming. Repairing the *Liebenfels* was strictly a shipbuilding mechanics' job, but there were none such in Massawa, either South African or American—all the iron-workers there were simply structural steel men with no experience on ships. Still they would have to do it.

So while a horde of Eritreans turned to in cleaning the entire *Liebenfels*, inside and out, of mud and barnacles, I shifted all the South Africans to her to cut away the bomb wreckage and that concrete patch the divers had installed in the number one hold. Williams who, alone of all those who had salvaged the *Liebenfels*, had elected not to go to Asmara for a rest, was put in charge. He wasn't a ship man either, but he was the best superintendent I ever had anywhere. I marked out for him where the damaged plates around that gaping hole in the *Liebenfels'* side and bottom were to be burned away. With the South Africans, he started in.

And then I had a bit of luck. The contractor's new construction superintendent ashore decided that Bill Cunningham, his ironworker, wasn't worth the trouble it took squabbling with the British M.P.s to keep him. Unless I wanted him, he was going to be shipped home. It seems some unidentified American had slugged a British M.P. in the Torino Bar the night before and broken his jaw with a single punch. While the American involved was unknown, Cunningham was strongly suspected by the British and the contractor was through with him. Did I want him?

Concealing my elation, I accepted responsibility for Cunningham with seeming reluctance lest any over-eagerness spoil the deal, and Cunningham officially joined my salvage force—a gift. Had the contractor only known it, I would have traded practically all the mechanics I had for him, so badly did I need ironworkers.

"Bill," I said to him, once he reported, "now you're a salvage man you've got to keep out of trouble. I can't be spending all my time keeping you out of British jails. What did you slug that M.P. for last night anyway? Why didn't you let him alone?"

"Honest, Captain, I tried my damnedest not to," pleaded Cunningham, "but he just wouldn't let me be. It being the Fourth of July, I was celebrating by having a beer in the Torino Bar just as quiet as a lamb, not bothering anybody, when in comes this limey M.P., and seeing I was an American, he starts to razz me about Pearl Harbor. I know I got a bad reputation 'round Massawa and can't stand getting in trouble, so I only shoves my beer farther down the bar to get away from him. What does he do but follow me up, harping on Pearl Harbor, so to quiet him, I told him what I thought about the surrender of Singapore. Then he lunges at me and I let him have it on the jaw. Honest, Captain, I only hit him once as light as I could so's I could stop him and get away without a fight, and then I hauled out of there! Nobody but you knows for sure I did it. How'd you find out?"

I didn't tell him, but it was easy. No one in Massawa but Cunningham could have broken that man's jaw with one punch, "light" or otherwise.

"See here, Bill, I'll be honest with you. I need you badly. You're no good to me in jail. I'm not blaming you for this so I'm saying nothing. Now for God's sake, do me a favor and behave! But if you do get in trouble, let me know. I'll do what I can for you, and you do the same for me."

"Aye, aye, Captain," answered Cunningham. "You watch me. What d'ye want me to do now?"

"You report to Lloyd Williams on the *Liebenfels*. He's got plenty of use for you."

So Bill Cunningham, a fiend for work when any steel was in sight, turned to with the South Africans on the bomb damage.

To repair that huge hole, I had to take practically all the scanty stock of steel I had accumulated in Massawa. But there was no alternative; I couldn't keep the dock tied up with a wreck; I couldn't take her off with a hole in her.

Lloyd Williams, Bill Cunningham, and the South Africans went at that damaged ship like demons, cutting away wreckage, then heating and bending to shape the new steel framing required. Most of the new ship plates went on flat, but with one of those new plates, I was in a dilemma. The hole went through the bilges, where the steel plating (called the bilge strake) joining the side and the bottom was bent round in a 90° curve. To get that curvature into a new steel plate one inch thick required passing it through heavy plate rolls, normally the biggest and most massive piece of machinery in any shipyard since the plates are thirty feet long and the heavy iron rolls have to be even longer.

But the longest set of plate rolls the Italians had left in Massawa (sabotaged, of course, but since repaired) would take a plate only five feet long; it couldn't start to take a plate thirty feet long. There was nothing for it, except to cut my long bilge strake plate into five-foot pieces, roll each piece separately to the required curved shape, and then weld the six curved pieces together again into one plate; an operation which vastly added to the work, since I had only a few welders. Then assembling all the new plating for the sides and the bulkheads so they would be watertight, with only ironworkers who knew none of the tricks of the trade in the shipbuilder's art, was a heart-breaking task.

Still we did it. In eight days, the *Liebenfels,* with all trace of that huge hole vanished, with her sides cleaned and painted and her underwater hull once more sleek and fair and completely watertight, as sound a hull as ever, went off the dock, erect and safely afloat once more.

But Lloyd Williams, who had moved from the salvage of the *Liebenfels* to her repairs with never a break between, was practically dead. I shipped Williams to Asmara to cool down for a week, together with all the ironworkers, who also were in a bad way from the extraordinary exertions required of them in that furnace of a dock in the middle of a Massawa July.

I should have known better. The fourth day of their vacation, Williams telephoned me from Asmara at 3:00 A.M., with bad news. Bill

Cunningham and another ironworker, one of the South Africans, a corporal, were in the military jail; eight British M.P.s, who had recklessly tried to arrest them, were in the military hospital; and most of the other M.P.s in Asmara were in bad shape. What should he do?

I thought hurriedly. When morning came and those two were dragged up before a British military court, that would be the end; I would never see either one of them again. No charges could possibly have been filed yet; there hadn't been time, and probably no complainants in good enough shape yet to file a complaint. At that moment my two ironworkers were probably booked on the night ledger as just two drunks in the jug.

I told Williams to get hold of the American military provost marshal in Asmara immediately, tell him there were two drunks belonging to the Massawa Naval Base whom I wanted released at once to American custody for the severest punishment I could inflict in Massawa, and if it worked and he got his hands on them, to put them instantly in a car and start with them for Massawa before dawn. He must not delay. If ever the wheels of justice started to grind on those two men, I was out two ironworkers, and so was Williams. As for the two culprits, I would punish the pair of them, all right; I would turn them to again at hard labor on the Massawa dry dock, a punishment which in any other jurisdiction would have been barred by law as cruel and inhuman. He could assure the provost marshal they would both be punished terribly. Nothing a military court in Asmara could do to them would equal what I was going to hand them for massacring all those M.P.s, only he wasn't to say what the punishment was to be—just say it would be swift and adequate to their heinous offense.

As for the British M.P.s, after their assailants' punishment had started, I would apologize to the British Military Governor for the conduct of my men, and extend my sympathy to the victims.

Williams said he understood and would get to work. He must have been a persuasive talker, for by 7:00 A.M., just in time for breakfast, he rolled into Massawa with my two bad boys. I looked them over. They were somewhat under the weather, somewhat bruised, but not badly, and in fair shape to go right back to work. Neither looked as if he had been in a bloody riot, such as must have occurred.

"Well, Bill," I said as I welcomed my lost sheep, "can't I even send

[296]

you on a vacation without your causing me trouble? What happened this time?"

"Honest, Captain, nothing at all, so far's I know," Cunningham explained in his lamblike voice. "Tom here," indicating the South African corporal with his thumb, "and me had just been circulating down the Viale Mussolini last night, having a few drinks to quiet our nerves after that repair job on the *Liebenfels,* when we figured finally we'd both had enough an' started for the hotel. But we was too tired to make it, so we just lay down in the gutter in the dark, out of the way o' everything, for a nap. I don't remember no fight. The next thing I knew, there was Lloyd shaking me to wake me up, and I was surprised as Tom was to find I was in the jug instead of still sleeping somewhere along the Viale Mussolini. Lloyd said you wanted him to drive us down here, and that's every blessed thing I know about it. Thanks, Captain, for getting us out o' that jail; I don't like jails."

"Get back out on that Italian dry dock, both of you," I muttered wearily, "and if you get me out of bed again, I'll have you shot for it. Don't you know I need some sleep, too? I'm as tired as you are. Get to work; you both lose the last two days of your vacation."

They left. I turned to Williams.

"Thanks, Lloyd, for saving them for us. Never let Cunningham out of Massawa again. The British Army can get lots more M.P.s, but where in hell we can get any more ironworkers I don't know. Now you go back to Asmara once more."

But Williams declined; he had had rest enough. Besides, getting out of Massawa, now he was here, just to have to come back again after a couple of days in the hills would only make him feel worse. So he also, after breakfast, went out to resume work on the Italian dock with his two ironworkers who officially now were serving time on it for their crime.

That day, July 16, turned out to be my day for difficulties with the British Military Government. Hardly had I had breakfast myself and sat down at my desk overlooking the Naval Base to scan what papers there were lying for me to sign, when Mrs. Maton informed me there was a young man, some civilian but not one of our workmen, urgently wishing to see me. He wouldn't state his business; all she could get out of him was that he *must* see me; he was very agitated, she said. I told her to show him in.

He entered; I looked him over. He was young, all right, probably about twenty; tall, very gaunt, and quite bronzed; to say that he was agitated was putting it very mildly. The moment he opened his mouth, I judged he was on the verge of hysteria; his words, in a high-pitched, youthful voice, poured out in an incoherent torrent. All I could gather from his excited statements was that he was appealing to me, the Commanding Officer of the American Naval Base, as his last hope; if I didn't help him, he was doomed.

Finally, mainly by showing a sympathetic willingness to listen rather than indicating that I was too busy, I got him calmed down enough to gather what his trouble was and what he wanted of me.

His name was Eugene Zeiner; he was a Czech, a Czech Jew, he informed me. In 1938, after Munich, but before the Nazis entered Prague, though then only sixteen, he had fled to France to escape them. His father, his mother, his younger sister, who had stayed in Prague, he told me in heart-broken tones, must now all be dead—in four years he had heard nothing from or of them.

In September of 1939, when the Nazis attacked Poland, he had crossed from France to England and had enlisted as an infantryman in a British regiment. He was burning to kill Nazis for what they had done to his family.

"See!" he cried, dragging from his pocket some soiled papers and tremblingly spreading them out before me. They were his official service records as a British soldier, starting in September, 1939, when seventeen-year-old Eugene Zeiner had volunteered. "I served all through that first campaign in France, through the collapse in Belgium, the retreat to Dunkirk. I was evacuated under fire on the beach at Dunkirk!" His shrill voice rose almost to a shriek as he pointed to the record. It was so entered there.

"Then after a few months in England, they gave us new rifles and I came to Libya. I fought with the Eighth Army in the desert under Wavell. See, again?" He pointed to the entry. "We did well, we got to Benghazi, we nearly drove the Fascists out of Africa, only suddenly we were all shipped out of Libya to stop the Nazis in Greece. Look!" Once more he pointed to the record. "Greece was terrible, a few thousand Englishmen against a million Nazis!" His piercing voice broke, he paused a moment, then excitedly went on. "We fought hard, but we were crushed. We had to retreat. Then from Greece another evacuation under fire on the beaches. It was worse than Dunkirk!"

Completely broken up by the recollection, he mumbled incoherently while he fumbled with the record, then pulled himself together a bit and pointed to the next entry.

"See, Crete next!" Now indeed his shrill cry sounded almost that of a madman's. "Crete, Nazi paratroopers, skies full of Nazi bombers and fighter planes strafing us, and we had hardly our bayonets to oppose them! Crete! That was worst of all! We fought like tigers. But once more we had to be evacuated from the beaches, those who were left!" He began to sob. I said nothing; there were several British naval officers in Massawa who had been at Crete; they had assured me that nothing in the whole war, on land or sea, had equaled Crete in hellishness.

"Look, Captain!" Zeiner finally managed to ejaculate, pointing to the last entry. Private Eugene Zeiner had been evacuated from Crete to Alexandria. Immediately after, in June, 1941, already at nineteen a veteran with four of the war's most horrible campaigns behind him, a medical survey had adjudged him unfit for further military service—shell shock, psychosis, whatever it was the surgeons had called it, had made a wreck of the lad and he was honorably discharged from His Majesty's Forces. The closing entry went on to note that he had been a good soldier, that for his disability he was entitled to a pension of four shillings a week or four shillings a month, I have forgotten which.

"Well?" I asked, looking up at him after I had read that. What did he want of me?

"They wouldn't let me fight any more, though I was willing! I hate Nazis!" he shrieked. "But all the same I was discharged, a civilian in Egypt. I couldn't go home; I had no home to go to. Of course I couldn't live on the four shillings but other soldiers helped me. It was hard getting a job in Egypt; people looked at my military papers and decided I must be crazy—maybe I am! At last I got a job as a clerk with the contractor for this American Mission in Cairo—they needed clerks so badly who could understand English that they would hire anybody. I worked hard; I did all right there in Cairo with them. Then came Rommel to El Alamein and this 'flap'; everybody American in the office fled in an instant! But I could not flee, I was not American; so I stayed in the empty office to straighten things out till quitting time anyway. On one desk I found lying ten thousand dollars in American bills; so fast had everybody gone they had not even bothered over all that money! I wrapped it up and took it to the American Ambassador's office; he was almost the only American left in Cairo. Then I was out of a job again, and besides Rommel was expected in Cairo almost every hour. Rommel and his Nazis! What would they do to me—a Czech Jew who had escaped Czechoslovakia to fight them as a British soldier!" Again Zeiner's high-pitched voice rose to a shrill crescendo.

Fascinated now, I listened to him, as unable to interrupt his discourse (even had I wanted to) as The Wedding Guest clutched by The Ancient Mariner in Coleridge's rime.

Zeiner got his breath again, continued excitedly.

"I had to get out of Egypt, but I wasn't British, I wasn't American, I had no passport of any kind, nothing except my military papers. I went to the Egyptians; without a passport, I could not leave. I went to the British for a passport; they said they couldn't give me one since I was not British. I showed my British military papers. That didn't help; being a British soldier didn't make me a British citizen. I was desperate; all the other civilians were gone. When the Nazis came, I should stick out among the Egyptians like a lighthouse to be seized instantly. I begged of the British to do something for me. But God save bureaucrats and red tape! There was nothing in the official books that covered a case like mine, so they could issue no passport.

"I refused to leave that office—two years I had served their king; now his servants *must* do something, even to breaking their rules, to save me! Finally one of them had an idea. They couldn't issue me a passport, but they could give me a transit visa through all British territories to Addis Ababa in Ethiopia (God himself only knows why Ethiopia); it would look enough like an official document in place of a passport that I might get out of Egypt on it. Would I take that? I was frantic! To get away from the Nazis and maybe fight again some day, I would take a transit visa to Ethiopia, to hell, to anywhere! Of course I took it. I went to Alexandria. There was much excitement there, refugees, bombs, Stukas; it was almost like another evacuation. My paper had a big enough red seal on it; the Egyptians were not paying close attention; I was permitted to board a freighter for Massawa on my way to Addis Ababa. So I came at last to Massawa, Captain!" finished Zeiner breathlessly.

"Yes, I understand that all right, Mr. Zeiner, seeing that you're here right now. But still what has all this got to do with me or this Naval Base?"

Zeiner clutched my arm, as if to hang on, fearful that I might order him thrown out, while he thrust still another paper down on my desk.

"Read that, Captain! You must save me! I can't go there!" he screamed.

I read it. It was on the O.E.T.A. stationery I knew well, a letter from the Occupied Enemy Territories Administration in Asmara, the British Military Government, to Mr. Eugene Zeiner. He was advised that already he had overstayed the brief period in Eritrea allowed him on his transit visa to Addis Ababa; unless he proceeded immediately on his journey to Ethiopia, he would be deported there. It was signed by one of the British officers in O.E.T.A. whom I knew slightly.

Now indeed Zeiner became hysterical; I felt as if I were listening to one of the damned as he shrilled out,

"I'll die in Ethiopia! What is there for me to do there? There's no way out of Ethiopia! Where could I go from there? I saved ten thousand dollars for the Americans in Cairo. You're American; for God's sake, do something for me! You are the American Commandant; the British will listen to you! Make them let me stay in Massawa at least! Maybe here I can find work, perhaps even for the Americans. But don't let them send me to Ethiopia! I can't stand any more!" and very evidently on the verge of utter collapse, he began sobbing violently.

Now I saw his reason for pouring out his story to me, a heart-rending one truly. And his papers backed it up. This broken lad, who had fought our enemies till the disasters he had been through had turned him into the hysterical wretch I had before me who could fight no more, was going to get all the help I could give him, if I had any influence in Eritrea. I told Mrs. Maton, standing near with tears in her own eyes, to get me on the phone the O.E.T.A. officer in Asmara, a major, who had signed that deportation letter.

It took some time. Meanwhile, I seated Eugene Zeiner in a chair, got him some water to cool him off, and calmed him down a bit by telling him to quit worrying—he wasn't going to Ethiopia. No matter what it took, I would see to that.

Twenty minutes later, Mrs. Maton, who had been patiently working on the phone, looked up at me and announced,

[301]

"You're through, Captain."

I took the phone.

"Hello, Major, this is Captain Ellsberg, Massawa Naval Base. There's an ex-British soldier, a Eugene Zeiner, in my office with a deportation order from you. He did something for us Americans in Cairo, and I'm taking an interest in his case. Can't you cancel that letter?"

"No, Captain Ellsberg. I know that case; the man's an alien with only a transit visa through Eritrea. He's already overstayed his transit time. We've been easy on him over that, but he's got to get cracking. He can't stay any longer."

"But, Major, you'll kill him if you deport him to Ethiopia! That man's fought for you till it's made a wreck of him. He's entitled to consideration. You saw his papers, didn't you?"

"Yes, Captain, I saw them."

"They're in order, aren't they? Anything wrong with them? Are those service records correct?"

"Yes, his military papers are in order. But except for that pension, they don't entitle him to anything. You don't understand, Captain. The man's not a British citizen; he's an alien, and he can't stay in Eritrea on only a transit visa through to Addis Ababa. He's got to move on. The regulations don't permit his staying."

"I'll say I don't understand, Major!" I answered bitterly. "Neither will anybody else in America, when I give this story to the American newspaper men from Cairo who're all in Asmara right now because of this flap! There's not much news in Asmara; those reporters will all fall hard for this Zeiner story. It'll sound fine in the American press, won't it? Broken-down British soldier, a mere boy, veteran of Dunkirk, Libya, Greece, and Crete, kicked out of Eritrea to his death against the protests of the American Commandant because British red tape can't be cut! That'll certainly encourage Americans to go all out to help Britain! There'll be an explosion in London over it; London'll hop your boss, Brigadier Longrigg; and the Brigadier will fall on you like a ton of bricks for being such a dumbbell as to let that story break! You deport that man, and by God, I'll do it!"

"Really, Captain, I trust you won't do anything like that!" came in a horrified voice over the wire. "It wouldn't be cricket, you know, old chap. I didn't make those regulations; it's only my job to see they're enforced. Really now, I sympathize with the poor blighter as much as you do, but what can I do? He's not all there, you know; you must have observed that yourself in talking to him. If I let him stay, nobody'll employ him, he'll become a public charge, and I'll be held respon—"

"Is *that* all that's worrying you?" I broke in. "Why, Major—" And the next instant I found myself suddenly listening to someone talking to me in Italian. Somewhere between Massawa and Asmara, as usual, some local operator had crossed the wires. But for once, instead of swearing over it, I blessed the operator who had done it. It gave me a few minutes to ponder that O.E.T.A. Major's last remark.

I gave the phone to Mrs. Maton.

"Connection broken as usual, Mrs. Maton. Please try to get it again."

I turned to Eugene Zeiner, and hastily sized him up. He looked like a well-educated young man; his English was perfect.

"What can you do if I give you a job?" I asked.

"Anything, Captain!" he burst out excitedly. "Clerk, maybe interpreter; I know five languages. I know even a little about machinery I learned in the Army! Anything at all you want, I'll try! Digging trenches for pipes even! I've had lots of experience digging foxholes; I can—"

"You're through again, Captain," interrupted Mrs. Maton, passing the phone towards me.

"That's enough; you're hired!" I informed Zeiner as I took the phone.

"Sorry, old chap," I heard, "some one of these blessed Eyties broke in on us. What were you saying, Captain?"

"I was going to say there was another factor in the case I'd overlooked. It didn't occur to me it meant anything till your last remark. Brigadier Longrigg knows how devilishly short-handed we are down here, and that man Zeiner's employed at this Base. If you deport him, I lose an employee, and I'll not stand for it; I'll go right to Brigadier Longrigg myself, on top of what else I promised to do, over your robbing me of one of my men when I'm breaking my neck to get ships out for the Royal Navy! He'll flay you alive for it!"

"He's your employee, you say? My word, that puts a different light on the case!" I heard a much relieved voice saying over the phone. "Too bad you didn't tell me that right off; I would have fixed it all up without bothering you so much over it, Captain. Your employee, eh? That's topping! That settles everything with no need of troubling anybody about the case. You just write us an official letter as Commandant of the Naval Base saying he's one of your employees, and we'll cancel that deportation notice and give him a permit to remain in Eritrea as long as he works for you. Happy to oblige you, Captain. Anything else?"

"No, thanks, Major. That fixes everything. Good-by!" and I hung up the phone.

"It's all right, Zeiner," I said, looking speculatively over my newly acquired employee. "They're canceling that letter. You can stay and work here."

Eugene Zeiner, with a light in his boyish eyes very like what I imagine might shine in those of a man suddenly pardoned as he stood with the noose round his neck, was too inarticulate for any words. He merely straightened stiffly up to attention, saluted in the British fashion, and looked at me as if awaiting orders.

"You take Mr. Zeiner down to the pay office, Mrs. Maton," I said to her, "and see he's entered on the Naval Base rolls as a clerk. I'll see about his actual assignment this afternoon, when I've had time to think over where we can use him best. Probably in the machine shop office."

Once more Zeiner saluted, faced about, and followed Mrs. Maton out of the office. So now, by the grace of Field Marshal Rommel, I had a clerk; the first male clerk the Naval Base itself had been blessed with. I could use one.

CHAPTER

37

I HAD A BUSY DAY FROM THEN ON. Already it was nearly 10:00 A.M.; I had promised to be on the Naval Base pier for a discussion with Brown on the *Intent* before he shoved off to start his second salvage job. I hurried down there.

Brown and his men had returned a few days before from their excursion to the Asmara plateau, somewhat rested again. They had since been overhauling the *Intent's* salvage outfit, particularly her pumps. Now everything was restowed, cleaned, dried out, and ready for business as before, except the crew themselves—they weren't the men they had been when first they had arrived—Massawa and the *Liebenfels* had already cost them plenty.

Inside the little bridge of the *Intent,* I went over briefly with Brown his second assignment—the scuttled *S.S. Frauenfels,* also Nazi, a slightly larger sister to the *Liebenfels.* She was sunk as the third ship ahead of where the *Liebenfels* had once lain, right in the center of that long line of wrecks in the south harbor. The salvage job would be practically the same as that on the *Liebenfels* except for three things which made it harder—the *Frauenfels* was in deeper water; she had two holes blasted in her, one forward and one aft, which meant twice as much patching under water; and Brown's crew, including Brown himself, weren't what they used to be, while one of his three divers, Wiard, was now on a shore job with the contractor.

On the credit side of that ledger, however, there were some offsets. A freighter from America had come in a few days before with a considerable number of portable air-conditioning units, some new salvage pumps I had ordered in New York, and a large number of cases of small hand tools of all kinds for me.

With the air-conditioners, I could fix up not only our quarters completely, but also the barracks for the men so all hands might have a chance to sleep at night without perspiring—that would help alleviate the prickly heat which was driving us all wild.

The new American salvage pumps, a consignment of big ten-inch and six-inch pumps, would give us vastly improved pumping capacity on the *Frauenfels*, allowing us to cut the pumping time so low we should get the ship up and dried out before moisture could kill off all the magnetos, avoiding the battle we had had on the *Liebenfels*.

And all the hand tools—torches, drills, diving telephones, that were in those new cases—should greatly help both the salvage crews and the Naval Base shops in working—at last we should have enough small tools to work with.

So without trepidation, I looked forward to the lifting of the *Frauenfels*, though undoubtedly it would take considerably longer than the *Intent* had spent on her sister. In addition to two holes to patch, because of the greater depth of water and the resulting greater load coming on the main deck of the wreck when we started to pump out the submerged holds, Brown would have to have the divers shore up inside underneath the main deck of the *Frauenfels* before we started pumping out. Otherwise that deck, with the weight of thousands of tons of sea water on top of it, would collapse on us and ruin everything, once the water inside the holds fell away from the main deck and no longer supported it from below.

All that I went over with Brown—the shoring, the patching, the hatch cofferdams, the sealing up of the sea chests, the closing of all interior valves. It was all clear, and the *Intent* could shove off for the south harbor to commence, but Brown seemed to have something on his mind distracting him from the job in hand. I asked him what was the matter; was he too worn out for another raising?

"No, it's not the *Frauenfels;* we'll get her up, Captain. It's that gang up on the hill! They're enough to drive anybody crazy!"

I supposed he meant the American contractor. While that contractor was causing me more mental anguish than anything I had to battle in Massawa, still why should Brown be concerned over those people? I looked at him, puzzled.

"I went to see them while I was in Asmara for our rest, Captain, to go over with them some claims my crew has got for pay on the voyage round from Port Arthur, and did I get a going over! But the boys are entitled to that money, and I wasn't taking no for an answer from anybody. Finally I finished up talking to just about the top mogul, and do those people up there think they're God! You should have heard what their foreign manager said to me. I didn't get the money due my men, but take it from me, Captain, I told them off! Read that!"

Brown shoved a carbon copy of a letter into my hands. I glanced at it. It was dated in Massawa, July 13, three days before, addressed to the contractor's foreign manager in Asmara.

My dear sir:

I wish to thank you for the very enlightening interview that you so graciously gave me at your Asmara office on July 7, 1942. Until I was so informed by you I had not realized that I was just a "camp follower."

It was extremely kind of you, a busy man of affairs, to take the time to inform me in such a courteous and tactful manner exactly what I was, and make clear to me the small and insignificant part that the men in Massawa were playing in the extremely large scale operations under your jurisdiction.

Until pointed out to me by you I had not realized that Captain Ellsberg, U.S.N.R., was "a small pebble on the beach" and the operations at Massawa "just a drop in the bucket."

If you put all the supervisors in your company in their places as deftly and efficiently as you did me, I am sure they would co-operate to the limit of their endurance for your company in the war effort.

Sincerely yours,

Edison D. Brown,
Salvage Master

c.c. Capt. Edward Ellsberg

I shoved my carbon copy of his letter into my shirt pocket, trying not to grin.

"You certainly told 'em off, Brown," I had to admit. "Now I'm a naval officer, and I couldn't write letters like that to anybody, but since you're still a free and equal citizen of the United States, I suppose you can. However, don't lose any sleep over that crowd. We'll do our bit for the war effort in Massawa even if you are only a 'camp follower' and I'm only 'a small pebble on the beach.' Now if you have any more problems with that outfit, let me handle them while you tend to the *Frauenfels*. I'm used to being kicked around by their big shots in the high hills over the telephone (Massawa's too hot for em to come down here much to bother me) and I see you're not.

Leave them to me, and you at least will have fewer headaches. You can shove off now, and good luck to you, Brown, and your men on the *Frauenfels*."

"Aye, aye, Captain." Brown reached for his bridge controls to start maneuvering his tug away from the pier while I hastily slid down from his superstructure onto the wharf, an exit which on that tiny craft required no more than two good jumps.

I waved to the salvage men on the *Intent's* fantail as their vessel fell away from the pier and her powerful propeller started to push her ahead on her way to the south harbor and the scuttled *Frauenfels*. Next day I should be with them there.

Back in my office, I took up other problems again. I had managed to get turned over to the Naval Base the huge masonry barracks that shortly before Britain's Indian troops had been occupying. Part of the Bengalis and the Sikhs had been hurriedly shipped east to fight the Japs; the rest I had persuaded Colonel Sundius-Smith, commanding the British forces about Massawa, to move out of Massawa to some ex-Italian wooden barracks in the hills halfway to Asmara.

That massive building would make fine quarters for all the American (and South African) workmen in Massawa; it was the one place which (once all its shuttered windows were sealed off airtight with masonite sheets) could be air-conditioned.

For now we had quite a number of air-conditioners. A few sets, the first to arrive, had already been installed in Building 35. There we had sealed up tightly every shuttered window and door, put a portable air-conditioning set in each room, and the results had been marvelous. In my room, for instance, the air-conditioner, running night and day, of course, with never a shut off, had managed to knock the inside temperature down to 90° F., and the humidity down to 65 per cent. It was unbelievable what the effect was. Entering that room at night after a regular day under the Massawa sun, it felt as if I had suddenly entered a refrigerator, and for a while after entering I always had to slip on a coat to avoid a chill till I got used to it indoors.

Then there was another gain. With all room openings tightly sealed off and the only air now coming in blowing first through the filter of the air-conditioner, I no longer had to sleep under a mosquito net enveloping my bed. That was wonderful. Between the absence of the mosquito net and that beautifully cool 90° F. air in my room with only 65 per cent humidity in it, I could now wear pajamas again at night without perspiring; I didn't have to sleep naked any more.

The effect of all this was heavenly. No longer bathed in sweat all night through, the prickly heat from the day's exposure outside subsided a bit, leaving the sufferer to start from scratch, so to speak, each morning in accumulating a fresh crop of prickles in his prickly heat instead of having it build up as before without intermission, day or night. Every night I blessed the Westinghouse Company which had made my air-conditioner and wished them unending prosperity for what their machinery was doing for me in Massawa.

Now to talk about heavenly comfort in a room with the thermometer at 90° F. and the humidity at 65 per cent (conditions which in any American city would be headlined in the papers as a heat wave, with the prostration victims listed daily) only goes to show that everything is relative. In Massawa, my air-conditioned room was the nearest thing to heaven that existed.

Of course, it goes without saying that there was a catch to all this bliss—the catch came when every morning between 5:00 and 6:00, I opened my door to step out and begin my day's work. Some day, somewhere, somehow, there may arise another Shakespeare with words graphic enough to convey the shock resulting each morning when I emerged from my cool room to meet again that soul-shriveling blast that was Massawa in midsummer; I can't do it.

At least, in air-conditioned rooms, we could sleep at night now; that was something. Now the problem was to get my ex-Italian barracks building sealed up, air-conditioned, and our American workmen moved into it. How was that going?

Captain Morrill came in to report to me on the subject; progress was not too fast. Overhauling the plumbing system and rewiring the building with electric circuits heavy enough to carry all the new air-conditioners, were the major difficulties. There were available in Massawa to hurry the job neither enough plumbers nor enough electricians; most of the Americans in those trades were still engaged at Ghinda in finishing up that magnificent housing project in the hills (against which I had futilely protested many times), which would be utterly worthless to us when finished, and which as an actual fact never was used by anybody in Massawa.

I listened to Morrill's report. With difficulty I avoided a hysterical outburst myself over the tragic waste of money, men, and material at Ghinda.

"Well, Morrill, let's hope they finish it soon, so it can be abandoned to the natives, the Eyties, or the goats up there, whoever wants it, and the workmen in Ghinda at least moved somewhere they'll do some good. Anything else?"

"Yes, Captain; there's that man you hired this morning. Anywhere special you want him assigned?"

"Oh, Zeiner, you mean? I'd forgotten about him. You got any suggestions?"

"Yes, if you've got no objections. I've talked with him while you were out. Looks like a very bright youngster to me, and maybe he can fix something that's been giving me and Woods a headache. You know all those cases of small tools that came in last week? We've got nobody to inventory them or keep track of their issue, and Lieutenant Woods tells me the stuff in the few cases he's already opened has disappeared like a snowball would in this place, with no trace of where it's gone. There's a swell black market around here for everything these Eyties steal. Now suppose we give that Zeiner to Lieutenant Woods, give him a few Eritreans to help, and let him crack open all those cases, inventory what's in 'em, and after that make him responsible for issue and return of all those tools. That boy can talk both Arabian and Italian; none of these Arab or Eytie mechanic will put anything over on him. I'll bet you, Captain, he'll save us his whole year's wages in one day!"

"O.K., Morrill; it sounds fine. You turn him over to Woods and let me know in a few days if it works out."

CHAPTER

38

NEXT MORNING ON ARRIVAL AT MY office, I received a telephone call from Captain Lucas at the Royal Naval Base. He had something of a top secret nature he had to talk with me about; he couldn't, of course, mention it over the phone. Would I be so kind as to drop over at once to see him? I would.

As I went over to Lucas' office, I wondered what on earth was up now. Were the British going to haul me over the coals for Bill Cunningham and his riot in Asmara? Then I decided it couldn't be that; nothing connected with that riot could possibly be considered top secret. Perhaps it might be my harsh words to Brigadier Longrigg's major in the Zeiner case if he didn't meet my wishes. That seemed more likely.

But after I got a look at Lucas' face, I decided it was for none of my crimes. Lucas was serious enough but not in the manner I'd seen him each time he'd had to call my attention to some dereliction on the part of my obstreperous Americans (which had been often).

So it turned out. Posting his orderly to keep everyone out of earshot of his office, Captain Lucas informed me of what was up. The Duke of Gloucester, Lieutenant General in the British Army, brother to the King, and his official representative, had manifested an interest in what was going on in Massawa. The next morning, by car from Asmara, he would arrive at ten o'clock to inspect the U.S. Naval Repair Base and the salvage operations.

Naturally Captain Lucas was perturbed, and I didn't blame him. Here was a member of the Royal Family, third in the succession, and likely suddenly to awake any morning as King of England himself should one of the many bombs aimed at Buckingham Palace strike it, thrust into our hands to inspect a naval station manned to a high degree by enemy aliens and P.O.W.s. If anything unfortunate happened to the Duke of Gloucester while in Massawa, the responsibility would be on our heads. It was absolutely imperative to keep the Duke's coming visit top secret to the last minute—till too late for any plots to be hatched. After the last minute, we should have to be prepared against any impromptu episodes.

I nodded in agreement. Captain Lucas undertook to look out for the Duke everywhere on the Abd-El-Kader Peninsula except when he was actually within my Base and afloat; during those periods, it would have to be my task. No one knew of the matter at the Royal Naval Base except himself and his executive officer; I could inform my own exec, Captain Morrill. But in neither case, till about sixty minutes before the Duke's arrival would either of us inform even our major assistants.

There was one other thing. Colonel Sundius-Smith, commanding officer for the British Army, was also in on the matter—he would furnish several battalions of Sudanese and Indians to be reviewed by the Duke on his arrival on the grounds of my Base, though none of his men were to be informed in advance as to the why of the parade.

I thanked Captain Lucas for his information, promised to let him know that night of my preparations, and started to depart. Then one other matter occurred to me, and I paused. I had to take the Duke around on the water to show him our salvaged craft and our wrecks; all I had for the job was the *Lord Grey,* a terrible scow to ask the Duke to ride in. Would Captain Lucas be so kind as to lend me for the occasion his own boat, the ex-Italian admiral's barge which the British had promptly seized on the surrender? For this occasion she would have to fly an American flag; would Captain Lucas mind? Lucas agreed cordially to lend the boat and not to object to the flag.

So I went back to my own Base to call Morrill into our own top secret conference. Hurriedly we arranged matters. An hour before the Duke's arrival, Morrill would inform Lieutenant Woods and our shop superintendents of who was coming. In every shop immediately thereafter, every overhead crane was to be run to one end of the shop, the crane hook trolleyed all the way over to one side, the Eytie operator removed from the overhead crane cab, and the power cut off the crane. I was taking no chances on anyone accidentally dropping anything from above on the Duke's head as he passed through; I had seen such accidents happen before.

Ten minutes before the Duke's arrival, each foreman was explicitly to warn all his workmen that visitors were shortly expected; the warning was to be in all appropriate languages so no one could possibly misunderstand. The men were to be told then also that just before the arrival in that shop of the visitors, a whistle would be blown. After that whistle all hands were strictly to tend to their machines; any man who made a move from his task before the visitors had departed from that shop was likely to be shot instantly and without discussion.

Finally there was the question of who should stand by to do the shooting if necessary. As an American Naval Base, it would look well if only we had some American bluejackets in each shop as a guard, but our American Naval Base didn't possess even one American yeoman, let alone a more seagoing bluejacket. Captain Lucas had plenty of British bluejackets, whom doubtless he would be very willing to lend us, but I would have died of mortification if the Duke of Gloucester should see that the United States had not even provided its Naval Base with at least a few of its own seamen.

That was a tough one, but we solved it. In the commercial harbor were now a number of American freighters discharging. They were all armed; they must have Navy Armed Guard detachments aboard. Morrill was to go over to the commercial port, and in my name borrow at least twelve American bluejackets and two Armed Guard naval officers, all to come armed with Colt .45s by 9:00 A.M. next day. Then Morrill would instruct them in their jobs; they would be divided into two squads, each under an officer. One squad would guard the shop being visited; the other, the next shop to be entered. As soon as the visitors had left a shop, the guard there was to leapfrog to the second shop beyond, and so on alternately. It ought to work, and if the Duke were not too observant, he would think the United States really had a well-manned Naval Base in Massawa.

There was one other trouble for me. The uniform for the occasion for all naval officers, set by Captain Lucas as Senior Officer Present, was to be whites—white shorts, of course, white shirts, white shoes and socks, and white sun helmets. I didn't have any white sun helmet, but that I could get around by wearing my white gold-visored naval cap; damned uncomfortable in place of a helmet, but at least suitable in appearance. What stymied me was that I had no white shorts —nothing but the khaki that had served me on wrecks and everywhere else. And in Massawa I could neither buy any nor have any made. It looked as if I were going to be a disgrace to the United States.

In that dilemma, Captain Morrill, who as an Army officer would wear khaki along with all others, came to my rescue—remarkably enough he had a pair of white shorts, though they were no part of any Army uniform. Someone somewhere had loaned him a pair for something, he couldn't remember what, and he had forgotten to return them. I was welcome to them permanently. Later that day I tried them on; they were quite large for my much-reduced Massawa figure, but by heavily reefing in, I could keep them up. I accepted them gladly, all set now to receive the Duke of Gloucester in borrowed shorts, borrowed sailors, a borrowed boat, and under what had once been a borrowed American flag. I may add that the Naval Base itself was also all borrowed from the Eyties, including most of my skilled workmen in it.

Next morning, the show started off at nine as scheduled—there were three battalions of Sudanese, Bengalis, and Sikhs, all lined up on the parade ground in front of my electric shop, with our one large American flag, somewhat faded and dusty by now, proudly displayed above them. In front of them were all the naval officers, British and American (twelve British and one American) from both naval stations. Then there were Colonel Sundius-Smith, and various British and American Army officers, all except Morrill and Woods, who were having their hands full in the shops, instructing both the foremen and our borrowed sailors.

It was damned hot out in the sun; to avoid being knocked out, I was wearing my khaki sun helmet over my whites, reserving my white naval cap till the last minute before the Duke showed up.

Nine-thirty rolled around. The news of who was to be received was passed out to all officers. It caused quite a stir—among the British because of their natural respect for the Royal Family; among the Americans because Dukes were *rara avis* to them.

Ten o'clock came but no Duke nor any sign of him or his cavalcade. Meanwhile, here and there men in ranks, though all allowed to stand at ease, were keeling over one by one—a startling thing considering they were all colonial troops, brought up in the tropics. Evidently neither India nor the Sudan was any proper training for the Massawa sun in July. I thanked God I'd had sense enough to be non reg

[314]

for a while and wear my khaki sun helmet, otherwise I should myself long since have collapsed.

At 10:20 A.M., a British dispatch rider raced in on a motorcycle to inform us the Duke would be along in a few minutes, would we be patient? The Duke was late, but it wasn't his fault; he had started in plenty of time from Asmara. Unfortunately, he was being transported in a British Army Ford, brought from the Libyan Desert and fitted out for desert service. But that Ford never knew what deserts were till it struck the Massawa desert this side of the mountains. Then its radiator water had all boiled out, the engine had frozen up, and with all its pistons seized in the cylinders, the engine had curled up and died in the middle of the desert. After vain attempts to unfreeze it by pouring in a fresh charge of water while the Duke cooked inside the car, the attempt had finally been abandoned, the Duke had been taken aboard Colonel Chickering's Chevrolet, and the procession had started again, abandoning the Duke's Ford. He should shortly arrive.

He did. At 10:30 A.M., I hurriedly tossed aside my khaki sun helmet and donned my white cap, as amidst appropriate flourishes, the Duke himself descended from his borrowed American car, and my conscience ceased to trouble me about all my borrowed accessories. Apparently even Dukes could borrow under sufficient necessity.

Everything went off beautifully. The colonials (that is, those still left on their feet) paraded in amazingly soldierly fashion, considering the long preliminary roasting they had received. However, all hands were even that way, for the Duke had baked in the desert while we had roasted on the parade ground, and he looked it, with his khaki shirt unbuttoned well down from his throat and thoroughly soaked from head to foot in perspiration.

After the parade, I escorted the Duke through all the shops, where he gazed with great interest at the previously sabotaged machinery and at our all-nations workmen, busily attending their machines. Morrill had done a splendid job in the shops, backed up by Woods. In every shop was presented a scene of native and Eytie workmen so thoroughly engrossed at their tasks they hardly looked up at the Duke as he slowly passed through, asking how this or that damaged machine had been repaired, and being introduced to the American superintendents who had done it. Meanwhile, my borrowed bluejackets were leap-frogging magnificently; one would never have guessed there

[315]

wasn't a permanent American naval guard in every shop.

After the shop inspection, we moved briefly over to the Royal Naval Base where at the Officers' Mess, lunch was served for the Duke and the senior officers.

That over, back at my Base, we shoved off in the boat borrowed from Captain Lucas, disguised at the stern with a small American boat ensign. Fortunately, there was a little breeze, and it was cooler out on the water. I'm sure the Duke appreciated it.

By this time I had seen enough of the Duke to conclude he was a very unaffected human being, in no way trying to be regal, and honestly interested in what was going on. He manifested tremendous enthusiasm over our achievements on both the *Liebenfels* and the salvaged Italian dock, insisted on boarding both, laughed over how the Persian dry dock had been finessed as a prize of war, and was as startled as I had been at first viewing the rows on rows of scuttled ships with which the Nazis and Eyties had festooned the harbor waters.

About the middle of the afternoon, we came back to our Base and the Duke was ready to leave. But he had had enough of traversing the desert outside Massawa, so while we were inspecting the Base, a plane had hastily been flown down from Asmara to the little-used Massawa airfield to take him back to Asmara. The Duke didn't say farewell; instead he invited me to fly back with him to Asmara to have dinner there with him as his guest, and later to attend an evening reception he was giving.

I accepted with great pleasure. While the Duke was being transported to the airfield, I rushed to my room to get an overcoat lest I freeze in Asmara, then joined him at the airfield.

The plane ride I thought was a great improvement; in twenty minutes we had covered the forty airline miles to Asmara, instead of putting in at least two and a half hours on that terrible seventy-mile combination of desert and mountain road. And the more I saw of the Duke of Gloucester, the more he seemed to me to resemble his brother, King George, whose coronation five years before I had attended.

The conversation at dinner ran mostly to the story of Massawa. At the reception afterward, I saw little of him, for all British and American officialdom in Asmara was there. Late in the evening, I managed to squeeze through the crowd about him to thank the Duke for his interest and to say good-by. On his part, he thanked me for my help to Britain and promised that if ever he might put in a word to help us, he'd not forget Massawa. I was quite willing to believe that; never would he forget Massawa, if for no other account than what he had suffered there.

CHAPTER

39

THE LAST FEW WEEKS OF JULY moved unexcitedly along while endlessly we labored and sweltered. We got the barracks building finished for the men and moved all the American workmen—the slight Naval Base force, the contractor's men, my salvage crews, and the South Africans—into it, where they also could get the blessings of air-conditioning. Our cases of hospitalization for prickly heat immediately dropped sharply.

Out on the Persian dry dock, we were pushing ships through steadily, one every day and a half. My major troubles on that dock were now meeting religious requirements—I had to furnish a goat every five days to the Persians to meet their necessities and it seemed to me that every day was the Sabbath for some group on that dry dock—I never knew there were so many religions in the world.

Lloyd Williams, assisted by Bill Reed and his divers, and by Cunningham and the South Africans, was repairing the salvaged Italian dry dock as fast as his skimpy stock of steel allowed. All of us were going around the Naval Base now with our eyes glued to the ground, looking for odd scraps of steel plate or bars we might somehow use. And I had one more American ironworker, Horace Armstrong, who, five months in transit by sea, had finally arrived as an additional salvage mechanic. He was, according to Williams, another tough guy, more pugnacious even than Cunningham, who was pugnacious only when he was drunk, while Armstrong tended toward pugnacity all the time. But he showed himself to be a good ironworker, and I could pardon much for that. He and Cunningham now worked as a team.

Then there was the *Liebenfels*. Her hull was repaired, but her boilers, her engines, and her electrical outfit, submerged in the Red Sea more than a year, had all to be cleaned and her machinery dismantled, oiled, and reassembled before she could steam again.

For this task, a terrific one, I took Hudson, the English engineer on the Persian dock, and put him in charge of all machinery repairs on our salvaged wrecks, helped by such miscellaneous Italians as I could spare and a few Danish, Jewish, and Greek engineers as could occasionally be hired off some ship coming into Massawa. I never had any Americans at all on that task.

Hudson proved to be a wonder—a hard worker himself, a fine engineer, and a good leader. Under him, considering the few men he had, we started to make excellent progress in getting the machinery of the *Liebenfels* ready for sea again.

Finally aside from everything going on in the naval shops, there was the *Intent* working on the *Frauenfels*. I visited her every few days, made a few dives to inspect her damage, and left the rest to Brown. There was nothing novel on the *Frauenfels*—just the day by day torture of working on her under the July sun, undersea and on the surface. Brown and his men kept steadily at it.

For well over two months, I had been bombarding Cairo to get me more workmen for repairing my salvaged wrecks—first, for the Italian dry dock, then for the *Liebenfels* also. America swiftly passed the problem to the British; the British said they couldn't help. But now with the Naval Base at Alexandria shut down, it seemed to me there *must* be men from there available to be sent to Massawa, if only temporarily, and I had commenced a second barrage of requests along those lines.

Seemingly I was getting nowhere with this either, and I began to get morose, particularly with everybody's personal troubles, native or American, being landed in my lap for solution.

For instance, Mrs. Maton complained to me about the Sudanese laborers in the carpenter shop. They were parking the goat for their Sabbath dinner right alongside the office building all through the week and then slaughtering and roasting him right there in the open. As she had to be in the office all day long, smelling that goat all week, not to mention witnessing his piteous demise and the ensuing rather savage feast, she felt that after three goats, she was fed up. Couldn't I do something about it?

A cursory investigation showed Mrs. Maton was in nowise exaggerating, so I declared a moratorium on all goats ashore within the limits of the U.S. Naval Repair Base.

Then Doc Kimble, diver, came to me to complain that the circulation of air in the corner of the barracks where he now slept didn't suit; would I do something about it? Of course, for a diver I'd do anything. I personally investigated that corner and had the fans changed.

Then Bill Reed, salvage master, had a complaint also. It appeared that he had only a station wagon to haul his men about, while one of the contractor's superintendents ran around in a sedan. Bill felt there was no justice in that situation. I agreed with Bill heartily on that; he was as much entitled to a sedan as that construction superintendent—more even, maybe, for he certainly worked harder—but where could I get the sedan? All I could do (and did) was to tell Bill he could use my sedan whenever I wasn't (which was most of the time).

Then Mohammed Ali, with God alone knows how many children and wives, needed a job to keep them all from starving. Mohammed, of course, came to see me about it. I hired Mohammed.

Next Garza, my Somali chauffeur (who had long since superseded the Italian driver I had originally) felt decidedly aggrieved over his rate of pay and I must do something about that. Garza, as a Somali, was on the payroll as a native at twenty-five lira a day. Garza assured me that he had some European blood in him, and was consequently entitled to be paid as such—say, at fifty lira a day, the same as the Italians. I looked at Garza, but I was stumped; what he said might well be true, but who was I to pass on how much European blood, if any, Garza had in his veins, and what between twenty-five and fifty lira a day that entitled him to? For once, with great glee I passed a problem on to the ponderous board of bureaucrats sitting on wage matters in Asmara—let them struggle with that one.

Then came Buck Scougale with fire in his eye and a fist full of figures to prove to me that the paymaster was trying to gyp him out of some of his money due for dives made, and would I please wring the paymaster's neck for him. Seeing all the trouble the pay office had once caused, I should once have been glad to oblige Buck, but now could I see his figures anyway? I was under the impression that under a new paymaster the pay office was doing better since the strike, which was before Buck's time in Massawa. I audited Buck's figures. Undoubtedly Buck was right; I knew he had made the dives he claimed; his pay envelopes failed to show any pay for them. I promised

Buck I'd see the paymaster did right by him. Buck left, a little skeptical. Buck was naturally a pessimist; till he actually had his hands on his money, he'd remain dubious. He'd heard too many tales about that pay office.

Then along came Ahmed Hussein, my own Sudanese houseboy, dragging an interpreter, through whom I heard a lugubrious tale of woe from Ahmed, also involving the paymaster. Ahmed claimed that for two weeks he had gone unpaid; Allah would bear him witness that all that time he had been always on the job; there was no reason why he should not have been paid. Leaving Allah out of it, I knew that except for the hours spent shining my car (which to Ahmed was pleasure, not work), I could bear witness myself that he had always been sleeping across my doorstep, which was about all Ahmed ever did to earn his pay.

Still, since he had faithfully been doing that, there was no reason why he should not have been paid as usual and I was perfectly willing myself to bear witness to that. Here was a case that could quickly be settled, so with the interpreter tagging behind, I escorted Ahmed into the pay office, to see what was the matter. We had a new paymaster since the strike, Ed Mahoney, a very energetic, a very capable, and a very co-operative person, who in my mind made only such errors as even the best of human beings make. I explained Ahmed's case to Ed. He started to thumb his pay sheets—he had only about two hundred Ahmeds on his payroll; most of his other native laborers went by the name of Mohammed.

Finally Mahoney's finger came to Hussein; he looked at Ahmed puzzled. The pay sheets indicated that for the two weeks in question, Ahmed *had* drawn his pay. Through the interpreter Ahmed was taxed with this: why was he trying to draw his pay twice over?

Ahmed stood mute. He had nothing to say in explanation, but Ed Mahoney who, like a good paymaster, had been scanning Ahmed closely, didn't stand mute.

"Captain," he averred finally, "that black boy is also on my payroll under the name of Mohammed Bayumi. I recognize him." He thumbed through the Mohammeds till he came to Bayumi, who had also been paid for those same two weeks.

I looked at my houseboy in horror. Apparently Ahmed was not as dumb as he looked, or perhaps he was even dumber, trying to push a good thing entirely too far. Through the interpreter, Ahmed was

[321]

taxed with this duplicity. Why had he been trying to cheat Uncle Sam? Ahmed still had nothing whatever to say, so he was fired on the spot for a payroll fraud, and promptly (with what pay was due him for the current week) escorted out the gate by a sentry. Never would Ahmed darken my doorstep again, over which I shed no tears. No longer would I be in danger of stumbling over his black torso when I came in late off some salvage job; and as for shining up my car, it could get along with Garza's attention. I decided for the future to dispense with any houseboy.

Finally there came the worst problem of all. Lieutenant Winfield, who had come down from Asmara to help Morrill drill the civilian volunteers, had also been assigned Intelligence Officer and Provost Marshal at the Naval Base. He came to me one day with a red-hot situation.

It appeared that the warehouse foreman, an American employee of the contractor, Barton (which wasn't his name), was about to marry an Italian girl (a bleached blonde, as is usual in such cases) working as his warehouse typist. Winfield pointed out it couldn't be done—she was an enemy alien, and all fraternization with enemy aliens, let alone marrying one, was strictly forbidden by Army regulations in wartime.

To make the situation worse, the girl's dossier, which Winfield had checked in the British files in Asmara, showed a very disturbing state of affairs. That girl, according to the Italian records, which the British now had, had come to Eritrea in 1935 as one of a batch of Italian prostitutes sent by Mussolini to serve with the Fascist army in the campaign against Haile Selassie. That service completed, she had settled down in Asmara as the mistress of an Italian civil official, an ardent Fascist, now in an Eritrean concentration camp. She herself was suspected of being a Fascist transmission belt, if not an active espionage agent. That was the girl Barton wanted to marry.

"Tell the damned fool he can't do it, it's against the law," I ordered Winfield. "He's under military law here, civilian or not, and he can't do it without my permission as Commanding Officer here. I'll not give it."

That, I thought, ended it, but it didn't. Barton swiftly came to see me to get my permission.

"Don't be an idiot," I told him. "The rule's sensible. I'll not waive it. Besides, don't you know that girl's record?"

"Lieutenant Winfield told me. I don't believe it."

I looked at Barton. He was certainly well over thirty and old enough to have more sense; I had seen that Italian girl in the warehouse, and from her bleached hair down, she matched her dossier. But there was no use, apparently, arguing with Barton.

"No permission will be given you to marry any enemy alien. That settles it. I don't care whether you believe it or not. Now get back to work," I ordered him. Barton left.

But it didn't settle it. A few days later Lieutenant Winfield advised me he had learned via the underground, that there was more to the case than he had suspected before. Barton was arranging secretly to marry the girl at 4:00 P.M., the coming Sunday, permission or no permission. The girl was pregnant. But to complicate matters, the friends of her Fascist paramour who was sequestered in a concentration camp, were threatening to knife Barton if he married the mistress of their temporarily out-of-circulation associate. On the other hand, the Italian friends of the girl were threatening to knife him if he didn't marry the girl he had made pregnant.

Barton was apparently in a dilemma. So also was I, who had to do something or Romeo Barton would surely be murdered either by the Montagues or the Capulets in this strange Italian vendetta over a prostitute, certainly no very attractive modern substitute for Juliet.

Here was a situation in which even Beatrice Fairfax might have been stymied in giving advice to the lovelorn, and I certainly had no claims to being any "expert" in that field. The only proper thing for me to do as Commanding Officer was to see that the wartime regulations were enforced, and as that seemed to be the best way out for Barton also, who was the only party involved for whom I had any responsibility, I acted accordingly.

"Winfield, your orders are to see that Saturday afternoon, Barton is suddenly called out of Massawa and that he doesn't get back Sunday. How you manage it is quite up to you. And then see our Army headquarters in Asmara and see that the contractor transfers Barton to Egypt or Palestine or Arabia or wherever suits them. I won't have him back in the Naval Base warehouse here again under any circumstances. He's undesirable."

Winfield promised to attend to it. The week rolled along and I forgot all about it in the press of salvage and repair work. That Sunday afternoon for once I had free, and I was in my room writing a letter home, when outside Building 35 I heard what sounded like an antiquated automobile falling to pieces. Then followed the rush of feet up the stairs, a bang on my door, and the next I knew in burst four disheveled Italians I'd never seen before.

Without any by your leave, they hurriedly scanned my room, which, bare as Mother Hubbard's cupboard, could be taken in at a glance.

In broken English, one Eytie demanded,

"Signor Barton, where ees he?"

"He's not here, and I don't know where he is! Get the hell out of here, all of you!"

But they needed no invitation to leave. Satisfied I wasn't concealing Barton, already they were on their way out on the run, heading pell-mell down the outer stairs into their rattletrap machine in which they vanished in a cloud of coral dust, headed for the old town of Massawa, before any Sudanese sentries could be alerted to stop them.

They left me gasping an instant at their audacity, till I reflected that when you are out to murder someone, a little added misdemeanor like trespass is of slight moment. Whether they were the friends of the bride, ready to stiletto Barton if he didn't show up at the wedding at 4:00 P.M., or whether they were the friends of her paramour, trying to locate him to stab him if he started for it, I never found out.

There never was any wedding. And Barton shortly was working for the contractor far away from Eritrea.

And so it went as July melted into August in Massawa—British, Americans, Somalis, Italians, Sudanese, Arabs—everybody came to lay their troubles in my lap. Sometimes I solved them, sometimes I soothed them, sometimes I couldn't do anything but wish for a less patriarchal country where all hands didn't look on the Commanding Officer as the father who had to concern himself with all their problems, their amours, and their personal frustrations. I had frustrations enough of my own, and no one at all closer than 13,000 miles away by sea on whose shoulder I could lay *my* head and shed tears.

CHAPTER

40

ON SUNDAY, AUGUST 2, I RECEIVED A surprise; for once, a pleasant one. It was in the form of radio orders from General Maxwell to proceed immediately to Cairo for a conference with him there and with the Royal Navy command in Alexandria over furnishing British labor for Massawa—something I had been trying hard to get. I was to expect to be gone for a week to ten days; I should arrange my Massawa affairs for such an absence.

Hurriedly I got hold of Captain Morrill, Lieutenant Woods, and Commander Davy, liaison officer, and informed them all of it. Then I turned my command over temporarily to Captain Morrill, as senior American officer remaining, warned him against allowing any changes to be made in my absence, instructed him in detail as to keeping things going (fortunately over that period we were starting nothing new), and told him jokingly we would now have a chance to see how the Army could run a Navy. And would he please also start phoning Asmara to get me a seat in the plane next morning for Cairo? Then I left them, to pack my aviation bag for a ten days' trip while Garza rushed my car over to the garage to fuel it up for the trip to Asmara.

In an hour I was ready to leave. I stopped a moment on my way out at my office to see what luck Morrill had had with my plane reservation. He informed me he had managed to get Asmara, and while the Army transportation officer there could not immediately give him the seat, I could rest assured the Army would see I got one, even though the plane was going to be a British BOAC.

And in addition, Morrill with a wry grin informed me that already the news of my departure was all over the Naval Base (though how it had got out he didn't know; from Asmara probably). That didn't matter much, but what he thought might interest me was the accompanying rumor that I wasn't coming back, which he had already heard from several Americans who had dropped in at the office to say good-by to me. They had the straight dope, they said, right from the horse's mouth—the contractor had finally succeeded in having me kicked out of Massawa as a nuisance; the conference business in Cairo was just eyewash to camouflage the situation a bit. Could that be true, Morrill asked of me? I knew, didn't I, that the Army Air Corps colonel at the Gura air base near Asmara, who had apparently become *persona non grata* to the contractor there, had suddenly departed from his command, never to return?

"The air certainly gets hot around here, Morrill," was my only comment. "You just see nobody puts anything over on *you* till I get back, and that's all I ask. And you might advise those who seem too interested, not to start celebrating. So long; I'll see you again in about ten days," and sliding into the car alongside Garza, I motioned him to shove off for Asmara.

It was a hot ride. Shortly we were out of Massawa and racing at seventy miles an hour across the thirty-mile stretch of flat desert that lay between Massawa and the mountains. Garza's one shortcoming as a chauffeur was that he also, like the first Italian who had ever taken me over that course, had a speed mania. But on the desert stretch, I didn't mind. It would allow my Somali to get some of the speed germs out of his mixed blood before we hit the mountain switchbacks. Then in addition we would that much sooner get over that terrible desert.

To satisfy my curiosity as to exactly what we would have faced twice a day had we ever attempted to drag our Massawa workmen in lumbering buses back and forth to that housing project in Ghinda (and also what the Duke of Gloucester had been subjected to while stuck there), I had brought along with me my special thermometer. It had not seen the light since that day, nearly two months before in early June, when I had exposed it on the dry dock. Now I laid it down on the seat beside me, in the shade this time since it was inside the car, and left it a few minutes.

When I picked it up, it read 160° F. Fairly warm, I thought, for the shaded inside of an automobile with the breeze streaming through all its open windows at seventy miles an hour. What it might have read had I told Garza to stop while I exposed the thermometer to the still air in the sun outside, I had no idea. Nor had I any desire to tell Garza to stop long enough to find out.

It didn't take us long at the rate we were going for our Chevrolet to get across that desert. Once we hit the mountains, I slowed Garza down considerably, aided slightly in my endeavors by the mountain grades we were climbing. Thirty miles an hour suited me there, with reductions to twenty around every switchback. I had considerable difficulty in holding my speed-mad Somali, with all that horsepower at his feet, down to what I wanted. But I succeeded, principally, I think, because Garza knew his only chance of ever getting any part of that increase to fifty lira a day he had his heart set on, rested with my continued existence.

Before long, we had climbed to over 3000 feet, it had cooled off considerably, and we were in the mountains passing Ghinda and its vast array of now completed and deserted buildings. I could hardly restrain bitter tears as I passed it—supposedly built to help us at Massawa! Permanent brick residence buildings, elaborate recreation hall, huge mess hall—everything to house around a thousand men—completed now and useless except perhaps as quarters for occasional passers-by, stray Eyties, and casual Eritrean goats. I had been forced to slave in Massawa in the heat with little help, begging occasionally for the loan of a single mechanic. I supposed I *had* made a nuisance of myself everywhere objecting to Ghinda's continued construction, once I had seen Eritrea. But when I thought of what I might have been able to do on urgent war work with all the wasted American labor and materials on which my eyes now rested, I became almost hysterical. My nerves weren't as cool and calm any more as they had been when first I came to Massawa. For once, I urged Garza to go faster as we passed through Ghinda; I couldn't stand the sight of it.

It took us over two hours to cover the remaining forty miles, more or less, to Asmara, and by that time, I had cooled down considerably, both mentally and physically. By the time of our arrival on the high plateau 7500 feet up, I was completely dressed for the first time in months—jacket, shirt, undershirt, long trousers, and my naval cap instead of a sun helmet—and had laid aside the sun glasses which had practically become a permanent part of my face.

I went to the Army Officers' Mess in Asmara for the night to learn there that BOAC had reserved a seat for me next day in the plane. On General Maxwell's orders, I had the top priority for the plane; there had been no argument. We were to take off at 9:00 A.M.

Asmara, I noted, was rather cold. All the Army men were wearing woolen O.D.s. As I had with me only the khaki I needed in Cairo and the white naval uniform (with my borrowed shorts) which I felt I must use in Alex where all the Royal Naval officers would be in white, I elected to stay indoors all evening rather than to freeze to death.

Next morning, Garza drove me to the Asmara airfield and then returned alone to Massawa, to him a heaven-sent opportunity to go as fast as he liked. I could only hope for the best with regard to the car as I stepped into the little BOAC plane and waved him a farewell.

In a few minutes, we took off on our way to Cairo via Khartoum; our first hop in the little plane would be only the few hours' ride to Khartoum on the Nile, where after laying overnight, I would board a much larger plane for the long flight to Cairo itself.

I seized the opportunity while in the air to write a letter home; before it was finished we were circling for a landing over the Khartoum airfield which I knew so well. I looked curiously down on that hard-baked Khartoum field shimmering in the sun, where twice before in March I had nearly expired with the heat. How would it feel to me, now that it was midsummer and August instead of early spring and March?

I got a pleasant surprise—that Khartoum airfield, when I stepped out of the plane, felt only moderately warm.

A car was waiting for me to take me into Khartoum itself where perhaps because of the added dignity of my rank as Captain, I was to spend the night in a hotel, the *Grand* Hotel, of course, instead of that ex-girls' college dormitory of unblessed memory near the airfield.

The Grand Hotel in Khartoum, I found, was really grand; it had hot and cold running water and the usual plumbing of any ordinary, good hotel. As I gazed on the white porcelain equipment of my bathroom, my mind went back to my last stay in Khartoum. Why, when I had "gyppy tummy" and badly needed that bathroom, had I been quartered in that cursed dormitory with its little well-detached brick cubicles, instead of in this grand hotel where I was when I had little need of it?

After lunch, I wandered out into Khartoum to do a little shopping, as Massawa offered no such opportunity. To my astonishment, I found every shop in the city closed until after 4:30 P.M., because of the heat. What heat, I wondered?

I gave Khartoum up in disgust, and went back to the Grand Hotel to spend the rest of the day and all the evening catching up on my home correspondence.

In the morning, I took off for Cairo on the thousand-mile flight north over the desert bordering the Nile. Having seen already too much of that desert, I ignored it to continue writing home, trying to make up for all the nights in Massawa when I had come in so dead and so hot, I couldn't do anything but collapse on my bed. Circumspect as I was about mentioning anything, even that I was in Egypt again instead of in Eritrea, I couldn't help wondering how those letters would look when they finally arrived home after the censor's razor blades got through cutting them up.

We landed at Heliopolis military airport and I learned with interest that instead of going into town to a Cairo hotel, I was to be billeted with some Army officers in an Egyptian mansion just on the edge of that military airfield, a very convenient arrangement for me, I thought. The "flap" was over, so far as the Army was concerned. All military personnel evacuated early in July had been returned to Cairo for duty.

As it was practically evening and too late for any conferences that day, I didn't go out, instead spending the evening swapping my Massawa experiences for those of half a dozen Army files who had been out in the desert as observers with the Eighth Army in its Libyan vicissitudes. But the round table didn't last very long. Hardly had nine o'clock struck when all my Army companions got up and prepared to go to bed.

"What's the matter with you fellows?" I asked. "The evening's young, and I'm willing to hear lots more yet on how Rommel chased you all a thousand miles or so way across Libya."

"No," one major answered me, "we better turn in now if we want any sleep. There'll be an air raid tonight about 1:00 A.M. We won't get any sleep after that. We're the target out here, alongside the airfield."

"So?" I inquired skeptically. "How do you know what Rommel's planning tonight? Been decoding his battle orders?"

"No, Captain, but it's easy to figure. There was a Nazi snooper plane over at 40,000 feet this noon, taking pictures. That always means bombs that same night; as for the 1:00 A.M., that's the optimum time for attack, considering all Rommel's conditions. You'll see. By the way, I'd better lend you a spare tin hat; I see you didn't bring any."

I had to confess that the omission was due to the fact that in Massawa I didn't even own one; we had next to nothing out there in the sticks. So I was provided with a tin hat and trooped up to the second floor to bed with my companions.

Sure enough, at about 12:40 A.M., air raid sirens began to wail all over Cairo. I dressed hurriedly, seized my newly acquired tin hat, and started for the roof to get a good view of what happened, but I was restrained.

"You can't go up there," the major who had fitted me out with my headgear sternly ordered. "It's too dangerous! Didn't I tell you before we're the target here? This building might just as well be in the center of the airfield, so far as the bombers are concerned. We're right behind the main hangars, and they're such poor shots they're as likely to hit us as the hangars. Hell, we'll shovel a couple of buckets full of shrapnel and bomb fragments off that roof when the raid's over. We always do. You'd better go down in the basement."

"Well, what's the tin hat for, then?" I queried. "If I go down in that basement you've got rigged as an air raid shelter, I won't need it for shrapnel. And if a bomb gets a direct hit on this house, the whole place will collapse right on me, and a hell of a lot of good a tin hat'll do me then!"

"It's if you want to go out on the portico," explained the major patiently. "There's a fair roof over that which'll catch most of the shrapnel, and the tin hat may take care of anything heavy that manages to get through the roof. But you'll be safer in the basement, Captain," he cautioned, "except, of course, if we get a direct hit, when it won't make any difference where you are."

I thought to myself that if safety had been my major consideration, I should certainly never have gone in for diving, let alone volunteering for a war when I was over fifty.

"Does the portico face the airfield?" I asked.

"Yes, partly."

"Well, Major, I'll settle for the portico then. I'm not looking for maximum safety; a reasonable amount'll do me. This is my first air raid and I'm not going to miss it. You coming along?"

"Sure thing!" exclaimed the major. "I always watch 'em from there. Let's go!"

So, escorted by the major, I went downstairs instead of up as I had first intended, and out on the portico. The roof, which seemed quite substantial, interfered with the view directly overhead; still a fair view out and up over the airfield, as well as over a considerable part of Cairo, was possible.

By now, the air raid sirens had quit screaming and a dead silence reigned over very thoroughly blacked-out Cairo. But why it should have been blacked out, I couldn't see. The Nile, gleaming against the desert, running north and south through Cairo, gave any bomber an excellent marker for compass direction, and the Pyramids to the west of the Nile, clearly visible even at night, gave an excellent point of departure from which to lay out a bombing run. Heliopolis airport was the only target in (to the Nazis) otherwise friendly Cairo. Any navigator, with all that to guide him, who couldn't get over it, blackout or no blackout, should have been sent back to kindergarten.

Then there were the searchlights. A vast ring of searchlights was fingering the night sky over Cairo, each an immense bluish pencil of light sweeping its own arc of the heavens. Again the blackout puzzled me; if the Nile and the Pyramids didn't show where Cairo was, how could anybody fail to locate it with all those searchlights encircling it? But whether useful in defense or not, Cairo was still thoroughly blacked out. Maybe it had a psychological value somewhere, either on the attacking bombers or on the Gyppos.

"Here they come," whispered the major. In all that silence and darkness out on the portico whispering was certainly natural, though it never struck me till later how grotesque it was really. I strained my ears, heard the distant roar of high-flying engines. A moment later, three searchlights suddenly swung together toward the west in a vast pyramid, apexing far up in the dark sky and something glimmered in that apex.

"They've got one! They've got one!" shrieked the major, forgetting all about whispering now, which was probably just as well, for in another instant hell broke loose right under our noses. I hadn't realized an anti-aircraft battery was that close to us. All the guns in that heavy battery let go simultaneously with a roar, and the battle was on.

Other groups of searchlights swung over eagerly, joining in the search; other batteries of guns, not so near to us, commenced firing. Long streaks of heavy tracer fire streamed skyward at targets, seen and unseen, some batteries probably firing on radar bearings at planes the searchlights hadn't picked up.

On came the bombers; the throb of engines could be heard more plainly now in spite of the concussions of the rapidly firing guns. Next, a new note entered; it sounded as if it were hailing. That, I supposed, was the shrapnel from shells exploding far above us, coming down on the roof.

Then a shrill whistling, rising to a shriek, suddenly overrode every other sound.

"Here come the bombs!" I thought. I couldn't help wondering how good the aim of the Nazi bombardiers, sighting downward at the hangars amidst that inferno of shells bursting about them, would be.

It wasn't so good. In terrific eruptions, the bombs hit and exploded, a dozen of them perhaps, one near a hangar, the rest mainly over the open airfield which was vast in extent. A few may have missed the field altogether, but except for that one near the hangar, none struck very close to us.

The guns and searchlights kept on tracking and firing as the noise of engines faded away; then suddenly all the lights were switched off, the guns quit blazing, and unbelievable silence ensued. Apparently the raid was over. Perhaps night fighter planes, certainly up by now, might track and knock down some of the Nazis on their way home, but we were unlikely to see anything of that.

So far as I could judge, for both sides it was a scoreless tie—unless that bomb exploding near the hangar had done some damage. Certainly the guns had knocked down no planes, though they might have damaged some; we would never know. And as for Heliopolis airport, we could see that no hangars had been squarely hit and probably no parked planes either, as no fires had resulted anywhere after those volcanic blasts. Most likely only a dozen craters had been dug in the open field; a few bulldozers would hastily fill and level them off in the morning and all would be serene again.

"That's all tonight," announced the major. "We might as well turn in again. Only one wave; not much of a raid."

That may have been so. But as regards the half dozen R.A.F. men, six poor devils whom next morning we learned had all been killed by that bomb exploding near the hangar across from us, I imagine the raid was heavy enough.

I saw General Maxwell the following morning, to learn my visit had a double purpose—one was the labor matter he had mentioned, the other was to give me an involuntary vacation from Massawa for at least ten days in the relatively cool Nile Delta. Even though all my conferences might be concluded sooner, I was not to leave until about August 11 or 12. Aside from business, I could spend my time looking over the Suez Canal, the naval base at Alex, the preparations of Generals Alexander and Montgomery (who had taken over from Auchinleck and Ritchie) to smack Rommel, or stay in Cairo, just as suited me best.

General Maxwell was intensely interested in getting maximum results from the Massawa Naval Base, especially now that the worst had happened and Alex was practically shut down, unable to function effectively under continuous bombing. He regretted he had not succeeded in getting me any help, naval or otherwise, from the United States, but the situation with respect to the British, on whom he had also been working, looked better. Admiral Harwood, the British Commander-in-Chief, had manifested a lively interest. The major purpose of my visit was to go to Admiral Harwood personally, since I knew best what Massawa needed and what it could do, and negotiate directly with him. General Maxwell himself would not go to Alex; he would leave the matter wholly in my hands.

I thanked the general for all he had already done for Massawa, and incidentally for his glowing recommendation which had got me promoted so promptly to captain. But did he know I was facing considerable underground opposition to my program of Naval Base operations—more specifically that I was shortly going to be booted out of Massawa because I was spending Government money illegally? There wasn't one of my salvage or repair gang afloat that hadn't had that whispered in his ear—that I was taking American funds which otherwise could be used ashore to increase the wages and the overtime pay of all the American civilians in Eritrea, contractor's construction force and everybody, and using them to pay Eritreans, Eyties, all the flotsam and jetsam of the Middle East I could lay my hands on, to repair British ships. Who was responsible for setting that rumor afloat, I couldn't state positively, but with my men, as well as the contractor's men whom I had to deal with, believing that any minute I was going to be removed, my authority was definitely being undermined. I had troubles enough in Massawa without that one. Apparently my order to Cairo had brought that rumor to a head; those interested in tying

[333]

my hands afloat were bragging I wasn't coming back. Where did I stand?

"Rot!" stated General Maxwell incisively. "You're doing exactly what I want you to do! What's the Naval Base for except to keep British ships going? What other ships are there around here to fight this war? You'll be relieved only for failing to carry out my orders, not for obeying them. Don't concern yourself any more over that. Now make your own appointments in Alex to try to get some British workmen."

"Aye, aye, sir!" I acknowledged, somewhat relieved at hearing it stated so definitely, though I had never had any fears about being backed up by the general. I left to go to Admiralty House in Cairo to arrange the meeting in Alex with Admiral Harwood.

There, after some telephoning to Alex, the meeting was set for the third morning following. It appeared that Admiral Harwood's staff, especially some of the dockyard civilian superintendents, were considerably scattered now from Suez to Alex; it would take that long to get all those together in Alex he wanted there for the conferences.

So aside from that day, I had two free days myself in between. I decided to spend them looking over the salvage situation along the Suez Canal, which I had heard over the Axis radio the Nazis had blocked with mines.

Colonel Chickering, Chief of Staff for the North African Mission, fitted me out with an Army car, an enlisted man for a driver, and orders wide enough in their terms to take me anywhere in the Delta and the Canal zone, where of course there were innumerable military road blocks and all ordinary traffic was barred.

Early next morning, bidding my Army hosts alongside the airfield farewell for a few days, with the further hope that on my return that house would still be there to accommodate me, I started by car for Suez. It wasn't a long ride, eighty to ninety miles perhaps over fairly flat country, but between showing our papers at every road block and passing interminable convoys of loaded military trucks headed towards Cairo from Suez, we didn't get along very rapidly.

Meanwhile, as we drove, the whole desert on both sides of the road seemed covered with British tank squadrons, motorized infantry, and infantry on foot, all maneuvering endlessly in battle exercises on terrain similar to that over which they would fight. Apparently Montgomery was holding secret practice on a huge scale behind the lines, preparing a few trick plays of his own to spring on Rommel.

We reached Suez in the early afternoon. Suez as a city, whether a sink of iniquity or not, didn't interest me at all. I had eyes only for its harbor—the terminus of the long sea route around Africa into which America was pouring weapons and supplies to crush Rommel. My eyes opened wide—Suez harbor and the water front, including a considerable part of the wide canal stretching north, was jammed with ships unloading tanks, guns, ammunition, trucks, packing cases— all in tremendous quantities.

I didn't stop in Suez. Instead I ordered the driver to head north along the west side of the Canal for Ismailia, and Port Said where we would spend the night. Mile after mile we passed huge piles of war supplies stacked along the bank—the whole area was one vast open warehouse packed with fighting equipment and supplies for Montgomery at El Alamein.

At Ismailia, halfway up the Isthmus above the Bitter Lakes, the Canal really started, with steep straight banks cut through sand and rock. From then on, I kept a sharp eye out for all the wrecks, sunk by mines dropped from heavy Nazi bombers in the Canal, which over the Axis broadcasts from Berlin and Rome, I had heard were blocking the Canal completely. We got to Port Said; I hadn't seen a single wreck. The Canal was as open to traffic as in the quietest days of peace, though for other reasons, partly to save heavy Canal tolls, all ships were being unloaded at Suez, and only warships were transiting the Canal.

The British, though the Nazis didn't know of it, had developed a remarkable detection system to spot all mines dropped into the Canal. No sooner was a mine dropped into the Canal waters than the British had the exact spot where it had splashed downward marked, traffic stopped temporarily, and mine-sweeping crews and divers working on that exact spot to explode or remove the mine. In a few hours, all mines would be cleared, and ships moving again. The Nazis had dropped plenty of mines, all right, but with no results; there were no wrecks in the Canal. And the British were saying nothing to contradict the Axis claims; if the Nazis wanted to keep on wasting bombers on planting harmless mines in the Canal instead of using the bombers elsewhere where they might do real damage, it was all right with the British. Smart people, I thought.

It was evening when I got to Port Said. In Port Said I was taken to the largest hotel there for the night as the guest of Captain G. C. C. Damant, C.B.E., Royal Navy, Principal Salvage Officer for the Mediterranean Forces. Captain Damant, now over seventy-five and long since retired, was of course too old to direct salvage operations afloat personally. A much younger man, Commander Rithon of the British Navy, was doing that at Port Said, with Commander Wheeler, an associate, directing operations at Alex. Captain Damant, whom I looked on as the grand old man of diving, since thirty-five years before he had personally done the experimental diving work on which the science of deep diving rested, simply advised from shore on knotty problems when they came up.

Next morning, I accompanied Captain Damant, who really was in remarkable physical shape considering his age, along the Port Said water front to where Commander Rithon, the officer actually in charge of salvage there, was going to stage an experiment on underwater electric welding for my benefit. As my eyes swept the harbor, dotted here and there with the destroyers, cruisers, and submarines which could no longer safely be based on Alexandria, they fell to my astonishment on a British battleship, a huge superdreadnought swinging placidly at anchor not a quarter of a mile off the quay, standing out like a goose amidst a brood of goslings!

"Captain!" I exclaimed. "What battleship is that? I understood you didn't have a single battleship left in the Mediterranean, and there's one of the old *Iron Dukes* that fought at Jutland along with the *Barham* and the *Valiant* that used to be around here! What's her name?"

Captain Damant didn't even bother to turn his head to look at her as he replied,

"She's not a battleship; she's just a dummy. She's the old *Centurion.*"

A dummy? I looked again. That battleship was close to me and broadside on, easy to scan. If ever I was looking at 13.5-inch naval guns, heavily armored turrets, a powerful battleship stripped for action, I was seeing one then close aboard me under conditions where she couldn't be another mirage—it wasn't hot enough in Port Said for that. Besides, the *Centurion was* a battleship; her tremendous 13.5-inch guns had done heavy execution on Admiral von Scheer's German fleet at Jutland in 1916.

"Quit trying to fool me, Captain," I protested. "Why try to kid your Allies you haven't got a battleship? I know a battleship when I see one!"

"That's what our Eytie friends think, too," answered Captain Damant. "We're pulling their leg just the way we're pulling yours. Good job, isn't she? All those heavy guns you're looking at are made of wood! So's all the armor on what you think are turrets! The *Centurion* had all her real guns and gun turrets taken off years ago to change her into a target ship, though her machinery is still all there. So when the war came along and Admiral Harwood found himself on this station with every battleship knocked out, the Admiralty in a hurry fitted out the old *Centurion* with wooden guns and armor, mounted a good set of real A.A. guns on her topsides, and sent her down here. She does fine. Fooled you, didn't she? Well, she's fooling the whole Italian battle fleet, too, that's afraid to come out and meet what they think is one old British dreadnought. Any little Eytie gunboat that had the nerve to get close enough, could sink her easily, but she's keeping off at least four modern Eytie superdreadnoughts! She steams out occasionally, escorted by a few destroyers, to show the flag in the eastern Mediterranean and keep the big Eyties holed up in home ports. She gets strafed plenty on her cruises by everything the Nazis and the Eyties have got in the way of bombers, but she has a grand set of A.A. guns, including four "Chicago pianos," and she keeps 'em off. She hasn't been hit yet. Blessed lot of bombs she's cost the Axis! Quite a show the old girl's putting on, don't you think, Captain Ellsberg?"

I had to agree. So the battleship I saw before me was nothing but another Middle East mirage! Very bright of my British friends, I thought. I took a last look at the *Centurion,* not to meet her again till two years later on the Omaha Beach in Normandy right after D-day, where once more our paths were to cross and I was to tread her decks myself, both of us then engaged in outsmarting Rommel and his Nazis, far away from Africa.

Half a mile further along the quay, we came to the spot where Commander Rithon, actual British Chief Salvage Officer for the Port Said area, had a diver waiting for us with his underwater welding experiment. The experiment was of no great importance and interested me very little, but Rithon interested me a lot. Rithon, who seemed a very decent chap, blushed in considerable embarrassment when Captain Damant introduced him to me. For Rithon knew (and knew I knew it also) that his associate in Alex, Commander Wheeler, had made a considerable bet with another British engineer (the latter the source of my information) that I wouldn't raise the sunken Italian dry dock in Massawa—it was impossible. And then to Wheeler's great confusion, the dock had come up in only nine days! Wheeler, of course, had paid up, as the other party to the bet who had come to Massawa to see for himself had gleefully assured me, adding that the Italian dry dock was a sore subject in British salvage circles, best not to be mentioned to any British salvage officer.

I didn't mention the dock; neither did Rithon. Our discussion centered wholly on the salvage troubles Rithon was having around Port Said, generally with waterlogged ships ready to sink at one end or the other from actual or near miss bomb damage. The poor devil was being run ragged keeping his derelicts from sinking altogether before he could get them beached. He had my sincere sympathy.

The three of us went back to the hotel for lunch, with Captain Damant as host. It was a beautiful day, pleasantly cool, with the usual cloudless sky and azure blue of the Mediterranean spread out before us.

About half through lunch, with no warning at all, a battery of very heavy A.A. shore guns opened up near by. I jumped from my seat, but nobody else even quit eating.

"What's the matter?" I asked. "Isn't this another air raid on Port Said?"

"No, nothing to bother about this time of day," replied Commander Rithon. "There'll be no bombs. It's just another high-flying Nazi snooper with a camera, with the sky guns keeping him a respectable distance up. They can't reach him; he's got no bombs, so nobody worries on either side. The bombs'll come tonight, after he's got home and they've developed his pictures to show them what ships are in the harbor. Better sit down, Captain; your lunch will get cold."

However, I was much more interested in Nazi air tactics than in lunch, so I got out from under the veranda to where in the garden I could get a good look upwards. Sure enough, so far up in the heavens that the plane itself was completely invisible, was the snooper, his presence marked only by a lengthening trail of white in the stratosphere streaming from his plane—the vapors from his engine exhaust congealing instantly into a frosty plume in the cold and rarefied air up where that very specially designed high-flying camera plane was.

The ack-ack was tracking him, futilely it knew as well as he. For the guns could reach only 30,000 feet up, where in lazy puffs opening like flowers well below him and his trailing cloud, the heavy shells were exploding. But at least they were keeping him from 35,000 to 40,000 feet up, from which altitude his pictures would be none too good.

The trail of vapor made a complete circle over Port Said and then headed back westward, presumably to a field in Rommel's rear beyond El Alamein. The guns ceased firing. No one but me had bothered in the slightest. I sat down again, asked,

"What can you do about that?"

"Nothing at all, around here," replied Damant. "Even if we had a specially fitted out fighter that could get that high, before he ever got altitude enough to fire a gun, that snooper would be halfway back toward El Alamein. But we're discouraging 'em. The news of this has already gone to Alex, which is a hundred and twenty-five miles west of here, right on the path of that plane homeward bound. There'll be a special fighter up from Alex when he gets there, high enough to give him a fight. They've already knocked down about half of Rommel's Port Said snoopers on their way back over Alex; I imagine what's left of 'em will get discouraged soon and let us alone."

Lunch over, Captain Damant went back to his office, while I spent the afternoon with Commander Rithon, looking over several of his beached wrecks, his salvage crews, and his salvage gear. I was astonished to note that though his operation was all Royal Navy, the equipment he had couldn't start to compare with all the salvage gear the Admiralty had so plentifully placed at the disposal of the incompetent McCance and his commercial basis operations in Massawa.

In particular, Rithon bewailed how his shortage of underwater cutting torches, for burning away protruding steel on the hulls of his wrecks, had set him back. He had possessed several British make underwater torches, but they were cumbersome and slow for a diver to work with; he had needed far more to cover his work properly.

"Then I had a bit of luck with this underwater burning, Captain," he confided to me. "I've got one torch now that's tops; it does more work under water itself than all the torches together the Royal Navy's given me. And where do you think I got it? Out of the junk heap! Along with some other gear shipped here from home, there was a box full of junk of all kinds; stuff perhaps they had an idea in England I might find useful in repairing something else. I was pawing that box of junk over—bolts, nuts, copper piping, old brass valves—when I came across an old underwater torch I'd never seen before. Worn out, all green with verdigris it was, evidently discarded as junk itself. My men and I took it apart, cleaned it up, repaired it a bit, put it together again, and took it down on a wreck to try it out. Mighty handy torch it proved; beat everything we had all hollow! Let me show it to you."

Commander Rithon drew forth from a tool kit an underwater torch, considerably battered from long years of hard use before he salvaged it from the junk pile, and proudly handed it to me.

I took one look and laughed. If the *Centurion* was a British joke on me, that torch was my joke on them. It was my underwater torch—one of the original torches I had invented over fifteen years before for my first salvage job on the submarine *S-51!* How it ever got to England and then to Port Said, I couldn't imagine. But it was an Ellsberg torch, all right; the most battered one I'd ever seen, still doing its bit under water in Port Said to help win the war.

"Well, that's certainly interesting! Thanks for the unexpected compliment!" I told Rithon as I explained to him what that unknown torch was. "Now if you're still in trouble over torches, I can help you out. In a shipment I got from New York just lately, there's a whole case of these torches, half a dozen new ones, the very latest model. I can spare you one; I'll send it to you as soon as I get back to Massawa; the new ones are much handier even than this old model."

But with typical British conservatism, Rithon refused the gift. The one he had suited him fine; it wasn't by any means worn out yet and he didn't want anything better. Only in case some diver lost his most prized possession in the deep sea would he take me up on my offer to give him another and a newer one for nothing.

So Commander Rithon and I parted very good friends (in spite of his associate's bet on the dry dock which still remained unmentioned) and I started back for Cairo. From Port Said, while roundabout the whole Delta, going via Cairo was still the quickest way by road to get to Alex.

CHAPTER

41

THE NEXT MORNING I WAS SEATED at a long conference table in the Alexandria dockyard, facing an array of Royal Navy officers and British civilian dockyard superintendents.

I had already met Admiral Harwood—the biggest admiral I had ever set eyes on. I was willing to bet that when he walked out to the end of the flying bridge, his flagship heeled appreciably to that side. After a brief discussion with him and an invitation to come back and spend the night with him as his guest when I had finished, I was turned over to the Royal Navy captain serving as Superintendent of His Majesty's Alexandria Dockyard. The latter had already received his instructions from the admiral.

The conference opened. Admiral Harwood had instructed the dockyard superintendent to go all out in providing me what I needed at Massawa. The first need was the seven naval officers as assistants, whom America had stated to General Maxwell wouldn't be furnished me from home.

That was agreed on without argument—the need was obvious. The only question, a tough one, was which seven British naval officers should be ordered to go. Massawa was a highly undesired station. Finally they were selected—two Royal Navy commanders, two lieutenant commanders, three lieutenants. If the Admiralty in London approved, they would be ordered to Massawa.

Next came the problem of mechanics. I wanted two hundred shipyard men in assorted trades; I had a list of what I wanted. There wasn't any argument over that need, or over their distribution by trades, nor even over their availability now that the dockyard at Alex was functioning to a limited degree only. But didn't I understand that British dockyard workmen were like Americans; they were free and equal citizens of a democracy and couldn't permanently be shipped about from one city to another without their consent?

Now the discussion waxed really hot, with the civilian dockyard supervisors doing most of the discussing. Their men were scattered everywhere over the Middle East by the "flap"—Suez, Port Said, Beirut, Haifa—even getting in touch with them to canvass their willingness to go was no simple matter. Then Massawa had a terrible reputation. They doubted they could get any volunteers at all. Perhaps if a sufficiently high bonus were offered, they might get some. What bonus would be offered?

I offered to pay a very handsome bonus; one I thought would prove attractive; I would see that the men sent earned it. Then there was a fierce argument over that. Not that the bonus I suggested wasn't large enough, but that it was too large—it would cause repercussions on the wage scales at the Alexandria dockyard itself when the men finally came back to work again there. The conference became very heated. Finally the bonus was cut down radically to what wouldn't hurt Alex in the long run. I didn't feel it was enough to help Massawa much right then, especially as the wages all American workmen were getting in Massawa made the offer to the British mechanics, bonus included, look very sick. But I got nowhere on that; Alex and its future came first.

The Captain of the Dockyard ordered his civilian assistants to start canvassing their scattered workmen for volunteers to go to Massawa on the terms finally set; obviously it would take some time. The conference broke up. The civilians and most of the officers left. The Captain of the Dockyard and another officer, the fleet naval constructor, Commander Mann, R.N., began a private discussion over a damaged light cruiser they had on their hands.

I couldn't help overhearing them since apparently neither of the two regarded the matter as confidential so far as I was concerned, and immediately I pricked up my ears. It appeared that the light cruiser, *H.M.S. Dido,* was in serious trouble. Her stern, beneath her steering engine room, was flooded, apparently as the combined result of concussion from near-miss Axis bombs while she was bombarding Rhodes, and too light a hull structure aft. (This last was a result of lightening up her whole structure during the idiocy resulting from the Geneva naval agreements on limiting warship sizes, where the British, as we did also, had lightened up warship hulls so much trying to keep weights inside arbitrarily assigned class limits, as to get themselves in serious trouble now there was a war on and ships had to fight.)

The *Dido* had to be dry-docked for a considerable underwater repair job to her stern before she could fight again. Since they dared not dry-dock her in constantly bombed Alexandria, they were discussing the final arrangements for sending her 5000 miles to Durban in South Africa to dock her there and carry out the repairs. She would be gone from the fighting line in the Mediterranean well over a month, perhaps nearly two months. That was all too much for me, and I broke in on the discussion.

"Captain," I asked, "why send the *Dido* to Durban if she's only a light cruiser? She has to pass right by my front door in Massawa on her way through the Red Sea to Durban. Send me a few workmen right now, send her to me, and I'll dock her in Massawa, repair her, and have her back here again throwing shells at the enemy in less than a quarter of the time she can possibly get to Durban and back for that job!"

Commander Mann, the fleet naval constructor, explained to me why not. The "light" cruiser *Dido* was not so light; she actually displaced over 7500 tons in her fighting trim, somewhat more now that she was flooded aft. I couldn't possibly dry-dock her in my Persian dry dock, the only one I yet had operating, which could lift only 6000 tons at best. Besides that, the *Dido* was far too long for my floating dry dock. She was 530 feet long from stem to stern, my Persian dry dock was only 410 feet long. Even if my dock could lift the weight, docking a ship with such a terrific length of her hull overhanging the dock with no support, would break her back.

It was too bad, Mann added. They had considered sending her to Massawa at first, but once they had checked the size of my Persian dock against the *Dido's* dimensions and weight, of course they had dropped the idea. Now if only that large Italian dry dock I had salvaged were repaired already, that would be a different story, but of course it wasn't yet. Serious as sending one of the few major remaining Mediterranean warships away for so long was, there was nothing for it except to take the knock and send her to Durban.

I gnashed my teeth. If only someone, America, Britain, anybody, had sent me the modest quota of men and the materials I had begged for, I could long since have had that salvaged Italian dry dock back in commission, ready at that vital moment to dock this damaged warship! Now God alone knew what damage to the Allied cause might

[343]

result from her long absence from the weakened fighting line at sea while she went to Durban. But what Commander Mann had said was true—my salvaged Italian dry dock wasn't yet repaired. I said nothing further and left the conference room. I spent the rest of the day looking over the half-deserted Alexandria dockyard, the damage there to ships and naval shops the Nazis had already done with their constant bombing, and what damage the Nazis and the Eyties together had done to Alexandria itself.

But I wasn't seeing the bomb damage, even though I was looking at it. Hour after hour as I wandered on foot over Alexandria there kept running through my mind the picture of that cruiser, *H.M.S. Dido,* steaming 10,000 miles to Durban and back to be repaired, a terrible waste even in a war when waste is accepted as a matter of course. But her long absence from her fighting station—there was a danger nobody could laugh off! How could I fit that overweight and overlong cruiser into my little Persian dry dock and avoid both the waste and the danger? My eyes were looking at collapsed buildings, bomb craters, sunk or burned-out ships along the dockyard quays, but I wasn't seeing them; instead all my mind saw was every conceivable and inconceivable fantasy of the *Dido* and that Persian dock being somehow fitted together—truly a miracle if it could be done.

In the late afternoon, my steps turned finally toward the Egyptian mansion taken over as a shore residence by Admiral Sir Henry Harwood, K.C.B., O.B.E., R.N., Commander-in-Chief of the British Mediterranean Fleet (if anyone could still call it a fleet without blushing, seeing it was composed mainly of a few cruisers and one dummy battleship). There I was to dine with him and spend the night.

My bag was already at his house, left by my Army driver. I was escorted to my room by a British petty officer, apparently detailed temporarily as steward to me. He had already opened and been all through what I had in my aviation bag. Spread out on the huge Egyptian bed in that large room was my best white naval uniform, gold buttons already inserted, shoulder marks attached, campaign ribbons pinned on. My only white shoes, newly whitened, reposed on the floor alongside. That steward knew what was appropriate when one dined with the Commander-in-Chief; he was evidently taking no chances on any non-reg American from even more non-reg Massawa appearing in the wrong clothes.

"Anything else I can do to 'elp, sir?" he inquired anxiously as he pointed to what was laid out. "Your bath's already run, sir," and he indicated the bathroom with its well-filled tub.

"No, thanks, steward. You seem to have tended to everything; that's all, I think," and I waved him out, a little fearful he might insist on staying to dress me, which I doubted I could stand up under. After all, I wasn't too sure of what was customary from British valets.

I stripped and climbed into the tub, the first time in months I had used one instead of a shower. After drying myself on a huge towel, the like of which I never knew in Massawa, I started to dress for dinner. And then in a flash it came to me!

If only they would give me the *Dido,* I had the answer—I could dry-dock her in Massawa; repair her; return her swiftly to the Mediterranean! She need never go to Durban! The prospect positively dazzled me as it dawned on me how it could be done!

And then the first glow swiftly faded. My method would probably sound unorthodox, and I was dealing with the very conservative British. Would they ever let me try anything so unconventional on one of their precious cruisers? Hardly likely. There, for example, was Commander Rithon in Port Said, so conservative he wouldn't even let me give him as a gift a new and improved underwater torch to help him out—he was perfectly content to continue with that old model of mine I had discarded over ten years before.

But the idea was too good to drop without a fight, and then it struck me that after all, I might be in luck—my chance of getting the *Dido* might be excellent. For in a few minutes I was to dine with Admiral Harwood himself, who would have the last word on my proposal and Admiral Harwood just couldn't be the conventional Englishman—his bulk was unconventional and so also must be his ideas, for he had won his fame, while a commodore, by fighting off the River Plate, in 1939, the most unconventional naval battle a British admiral had ever fought.

There with simply three small cruisers, armed only with six-inch and eight-inch guns, he had fallen in with the Nazi pocket battleship, the *Admiral Graf Spee,* armed with six eleven-inch guns in heavily armored turrets. Against the heavy guns and the thick armor of that battleship, built by the Nazis with the boast that her guns could sink anything her engines couldn't outrun, and that her engines could outrun anything her guns couldn't sink, the guns and protection of Harwood's little cruisers were mere popguns and tinplate.

[345]

Had Harwood been the conventional admiral, he would have formed his three cruisers into prescribed line of battle ahead and engaged the *Graf Spee,* broadside to broadside, to go down with all his ships firing to the last, flags nailed to their masts, the very symbol of dogged British courage against overwhelming odds, while the *Graf Spee,* without a scratch on her after the battle, would have continued her career of destruction in the South Atlantic. Queerly enough, exactly that had happened in World War I, when another British admiral had fallen in off Chile on the other side of South America with a superior German force commanded in the flesh by the very Admiral Graf von Spee for whom Harwood's antagonist was now named.

But had Harwood fought a conventional battle? He had not. Did he go down in conventional style as he should have with guns still firing and flags flying? He did not.

Instead when all the smoke had lifted from over his very unorthodox tactics in that battle off the River Plate, the bewildered captain of the *Graf Spee* lay dead by his own hand, a suicide, and the battered and defeated *Graf Spee* lay on the bottom, also a suicide, scuttled in despair by her own crew!

The unconventional Commodore Harwood, all his own little ships battle-scarred but still afloat, had gone on triumphantly to become Admiral and Commander-in-Chief of the Mediterranean Fleet. With him I was to dine in a few minutes. I felt sure that with Harwood, my unconventional scheme for the *Dido* would get an O.K.

Dinner was soon announced, and I sat down to a very formally served meal at which the others present, aside from the host, were his Chief-of-Staff, Rear Admiral Edelstein, R.N., unlike his C.-in-C. very thin and gaunt; and his naval aide, Flag Lieutenant Sinclair, R.N.V.R., like all flag lieutenants, a paragon of attention to his admiral's guests.

The conversation roamed all over the world—from Block Island to Rabaul; from the River Plate to the Red Sea. While the soup was being served, Rear Admiral Edelstein, the Chief-of-Staff, apparently as well qualified for the diplomatic service as for the fighting line, asked the C.-in-C. whether he had ever read a book by me, "On the Bottom," relating to the raising of the American submarine, *S-51,* sixteen years before. But despite the obvious diplomacy of this opening remark, he came to grief with his question.

Admiral Harwood, whom I had found very human and very un-affected, also proved himself very honest. He confessed he had never heard of "On the Bottom," a terrible statement to make regarding any book in the presence of its author.

"My word, Admiral!" exclaimed the Chief-of-Staff. "You simply must read Ellsberg's 'On the Bottom.' It's one of the most thrilling books I ever read; a real classic of the sea! All the London critics so acclaimed it when it came out!"

Admiral Harwood promised that in between battles he'd get him-self a copy and read it.

Then the admiral steered the conversation down the Red Sea, praising wholeheartedly what he called my remarkable achievements in getting the Naval Base there going, in raising the Italian dry dock and the *Liebenfels*, and in putting his supply fleet in some decent shape for efficient action, all of which aid he highly appreciated. While he had to confess he'd never heard of my book, my reputation in salvage he well knew of before and he was deeply gratified to see it so much enhanced by my performance at Massawa.

"Tit for tat, old man," I thought to myself, so I told him that for three years I had glowed inwardly over his remarkable performance at the battle off the River Plate, even going so far at the time as to write a special article in an American seagoing journal calling atten-tion to it as not only a brilliant victory, but as one unique in the tac-tics which had brought victory to the side to which no naval "expert" would have given the slightest chance. Now that I had the oppor-tunity to tell him of my admiration in person, I wasn't going to pass it up.

So mutually admiring each other's efforts in our widely different fields, the dinner progressed through the fish to the roast, then finally to the coffee for which we retired to another room where the dismal situation in trying to provision beleaguered Malta by sea got some attention. All the time I was wondering how I could toss my scheme for the *Dido* into the admiral's prodigious lap. But since nobody else mentioned her or anything relative to her, I finally bluntly dragged her in myself.

"I understand, Admiral," I said, "you're sending the cruiser *Dido* to Durban for dry-docking and repairs."

"Why, yes, Ellsberg," said the admiral, a little startled at the sud-den change of subject. "She's waterlogged aft; the dockyard chaps say there's nothing for it except to send her away for docking. You see, Rommel won't let us dock her here."

"So I understand, Admiral, but Durban's a long way off. Why not let me do the job at Massawa? It's much closer."

Admiral Harwood looked at me somewhat puzzled, then turned to his Chief-of-Staff.

"Didn't the dockyard staff tell us, Edelstein, that Massawa can't take her? The dock there's too small, I thought they said."

"That's correct, Admiral. Our constructor, Commander Mann, has been all over that. She's too big for Massawa; she's got to go to Durban."

"I understand all that, Admiral," I interjected. "I've been over that part myself this morning with both Mann and your Captain of the Dockyard; fact is, I first learned of the *Dido* from them. They're right, the dry dock at Massawa is too small—ordinarily. But I've given it a little thought and I've figured out a way to do it at Massawa. You give me the *Dido* at Massawa, Admiral, and I'll give her back to you repaired in no time at all compared to Durban! Where's a pencil? Look!"

And with pencil and paper which the Flag Lieutenant hurriedly brought me, I drew sketches to show Admiral Harwood and his Chief-of-Staff how I was going to dry-dock a 7500-ton cruiser in a dry dock for which she was both far too heavy and far too long—a seeming impossibility.

Admiral Harwood gazed at the scheme in open wonder, but he was cautious. Would it endanger the *Dido*? He could take no chances. Did I know how few ships he had in his fleet now?

"Not many, I hear, Admiral. No battleships; that I know, but that's about all I know for certain."

"It's top secret information and if the enemy knew it, the Eytie fleet would slaughter us, but seeing your Naval Base is involved I'll tell you. My whole fleet, including the *Dido*, consists of exactly four light cruisers! And two others, the *Euryalus* and the *Cleopatra*, her sisters, out of those four, are damaged exactly as the *Dido* is, only not quite so badly. We're praying their sterns will hang together till the *Dido* gets back here; one ship at a time is as much as I dare send out of the Mediterranean for repairs. If you could only do the lot of them at Massawa, it would be a godsend to me!"

So? Now there were three cruisers instead of one Massawa could work on.

"Admiral," I assured him earnestly, "you send me those three cruisers in succession and I'll repair all of them for you! And fast, too! All I ask of you is that you furnish from Alex the steel and the men for the repair work; they can come down with the *Dido*. I've got no steel at all for the job, and next to no men in Massawa."

"Sinclair," ordered Harwood sharply, "send for the fleet constructor right away!" He turned to me while his flag lieutenant hurried out to send an orderly after Commander Mann. "You see, Ellsberg, I don't claim to know anything myself about docking ships, neither does Edelstein here; but Mann, of course, does. If he says there's the slightest chance of doing it your way, the *Dido* goes to Massawa. If you do her successfully, then you get her two sisters also. It will be wonderful! You'll have to pardon my sending for Mann, old chap, but I'm in a tight hole, and I've got to be cautious. You explain it to Mann; he'll understand you better than I; it's his business. When I've heard what he's got to say, I'll give you an answer right off!"

"Aye, aye, sir," I agreed. "If I can't convince Mann, then my plan's no good and neither am I. You can forget it."

While we were waiting for the fleet constructor who was quartered a considerable distance away, the talk went back to the River Plate. From his own lips, I listened fascinated while Admiral Harwood related to me his weird battle tactics in defeating the *Graf Spee*.

Then he told me how a short time before, two of his light cruisers escorting a convoy of freighters through the eastern Mediterranean to the relief of Malta, had found across their path in broad daylight an Italian superdreadnought, and in addition an Italian cruiser force in itself far outgunning them. Escape for anyone was hopeless unless the fast cruisers fled immediately, leaving their slow convoy to be sunk. By wireless the situation had been reported to him in Alex by his commodore at sea; he had wirelessed back what to do. And then while he waited in agony to learn what his losses were, he heard that his commodore had outbluffed the vastly superior enemy force and escaped without a fight, cruisers and precious freighters all saved!

At that moment the fleet naval constructor arrived and all other discussion promptly ceased while Admiral Harwood ordered Commander Mann to attend closely to my scheme for dry-docking the *Dido* at Massawa instead of sending her to Durban.

I showed Mann the sketches, explained the operation. Mann was evidently a skilled naval constructor; it took slight explanation only for him to grasp the novel idea. He gazed in admiration at the rough penciled sketches, then turned to his Commander-in-Chief.

"No reason at all why it can't be done that way, Admiral," he agreed. "Odd it never occurred to anyone else. All it requires is skillful handling of the dry dock during the lifting operation."

"Topping!" exclaimed Admiral Harwood. "That settles it, Ellsberg; the *Dido* goes to Massawa! Mann, you find out from Ellsberg in the morning what he needs at his dockyard in the way of materials and men for the job, and get cracking yourself on loading them all on the *Dido.* Edelstein, you change the *Dido's* orders to Massawa instead of Durban, notify them in Durban she isn't coming, and see the *Dido* gets under way as soon as Mann has her loaded. And now I guess we'd better all turn in; there'll be plenty to do tomorrow—for all of us."

After an early breakfast, I returned to the dockyard to work with Mann. He would send me the blueprints for the task, see all the steel necessary loaded on the *Dido,* together with one Royal Navy lieutenant commander to advise me, and thirty British mechanics, two British civilian superintendents, and four foremen put aboard the *Dido* to do the actual repair work under my direction. He offered to send me more men, but thirty, I thought, should be enough to work three shifts around the clock. It would be a close quarters job around that damaged stern; more men would only get in each other's way and slow up the work.

All that settled, I went to Admiral Harwood's headquarters to bid him good-by.

"Everything arranged regarding the *Dido?*" he asked.

"Yes, sir. It'll take your dockyard a few days yet to collect the men and the steel; after that, she'll be right along, Admiral."

Admiral Harwood shook my hand warmly in farewell, then added fervently,

"Good luck to you and my thanks for what you've already done for us. But for God's sake, Ellsberg, be careful with the *Dido!* She's one quarter of my whole fleet!"

CHAPTER

42

Hardly had I left the commander-in-Chief's headquarters and started in my Army car for his residence to retrieve my aviation bag, than the air raid sirens began to shriek all over Alexandria. When I got to the house, all the personnel there had already retreated to the shelters, but I was so treading on air myself over the prospect of what Massawa was going to do for the Mediterranean fighting fleet, that a minor thing like an air raid didn't concern me.

I went up to my room, heaved all the clothes in sight into my bag, and was about to close it when the ground guns opened up and the bombs began to explode. From all the noise, Alexandria was certainly putting up a terrific barrage with its guns—what I had heard in Cairo was nothing to this ack-ack. And for their part, the Nazis were surely unloading far more bombs. Presumably the Alexandria dockyard was a much more worth-while target to them than the Heliopolis airport.

I lugged my bag downstairs through the deserted house and tossed it into the back of the sedan the Army had given me, then hurriedly climbed aboard myself alongside the chauffeur.

"We'd better make knots away from this place!" I ordered the driver. "Let the limeys attend to those Stukas; I've got no more business here!"

In another moment, with no other traffic moving to bother us, we were racing out of Alexandria bound for the open desert, praying that no ill-aimed bomb would come our way. None did; very shortly we were clear of the city and its mingled roar of thundering A.A. guns and detonating bombs.

It wasn't long, however, before our progress was sadly impeded by endless convoys of military trucks headed for El Alamein, only forty miles to the westward of us. I should have liked to have gone there myself to look over the Nazi lines and I had all the rest of the day for it, but I couldn't. That was the one area my passes wouldn't get me into. Even Colonel Chickering by no stretch of his imagination could camouflage a naval officer into an American military observer, entitled to enter the British Eighth Army's fighting lines.

I tried to achieve it by indirection, purposely losing my way, taking a wrong turn, and heading for El Alamein to the west, instead of Cairo to the southeast. But the first military road block we ran into, ruined the scheme. There the British M.P.s, after examining my papers, very courteously pointed out my error, apologized for the poor road signs that must have caused it, indicated the roads to take to get back on the main road to Cairo, and then over my objections that they should go to so much trouble to help, obligingly put an M.P. on my running board to guide us till we came to the main road and were again headed southeast along it towards Cairo.

So I had to give up a visit to El Alamein, and after finally dropping our helpful M.P. to board a convoy headed west for his return journey, we kept on towards Cairo.

There I reported to General Maxwell what had happened in Alex—that I was to get seven Royal Naval officers as assistants, two hundred British workmen, also what materials they could spare. All, of course, subject to the approval of the Admiralty in London, which would take some time to get; and to the volunteering of a sufficient number of the dockyard civilians, which I feared would take a major miracle to bring about. Still it looked promising—I might ultimately get an officer or two, a couple of dozen mechanics, and perhaps a few tons of steel—it would all help.

My major news, I saved for the last—that Massawa had done Durban out of the cruiser *Dido* and was now to blossom forth as an actual Naval Base, directly supporting the fighting ships of the Mediterranean Fleet, taking the place of shut-down Alexandria.

General Maxwell glowed over that—that was what in his plans Massawa had been intended for originally. And to think that it had been achieved with none of the shipyard machinery supposedly required from America to make it possible, yet delivered in Massawa! The general wished me luck with my first warship, warned me to take care of myself and not crack up in the Massawa heat now at its midsummer height, and gave me permission to start back the second day following, August 11. That would give me just about a week's vacation from Eritrea.

He also ordered one other thing. I was directed to show up next morning at his headquarters for an interview with all the press representatives in Cairo (which they had just requested) on what had been going on in Massawa. A little perturbed at this, for I couldn't get by the censors in letters to my wife that I was even in Massawa, I asked him how free I should be to answer questions.

I learned to my astonishment that I was free to answer any questions whatever and the general would be pleased if I told the whole story.

"Don't worry," he told me. "Every war correspondent's story will be submitted to the censors here before anything goes out. Whatever the censors want concealed, they'll cut out. Leave that to them."

So next morning I met all the correspondents, American and British, in Cairo, plus a battery of photographers. They received free answers to their questions—the rehabilitation of the Naval Base, the salvage of the large Italian dry dock, the raising of the *Liebenfels.*

It was interesting to note what the censors passed—not a word on the *Liebenfels,* not a word on the re-establishment of the sabotaged base, but the story of my dry dock salvage went out in full. That night the air waves were full of Massawa. The British Broadcasting Corporation put it on the air from London, telling the world in English of that dry dock, and to make sure our enemies didn't miss it, beaming the news to Berlin in German and to Rome in Italian!

And in New York the same story went out over the air on all our networks and on short wave to the forces abroad. As I afterward learned, it made the front page in every New York newspaper, as well as the one in Cairo which I saw the next day.

After that, I concluded it wasn't a military secret any more that I was in Massawa, but nevertheless it still happened that whenever I mentioned the place in any letters home, the censors continued carefully to excise the name. Probably they were all too busy with their razor blades ever to listen to the home radio or read our own newspapers.

Meanwhile, Colonel Chickering took care of my transportation next day back to Massawa to see that BOAC should not suddenly pull my seat out from under me—it was arranged I was to go back via Port Sudan again, only a one day's journey as against the two days via Khartoum.

On the morning of August 11, I took off for Massawa. At Port Sudan where as usual we made an intermediate stop, the airfield commanding officer agreed to send a wireless to Asmara, asking to have my car sent up from Massawa to meet me at the airport.

When in the very late afternoon, I alighted at the Asmara airfield, Garza and my car were both there. Since I had no desire to run the mountain road in the darkness any more than was necessary, we started back promptly for Massawa. About two-thirds of the way down, darkness caught us. After that we went quite slowly with surprisingly little resistance from Garza; I judged my Somali must have raced up those mountains so fast he was content for the day.

We arrived at the Naval Base about 9:00 P.M. I disembarked in front of Building 35, bursting to find my assistants and tell them that our establishment was about to take over from Alex, and so enthusiastic over our prospects I totally ignored my sudden reintroduction to the blast furnace temperatures I had been spared for eight days. So I was delighted to find Captain Morrill waiting for me inside my own air-conditioned room when I entered it. But before I could tell him anything, he started to tell me instead.

"Damned glad to set eyes on you once more, Captain!" he burst out. "Till I got your radio this afternoon asking for your car, I never expected to see you again and was wondering where I should send your clothes. There's hell to pay around here! Look at that!"

He shoved a paper under my nose. It was on the stationery of our civilian contractor, dated at Asmara, August 10, 1942, the day before. It read:

To: All concerned.
From: Assistant Foreign Manager.
Subject: Assignment of Personnel.

Effective immediately, Capt. Edison Brown is placed in complete charge of all Red Sea salvage operations for this company.

Morrill continued angrily:

"Hell's sure popping around here over that! On the face of it, you're relieved, Brown's in charge! Of course I never expected to see

[354]

you again; neither did anybody else. Here the contractor, who everybody figured had eased you out of Eritrea, was already designating Brown as your successor on salvage! Was there an explosion over that! Captain Reed, Lloyd Williams, and all their men say they're quitting—they're damned if they'll work for Brown! Then you don't know it, but your big salvage ship, the *Chamberlin,* finally arrived yesterday from San Diego, and her skipper, Captain Hansen, says he never signed on to work for Brown, and he guesses he'll quit, too! Everything's in a hell of a mess around this Base! Thank God, you've come back; you're staying, aren't you?"

I had to have a few minutes to think, so I said nothing while once again I read that brief order from the contractor, addressed to all hands in Asmara as well as in Massawa. Whether rage or mirth was my predominating reaction at that moment, I still don't know. The idea of a civilian contractor working for the War Department issuing such an order in wartime and in the war zone! They were undertaking to relieve a naval officer designated both by the Navy Department and by the Commanding General in Africa as Officer in Charge of Salvage Operations, by one of his own civilian subordinates! Shades of "Alice in Wonderland"! Had they completely lost their senses?

Finally I turned from the typewritten order to look into Morrill's wrathful face again.

"Morrill," I said, "if it were not for the serious morale effect this has already had on my salvage crews, I'd say nothing I've seen in Eritrea since I first laid eyes on all those 'W il Duce!' signs on the road between here and Asmara, strikes me as so funny! I'll flatten this out so fast it'll make its sponsors dizzy! I gave them credit for having more finesse. The only thing I'm really concerned about is, What did Brown have to do with it? Is he any party to this thing?"

Morrill only shrugged his shoulders. I looked at my watch. It was a little after 9:00 P.M. Brown should be in his room, just around the corner on that same floor in Building 35.

"Bring Brown in here," I ordered Morrill.

I sat down at my desk, took another look at that unbelievable notice. Another mirage, perhaps? No, on the third reading, it still read the same.

Morrill returned, with Brown trailing him.

"Brown," I said abruptly, handing him the notice, "what do you

[355]

know about that? Are you any party to this proceeding?"

Brown gave the order only a perfunctory glance to identify it. He had, of course, seen it before.

"No, sir," answered Brown promptly. "I had nothing to do with it. I never saw it before till I received it yesterday like everybody else. I don't know anything about it."

"That's all then, Brown; you can go back to your room. Don't bother to act on that order. It's worthless and illegal; the contractor had no right to issue it. Just for the record, you'll see it rescinded in no time at all. Good night!"

Brown left.

"Well, that lets Brown out, Morrill. I should have been damned sorry to have found him mixed up in all this mess," I said. "Now all that's necessary is to squelch that order for what effect it'll have in undoing all the harm it's done."

I picked up the telephone to call Asmara, asking for Lieutenant Colonel Knapp, the Area Engineer, whose approval as contracting officer for the Army, the contractor had to have before he could issue any personnel change orders. Knapp, I knew, could never have approved any such order. I got Knapp, to find he didn't even know any such order was in contemplation, let alone had approved it.

The rest of the story was short, covered in two more brief orders.

Asmara, Aug. 12, 1942

Assignment of Personnel.
Assistant Foreign Manager.

1. Reference to your letter August 10, 1942, appointing Captain Brown in complete charge of the Salvage Operations.

2. You are directed to rescind this order at once as this change was not authorized by the contracting officer.

RALPH E. KNAPP,
Lt. Colonel, Corps of Engineers,
Area Engineer, Eritrea Area.

The next day the following order from the contractor reached Massawa:

[356]

To: All concerned.
From: Assistant Foreign Manager.
Subject: Assignment of Personnel.

Reference is made to memorandum from this office, dated August 10, 1942, assigning Capt. Edison Brown in complete charge of all Red Sea Salvage operations for this company.

Effective this date, the order is rescinded.

So that ended that. Whatever, I wondered, could have motivated that contractor in such a crudely conceived maneuver, so easily defeated? Was it simply to annoy me? Was it intended to get Brown in trouble? But I had a war on my hands and no time to bother my head over contractor maneuvers, crude or otherwise, regardless of how much time his men in Asmara might have on their hands with nothing better to do in the middle of a war than to think them up. And I had the shattered morale of my whole salvage force to restore, none of them in either Captain Reed's old crew or the newly arrived force under Captain Hansen on the *Chamberlin* willing to believe that their associate, Captain Brown, had not been mixed up in the scheme somehow, trying to make himself their overall commanding officer.

All of this was bad at that moment, for the *Chamberlin* had brought practically all the rest of my salvage equipment in her large holds, several more divers, and a moderate-sized crew of salvage mechanics; I had expected on their arrival to get salvage going on a much larger scale than before.

The effect on the *Chamberlin's* crew, from her captain down, was particularly bad. They had arrived the very day that order had been posted in Massawa, to find themselves in the middle of an uproar, with their expected Officer in Charge of Salvage vanished from the country, the wildest rumors flying about concerning him, and with all certainty as to who was running the operation knocked sky-high. If that was the way things were run in Eritrea, they had better look out for themselves—next time the contractor might be more skillful in his tactics and they would find themselves being directed by someone of whose qualifications for the task they were doubtful and of whose loyalty they were suspicious. It took their hearts out of their work; never was I able to make a really effective salvage force out of the *Chamberlin's* crew.

The only real assistance I ever got out of my biggest and most expensive salvage ship came from her as a repair ship, and from the materials she was carrying in her holds and the few men I was able to detach from the ship for assignments elsewhere.

In a material way, the *Chamberlin* brought me plenty. She delivered a beautiful set of salvage pumps of all sizes. She brought some air compressors, including one tremendous Sutorbilt low pressure salvage air compressor that could by itself deliver more compressed air than all four of the borrowed compressors I had used on the big Italian dry dock. In the way of salvage material, she brought practically everything I had ever ordered in New York; no longer should I have to bother about borrowing anything from reluctant Captain McCance.

Then further to help out, she brought several fine heavy motor launches for work boats for salvage, and a fast motorboat for me—this last a beautiful launch suitable for a captain's gig in which I could speedily get about on salvage work between all the harbors, and when I again had official visitors, take them out in it without apologies. With all those boats at my command, the *Lord Grey* was promptly relegated to the task of harbor workhorse, for which she had been built.

One of the men who had shipped out as a seaman on the *Chamberlin* was assigned as coxswain of my boat—he proved to be an unusual person. Glen Galvin, lately a backfield man on Howard Jones' University of Southern California football team and himself a participant in Rose Bowl battles, was trying his hand in an entirely different kind of broken field running and against decidedly different opposition.

I chose Galvin myself for the job; he seemed about the most intelligent and willing member of the *Chamberlin's* crew. From then on Glen, with his powerful athletic figure, was always alongside me on wrecks, clambering aboard to lend the salvage crews a hand whenever I boarded a wreck. I think Glen did everything in salvage except dive himself.

As my coxswain, Glen Galvin gave me a strong lift. He was proud of the United States himself and he both ran and rigged his boat so everyone who ever saw her in Massawa would have equal cause to be proud of his country also.

With the aid of two very black, very tall, and very thin Eritreans as his boat crew, both always immaculately rigged out in white turbans and breechcloths setting off their glistening torsos beautifully,

Glen Galvin made his boat and his boat's crew into something to make any skipper happy.

It took some weeks to unload the *Chamberlin's* holds and get her ready to try salvage work herself—a very unfortunate circumstance since it gave her salvage crew too much time to pick up all the gossip of Massawa.

And then as the final blow to the *Chamberlin's* salvage effectiveness, her best diver, Wilford Wood, went ashore shortly after her arrival looking for a secluded spot where he might hang his diving dresses to dry them out after a long sea voyage. Unable to read Italian, and unacquainted with the Naval Base, he wandered into the second floor of what he thought was an abandoned building but which actually was a live high voltage power substation. Hanging up his diving suits, he touched some power wires, and 3000 volts of high tension current hit him with a blinding flash. Fortunately that lightning jolt flung him clear of the wires, though unconscious; why he wasn't instantly killed no one could ever tell. His moans after a while attracted attention. Horribly burned, he hovered for weeks in the hospital between life and death; finally, badly crippled forever, he was shipped home.

If anything more had been necessary to destroy the effectiveness of the *Chamberlin's* salvage crew, the sad accident crippling Wood furnished it, both from my losing him as a diver and from the effect it had on his shipmates.

CHAPTER

43

IN THE MIDST OF ALL THIS TURMOIL, I received word *H.M.S. Dido* was on her way through the Suez Canal bound for Massawa and would arrive late on August 18. I had to make immediate preparations to quarter ashore somewhere the British supervisors and mechanics she was carrying. All the decent quarters I had ashore in the ex-Italian naval barracks were now well filled, mainly by our contractor's American workmen on shore construction projects. I couldn't put the Englishmen with the Americans; there was no room for them there.

It was undesirable also for various reasons to quarter the British coming temporarily to Massawa with the Americans—the major reason was my fear that should the newcomers hear too much regarding the horrors of staying long in Massawa, that on their return to Alexandria, they would effectively kill off any volunteering there with their tales of the place. Their personal experiences would be bad enough to combat; I didn't want them augmented by accounts of what had happened to various Americans.

There was only one possible place I could quarter the newcomers—one I long ago had had my eye on. So I went to Colonel Sundius-Smith of the British Forces and asked that he clear all the black girls out of the military brothel for colonial troops at the foot of the Abd-El-Kader Peninsula and give me the building. The colonel agreed; the building was hastily evacuated.

I turned to a large gang of native laborers in it, scrubbing it and disinfecting it thoroughly with chemicals furnished by our medical officer. Then a new set of cots, mattresses, sheets, and mosquito nets was hurriedly installed, and our new quarters building was ready for occupancy. It really was quite a fine masonry stuccoed building, equal in interior finish to the late-lamented Building 108, though not nearly so well located near the sea. The only reminder left of its former use was the barbed wire entanglement surrounding it. I merely had the gate removed and didn't attempt the nasty task of clearing away the barbed wire; I hadn't time.

On the early afternoon of August 18 we undocked our last supply ship; no more were to arrive until we reported the day the *Dido* would leave. Then with great care we prepared the keel blocks and the bilge blocks of the Persian dry dock to suit the shape of the *Dido's* underwater hull from a plan of her previously sent us. All was ready, ashore and on the dry dock, to receive the *Dido* and the workmen she carried.

About the middle of that afternoon H.M.S. *Dido* arrived and anchored in the outer roadstead, just beyond the wrecks guarding the entrance to the naval harbor. Immediately she sent ashore in her boats the civilian working force she was transporting and the steel she had brought.

My first concern was to house the British workmen—two superin-tendents, four foremen, and thirty mechanics. I loaded the workmen into trucks, the supervisors into my own car, and transported them to their waiting quarters where all disembarked with their baggage.

All hands from Alex were definitely pleased. They were sweltering —that they had expected to stand a while. But their murmurs of appreciation over the beautiful building they got for quarters—something they had never expected—were plainly audible, particularly when they saw the large refrigerator jammed with bottles of cold water I had provided for them. The supervisors received individual rooms. The mechanics were housed barracks style. All were told to make themselves at home till next morning when their labors would begin. Several were curious as to the why of all the barbed wire surrounding their new domicile, but on that I remained noncommittal.

Then I departed to board the *Dido* for a discussion with her captain on the work. I came aboard that British warship in my new boat, expertly landed alongside her starboard gangway by Glen Galvin and his two mostly naked but very nautical Eritreans, to be received on her quarterdeck with the usual naval ceremonies—side boys, bos'n's pipe, Officer of the Deck, and all the other accessories to life in the Navy whose existence my long stay in Massawa had almost made me forget.

I was welcomed aboard by the Commanding Officer, Captain

H. W. U. McCall, R.N.; we promptly retired from his hot quarter-deck to his not much cooler but much fan-ventilated cabin. There he sent for his Executive Officer, his Engineer Officer, and his First Lieutenant, and we immediately got down to brass tacks on what was to be done to the *Dido*. Also present was Commander Mole, R.N., of the engineering dockyard staff in Alex, sent down from there with the *Dido* to advise me technically concerning the design of that particular ship.

We went into the details of what was needed—the new steel stringers to be installed in the stern to make it stronger for the future, the new steel hull plating required to replace her cracked shell plates which now were allowing her stern to flood. I informed the ship of what was wanted of them in the way of assistance in docking the *Dido*.

Then I learned to my great surprise that after a careful diving examination of her damage by the British before her departure, we were to be allowed twelve days on the dock for the repair job before starting the *Dido* back to the Mediterranean.

I promptly vetoed that.

"Nothing doing on twelve days," I announced. "I can't spare the dock that long on one ship—too many other ships waiting to dock here. Right on that dock, we repaired a huge bomb hole in the *Liebenfels* with fewer men than you brought, all of them inexperienced in ship work, in eight days. The *Dido* can't be as bad as the *Liebenfels*. The *Dido* will go off repaired in eight days—no more. And maybe after I've lifted her and seen the actual damage myself, I'll cut that even further, but it'll *not* be increased."

There were immediate objections from Commander Mole and from the *Dido's* officers. Commander Mole pointed out that the Alexandria dockyard with all its machinery couldn't do the job in less than twelve; neither could Durban, had she been sent there. To figure that Massawa, far inferior in size and equipment to either of these dockyards and further handicapped by intolerable working temperatures, could do it in less, was unsafe.

Captain McCall, skeptical of my statement, pointed out the disastrous effects on his crew of an underestimate in time. Living conditions in the crew's quarters below decks on his ship, veritable steel ovens already in Massawa and bound to be worse when the ship was lifted out of water on the dry dock and more of her hull exposed to the sun, were so bad he was sending half his crew that afternoon in trucks to a British military camp in Asmara on the high plateau for the first half of the repair period. The other half of his crew was to be sent there during the last half of the repair time after the first party came back.

If my guess was wrong, as both he and Commander Mole of the Alex dockyard felt assured it was, and he brought his second party back at the end of eight days, he would have his whole crew jammed aboard during the remaining four days of the job—longer even than that if the task took more than twelve days which he thought possible. That would practically kill off his whole crew—when sailing day came, he wouldn't have men enough left on their feet to take his ship out of Massawa, still less any able to fight on their return to the Mediterranean if he ever got there.

"I'm sorry, Captain," I told McCall, "but I'm giving you the facts; you'll have to accept responsibility for how long you send your first party away. If you send your first party away for six days, the second party may never even start for the hills. At best they'll only have a day there before they must return. I tell you the *Dido* will be on the Massawa dry dock not over eight days. Tomorrow after I've lifted her, I'll tell you definitely how much less than that, if any, she'll be here. The pilot will be aboard at 7:00 A.M. to take you in; you'll go immediately on the dock. And remember, you'll be on the dock not over eight days!"

The next morning, early on August 19, *H.M.S. Dido,* the longest ship yet to make the passage, was cautiously piloted by Lieutenant Fairbairn through the line of wrecks and swung hard to starboard to clear the shoal spot and line her up for the dock. The Persian dry dock was, as usual for a large ship, fully but not abnormally flooded down. Excessive draft was not a problem in docking the *Dido*—it was her gross overweight and her excessive length that were the difficulties to be overcome.

The Persian dry dock could lift a maximum of only 6000 tons; her keel blocks could support a length of only 410 feet.

H.M.S. Dido displaced (or weighed) over 7500 tons; her length was 530 feet.

It was on the face of things my job to dry-dock a ship of 7500 tons displacement and 530 feet in length in a dry dock which could lift only 6000 tons and support a length of only 410 feet.

Of course, I could not do that. No one but God himself could have done it. I had no intention of even trying to do it. The thing that had struck me like a flash in Alex the day I was pondering the problem was that it wasn't necessary to do it in order to repair completely the damage to the *Dido*. It so happened that the damage to the *Dido* was wholly at her stern. To repair it, all that was required was that I lift her stern clear of the water. I didn't have to lift her bow out of the water also, as is normally done in docking any ship—there wasn't any damage to the bow. And not having to lift her bow out of the water (which I couldn't do simultaneously anyway) solved the other dilemma of the inability of the short dry dock to support such a long ship lest the unsupported part break off. The bow of the *Dido* was going to remain floating in the water at practically its normal draft forward, supported almost as usual by the sea, while I lifted only the stern clear of the water to repair the damage there.

The whole result was going to be that when docked for repairs, the *Dido* (and, of course, also the dry dock with her) was going to be on considerable of a slope as if sliding downhill towards her bow. The effect was to be about as if some titanic derrick had taken hold of that long cruiser at the stern and lifted that warship's stern well out of water while leaving her bow afloat and undisturbed.

In the actual operation, the dry dock would not have to lift even 6000 tons' worth to get the stern completely out of water; it would be easy for the dry dock. The only dangers involved were in getting too much of the lift needed, towards the bow of the dry dock—that might strain the ship there; and in getting the ship on such a steep slope that she would slide forward down the incline and capsize the keel blocks on the floor of the dry dock. The first danger could be avoided by not lifting too much with the bow compartments of the dry dock. The second danger could be eliminated by not lifting the stern any higher than necessary to repair the damage and by securing the *Dido* to the dry dock by stout fore and aft steel hawsers, hauled taut, so she had no chance to slide forward in the dry dock.

And that was how *H.M.S. Dido* was dry-docked in a dry dock too small to take her. She came into the dry dock as for any normal dry-docking, but was hauled through it till about 110 feet of her bow overhung the forward end of the dry dock altogether. Then the dry dock was pumped up with the ship level fore and aft, no trim on her, till the keel blocks of the dry dock touched for their entire length.

At that point, the sliding bilge blocks were run in under the ship and the side spur shores run in against her sides to keep her from listing to either side as her stern lifted. At the same time, the steel hawsers to keep her from sliding forward were hauled taut.

After that, the dry dock was pumped up on a slant, with far more buoyancy aft than forward, till the stern of the *Dido* came clear of the water, leaving the overhanging bow afloat practically as usual. I stopped lifting when the stern was clear, leaving about four feet of water over the dry dock floor aft—no more than a man could wade in and reducing the slant of the ship by that much.

At that point the docking operation was completed and the repair job could start. I must admit that anyone looking across the harbor at that crazily slanted cruiser and dry dock would have concluded there was something cock-eyed going on in Massawa. And he would have been right.

Once the sea had dropped far enough down around the stern, carpenters working from boats began to rig scaffolding on both sides around her after end. But I didn't wait for any scaffolding to stand on to make my inspection. Crossing in a small skiff myself, I got close in under her exposed counters, supporting myself first by her propeller blades, later by standing on her shafts, and made a close examination of her troubles. I found them worse than the British diving examination had reported.

In way of the starboard after propeller, a huge piece (about as large as a garage door) of her steel hull, made of two thicknesses of plating, was cracked completely through and through and all around; nothing seemingly supported it any longer. Why it had not fallen out already was a mystery. On the port side, a somewhat similar cracking existed in way of the port after propeller, but it had not gone quite so far.

Swiftly but carefully I went over the damage outside while the scaffolding was being rigged. Then I clambered back aboard the *Dido,* and dropped through a small manhole alongside her steering machinery into the stern compartment beneath, from which by now most of the sea water there had been drained out the way it had come in—through the wide open cracks in her sides.

In that confined stern hold, a devil of a place to try to get about in because of its narrowing triangular shape between the propellers outside, I crawled around over wet steel. With a flashlight I examined cracked girders which would have to be replaced, the difficulties in-

H.M.S. Dido docked, stern lifted, bow still afloat.

volved in building in the new girders wanted in a space already so full of interlacing steel one could hardly move about, and our chances of getting at the inside welding and riveting that would be required. It was going to be tough, much more difficult to get to than when the ship was first built, for then the workmen did not have the deck overhead to seal them in. We, however, would not only have that deck as an interference to our every movement, but in addition nearly everything needed in that cramped space, men and materials, would have to enter through a manhole so small a man had difficulty in getting through. In hot Massawa, once we started welding and riveting inside that jammed-up hold, the infamous Black Hole of Calcutta would be the very acme of cool comfort in comparison. But it could be done, and, of course, it had to be.

Back up on deck, smeared with rust and slime (I was wet through anyway from perspiration so the water in the hold had made me no wetter), I gathered up the two top British dockyard superintendents, Mr. Smith and Mr. Edwards, and also Commander Mole. With them all, I went to see Captain McCall of H.M.S. Dido to inform him how long his ship would be under repair on the dry dock.

"Captain," I said, "I have carefully examined the damage from all causes to your ship both inside and outside. It's worse now that it can be seen in the light of day than reported by your divers, whose ability to inspect was naturally limited. I've sized it up against other damage jobs I have handled, and particularly against the Liebenfels bomb repair job recently done on this dry dock. I find my estimate of yesterday of eight days for this job needs revision. The estimate was too generous. The Dido will be repaired and off this dry dock in six days. You can all make your plans accordingly."

I got repercussions. Captain McCall, who had been reluctant to arrange his leave parties to Asmara on an eight-day limit, felt that arranging them on a six-day basis was taking a grave risk of putting his whole crew out of action. If we failed, the results would be tragic.

I told him that was my responsibility as Commanding Officer of the Naval Base; I was informing him of what was going to happen; I would shoulder all responsibility in seeing it happened. He was going out in six days; it would be wise to act accordingly.

The two British dockyard superintendents—Mr. Smith, the elder, very wiry but grown grizzled in the British dockyard service, and Mr. Edwards, middle-aged, somewhat stout, but also a very experienced supervisor—both objected strenuously. They had considered eight days highly improbable but had made no vocal objection; they had been willing on that to try, and perhaps finish in ten. But six days for the job was completely out of question—they knew their men, all good mechanics, better than I did. They couldn't do it in six days; it wasn't even worth trying.

I had a simple answer to that.

"Gentlemen," I countered, "you've got four foremen and thirty good British shipyard mechanics with you for this task. Over on that salvaged Italian dry dock I've got one American superintendent, Lloyd Williams; about six American ironworkers and welders; and ten South African ironworkers. Not one of them, including Williams, ever worked on a ship before in his life until he saw Massawa. I know what they can do. If you and your men, twice as many as they, don't want to tackle this *Dido* job on a six-day basis, you can all start back toward Suez tonight without tackling it at all. I'll bring my Americans and South Africans over from that dry dock, and Lloyd Williams will see *they* do it in six days. It's going to be done in six days, whether you do it or not. I'm merely offering you the chance. If you don't want it, say so right now. I've no time to waste."

Those two Englishmen looked from me to each other, conferred privately a moment. Then they proved they were of the same breed as their countrymen facing Hitler alone after Dunkirk.

"We'll have a go at it, anyway, Captain," announced Smith, the elder, laconically.

"Fine!" I sang out. "That's all I ask of you. You'll do it, and no trouble. Now, you and your men get cracking; I'll be with you on the staging in a few minutes."

Both superintendents left. I looked at Captain McCall, who, of course, had been listening, but he had no further comment. So I motioned Commander Mole, who was as skeptical as the dockyard superintendents in spite of his silence while they spoke, and we both left the skipper's cabin.

"They won't do it," said Mole, who as an engineer commander, had had considerable experience in British dockyards.

"They'll do that job in six days," I replied, "unless I'm badly disappointed in what British mechanics can do."

"You'll be disappointed, then," answered Mole.

CHAPTER

44

THE NEXT FEW DAYS WERE VERY
hectic ones under the stern of the *Dido*. Night and day around the
clock, without intermission, three shifts of British mechanics labored
in the Massawa heat. Rivet guns rattled like machine guns firing in
action. Acetylene torches cutting away damaged steel sent trails of
scintillating sparks flaming across the dock like ack-ack tracers in the
night sky. Pneumatic drills groaned and hummed as they bored
through thick warship steel. Crackling electric welding arcs cast a
weird unearthly bluish light over everything as molten steel flowed
from their electrodes to knit steel plates together—electric arcs rivaling
the sun on which it was wise not to look unless one wanted to go
blind.

Inside and outside, the light cruiser *Dido's* stern was a tight spot in
which to work. On the scaffoldings outside there was room for only
a few men to stand at once, and that few had to be careful of their
every movement lest they knock a fellow worker off the staging into
the dry dock below. Inside the stern, where the ship narrowed down
practically to a knife edge at the rudder post, hardly two men at a
time could enter, and one of them normally had the other man's
elbows or his feet in his stomach. It was stifling in that confined space
from the outside heat, from red-hot rivets to be driven, from smoke
and gas fumes from cutting torches and welding arcs.

I did what I could to make it bearable. On the quarterdeck I installed an American electrically operated water cooler; one of two
just brought us by the *Chamberlin*. Cold water flowed on tap—to my
thirsting Englishmen a boon from heaven. Inside the lower hold, I
got what electric blower fans I could to force down fresh air and to
exhaust the gases. Otherwise the few men down there would have
been asphyxiated in short order.

I found all those Englishmen exceptionally skilled workmen—they knew ships, they knew their trades. I found all of them, superintendents, foremen, and mechanics alike, very willing workers, and soon I was calling them by their first names—Willie, Alf, 'Erbert, Eddie, or Tom—how could you do anything else when you were sweating with them cheek by jowl jammed together in a tight hole trying to figure out how a particularly impossible-to-get-at rivet was to be driven, or a piece of cracked girder cut away with an acetylene torch without burning also into a good steel plate that would be hell to renew if accidentally it were burned into also?

Very swiftly I ran into the reason why Commander Mole felt assured the job could never be done in six days—British trade union rules and British trade customs ingrained in all these men by a century of labor conditions and labor battles in England. I met that issue head on the first few hours when first it arose on the starboard scaffolding, over sending up on deck for another mechanic to perform the next operation on removing a damaged steel plate—it wasn't the trade of the man on the staging with me then, Alf, to do that operation, it was 'Erbert's trade. 'Erbert, who was on deck the *Dido*, would be sent for while Alf got off the staging to make room so 'Erbert could work when he arrived. Half an hour would be lost while the shift was being made, and another half hour also when 'Erbert got through and Alf had to be sent for to resume.

We lost the first half hour then and there, but it was the last half hour we lost on the *Dido* over that. I knocked off everybody, gathered them all, superintendents and mechanics alike, on the *Dido's* quarterdeck. I told them they'd work like everybody else that worked for me in Massawa—every man would do anything he could as well as he could every time he could regardless of his trade or anybody else's. This wasn't England, it wasn't a British dockyard—it was Massawa in wartime where neither I nor anybody else had time or energy to waste on trade union rules or customs, British or American. It was too damned hot where we were and we were fighting Hitler and Mussolini, neither of whom was paying any attention to rules of any kind, union or otherwise.

"That's all, men," I concluded. "You're good mechanics, every one of you knows enough of the other man's trade to do a bit of it when it means either doing it or stopping the job a while. Now get back to work, and nobody pulls any more rules on me! We don't stop for anything in Massawa!"

The men went back to work, and to the undisguised astonishment of very British Mr. Smith, veteran of many a trade union dockyard controversy over rule technicalities, they did exactly what I asked of them. He shook his head incredulously as he watched them.

"I could never get them to do that! You couldn't either, Captain, if this was a British dockyard. But even here, I can't see how you're getting by with it without their quitting on you. You don't know how sacred them rules is to all these men!"

But I didn't care. It wasn't a British dockyard; I wasn't interested in hampering rules. Massawa's resources were too limited ever to get anything done if I went by the rule book in labor or in anything else.

We got along with the job. Around and around the clock, night or day the same to us. The damaged steel was cut away; cracks which could safely be welded up again were welded; patterns (templets) were made to be sent ashore to the Naval Base shops from which to fabricate there all the new steel plates and girders required. The *Lord Grey* was busy all the time bringing us materials.

I had a careful schedule made of when each new plate, each new piece of girder had to arrive from the shops and be installed to keep us on my six-day timetable. Those Englishmen took as much interest in keeping on that schedule on their warship as I did.

The third day went by, all the damaged structure was removed and new steel began to arrive to replace it. The fourth day of that scorching August vanished and more steel came out. By morning of the fifth day, we had the holes in the sides of the *Dido* plated up and riveting guns and welding arcs going all over the stern securing the new plating and girders together.

My British workers were all tired and wan from the heat by then but since they were working only one shift a day each, at least they got ashore when their shift was over to sprawl out on their cots under their mosquito nets and get what rest they could in the heat (which wasn't any too much). I felt they would last out.

The fifth day, on the *Dido's* quarterdeck, I tried to do a little missionary work on elderly Mr. Smith and youngish Mr. Edwards towards getting them and as many of their men as possible to volunteer permanently for Massawa, instead of returning to Alex. There would be a good bonus in it for the volunteers. Mr. Edwards seemed interested and promised to give it consideration, but first he would go back to Alex anyway.

But with graying Mr. Smith there was not a chance.

"I'm too old for this place, Captain," he assured me. "And then I'm too old for you; you're too much of a driver for me to keep up with long. It takes younger men, like Mr. Edwards here." Then he seized me by my unbuttoned shirt near my throat as if to choke me, and continued. "Besides, what do you mean by deceiving a poor old man like me? Remember I asked you when we came here about the barbed wire around that fine building you've put us all in, and you didn't answer me? A fine building it is, all right! What'll my good wife back in Portsmouth say when she hears I'm living in Massawa in a brothel? And mind you, Captain, a black brothel at that! I'll never live it down!"

I had to laugh. So did Smith.

"So you've found out, eh? I wondered how long it would take for the scandalous truth to leak out!"

But both Smith and Edwards promised to do what they might to get me some volunteers from among the thirty men they'd brought, so with that we all turned to again.

The fifth day dragged along. Everybody—British workmen and British officers on the *Dido*—could see the task was so well advanced there was little doubt we'd finish within the six days set. Captain McCall, astonished but pleased, so reported to the Commander-in-Chief back in Alex and went about getting the second section of his crew which had gone to Asmara only the morning before, back aboard by next night in preparation for final undocking and departure.

Meanwhile, the Eritrean natives, who had already scraped clean the exposed portion of the *Dido* aft (she wasn't very foul), began to apply the first coat of underwater paint. The idea was that when all the repairs were completed and all the exposed stern painted, the cruiser would be floated, shifted aft inside the dry dock till the stern overhung about 150 feet, and then the bow end lifted out of water for swiftly scraping and painting that. When we were all through, except for a small part of the bottom amidships which would never come out of water during any part of the liftings, we should have the *Dido* not only wholly repaired but mostly freshly cleaned and painted also when she left Massawa.

Late in the evening of the fifth day, all the new plating was secured n place except the last plate on the starboard side, an outer course plate or doubler. This was an especially thick steel plate for which we could not lift a templet till all the plating beneath it was riveted and welded up.

The shipfitters went to work then against the side of the ship to make their templet, a pattern of thin wood strips to the exact size and shape of the required steel plate. On a large scale, the job resembled a dressmaker's laying out of a paper pattern for a section of a dress, cut to match all adjoining seams. It was a fair-sized steel plate we would need—about six feet wide, fifteen feet long, and around three-quarters of an inch in thickness. The shipfitters worked with great care on that templet; the rigid steel of the new plate would have to match exactly all the seams and rivet holes of the plating beneath it.

About midnight the templet was finished and sent ashore in the Lord Grey to the plate shop where the new plate was to be fabricated during the night. My plate shop, unfortunately, had rather scanty machinery; the Italians had had no great amount of plate fabricating machinery in Massawa and none of the beautiful equipment for that shop (or any shop) had yet reached us from America. The Italian plate shop in Massawa had been their most poorly equipped shop.

I saw that the shop foreman and his Italian assistants got started on the steel plate, and then went home to Building 35 for a rest myself. The new plate should be ready to ship out about 6:00 A.M.

About 6:30 A.M., beginning the morning of our sixth and last twenty-four hours, I was back on the dry dock. So also was that final steel plate, hanging from the traveling crane of the dry dock, ready to be swung into place against the Dido's starboard side. On the scaffolding in way of the starboard after propeller where that plate was to go, were all the workmen, but no one seemed to be doing anything towards swinging that plate over in place.

I clambered from the side of the dock over the wooden walkway bridging the water beneath me, to the scaffolding inboard of the propeller. One of the British foremen handling the early shift greeted me.

"That plate ain't right, Cap'n," he informed me, pointing to it as it hung from the crane hook. "We 'as to send it back to the shop ashore for 'em to work on it there again before we can erect it."

I looked at the plate. It looked all right to me.

"What's the matter with it?" I asked anxiously, for we had no extra steel, and if my shop ashore had cut that plate to the wrong size, especially if it had made it too small, it would be a major tragedy.

"It ain't got the knuckle in it," he explained. "Cast your eye over this, Cap'n," and he turned toward the *Dido* where right under our noses, the plate had to fit. "D' ye see? There's a sharp knuckle in the counter o' this vessel which'll come about six inches below the top edge o' that plate. We showed that knuckle on the templet Willie made an' sent ashore, only them Eyties o' yours in the plate shop there forgot to knuckle the plate to suit the templet. It's got to go back to be knuckled."

I knew that knuckle in the *Dido* he was referring to well enough. Her stern, from the quarterdeck down, was practically straight-sided till it reached a few feet below her water line; then the plating was sharply knuckled or creased inward to run at a considerable slope inboard and downward toward her keel. The top edge of our last steel plate came to about six inches above this horizontal knuckle line; of course, to fit the ship it also had to be knuckled over at the top so it could be riveted and welded there neatly and watertight against the plating already in place.

"Oh, is that all that's worrying you!" I exclaimed, much relieved. "Don't bother to send the plate ashore. We'll have to knuckle it over in place with sledge hammers. Just swing it over, secure it where it belongs, bolt it up, then rivet and weld the bottom and both sides up to near the top, and after that we'll do the knuckling with sledges with the ship as a jig to knuckle against."

The foreman looked at me as if I were crazy, or else perhaps knew nothing of shipbuilding.

"Knuckle that thick plate over by hand?" he gasped. "Why, they got power machinery ashore to do jobs like that! All you have to do is put that plate in a keel-bender, put about 500 tons o' pressure on it, and the keel-bender'll knuckle it over for us in no time!"

"Yes, yes," I admitted, slightly peeved at the time being lost. "I know all about keel-benders. You don't have to tell me how they work. Only there *isn't* any keel-bender in the plate shop ashore. That's why they didn't knuckle that plate for you in the first place. And there isn't any other kind of machine ashore either that could knuckle that plate, or I'd have it done. This is Massawa, not the dockyard in Alex. Now you get that plate swung over in place, secure it as I told

[374]

you, then get some acetylene torches to heat the plate up red-hot along that knuckle line and put two of the huskiest men you've got swinging sledges on the hot iron to knuckle it up against the ship's side. After that, we'll weld it in place along the top seam and we'll be all through. Now don't lose any more time. Get going! I'll be along again in about an hour to see how you're making out."

With as stricken a look in his eyes as if I had just sentenced him to Massawa forever, the foreman turned and waved to the crane operator on the dry dock far above him to lower the plate further and then to swing it in. As I left, I heard him muttering,

"No keel-bender? What kind o' dockyard is this they're wanting us to stay an' work in?"

I really could have told him, but I refrained. I ducked on the scaffolding to keep clear of the rapidly descending steel plate, climbed over to the side of the dry dock, and took my boat over to the Italian dry dock to see how Lloyd Williams and his crew were getting along in patching the bomb holes there. I had hardly been aboard that dock in five days; practically all my time since her arrival had been put in on the *Dido*.

I nodded approvingly to Williams as I went over his job. Already a number of the huge bomb craters had vanished forever, permanently sealed over with new steel plating. But about half the bomb holes were still left, all the damaged steel removed but the holes on top in the floor still yawning chasms waiting for steel.

"We'll just about run out of steel by tomorrow, Captain," Williams informed me. "Will there be any left over from that job"—he inclined his head toward the Persian dock—"that you can give us when she leaves?" he asked.

"Nothing to talk about, Lloyd; just some scraps, maybe." I sighed at our predicament. "I'll try Alex again tomorrow. Maybe with the *Dido* back in their laps, they'll feel grateful to us here and scrape up a few plates for us."

I got back into my boat and returned to the *Dido*. It was nearly 3:00 A.M.; I'd been gone somewhat over an hour. I disembarked and hurried over the side of the dry dock back on the starboard scaffolding, eager to see how much progress the men had made in knuckling that plate.

My heart sank as my eyes fell on that plate. No progress had been made in knuckling it. True, it was now in place against the sloping lower shell of the ship, with most of the quilting rivets driven to hold it there. But its top edge stood sharply away from the shell there, with not a sign of a knuckling yet in it.

I looked over the men on the scaffolding. It was crowded now with men—too many for anybody possibly to work. There were Smith and Edwards, their foreman, two English riveters who were certainly the huskiest Englishmen on the job, a torch operator, some sledges, and a torch. Everything was there that I had ordered to do that knuckling job, but there was no indication of any knuckling.

"We've been waiting for you to come back, Captain," said Smith somewhat apologetically as he noted my chagrin. "I've stopped 'em from driving any more rivets. We'll have to cut out the rivets they've driven already, take that plate off o' there and send it ashore somewhere to be knuckled. Nobody can knuckle it the way you said; it's too thick a plate. It's a job for power machinery."

"But there isn't any power machinery ashore!" I burst out exasperated. "I told your foreman here that and he must have told you. You shouldn't have stopped the job, Mr. Smith. I told 'em how to do it. Now let's all of us get off this scaffolding and give your men a chance to get to work with that torch and the sledges. We've lost too damned much time already talking about this!"

"It's no use, Captain," replied Smith, blank despondency written all over his grizzled face. "Here's the two strongest men I've got and they say they can't do it; nobody can. And I agree with 'em. It's beyond human strength. I'd expected you to have that plate knuckled in a keel-bender ashore here, or I'd never have agreed to let 'em send the ship here instead o' to Durban. Now we're in a pickle. We can't finish the job!"

I looked at Mr. Smith in dismay. There was no question—he wasn't being mutinous, he wasn't being obstinate—the job was just completely beyond him. I turned to his two riveters, huskies both of them, though I was sure I'd seen better.

"Can't you men do that?" I asked of them, touching the protruding plate about in line with our heads. Both of them shook their heads solemnly.

"No, Cap'n," said the nearer of the two, "nor nobody else neither."

I looked from the dejected men about me to that troublesome plate which *had* to be beaten in or we couldn't undock the *Dido*. If anybody was in a pickle, it was I. This was the last day. The captain o' the *Dido* had already radioed Alex that next day he was returning to the Mediterranean. No doubt already in Alex, the C.-in-C. was arranging his warship movements to take account of that. Now not only would she not undock tomorrow, as these men saw it, but no one could say when she would undock—probably not till that recalcitrant plate had been removed from the *Dido* and sent on a round trip to Alex to be knuckled under the keel-bender there. We couldn't get that big plate into a plane. If it went by freighter, it would take around two weeks for the journey.

What a lot of rot! I couldn't believe they couldn't do it. In the quarter of a century since I'd worked on my first ship, I'd seen men, many of them English and Scotch, do far more than that to steel.

"So you try to tell me it can't be done my way, eh? This is your last chance. Can you do it?"

Everybody involved shook his head again.

"All right then, boys; just move aside and clear this scaffold so somebody who can, gets a chance to swing a sledge! Pick out some seats along the side of the dock where you can all see without getting in the road, and I'll show you something!" I turned toward the near-by stern of the dry dock where my new boat was tied up waiting for me.

"Glen!" I sang out to my coxswain. "Get over to the Italian dry dock and tell Lloyd Williams to break Bill Cunningham and Horace Armstrong off whatever they're doing and bring 'em both over here four bells with the biggest pair of sledge hammers they've got on that dry dock! Bring all three of 'em back with you; I've got a little job here for 'em! Shake it up now!"

"Aye, aye, Captain!" With a wave of his hand to show he understood, Galvin shoved off and with the throttle all out raced away toward the other near-by dry dock.

Silently all the Englishmen started to clear the scaffolding. I restrained their top superintendent.

"You'd better stay here with me, Mr. Smith. You'll want a close view, so next time you'll know what men can do when it has to be done." His wrinkled face incredulous but silent, the elderly dockyard superintendent picked out a spot on the end of the scaffolding where he would be clear but still close by.

In ten minutes, the boat was back, and its three passengers disembarking. Galvin pointed out to them where I was up on the scaffolding over the starboard after propeller. In single file, Williams leading, with behind him Cunningham and Armstrong, each nonchalantly swinging a heavy sledge in one hand, they threaded their way past the British mechanics now perched on the side of the dry dock near by, and came over the walkway to the scaffolding where I stood.

I looked at Cunningham and Armstrong approvingly, both stripped to the waist, both glistening with perspiration. They were tough guys, and over Cunningham particularly I had had plenty of headaches in the past. But now I needed a couple of tough guys and they were going to repay me for all my troubles. I had no fears.

"Boys," I said, "you see this steel plate?" and I laid my hand on its protruding upper edge. "I want it knuckled in flat against the shell behind it to let us weld this top edge and make the stern of this cruiser watertight so she can go back and fight." I turned carefully around on the narrow scaffolding toward my late companions on it, now all ensconced some thirty feet away on various vantage points.

"Now, boys, you see those Englishmen over there? It was their job to do this, only they say they can't. And what's more, Bill, and you, too, Horace, they say you can't either!"

Cunningham and Armstrong both took a brief look at the thick steel plate, then gazed belligerently at the onlookers. Neither of them cared much for Englishmen; they were all potential M.P.s to them. Already Lloyd Williams was lighting up the acetylene torch which lay on the scaffolding at his feet, applying the hot flame to the plate at about the knuckle line, heating the steel.

"Them limeys say we can't do it?" as soft in speech as ever, Cunningham asked of me. "Is *that* all you want of us, Cap'n?"

I nodded in assent.

Cunningham looked at the spot Williams was heating, then at the narrow scaffolding to get a proper stance for his feet. The sledge hammers the Englishmen had left there were in his way. He glanced casually at them, then contemptuously kicked them both overboard into the water covering the dock floor below. Compared to the sledge hammer he was carrying, they were only toys, too small for a man to work with.

Lloyd Williams had a considerable spot of steel red-hot. Cunningham looked inquiringly at Armstrong.

"O.K., Bill," answered Armstrong, bracing himself while he raised his sledge, gripped it with both hands.

"All right, Horace, let's go!" said Cunningham, and with a terrific clang, his heavy sledge hammer came down against that hot steel plate. It sounded as if Big Ben himself had struck one.

As Cunningham's hammer swung back over his shoulder, Armstrong's cracked down, and from then on it seemed as if Hercules and Vulcan themselves were rhythmically sledging away on that steel plate as Bill and Horace plied those ponderous sledges.

Soon they had a gallery, with all the other British mechanics, practically the whole crew of the *Dido,* and almost everybody belonging on the Persian dry dock lining the rails of the *Dido* and the dry dock to watch them—everybody from Captain McCall of the *Dido* (whom someone had informed of impending disaster), immaculate in whites and gold-visored cap, down to practically naked Eritreans fouled with dirt and paint.

The reaction on everybody, cruiser captain to naked savages, was the same. They were witnessing something not often seen—they were seeing *men* work. Never was I prouder of being an American than while I watched my two fellow Americans, the center of the awe-struck attention of men of every race and every religion in the Middle East, beating that plate into place.

Pausing only periodically while Lloyd Williams heated up new stretches of steel for them to swing on, steadily they worked their way with their sledge hammers along the fifteen-foot length of that plate. The task took them an hour and a half. At the end of that time, from end to end that heavy steel plate along its upper edge lay neatly in against the plating under it, beautifully knuckled over.

With his last blow swung home to finish, Bill Cunningham rested his sledge negligently on his shoulder and turned again to me.

"Anything else you want o' us here, Cap'n?" he queried mildly.

"No, Bill, that's all. And thanks to both of you." I could have kissed him for what he'd done, and Armstrong also.

"C'mon then, Horace," said Cunningham to Armstrong. "We'd better get going back to that Eytie dry dock an' get some work in this morning."

CHAPTER

45

N<small>EXT</small> MORNING, AUGUST 25, COM-
pletely finished, *H.M.S. Dido* was undocked, having spent exactly six
days on the Massawa dry dock. We were through with her in just
half the time allowed us for the task in Alexandria. Hardly was she
off the dry dock when another of Admiral Harwood's armed supply
ships, waiting already outside the harbor, took her place on the keel
blocks.

That day the *Dido* started back for her station in the Mediterranean, having on her return been absent from it a total of eleven
days, as against the forty to sixty days she would have been missing
from the war zone had she gone to Durban.

Via Captain Lucas, R.N., NOIC in Massawa, the usual wireless to
the C.-in-C., announcing her completion, went out.

H.M.S. Dido undocked 0630 today. *Kythera* follows.

A few hours later, a sweating British seaman from NOIC's office
caught up with me to thrust into my hands a wireless from Admiral
Harwood in Alexandria:

Your 0802/25. Pass to Ellsberg. Well done indeed. Great work!

That, from a conservative British admiral, was certainly praise.
The United States Naval Repair Base at Massawa at last had come
of age.

Shortly we were informed that we were also definitely allotted the
cruisers *Euryalus* and *Cleopatra,* damaged sisters to the *Dido.* Our performance on the *Dido* had pushed Durban off the C.-in-C.'s list so
far as further wartime maintenance of the Mediterranean Fleet was
concerned. All the British mechanics who came down with the *Dido*
had already been ordered to remain in Massawa to await the coming

of her sisters—only Commander Mole and Mr. Smith had returned to Alex with the *Dido*. The commander went back to report firsthand on our performance; Mr. Smith because Massawa had proved too much for his aging body.

With only a few days overlap in the Mediterranean to change stations about, *H.M.S. Euryalus* was sent to us, arriving September 5. We cleaned up her damage and sent her back, only four days in dry dock, an even better performance than on the *Dido*, but, of course, by then we knew better what to expect and were prepared in advance for it.

Last of all came *H.M.S. Cleopatra*, namesake of that woman who never failed to cause trouble to everyone who crossed her path. The *Cleopatra* ran true to her name. We repaired her and sent her away in five days, commencing on September 19, but she nearly ruined the Massawa Naval Base and everything in it, including me.

She lost no time in causing trouble. Hardly was her stern half lifted out of water and I beneath it in a small boat scanning her half-exposed bottom for her damage while standing on the gunwale of my skiff, than a wave washing into the still partly flooded dry dock lifted my boat suddenly, bringing my left foot on the gunwale up with a terrible jolt right against the sharp lower edge of her bronze propeller blade there, nearly amputating my big toe and laming me severely.

That was only the beginning. I got the work laid out and the repair job going with the British mechanics now under the immediate supervision of Lloyd Williams, without any difficulty. But at that unfortunate time, I received a peremptory order to proceed instantly to Alexandria for a conference there on some top secret matter.

It nearly broke my heart to have to leave that cruiser docked in what I as well as everyone else in Alex and Massawa knew was a ticklish situation. I had no competent person I could really trust to shift the *Cleopatra* in dry dock when her repairs were done and it came time to drop her stern and lift her bow to finish the cleaning and painting job, which the *Cleopatra* needed more badly than her two sisters.

But the orders permitted no delay, the conference was for one day only, and on the face of it, it looked as if I could get back in time to do the shifting myself.

I had no fears about Lloyd Williams. I instructed him what to do on repairs, which had been already laid out as a five-day job. Where my knees shook was over Spanner, the English dockmaster. I warned him to watch the ship carefully and to let her alone; I would be back in time to shift her myself. Then I dashed to Asmara to catch an Army plane next day for Cairo via Port Sudan, the fastest route, where I arrived in the early evening.

From Cairo, I was hurried next morning to Alex by car, to find that my conference was, oddly enough, wholly with a Major Quilln of the Royal Marines, an officer attached to Admiral Harwood's staff for special missions.

It appeared that the Royal Navy was deeply interested in blocking the entrance to a certain enemy port supplying somebody (Major Quilln never mentioned either name, but I thought I could guess). The idea was to run in and sink a blockship under fire, something attempted many times before in many wars, and usually with as little success as attended the late Lieutenant Richmond Pearson Hobson's effort to block Cervera's fleet in Santiago Harbor back in our own Spanish War, in 1898.

What concerned Major Quilln was how to sink a blockship so she would stay sunk. The British were undesirous, after a number of Royal Navy men had sacrificed their lives in sinking the ship, of having some Nazi salvage officer swiftly remove the blockship and open the harbor entrance to traffic again. Since I had done a fair job in quickly lifting an important wreck that the Axis had sunk so she was thought impossible to raise, it had occurred to the British command to have me sent for to tell them how to sink a ship so she'd stay sunk, thus paying me the compliment of implying that the Nazis had no one who could outguess me in salvage.

I went over the problem with Major Quilln and pointed out to him how best it could be done; since the subject is still a top secret one and I have no wish that the information ever be used against us, I won't go into it here.

That was the reason for dragging me out of Massawa at an unpropitious moment. An important reason, no doubt, but one giving me little peace of mind when I knew I hadn't a single trained naval assistant in Massawa to take over in my absence, least of all when we were in the midst of a tricky docking operation.

When finally I had finished with Major Quilln, I breathed a sigh of relief, and in the late afternoon rushed back to Cairo. A seat had already been reserved for me in the Asmara plane via Port Sudan next morning. I should get back to Massawa the day before it was necessary, to shift the *Cleopatra* myself, which no doubt the C.-in-C.'s headquarters had also figured on.

Early on the morning of September 22, I was on hand at Heliopolis airport to catch the plane for Asmara, but there was no plane there. Then for the first time, I learned the BOAC plane flights for Asmara didn't originate in Cairo, the route started in Syria somewhere and the plane was late arriving at Cairo. It would take off for Asmara as soon as it got in and could be refueled.

The hours dragged on, the morning wasted away, my margin of safety in getting to Massawa shrank constantly and I sat there in Heliopolis, capable of chewing nails had there been any about available for the purpose. Finally the plane arrived in the early afternoon. It had had engine trouble somewhere to delay it.

Then the final blow was administered. The plane would not take off for Asmara that day—it was too late to start the flight, besides the engines needed attention. They would be tuned up during the rest of the afternoon; next morning we should take off.

There wasn't anything I could do except go back to my billet alongside the airfield and await the next day. So I did. The situation now would be that I might with luck arrive a few hours only before the *Cleopatra* had to be shifted. It was going to be nip and tuck.

On the morning of September 23, again I was early on hand at the airfield. The plane was wheeled out, our baggage was put aboard, we embarked. The pilot revved up his engines preparatory to the take-off. Apparently they didn't suit him. All passengers were disembarked while the mechanics were called back to work again on the tuning up supposedly taken care of the day before.

Whatever was the matter with the ignition system on that plane, I don't know. The morning drifted away, the sound of the engines never suited the pilot. Finally about noon, we were informed the flight was off for that day also. The mechanics would have to change completely something on the engines; tomorrow morning we should surely fly. For the first time I realized acutely the meaning of what previously I had considered only a flip epigram:

"If you've got lots of time, fly; otherwise go some other way if you want to arrive on schedule."

Once again I returned to my billet to impose myself unexpectedly on an overcrowded Army menage. Now I was in real agony—the tricky handling of the *Cleopatra* on the dry dock, something which on the *Dido* Admiral Harwood had begged of me for God's sake to be careful of, was going to be in the hands of a dockmaster in whose competence I had no faith. The Lord alone knew what now was going to happen, with me a thousand miles away, helpless to do anything.

Next morning, September 24, the third day since it was supposed to start, the BOAC plane took off at last. I arrived in Asmara in the very early afternoon, grabbed an Army car there, and raced for Massawa. This time so far as I was concerned, the driver could go as fast as he pleased; there was never a word from me to slow down. By 3:00 P.M., I was in the Naval Base, looking out over the water as I roared down the road. Something was wrong, I could see the moment I got a glimpse. The *Cleopatra* was off the dock, as she should have been, anchored now outside the wrecks. But the dock itself was empty—there was no supply ship lifted out of water on it as should have been there.

As I dashed through my office to the water front to get my boat and get out on the water to find out what the trouble was, I picked up Captain Morrill who told me, though he knew none of the details. There had been an accident, all right.

The *Cleopatra* had dropped off the keel blocks late the night before in connection with the shift; the dry dock was out of commission with all its keel blocks reduced to pulp; and what the damage to the *Cleopatra* was, no one knew yet. When she fell off the blocks, the dock had been hurriedly flooded down by Spanner to get her out of the dry dock. At that moment in the afternoon, the bottom of the *Cleopatra* was being inspected by one of my divers, Al Watson, to determine the damage to her.

So with Glen Galvin opening his throttle wide, with an anguished heart over this catastrophe I raced to the outer roadstead to board the *Cleopatra*. What had we done to the *Cleopatra*, a quarter of Admiral Harwood's priceless fleet?

Captain G. Grantham, R.N., commanding officer of *H.M.S. Cleopatra,* met me at the gangway and escorted me to his cabin, where very generously he offered his condolences. He knew apparently how I must feel over what had occurred at my Base during my unexpectedly prolonged absence.

He had other news for me. His ship, in spite of about a four-foot drop in the dock, had apparently suffered slight damage—his Engineer Officer and his First Lieutenant had reported that at most there was only one minor leak in her bottom that would cause no trouble. Redocking, which was impossible anyway with my dock out of commission, would not be necessary.

As for the appearance of his bottom, that he couldn't tell me, since the diver hadn't reported yet. Regarding other matters, fortunately no one had been injured; when she went down, no one, native or otherwise, happened to be under her or he would have been crushed to death.

Very shortly, Al Watson, who had been examining the *Cleopatra* for some hours, came up to report. There were only four minor dents in the bottom plating; nothing was ruptured anywhere; the leak reported was through a sprung rivet in one of the dents—it was of no great consequence.

I breathed a sigh of relief. The *Cleopatra,* at least, had suffered insignificant harm. Her stern repairs had been completed, most of the painting finished, she could sail back for the Mediterranean in good fighting trim. To Captain Grantham and to me, that, of course, was the major matter. We shook hands and he prepared to sail. He would be all right.

I re-embarked in my boat for the long run back into the naval harbor. The *Cleopatra* was all right, but how about my dry dock, the only one I yet had working in Massawa? Already two ships were waiting for the dock; at least three more were on the way.

On the trip, carrying Commander Davy and Lloyd Williams, both of whom I had picked up on the *Cleopatra,* I learned a little more of what had happened and why.

Williams told me he had finished the repair job early the evening before, according to schedule. It was time to flood down, shift the cruiser aft, and lift her bow out of water as we had done on her two sisters, so her bow might be cleaned and painted. In my absence, Spanner had undertaken to do that and apparently had succeeded. He had lowered away the stern, floated the cruiser, shifted her well aft till her stern overhung the dock, then lifted the bow out of water while the stern floated, so the Eritreans could scrape and paint her bow, which they had started to do. They had finished beneath her and were working on her sides. She had been that way an hour, perhaps longer, when calamity struck.

The steel hawsers had not been secured taut to the dry dock to hold the *Cleopatra* tightly in position against sliding aft as she lay sloping aft on the dock. At about 11:00 P.M., she suddenly went aft down the slope, capsizing all the keel blocks and crushing them into matchsticks as her heavy hull came down on top of the mass of toppled blocks. Fortunately, in crushing the blocks as she seesawed aft, she had made a soft cushion for herself on the dry dock floor which had taken the shock and saved her. But what she had done to the dry dock was terrific—there wasn't a wooden keel block in the dock left to support anything; they were all just rubbish now. The dock was out of commission; that, of course, was why the next supply ship waiting to go on when the *Cleopatra* undocked, had not been lifted.

Grateful that the *Cleopatra* had only been dented slightly and that no one had been hurt, I began to feel somewhat better, even towards Spanner who had been in charge of the shifting. After all, the keel blocks in that Persian dock had had a tough life since May 8, when we had docked our first ship, the *Koritza,* on them. Some sixty-five or more ships had passed over those blocks in that short time. Perhaps from constant heavy loading, the blocks had finally come to the point where they might have collapsed under the *Cleopatra* even though Spanner *had* hauled taut those hawsers. However, I was skeptical of that; the keel blocks had looked in fair shape to me when we were preparing the dock for the *Cleopatra*. Still I was willing to give Spanner the benefit of the doubt.

Then Commander Davy's next remark sent all my altruistic feelings towards Spanner whistling down the wind.

"When we get ashore, Captain," he said, "I'll take up with Alex the return there without docking of the supply ships already here, and the cancellation of all future sailings for docking here for the next six weeks."

"Six weeks?" I asked, puzzled. "Why six weeks? That dock'll never be out of commission that long. Where'd you get that?"

"Why, from Mr. Spanner, Captain. He went to Captain Lucas at the Royal Naval Base this morning and asked him to send a signal to Alex reporting that the Massawa dry dock would be out of commission for from four to six weeks and to cancel all dockings. Captain Lucas took his word for it as dockmaster, since you weren't here, and sent the signal. It's gone already. And Spanner says it'll take longer than that unless Alexandria sends us immediately the new heavy timbers to saw up into keel blocks. There's no timber here."

Six weeks to replace a set of crushed keel blocks, while that invaluable Massawa dry dock lay idle all that time! Was Spanner crazy? And to think that he should have dared to send such a calamitous signal in my absence! Had he been present in my boat at that moment, I could have wrung his birdlike neck for that! I had suffered enough already from Spanner and his timid flutterings. Now this! What would they think of me in Alexandria!

Savagely I faced Commander Davy in the cockpit of the boat, though he was in no way to blame.

"Commander, I'm getting off on the Persian dock, but you take the boat ashore. Send out instantly a signal to Alex, canceling that signal from Spanner. Then send another to the C.-in-C. signed by me as Commanding Officer of this Base. Tell him that on the fourth day from now, that's the morning of September 28, the Massawa dry dock will dock its next ship. We'll be out of commission four days only, including today. We're returning no ships undocked. He's only to delay those that haven't started yet, by four days. Do you get that, Davy? And find out if the C.-in-C. can send me another dockmaster instead of Spanner! It makes me ill to think of having to keep him any longer!"

"Aye, aye, sir," acknowledged Davy. "I'll start on it immediately I'm ashore. But, Captain," he asked, frankly puzzled, "where are you going to get all the new keel blocks? There isn't a stick of heavy timber in Massawa to cut them from. Spanner's right about that."

"Spanner's a plain damned fool!" I exploded. "He's supposed to be a shipwright as well as a dockmaster, so if he weren't blind, he'd see. They're right under his nose. Look!"

We were passing the salvaged Italian dry dock, floating only a couple of hundred yards from the Persian dock which was disabled for want of keel blocks. Stacked in neat layers out of the way on the floor of that Italian dry dock were hundreds of already cut keel blocks which the bomb explosions had tossed all over its floor. I knew those keel blocks well; I had stumbled over them as they lay scattered on the floor of that dock on the bottom of the sea when I had made my very first dive in Massawa to start off the salvage work. We couldn't use those keel blocks again on the Italian dry dock till all the holes in her were repaired, which meant till I got steel I didn't have. Long before I got that steel, I was sure I could get timber for new keel blocks for *that* dock.

"All we have to do is to clean up the wreckage of the smashed blocks on the Persian dock, transfer those Italian dock keel blocks a few hundred yards over the water, and set them up in place of the crushed blocks. There're twice as many blocks available as we need; that Italian dock's much longer than the Persian one. Davy, if Spanner had only been what he's supposed to be in his trade, a shipwright, instead of being an empty-headed fool, he'd never have sent that signal this morning! He's been passing right by those huge stacks of idle keel blocks twice a day in a boat now for weeks, and he's got the nerve to tell the C.-in-C. there're no keel blocks in Massawa! And that for want of them, the only working dock within thousands and thousands of miles of Alex is out of commission for six weeks, maybe more unless they give us keel blocks. With technical assistants like that, no wonder commanding officers break down in the tropics! I could shed tears myself!"

Glen Galvin was maneuvering the boat in against the stern of the Persian dry dock for our landing. The naked Eritrean on the bow reached out with his boathook and hooked the dock. A brief glance down what had once been the four-foot-high row of keel blocks showed me all I wanted to know. Those blocks were lying now, a pathetic mass of crushed pulp perhaps a foot high, all along the length of the dock floor.

As soon as we were close in, I leaped onto the dock floor, motioning Lloyd Williams to follow me. Commander Davy stayed in the boat, which immediately shoved clear to go ashore.

Mr. Spanner was on the stern of the dry dock floor to meet me. At once, in his chirpy manner, he began to explain what had happened, why it had happened.

"Get the hell out of my sight, Spanner, and keep out of it for the next four days! I'm not blaming you for anything except that idiotic signal you sent the C.-in-C. this morning. There's no excuse for that, and it cooks your goose with me. This dock's going to dock its next ship four mornings from now, and I don't want you balling things up by getting in the road. Lloyd Williams is taking charge of this dock for the next four days, and if you get in his way, it'll be just too bad for you. Lloyd hasn't got the patience that I've got. Now get

[388]

out of here!" Spanner looked at me, then like a startled sparrow, he fluttered away.

"Now, Lloyd," I said to Williams as soon as Spanner had departed, "I mean just what I said. You're in charge of this dock for the next four days. Hudson, the engineer, will help you with that overhead crane in laying the new keel blocks, and Hudson's a man—he'll help you. If anybody else on this dock attempts to interfere with what you want, don't argue, smack him one. Now this is what I want. Start all the Eritreans on this dock and every man you've got on the Italian dock cleaning up here and moving blocks over from the salvaged dry dock. I'll get you all the carpenters I can steal from the contractor ashore out here to help. Take everybody you can lay your hands on— it's a hell of a big job. This is Thursday afternoon. On Monday morning we flood down to dock the next ship. Now don't stop for anything; your gang will have to work night and day. Do it your own way, Lloyd; I won't try to tell you how, only do it. If you want any help from me, sing out; otherwise it's all up to you."

"Aye, aye, Captain; just leave it to me," Williams assured me in his usual solemn tone. "If you say it's got to be done in four days, it'll be done."

The next few days and nights were a veritable tornado of activity between the salvaged Eytie dry dock and the Persian dry dock, with Lloyd Williams the center of a frenzied conglomeration of Eritreans, Hindoos, Maltese, Americans, Eyties, South Africans, Englishmen, Sudanese, and Persians.

It was done. On Monday morning, September 28, with Lloyd Williams wan and haggard but triumphant, the dry dock was flooded down and the next ship landed on a completely new set of keel blocks.

The Massawa dry dock was going again.

That same day, with H.M.S. Cleopatra, the third and last of his three damaged cruisers back on her Mediterranean war station and his whole fleet of four light cruisers now for the first time in several months again all fit for action against the enemy, Admiral Harwood sent the following message to General Maxwell:

Office of the Commander-in-Chief
Mediterranean Station
28 September, 1942

For GENERAL MAXWELL from C.-in-C. Med.

Very many thanks for splendid work done recently at Massawa. Quick dockings of over 50 merchant ships, raising of Italian docks, and emergency dockings of three cruisers are great achievements, and I know largely due to ELLSBERG's own great energy. Damage caused in last docking was a risk we accepted and I am glad it was not more serious. Please congratulate ELLSBERG and all his staff.

With great gusto I posted that message at the Naval Base and sent another copy to Asmara, so all who had struggled to make it possible might know their efforts were appreciated by the top command, and those others who had been just as busily engaged in heaving monkey wrenches might make of it what they pleased.

THE PRESENCE IN MASSAWA OF THE British mechanics, sent down with the *Dido* for work on the light cruisers, gave me an opportunity. They were all to go back to the Middle East upon the completion of the third cruiser, the *Cleopatra*, but, in between jobs on those warships, I had them available for other work around the Naval Base.

Consequently, after the completion of the *Dido* on August 25, I shifted the lot of them over to repair work on the Italian dry dock till the *Euryalus* arrived, and seized the chance thus afforded to take two out of three of Captain Reed's crew of divers, plus the remnant of the salvage mechanics who originally had worked with them, off repair work on that dry dock and start them again on salvage. The third diver, Ervin Johnson, was left on the dry dock to tend to what underwater repair work was necessary as that dry dock rehabilitation job proceeded.

So now I had two divers, Al Watson and Doc Kimble, and five salvage mechanics available under Captain Reed for another salvage job. I started them on August 31 on the salvage of the smaller Italian dry dock which lay in the naval harbor completely submerged about a hundred yards to port of its salvaged sister, where the Italians had scuttled it.

Reed made a swift diving survey of his new task. We found the smaller dock had been built in six sections, of which five had been blasted open by bombs. Here again, however, one bomb had misfired, only this time it was the second compartment from aft which was still intact.

Except for this difference, which was not important, the salvage problem was identical with that of the first dry dock, and Reed tackled it in the same way. There was, however, one other variation which forced more mechanical work. The upper decks of the side walls of this small dock were some nine feet under water, so we had nothing to stand on while we worked, and Reed had no salvage ship to work from. To overcome this, two wood scaffoldings, about eleven feet high and each over a hundred yards long, were built by Reed's carpenters and set on the submerged decks of the two side walls, thus giving the men a walkway about two feet above water.

For air compressors, I was somewhat better off than before. As a main source of air supply for the job, I had a huge Sutorbilt low pressure air compressor, capable of delivering 1200 cubic feet of air a minute, by itself more than one and a half times the total capacity of all four compressors on our first task. This machine was so big, it took two 200 horsepower Waukesha engines to drive it, and the whole assembly—driving engines, starting engine, belt drives, and compressor —took up about as much space as a small-sized room and stood about as high. As a matter of fact, the massive crate that this machine came in on the *Chamberlin* might well have served as a one-room cabin. This air compressor we mounted on a barge secured about amidships and outboard of the starboard side wall of the sunken dock, so that as the dock floated upward, it would just clear the barge.

It had been my intention to use two such compressors when I started salvage on the second dry dock. I had ordered two in New York, one of which came out on the *Chamberlin* and which I unloaded myself in the naval harbor in Massawa, and the other of which came out on an American freighter and was unloaded in the commercial harbor by our contractor. Our contractor insisted on handling himself everything that came into Massawa; insisted on sending everything arriving in Massawa up to Asmara first, ostensibly for checking, regardless of its use or destination; and insisted also on keeping me completely in the dark as to what had arrived by freighter till it suited his plans to inform me of it (if ever).

All this was one reason why I had the *Chamberlin*, which was my own salvage ship, brought to the naval harbor for unloading, even though the unloading facilities at my Base were vastly inferior to those in the commercial harbor. At least when something of my salvage equipment was unloaded at the Naval Base, I knew I had it, without either first searching all over Eritrea to discover it and then battling the contractor for possession of salvage equipment I had ordered for my salvage work.

At any rate, in the present instance, my intelligence service informed me that the second Sutorbilt air compressor had arrived in Massawa and had been unloaded there. With this information, obtained *sub rosa,* I requested the contractor's office in Asmara to deliver the compressor to me at once as I needed it badly for salvage work. What happened then would have been unbelievable outside an insane asylum.

After some checking, the contractor informed me the air compressor had been received some time before, as stated (although he had never informed me of that), but that it had been shipped from Massawa to Asmara first for inventorying there as per his usual custom. As soon as that was completed, it would be shipped back to me. I made no comment. How any supposedly sane person could undertake to ship an air compressor assembly literally as big as a house over that tortuous mountain railroad 7500 feet up to the summit plateau, just to check the markings on its crate, and then ship it back where it started from for use, about a hundred and fifty mile journey, was beyond me. That was certainly American efficiency at its best in conserving Eritrea's scant resources in labor in prosecuting the war. And yet some Americans were criticizing the British for inefficiency!

A few days went by. I had started my salvage job and I needed that second Sutorbilt compressor, so once again I inquired by telephone as to when my salvage compressor would be sufficiently inventoried up in the mountains to be returned to me for use down on the seacoast. In some embarrassment, the contractor informed me they were still trying to locate the compressor in Asmara but hadn't found it there yet. All their shipping papers showed its receipt in Massawa, its dispatch by rail to Asmara, but they couldn't find any record of its receipt in Asmara, and they couldn't find any air compressor there either. They were still searching their Asmara warehouses.

Whatever happened to my mammoth air compressor assembly, I never found out. The ship's papers showed its delivery in Massawa; the contractor's check sheets showed its receipts there and its dispatch to Asmara, and after that it vanished from the sight of men (particularly from mine) forever. The contractor could never find it and couldn't offer any explanations except that probably it had been stolen by the Eyties off the train on its way to Asmara (to which, in any sane establishment, it would never have been sent).

When I manifested incredulity over that, maintaining that even the rapacious Eyties would have been as badly stumped in stealing that ponderous compressor assembly as they might have been in attempting to get away with the Washington Monument, I was informed by the contractor's Massawa warehouse manager that a whole train of freight cars bound for Asmara not long before had vanished completely—cars, freight, and all—and had not since been found. Whether I was supposed to believe that or not, I couldn't tell. By now, however, I was getting to the point where I could swallow anything, however fantastic, relating to goings-on in Eritrea.

Nevertheless, my invaluable compressor was gone and I could never find a trace of it. Doubtless I made of myself a considerable nuisance to the contractor, insisting that since his scheme of keeping me in the dark while he thus handled my salvage equipment had culminated in this unbelievable disappearance, he must find it for me. But the contractor was too busy all over the Middle East with vast projects on a vast scale to be overly concerned with a minor matter like the strange evaporation while in his hands of the biggest piece of machinery in all Eritrea. He never found it for me. And except perhaps to make a note that there was a disturbing influence in Massawa to be gotten rid of at the first convenient opportunity, he seemed wholly unconcerned.

So with only one big Sutorbilt air compressor to carry the main load, and one very much smaller Ingersoll-Rand air compressor available to act as a stand-by when the big machine had to be shut down for servicing, we started our salvage job.

By now, Al Watson and Doc Kimble, the two divers, knew their Italian dry docks; so also did all the mechanics, particularly one fine new carpenter, a mountain of a man named Bill Oyea, who had come to us since the lifting of the first dock. He was even bigger than Buck Schott, whose place as carpenter he was taking, Buck himself having been promoted to foreman under Lloyd Williams for general repair work on already salvaged wrecks.

Captain Reed and his little crew of seven Americans all told, aided by a moderate number of Eyties and Eritreans, turned to enthusiastically to duplicate their initial exploit. They did, too. Starting on August 31, with only half as many divers and mechanics available to him as the first time and more work to do, since here the decks were totally submerged, by September 10 Reed had everything rigged and sealed up, ready to start the compressors.

[394]

On September 10, we started pumping compressed air from the big Sutorbilt compressor to starboard and the small Ingersoll-Rand to port. Immediately air leaks showed up, air bubbling upward through the sea all over the dock structure where the steelwork was improperly caulked by the Italian builders. This time we could caulk leaks only by diving, so Al Watson and Doc Kimble had a busy time under water for some days with caulking tools, making good enough of the leaks so the dock would hold air, particularly on the starboard side wall, which I intended to lift first. Doc used a regular diving rig; but Al, who was a marvelous swimmer, did practically all of his diving in a face mask only, which, in that shallow water, was less of an encumbrance to movement.

On Sunday, September 13, the starboard side of the dry dock floated up, exposing all the deck hatches. I brought aboard the barnacled deck some small 3-inch gasoline-driven pumps, with which we then swiftly pumped free of water all the storage and machinery compartments in the upper part of that side wall, thus floating it up further till about three feet of the starboard side wall was completely out of water.

All the deck hatches in the starboard side wall deck leading downward to these upper compartments we found worthless for watertightness, as their gaskets were all rotted away from long submergence. As we were unable to close these hatches therefore to retain compressed air, and the next deck down was leaking air so badly the compressors were unable to gain further on the water in the lower holds, it became necessary to get into these freshly pumped-out upper compartments and work inside them to plug leaks in the steelwork below.

For that purpose, I brought over from the big Italian dock a small gang of ironworkers composed of Armstrong, riveter; Larsen, welder; and Jones, shipfitter. Armstrong and Larsen were Americans; Jones was a very tall, very thin Englishman, one of the mechanics just through with the cruiser *Euryalus* repair job on the Persian dock near by.

With hand tools, this small crew started forward inside the newly exposed and pumped-out upper compartments of the starboard side wall, plugging all the air leaks they could find, and gradually worked their way aft.

Meanwhile, the air compressors, which had been running night and day in much hotter weather even than we had had in mid-May when we raised the first dock, were having troubles. This was particularly true of the big low-pressure Sutorbilt compressor, which, never designed for service under any such conditions, was running with its compressor main bearings smoking hot all the time, literally so hot it would have been simple to have broiled steaks on them. We used the best hard grease available for lubricating those bearings, but it always melted swiftly and ran out like water, to fry odoriferously on the hot metal, giving to all the surrounding atmosphere a smell of cooking going on on a major scale. That odor of frying grease, mingled with the smell of rotting mussels on the now exposed starboard wall of the dry dock, gave an unforgettable aroma to the whole salvage operation.

But as well as we could we kept both our compressors going and kept the air going down. I was holding the water level steady in the afloat starboard side and sending most of the compressed air through the cross connecting mains to the port side, hoping soon to get buoyancy enough on that side to float it also off the bottom.

In this situation, the dry dock was on a considerable slant to port, with its port side still resting in the mud on the bottom of the harbor and nine feet of water over its port side deck, while the starboard side was afloat, about three to four feet out of water along its whole length from bow to stern.

What I was working for was to get an even amount of buoyancy all along the port side so it would finally float up evenly, bow and stern together, with no trim. Of course this could not be assured for there was no way of telling whether the side still in the mud was more firmly stuck to the bottom at one end than at the other; also the only set of air pressure gauges we had or could get was none too reliable in showing how far down the water had gone inside any port side compartment.

All Sunday and Sunday night, and on into Monday, we kept on plugging leaks and pumping air. My three ironworkers finally arrived by the middle of Monday afternoon at the after compartment in the afloat starboard side in their quest for leaks, and there they found a very bad one. They sent Jones, the English shipfitter, for me to look it over.

I followed Jones, who very much resembled a bean-pole in build, aft along the barnacle-encrusted deck to that stern compartment. While all the other hatches in the deck were on low horizontal coamings, the hatch to this after compartment was different. It was a booby hatch; that is, it was a vertical steel structure rising above the deck to the height of a man nearly, with a rather small vertical steel door opening on its forward side to give access to a steep ladder going below from just inside that door.

Jones had to duck his lanky figure considerably to get through the opened door; then he descended the steep steel ladder inside. Even I had to duck a bit to avoid bumping my head on the steel door frame above; then I followed him down the ladder to find myself in an elongated watertight compartment, steaming hot inside, with no openings for ventilation except that booby hatch at the forward end by which I had entered.

Lighted only by my flashlight, I followed Jones through the water-logged rubbish of what perhaps had once been used as an Eytie storeroom, some forty feet aft to the very after end of that compartment. There was Larsen alongside Horace Armstrong, who in the cramped space overhead was futilely trying to get a decent swing with a hammer on his caulking chisel.

Armstrong paused to indicate to me the trouble. A strong stream of compressed air from the still-submerged dry dock section below was whistling out past an atrociously driven rivet in the top bounding bar of the after bulkhead. It wasn't just a little air leak; it was a big one. The rivet, very loose, came nowhere near filling its hole; evidently the Eytie riveters, in originally driving that rivet, had had difficulty getting at it and had left the job badly botched.

Armstrong, Jones, Larsen, and I held a conference on that rivet. It was finally agreed to accept Armstrong's solution—give him time and he felt sure he could get that rivet point sufficiently caulked to stop the leak. It would be a slow job since he could hardly find space overhead amidst the cramped steel bracing for a fair swing with a hammer, but he felt he could do it. So, leaving Larsen and Jones to hold the light for him and spell him on the caulking, I left them fairly cooking in the hot vapor surrounding them and, with difficulty, threaded my way forward through the inside wreckage to the ladder, climbed up it, and squeezed out the booby hatch door to the deck.

When I first went down that booby hatch, dressed only in a khaki shirt, khaki shorts, and some old shoes, I had already been thoroughly soaked with sweat; when I came out, however, I was positively dripping. I felt sorry for the men below.

It was several hours after lunch and everybody was hard at work. As I went slowly forward along the starboard scaffolding reading the pressure gauges, I noted that the Eritreans were as busy as usual, scraping away from floats alongside at the barnacled side wall of the dock. Back aft was the thirty foot boat which we had fitted up with a small compressor for diving. Doc Kimble, fully encased in his diving rig, was descending the ladder over the stern of the boat to caulk some underwater leak, while Al Watson, in bathing trunks only, and Lew Whitaker were acting as his tenders.

Bill Reed, salvage master, was in the boat with them to receive whatever reports Doc had to make over the diving telephone from below. On deck the dock itself below me, Lloyd Williams was working with various mechanics engaged in trying to make watertight and airtight the ruined gaskets on the deck hatches and on some other hatches which needed bracing to hold the air pressure below them.

When I finally came amidships, Jim Buzbee, pump mechanic, who was standing watch on the air compressors, called to me to come down off the scaffolding and take a look at our big twin-engined air compressor; it looked to him as if we were in for serious trouble soon.

I clambered down off the scaffolding; went by the air valve manifold, an intricate array of valves by which the flow of compressed air was directed from our Sutorbilt compressor to various parts of the submerged dry dock; and then crawled down the vertical ladder on the outboard side of the dry dock to the barge on which the throbbing Sutorbilt compressor stood.

It was certainly a huge array of machinery. The two massive Waukesha engines, side by side, which furnished the power, were far too big ever to dream of starting by hand cranking. Instead, in between them stood a small gasoline engine whose sole purpose was to start the big ones. After they were both unclutched from the compressor, the little gasoline engine was started by hand cranking, then clutched in to the big engines one at a time to start them; then, when both the big engines were running, they were clutched in on the compressor to carry the heavy compressor load. It was quite a slow and complicated arrangement, but workable; by hand alone, no one could ever get the rig going.

However, it wasn't the engines that were bothering Buzbee; they were doing all right in spite of the heat. It was the compressor itself.

Specifically, he called my attention to the main bearings at each end of the compressor casing—they were smoking as never before.

"Cap'n," complained Buzbee, "I was just about to go looking for you. If we don't shut this machine down quick, she'll shut herself down. I've never seen those bearings so hot before. I've been shooting grease steadily into 'em, but it's no use. She's running hotter'n blazes, and why that bearing metal hasn't wiped out already, I don't know. Better let me shut her down right now so she can cool off, or we won't have any compressor left!"

I looked at the bearing housings. The iron had a peculiar gray tinge I hadn't seen before. Buzbee was certainly right; they were far too hot to continue operation. It wasn't any use to try feeling the bearings to test whether they were too hot or not; I should only get a seared hand from that. I would have to go by sight alone and by the odor of that sizzling grease as it ran from the bearings, smoking as if it were on the point of spontaneous combustion.

"O.K., Jim, you're right. Shut her down. Only give me a few minutes to get up at that air valve manifold to close off the valves to this machine when you stop her, or the compressed air from inside the dock'll blow back through this compressor and run it in reverse."

I climbed hurriedly up to the valve manifold above and stood by to shut off both the four-inch valves there. As soon as I was set, I waved to Buzbee below me, who promptly unclutched the compressor and shut down both engines while I hurriedly, with both hands, screwed shut the air valves to prevent blowing back and losing the valuable compressed air we already had pumped into the dry dock.

Immediately, a strange silence fell over the dock, now the roar of those two huge engines was stilled, broken only by the comparatively trifling exhaust from the smaller Ingersoll-Rand compressor still running across the water in its barge outboard of the submerged port side of the dock.

I sighed regretfully. We had lost about 80 per cent of our air supply; it was doubtful if the Ingersoll-Rand by itself could even make good the leakage from all over the dock. I could now expect the afloat starboard side of the dry dock to start to sink slowly as the air leaked out from below. To minimize that, I set the air valves to throw all the air from our remaining compressor over to starboard to make good leakage there and hold the starboard side up as well as possible till the Sutorbilt compressor had cooled enough to hold grease in its bearings and make it safe to start it up again.

Hardly had I finished setting valves, when I felt a tremor in the dock beneath my feet. Startled, I looked up, to see that the wood scaffolding atop the submerged port side wall of the dry dock had lifted higher above the water!

The sunken port side of the dry dock was coming up, and at no slow speed either! Swiftly my eye ran along the hundred yard length of that scaffolding to port of me, to note to my dismay that it wasn't coming up evenly fore and aft; that whatever the reasons, it had already risen farther at the stern than at the bow, and that that already bad situation was getting worse as she rose.

I gazed in agony. At this moment of all moments when I had just lost my big air compressor and with it all chance of controlling the movements of that dock, the port side with no air at all going into it any longer, had broken free of the mud at last and was on its way up, stern first instead of evenly, throwing the whole dry dock out of balance and heading for possible catastrophe!

By now the port side had risen three or four feet, easily visible to everyone anywhere on or near the dock. All around I heard men begin to cheer at the sight, but to me it was nothing to cheer over. In anguish, I sang out to Buzbee below me to starboard, just beginning to inspect the dead compressor.

"For God's sake, Jim, start that compressor up again! Never mind if we ruin it now! START IT UP!"

Buzbee, masked by the starboard outboard side of dry dock near him from any view of what was going on to port, couldn't understand my sudden reversal of his orders, but like the faithful helper I had always found him, asked no questions and dashed for the little starting engine to crank that up first and get things going, while I stood by the compressor air manifold valves to twirl them open the moment the big compressor started to roll over, and shoot all the compressed air I could get forward into the starboard bow of the dry dock to hold that up. We were going to need it there.

For already I could see that the starboard bow of the dry dock was trimming lower into the water as the port side rose, high by the stern. A few seconds more and the stern on the port side broke above the surface while the starboard bow directly ahead of me, previously three feet or more out of water, slowly sank lower and I could see the ocean gradually rising toward the deck.

[400]

Below me to starboard, Buzbee was frantically working to start up the compressor engines, but it was an involved and a slow job. I looked to port. The whole deck of the port side wall was now above water, still stern high, with the entire skeleton of that eleven foot high scaffolding standing on it completely exposed.

But now I could see also that on the depressed starboard bow the ocean was already lapping aft along the deck and water was starting to pour down the forward hatches into the bow compartments of the dry dock. For me, that spelled the end. Even if I got air now from the compressor, it was too late. Nothing could save the entire dock, now all afloat, from swiftly sinking again as those bow compartments flooded and the water ran swiftly aft to flood other compartments in succession.

There was no longer any hope of keeping the dock afloat. All I could do was to see no one was trapped inside when it went down. I left my useless station at the air manifold to run aft along the scaffolding shouting for all hands below to get up on deck. Whether Jim Buzbee ever got that air compressor started then, I don't know yet. It made no difference any more.

Long before I got near the stern along that stretch of starboard side scaffolding, the whole dry dock had submerged again, both sides. Nothing of it was visible any more except a foot or two of the tops of the scaffoldings which a moment or two before had all been completely above water. All about, swimming in the turbulent sea, were the men who had been working before on deck the starboard side, and, I fervently hoped, those who had been working below decks. The broken water all about, badly disturbed by the sudden rising and the even more sudden sinking of the dry dock, was a mass of foam in which heads were bobbing about, striking out for the scaffoldings or the boats for support.

I had only one worry—had everybody got clear from below? Hurriedly I looked about me, but with mainly only unrecognizable heads dotting the foaming sea, there wasn't any way of taking an immediate muster.

But one thing I knew—whether anyone else had been below when the trouble started, Armstrong, Larsen, and Jones certainly had been. They had all been far aft inside the very compartment at the stern now submerged beneath my feet, into which I could see a flood of water must be pouring through the invisible booby hatch leading down to it, marked at that instant by a swirling vortex of water going down and of air bubbling up. Had those three men got out before the dock submerged aft, the last part of it to vanish?

In agony I looked about. I saw nothing of any of them on the scaffolding, in the few boats or floats near by. They might indeed be among the swimmers I couldn't recognize; that I couldn't tell.

My eyes fell on Lloyd Williams on the scaffolding near me. He had been on deck of the dock near that booby hatch when the dock started to submerge. He might have seen whether those men had escaped or not.

"Lloyd!" I shouted. "Where's Armstrong and his mates? Did they get clear?"

"Don't know, Captain. I didn't see 'em get out. All I think I saw was a hand waving out that booby hatch when she went down, but I can't swear to it!"

So probably they hadn't escaped; they were trapped below by the inrushing water. If we would save them, we must act swiftly. Close by me at the stern now was my diving boat. In it, still fully dressed in a diving rig except for his diving helmet and his partly unbolted breastplate, sat Doc Kimble, apparently up from his last dive and being undressed when catastrophe struck. Near him in the boat were Captain Reed, with Al Watson and Lew Whitaker who had been undressing Kimble.

"Bill!" I shouted to Reed. "Clap Doc's helmet back on him again and get him overboard! There're three men trapped in the stern here!"

"No use, Cap'n," shouted back Reed. "It'll take five minutes to get Doc dressed again. They'll all be drowned by then!"

Reed was right. That couldn't be done swiftly enough to matter. But alongside Kimble was Watson, a fine swimmer and an expert diver in a face mask, which would take him only a moment to slip on and go overboard.

"Al!" I shrieked. "Get on your face mask and get overboard to help those men!"

Watson took a look at that veritable maelstrom of water and air over the booby hatch, then answered briefly,

"Can't be done, Cap'n. Anybody going in there now'll only be sucked through and killed himself!"

My heart turned to lead. There was no absolute certainty that those three men were trapped below, but they probably were. And if they were and we waited either for Doc to get dressed or the water to calm enough for an expert swimmer like Al to dare that whirlpool in a face mask, it would be too late. I wasn't much of a swimmer myself, but those were my men trapped inside that submerged dry dock and I was responsible for them. They couldn't be allowed to die without at least an effort, poor as it might be, being made to save them. I plunged overboard from the scaffolding into the boiling vortex marking the booby hatch.

It was nine feet down through the water to that booby hatch and the instant I submerged, I could no longer see anything—just a mass of swirling water, milky with air bubbles, impossible to see through even an inch. Fortunately, my plunge took me straight down where I wanted to go; possibly the inward rush of water helped suck me to the right spot.

At any rate, completely blinded, I still by feel spotted myself in front of the booby hatch, over toward the latch side. I turned right side up, felt the door was open a bit, not much, and grabbed its edge with one hand to hold myself down while I felt round the steel door with the other. My fumbling fingers came across something soft, an arm, jammed between the door and its frame. There was somebody still down there! One man at least!

I tried to swing the steel door open but still there was some pressure of water pouring through to hold it closed. Frenziedly I braced both my legs somehow against the unseen barnacle-encrusted booby hatch, clinging to that arm with one hand lest I lose it in the rush of water when the door opened, while with the other I heaved with all the strength I had against that steel door. It swung back.

With both hands then, I got a good grip on the shoulder of the arm I had and dragged a completely limp body out of the hatch, though still I could see nothing of it. Gripping that body tightly now, with one arm and both legs, I pawed my way up through the sea to the surface.

Immediately I came up, gasping for air, a dozen arms reached down to grip me and my burden. I was alongside a boat which apparently had got there while I was below. Willy-nilly, I was dragged up into that boat, still clinging to whoever I had in my arms. In the process, the whole right half of my khaki shirt was torn from my back by someone heaving on me. The next moment, I was inside the boat, half strangled, gasping for breath and looking down at Horace Armstrong unconscious at my feet.

If Armstrong had been caught below, the two others with him probably still were there.

"Give 'im first aid, quick!" I mumbled, and then went overboard again.

Once more I brought up alongside the booby hatch, to grip it with both legs while I felt about in the milky swirl inside the now opened door. My hands came across another body, just as limp as Armstrong's, jammed in the upper part of the booby hatch against its curving steel back. With a strong tug, I dragged it clear, and shoved off for the surface again with whoever it was clutched tightly against my breast.

I saw it was Lloyd Williams who dragged me into the boat this time, while others helped. I dropped my lifeless burden on the floor boards, looked at it. It was Larsen. A little aft in the boat several men were already working on Armstrong. Only Jones could be left now. I jumped overboard a third time to get him.

For the third time I went down. The water around that booby hatch door was quieter now but as impenetrable to sight as ever. I felt through the door. My clawing fingers touched nothing. I jammed a whole arm and part of my body inside, clinging somehow with my legs to the framework of the booby hatch to keep from going through into what must now be that wholly flooded compartment, and thank God, my fingers closed on another body in the upper part of that booby hatch, apparently as lifeless as both the others. This must be Jones; there were only three men there.

With considerably more trouble than before, I managed to drag Jones' limp figure out through the little door into the clear and start up with him through the sea.

For the third and last time my head popped through the surface, there finally to be dragged into the boat to stay. Exhausted, I sank down on a thwart, while others began first aid on Jones, when to their surprise he opened his eyes languidly and looked around. The other two, who had been brought up first, were completely out, perhaps dead, but Jones, who had been down longer than either, was semiconscious! The only way I could ever explain that was that being so very tall, his nose may have come into a little pocket of air in the top of that booby hatch above the door frame, allowing him to get at least a few whiffs of air while the others, completely engulfed in water, strangled.

But there was no time for speculation. Hurriedly all three men were put in separate boats where they could all conveniently be worked over at once, and first aid for drowning proceeded on all of them.

In a few minutes, Glen Galvin and my boat, which had raced ashore for the surgeon, was back with Lieutenant Salmeri (who had lately relieved Captain Plummer as our surgeon), together with several Army hospital corpsmen and their pulmotor equipment. Out in open boats over the now wholly sunken dry dock, they went to work.

Jones was speedily restored to full consciousness. Within an hour Larsen also had been brought to, was breathing regularly, and was out of danger. Only Horace Armstrong, the first man I had brought up, still was not revived, though Dr. Salmeri thought that he could detect a faint heartbeat in his stethoscope. They would keep on working on Armstrong.

With a heavy heart and my prayers following him, I watched Horace Armstrong, still limp, still steadily being worked on with a pulmotor, taken ashore in my boat (together with the now revived Larsen and Jones), there to have resuscitation methods continued in the sickbay.

For the first time, now that the three men were gone from out in the harbor, I took a look at myself. I was a mess. I had on only half a shirt, the left half; the right half of my shirt, together with the gold-striped shoulder mark that belonged there, was gone completely. But what surprised me was that the left leg of my khaki shorts was cut wide open, and my left leg inside from knee to groin was a mass of gashes, looking as if a razor had slashed deeply into it vertically at least a dozen times. And I hadn't even noticed it before! Apparently at some point below while I was gripping that booby hatch between my legs to hold myself, the barnacles encrusting it had gone to work on me.

Lew Whitaker had in his diving boat a bottle of some special antiseptic he had brought from Los Angeles, used by the fishermen around Catalina Island to avoid infection from cuts on fish. We had found it helpful in Massawa. A good part of the liquid in that bottle went on my leg into all those gashes; then Doc Kimble (who actually was an M.D. but preferred diving for a change) bandaged up the whole inside of my leg and I was ready to go to work again.

It was around 5 P.M. Still out on the scaffoldings or in boats near by were all my men (except the three Dr. Salmeri had taken ashore) gazing mournfully at what little of the scaffoldings still showed above water. So far as I could judge, nothing of our air main setup or of the scaffoldings supporting it had been injured during the wild gyrations of the dry dock in rising and sinking again.

My men were still all more or less in a state of shock over what had just occurred; when they got over it, what their reactions might be to continued work on that unfortunate dry dock would be difficult to estimate. But at the moment, all were too numbed to do much thinking, so before their wounds could stiffen, so to speak, and slow them up, I started all hands immediately on the re-raising of that dry dock.

The bearings on the Sutorbilt compressor had cooled somewhat; we packed them with fresh grease and started it up, sending all its air down to the sunken starboard side. That done, I busied all hands in getting out from shore and from the big Eytie dry dock another set of gasoline-driven 3-inch pumps to replace the ones now on the submerged dock beneath us, which would be waterlogged and useless even when they emerged once more from the sea.

At 10 P.M. that Monday night, lighted only by the stars and the glimmer of a few electric lights, the starboard side of the dry dock floated up again. All hands turned to with the new pumps to dry out for the second time all the upper compartments, including the after one where stood that now innocuous-looking barnacle-covered booby hatch in which our three shipmates had been trapped.

There was no cessation of work, even in the darkness. Once the starboard side upper compartments were pumped dry and that side again as high out of water as it originally had been before our accident, I swung most of the compressed air over to the port side.

We had one thing in our favor. Now at least it was night, and hot though it was, we were spared the radiant heat of the sun playing on our big compressors. If only I could get the port side up again while still I had that big Sutorbilt compressor running, I would be all right. Hour after hour, I kept pouring compressed air into the port side, praying for action before dawn, while yet we had the night to favor us.

At 3:30 A.M. the port side showed signs of movement, then began to float up as before somewhat by the stern. Instantly, with Bill Reed

[406]

helping me twirl valves, we shut off air from the port side, shot everything we had in the way of compressed air from both compressors forward into the bow compartment on the starboard side to hold it up in spite of the tendency of the rising stern to trim it down into the sea again.

It worked. This time the bow never went under as the port side broke surface and then after bobbing about in a mass of broken water settled down with the whole dry dock on a fairly even keel.

Savagely, in the darkness the salvage crew shifted our 3-inch pumps across the water over to the port side, hurriedly to pump out the now exposed upper compartments there and ensure enough buoyancy to avoid that side's sinking again. Meanwhile, to help the same end, I redistributed the flow of compressed air all over the dry dock to hold it as level as possible.

When dawn came not long afterwards and the flaming sun went to work on us again, we had won. Both sides of the dry dock were high out of water, all danger past, and rising rapidly from all the compressed air now being poured in. The salvage task was over. In sixteen days, by September 15, with somewhat less than half the men used to raise the large dry dock in nine days, Captain Reed and his little crew had salvaged its smaller sister, just as badly blasted by bombs.

But the dawn brought us no feeling of triumph as we gazed on our handiwork. For Horace Armstrong was dead. At midnight my boat had brought out to us the sad news. At 11 P.M., after seven hours of continuous first aid in resuscitation, at first by hand in the boat, later by pulmotor ashore, whatever faint signs of life Armstrong had manifested had vanished completely, and Dr. Salmeri sadly had to admit there was no longer any hope of revival. Our shipmate was gone. As I remembered Horace Armstrong, swinging a huge sledge hammer under the stern of *H.M.S. Dido,* together with his comrade Bill Cunningham, showing the Middle East what an American could do when it was necessary, I wept when I heard that he was dead.

CHAPTER

47

On SEPTEMBER 3, JUST AFTER WE
had started salvage on the smaller Italian dry dock, my second salvage
tug, the *Resolute,* finally arrived in Massawa, some three months out
from Port Arthur over that same 13,000 miles of open sea that her
sister, the *Intent,* before her had successfully traversed.

I gazed on the *Resolute* with mixed feelings. Her skipper, Captain
Byglin, while a good seaman, knew nothing of salvage, and was of no
help to me that way. Acting as her first mate was Captain Frank Roys,
hastily flown to Trinidad to join her there for the rest of the voyage,
and to serve as her Salvage Master on arrival. Roys was a good salvage
man; I knew him and had tried myself to engage him before my departure from New York, but he was then not free to go. Now he
had arrived with the *Resolute* but the *Resolute* had brought not a
single diver with her! What good to me was another salvage ship and
even another salvage master, when they had no divers with them to
work on salvage?

My predicament regarding divers was distressing. I had fewer available to me than in early June. The *Chamberlin,* having lost her best
diver, Wood, was in a bad way for divers herself. After several weeks
spent unloading her holds, she was ready to go to work, but being
highly unmaneuverable, she could not safely be moored alongside any
wreck. So I had selected for her to work on, the *XXIII Marzo,* one of
the wrecks to the right of the entrance to the naval harbor, a ship
which had her bottom badly blown out fore and aft and was a tough
wreck to raise. But she was one of the few where the cumbersome
Chamberlin could moor herself safely close enough to send boats over
to work from without fouling up any channels needed for harbor
entrance.

Captain Hansen of the *Chamberlin* had now only four divers for his task, not enough for the vast amount of underwater work required; of these four, while two were very willing workers, none were expert divers. Hansen was going to have a rough time with his wreck, I knew; he couldn't spare any divers for the *Resolute*.

By now, I had already lost four divers permanently, but I had received one other good diver, who had applied by mail to me for a job while I was in New York. However, before his letter reached me, I had sailed. So Mr. Flanagan, my dynamic assistant in New York, had hired him, and sent him out by ship alone. He had finally arrived a short time before and had turned to temporarily with Reed's crew, proving himself a fine diver. I had hoped to use him on the *Resolute*, which I had been informed was coming without divers.

But that scheme had shortly blown up in my face. He had come to me to quit; he could go home and make more money diving than he was getting in Massawa; or, better yet in his eyes, the contractor had agreed to give him a job as a construction foreman ashore at considerably more than his diving pay. Unless I could better either offer, he was through diving for me.

I refused. I couldn't pay him more than the other divers were getting. And as for letting him go, that I wouldn't either. He had asked for the job himself; he had signed a contract to dive in Massawa for nine months on the very terms he was getting; besides, I desperately needed him as a diver; he couldn't back out.

But he and the contractor between them quickly showed me that he could. Contract or no contract, he quit and walked off the job. Short of trying to put him in jail, I could do nothing about it. Then strangest of all, in spite of my violent protests, the contractor himself who was a party to the very contract my diver had so cavalierly disregarded, after a brief interval took him on as one of his supervisors at a considerable increase in pay. So the rest of my divers got a stiff jolt to their morale—while they dived under heartbreaking conditions, there was one of their former mates in a cushy job ashore at more money—truly an excellent situation to encourage them in risking their lives undersea.

At any rate, there I was with the salvage ship *Resolute* and no divers for her. All I could do was to break Ervin Johnson off diving work on the repairs to the large Italian dry dock whenever he could be spared there and lend him to the *Resolute* for her to work with Johnson on what could be done under such conditions on the wreck of the *Moncalieri,* scuttled ahead the *XXIII Marzo* on which the *Chamberlin* had started.

So from the beginning to near its end, the month of September drifted hectically along. The *Resolute* arrived on September 3 and started on the *Moncalieri* the same day the *Chamberlin* began operations on the *XXIII Marzo.* Over in the south harbor, all through the month the *Intent* was struggling with the *Frauenfels.* On September 5, we dry-docked the *Euryalus* for repairs; on September 9, we undocked her. On September 14, the wreck of the smaller Italian dry dock came up and sank again and Horace Armstrong was killed; on September 15, we finally raised that dry dock. (I might add here, that the day after Armstrong's death, I had learned that he had not drowned, which at least eased a bit my mental torture that if only I had been a little quicker, he might have been resuscitated like the two men I had brought up after him. Dr. Salmeri, after an autopsy, had discovered that Armstrong had died, not of drowning, but of ruptured lungs. Apparently, first man at the steel door of the booby hatch, as he was emerging, the rush of water pouring down had slammed the steel door to on him. The closing door had hit him a terrible blow across the chest, injuring his lungs so he died as a result. Then the swinging door had jammed closed on his arm, blocking the solitary exit to Larsen and Jones behind him.)

On September 19, I dry-docked the *Cleopatra* in the Persian dry dock and then had to fly to Alexandria for a conference. On September 24, I returned to Massawa to find the *Cleopatra* had made hash of my Persian dry dock. From September 24 to 28, we worked frantically to restore that dry dock to service. On September 28, we succeeded and resumed docking on the never-ending stream of supply ships flowing to us from the Mediterranean.

Normally, that might have been considered a sufficiently full month for any naval base, even for far better manned ones than ours, but more was added.

I have previously mentioned that the British had another salvage operation going in the commercial harbor, which harbor was exclusively assigned for salvage to Captain McCance and his British co-workers. His company had received its contract in October of 1941; in December, 1941, it was reported to the British Admiralty that excellent progress was being made; by early September, 1942, nothing had yet been floated and the Admiralty, considering all the salvage equipment furnished and all the money it had paid out, was becoming somewhat discouraged with the results McCance was achieving.

To make matters worse, McCance had twice tried to salvage the huge floating crane sunk alongside the Massawa commercial wharfs, and twice had failed. That crane was a sore point with me. It had been scuttled simply by opening its sea valves; no explosives had been used in it to damage its hull. As it lay in about forty feet of water alongside the quay, it should at most have been a few weeks' work or less for any competent salvage master to recover, undamaged as it was, and restore it to service where it would have been of tremendous value on the multitude of small salvage jobs in Massawa.

But McCance was not competent, or if he was, he was never on the scene long enough properly to supervise. Whatever the cause, nine months after salvage operations had started on that crane, it was still on the bottom. And what was worse, in his two bungling attempts to raise that crane, McCance had thoroughly ruined the watertightness of its previously undamaged main deck, and had finally, after his second failure, given it up as hopeless of salvage.

At that point, in late August, he had cabled his company in London, reporting the crane impossible to raise. He recommended that it be demolished by explosives as it lay on the bottom, thereby at least clearing the berth alongside the quay which it was blocking, as the Italians had intended.

The Admiralty demurred at granting permission for demolition. Next to the two Italian dry docks, that huge crane was the most valuable piece of marine equipment in the Red Sea, if only it could be recovered. Instead of acquiescing, they cabled Captain Lucas, ordering him to get in touch with me to request me to advise McCance on how to raise that crane, assuming I still thought it possible after all the added damage to it.

So Captain Lucas, laying the whole sad tale before me, asked me if I thought the crane could still be lifted. I told him I did. Then he requested me, as the Admiralty had ordered him, to advise McCance on how to do it.

I refused. I told Captain Lucas he could advise the Admiralty I saw no value in giving McCance any advice. I had no authority over McCance and couldn't make him take my advice after I'd given it to him. All that would happen would be that the bungling McCance would by distant control from Asmara bungle the job a third time and then blame my plan for failure. I could carry out my own plan to raise the crane with men over whom I had authority. I wouldn't trust it to McCance under any circumstances, nor to any others whom I could merely advise, not direct, regardless of who they were. If the British Admiralty wanted to turn the lifting of that sunken crane over to me, though now it was a far harder task than originally, requiring peculiar methods to overcome the damage McCance had inflicted on that crane, I'd lift it for them. Otherwise, they could leave me out of it.

Captain Lucas reported by cable to the Admiralty the results of his discussion. But nothing happened. Apparently the Admiralty couldn't turn over to me the salvage of that badly needed crane without canceling wholly the contract McCance's company held. And they couldn't bring themselves to that. Neither would they acquiesce in the demolition by explosives of the crane. So matters remained in the status quo. The crane stayed on the bottom, all work on it abandoned. The berth it was blocking remained blocked. McCance, monocle and all, continued in misdirection of salvage in the commercial harbor of Massawa, operating mainly from Asmara, for it was damned hot in Massawa where I was laboring under the hallucination that the place for a salvage officer is where the wrecks are.

Then early in September, a remarkable thing happened; something I should hardly have believed had I not witnessed it. McCance and his men almost salvaged a wreck!

What happened, had it not been tragic, would have been humorous. Lying in the middle of the commercial harbor was the scuttled wreck of the Italian steamer *Gera,* a little smaller than the *Frauenfels* on which Brown was then working with the *Intent* in the south harbor, and almost identically damaged—both had two bomb holes blasted in their sides. But whereas I expected Brown and his little crew to finish so we could lift the *Frauenfels* about ten or eleven weeks after he started on her, McCance's company, with a far larger force than Brown had, had been working on the *Gera* over six months, and more probably around nine.

After six to nine months on what should have been about a six to nine weeks' job, McCance's men finally got the holes in the *Gera* patched up with cement, and McCance came down from Asmara, monocle and all, in white as usual, to supervise the pumping out of the *Gera* to lift her. As McCance, I knew, had a whole warehouseful of

British pumps, I saw no reason why he shouldn't, assuming his men had done a decent patching job, which they certainly had taken time enough to do.

About September 4, the pumping on the *Gera* started. Since I wasn't invited to witness the operation and would have been too busy anyway to have accepted even had I been invited, I noted it only casually morning and evening, looking out from the second floor of Building 35, which had a good view over the commercial harbor about a mile away on the west side of the Abd-El-Kader Peninsula.

Roughly on September 5, the *Gera* lifted her main deck above water. If McCance had got that far, the ship should soon be high enough to tow around to the naval harbor for docking to repair her damaged hull, and I began to wonder vaguely where I might fit her into the docking schedule between the *Euryalus,* due to arrive in a few days, and the *Cleopatra,* soon to follow the *Euryalus.* I wanted to dock her in the brief interval, ten days, between those two cruisers, while still I had all the temporary British mechanics in Massawa. Otherwise, repairing her would put a severe crimp in the other Massawa repair operations.

But I soon found I had no cause for concern. By September 7, the *Gera* was fairly afloat but very badly heeled over, unfit for dry-docking, and that was as far as McCance ever got with her. The next ten days, every time I looked out over the commercial harbor, the only matter in doubt was whether the *Gera* was about to capsize to starboard, or whether this time it was her port side she was about to roll over on, making of her a worse obstruction to traffic in the harbor than originally she had been.

Considering that McCance had plenty of men and plenty of pumps, within four days at the outside he should have dried her out and straightened her up, light enough for dry-docking. But it didn't happen. Day after day she wobbled from side to side, making everyone about the harbor seasick to look at her. The cruiser *Euryalus* came and went; the small Italian dry dock came up, went down, came up again; all the period in which I might have dry-docked the *Gera* faded day after day; finally came September 18, the day before the *Cleopatra* was due. When she left, all my extra British mechanics were going with her. It was too late now to dry-dock the *Gera* before the *Cleopatra;* and after that warship left I should no longer have workmen to handle the job conveniently.

On September 18, I received a telephone call from Captain Lucas at the Royal Naval Base. From him I learned that McCance was in desperate straits with the *Gera;* every pump he had in his overflowing warehouse had in succession been put aboard the *Gera* in the past two weeks and every one of them now was broken down, leaving him helpless with his wreck, which now he was sure was going to capsize on him unless he got more pumps. Would I be so kind as to lend McCance four salvage pumps to save the situation? I told Lucas I'd be glad to and as swiftly as possible deliver them to him aboard the *Gera.*

Hurriedly, I dragged the *Resolute,* my nearest ship, away from her wreck, loaded four new American pumps, two 6-inch and two 4-inch Jaegers, aboard her, steamed at full speed out of the naval harbor and around the Abd-El-Kader Peninsula into the commercial harbor to deliver them. We steamed in alongside the *Gera,* which was badly heeled to port, and there was McCance, monocle still in his eye, but his beautiful white clothes rather soiled, clinging to a bulkhead grab rod to avoid sliding overboard.

"What's the matter?" I asked, curious as to why in two weeks' time he hadn't got his wreck erect and pumped dry. It should long ago easily have been done with far fewer pumps than were in sight on deck the *Gera.* McCance mistook my question.

"All my pumps have broken down," he answered. "The blighters I've got aboard here have been dipping salt water up out of the holds and putting it into the radiators instead of coming up the ladders to get fresh water; every pump engine below has frozen up as a result of all that salt in its cylinder jackets."

I said nothing. If McCance didn't know enough to observe what was happening before it went too far, it was his funeral, not mine. And if he didn't have sense enough as salvage officer not to wear white aboard a wreck, he probably was spending too much time trying to keep his clothes clean to notice what kind of water went into the radiators.

"Where do you want these pumps?" I asked, preparing to have Frank Roys, salvage master on the *Resolute,* swing them over with his boom.

"Just a minute, Captain Ellsberg," answered McCance. "What are your conditions? I've got to know them before I can accept the pumps."

I stared at McCance in blank amazement. Conditions? I hadn't thought of any conditions; I was merely lending a man in trouble some desperately needed pumps. Then it dawned on me. As a commercial salvage man himself, McCance was afraid I might enter a salvage claim against the *Gera* for salvage for having helped save a vessel in desperate condition from capsizing, and thus force him to divide his salvage fee for the salvage of the *Gera*. He wanted to know how much I was going to hold him up for before he took the pumps.

"There aren't any conditions," I replied angrily. What did he think I was, anyway? "I'm just lending you some pumps, that's all. It's in return for some air compressors and a couple of pumps Captain Lucas once got from your warehouse for me. All I ask of you is that you see your men don't put any salt water in these radiators and ruin them too." I turned to Captain Roys. "Swing those pumps aboard her, Frank, and let's get out of here. They seem to think we're a gang of pirates!"

We delivered the pumps and steamed away from the terribly heeled over *Gera*. Those were four fine new pumps. If McCance couldn't straighten up his wreck with them, he wasn't any good at all.

He wasn't. Over the next couple of days, the *Gera* careened as crazily as ever from side to side. On September 19, I departed on my way to Alexandria, leaving the *Cleopatra* just dry-docked. On September 24, I got back; the *Gera* was no nearer safety than when I had left. That day and the following day, I could pay little attention to her antics; I was too busy seeing to the rehabilitation of the crushed keel blocks in the Persian dry dock. When I left my room in Building 35 early on September 25 there was the *Gera* still badly over to port.

It seemed unbelievable. Three weeks had gone by since that ship had lifted off the bottom and she was now no nearer safety from capsizing than the day she had lifted. At least by accident in all that time, one would have thought they might have got her straightened up. Evidently McCance had a far greater capacity for blundering incompetence than I had given him credit for.

In the early evening of that day, Friday, September 25, Captain Lucas phoned me to ask if I could come immediately to see him. I went, leaving Lloyd Williams to struggle alone with the keel blocks in the Persian dry dock.

Matters in respect to the *Gera* had apparently reached a climax. McCance had just sent a message to inform Captain Lucas that again

[415]

all the pumps, including mine now, were broken down and he was helpless to do anything further to save the *Gera.* Whether that meant he was voluntarily throwing up the sponge, I didn't learn, but I believe that was what was meant. At any rate, Captain Lucas, acting on cabled authority from the Admiralty to use his discretion, had decided the time had come to use it—he was canceling completely the contract held by McCance and his company in London. Would I be willing to take over everything, and particularly was I willing to take over instantly and try to save the *Gera?*

I told him if he would give me an official order canceling the British contract and authorizing me to take over, I'd take over at once. He had the order already made out—he handed it to me. It was about 6 P.M.

I hurried from his office to organize an emergency salvage party for the *Gera.* Hastily I started the crew of the *Resolute,* just in from her wreck and alongside our Naval Base pier, out to both salvaged dry docks to pick up from them all the salvage pumps still on those docks; rounded up Captain Reed and all his salvage men; got hold of Bob Steele to help on stability calculations, and at 7 P.M. everybody steamed away for the commercial harbor on the *Resolute* with half a dozen assorted pumps on her fantail.

At 7:30 P.M., we were alongside the port side of the *Gera,* listed now so badly to port it was impossible to stand on deck without holding on to something and with her port gunwale very nearly awash. She was in a very bad way; no pumps of any nature were running on her.

Far up on the high side, clinging there to the railing, I spotted Captain McCance. Telling Captain Reed only to start unloading pumps, to get them down inside the hatches, and to get some running in one hold forward and one hold aft as fast as possibly he could, I left him. I clambered with great difficulty up that inclined deck to where McCance stood, bedraggled in his white clothes, for once without his monocle, looking wan and haggard as he clung to the upper rail to keep from sliding down the deck and overboard. I was sorry for the poor devil; nobody looking at him then against a background of complete failure could help pitying him.

Hanging to the rail with one hand myself, I handed him a copy of the order from Captain Lucas, acting in the name of the Admiralty.

"We'll take over now, Captain," I said, as sympathetically as I could. "Better luck to you elsewhere in the future."

"What do you want of me?" asked McCance, reading the brief order.

"Nothing at all, Captain. You're all knocked out. Better get off and go home to get some sleep. We'll take care of this ship. Don't worry any more."

But I was wasting my sympathy on McCance, I swiftly found. He began to insist that I give him a receipt for the *Gera*, afloat in safe condition. I looked at him in astonishment. He wanted me to sign a certificate which, if the *Gera* immediately capsized on me before I could do anything to her to save her, would put all the blame on me? I promptly quit feeling sorry for Captain McCance; even if he'd lost his monocle, he hadn't lost his monocle manner.

"If you'll get down this deck after me, on to the *Resolute* where I can get a hand free to write without breaking my neck, I'll give you a receipt for the *Gera* 'as is' and no conditions. And that's all you'll get! Take it or leave it!" Very cautiously, hand over hand, I worked my way down that dangerous slope on to the *Resolute*, wrote out the receipt as promised, and saw McCance off. Then I turned to.

But I had little to do myself. Captain Reed, elderly as he was and with only one good eye for observation in getting about, knew his business; so did Captain Roys; so did all the salvage men I'd brought out. To all of them the *Gera* was a challenge—for three weeks they'd all observed her teetering crazily on the verge of going over, itching to get their fingers on her. Now at last she was theirs—they would show everybody round about that harbor in Massawa what *salvage* men could do.

On careened decks on which a monkey would have had difficulty in getting about, they manhandled the pumps aboard, got them down terrifically inclined hatches, coupled up discharge and suction hoses. Then in one hold forward and another aft, I got pumps rolling over and pumping out water, so as to get two holds dry and give the ship some stability before she rose high enough to make her topheavy and capsize her—the one thing McCance, trying to empty all holds together, hadn't had understanding enough to do.

Of course it was an all-night job; we didn't start until 7:30 P.M. Our greatest hazard we found as darkness caught us was to avoid breaking our necks on those sloping decks falling over McCance's collection of broken-down pumps littering the *Gera*. Every kind of pump

I'd ever seen or heard of was there in profusion, every one a piece of junk at the moment—gasoline-driven pumps; steam-driven pumps, both reciprocating and centrifugal; diesel-driven pumps; electric-driven pumps, both ordinary motor-driven centrifugals and special submersible units; together with donkey boilers to furnish steam and massive diesel-driven generators to furnish electricity for their special pump units. There was nearly enough broken-down salvage machinery on the *Gera's* decks to make her topheavy enough to capsize from that cause alone. And that was only what was up on deck. There was plenty more broken down inside the holds, including, from what causes I didn't know, the four new pumps I had loaned McCance.

We worked all night. By noon on Saturday the *Gera* was fairly well dried out in all her holds, floating erect, and no longer in any danger. At noon on Sunday, September 27, with all holds and machinery spaces dry, we towed the *Gera,* stable and upright for the first time in three weeks, out of the commercial harbor and around inside the naval harbor, to moor her there, waiting a propitious moment when from somewhere I could get men enough to repair her damaged hull when I docked her. All my temporary English mechanics had departed with the *Cleopatra* three days before. Perhaps soon I should get some of that batch of 200 mechanics promised me from Alex, and for whom, with Captain Lucas' co-operation, I was already preparing quarters.

At any rate, there in our harbor near the *Liebenfels* lay now the *Gera,* on which Captain Reed and his men, together with Captain Roys and the *Resolute's* crew, gazed with much pride. In two days, aided by a little knowledge, they had accomplished what all McCance's men and machinery had failed to accomplish in three weeks. Seeing that it was already Sunday afternoon, I let Reed and Roys and all their men have the rest of the day off as a reward, and decided to take the rest of the day off myself. So far, September had been rather wearing.

September, however, was not quite through with us. Next day, Monday, September 28, with all work on the keel blocks of the Persian dock completed by Lloyd Williams, I dry-docked the next supply ship and then settled back for a few days of only routine work till on October 1 the *Frauenfels* would be ready for lifting and all hands would go to work again.

Everything seemed propitious. The weather was as hot and humid as ever. But September, at least, the month (so I had been assured by my British friends who knew Massawa better than I) which would certainly knock us out with the heat even if June, July, and August hadn't, was practically gone and we were still on deck with a considerable amount accomplished. I no longer had any cause to worry about the Massawa heat stopping operations at my Naval Base, though the contractor had long since cut off working in the middle of the day on his construction jobs.

Monday ended in the most gorgeous evening I had ever seen in the Red Sea. I can't describe it better than by a direct quotation from the end of a letter I wrote my wife that evening (and finished next morning):

However, it is Monday night now and all is calm and peaceful on the shores of the Red Sea. I went down to the waterfront in the night to look over my collection, and we had a most marvelous harbor scene—no moon, but the brilliant stars glowing over the dark water which was absolutely smooth and like a mirror in which was reflected the inverted image of the nearest ship, our first salvage prize. And farther off sparkled the lights of the salvaged dry docks and our other salvaged ship. A lovely night—but utterly wasted here alone by your devoted

NED.

P.S.
Tuesday morning, September 29

About 2 A.M., our quiet night went all to hell. It started to rain (very unusual here) and blow like the devil. Our first ship [the *Liebenfels*] dragged its anchor down the harbor about half a mile before I could get some tugs alongside and drag her back to a safe anchorage. And our second one [the *Gera*] parted her stern mooring and swung round on her head mooring till she grounded astern. We'll have to pull her off at high tide tonight.

Quite an exciting life.

It was.

When high tide came, late at night on September 29, with the *Resolute*, the *Intent*, the *Hsin Rocket*, and the *Pauline Moller* all tugging together on heavy hawsers, we managed by morning of September 30 to drag the stern of the *Gera* off the mud flat on to which the sudden gale had driven it hard, but fortunately not damaged it. Most of September 30 was spent in remooring her again with such steel hawsers as Massawa afforded.

And so ended September. September had been a very hectic month for me.

CHAPTER

48

On THURSDAY, OCTOBER 1, ALL UN-
derwater work on the scuttled *Frauenfels* was completed, as scheduled,
and with practically everything I had at my command, I started out
to lift her.

During the eleven weeks since July 16 when he had started, Brown
and his little crew of twelve had struggled faithfully, underwater and
on the surface, to patch up with cement the two large holes, one forward and one aft, which Nazi bombs had blasted in her, and to seal
up watertight all seachests, close or plug all inside valves, build cofferdams around the submerged deck hatches, and rig up the pumps.

In every way, the *Frauenfels* was a harder task to salvage than the
Liebenfels had been. She was somewhat bigger, she had twice as many
holes in her, she lay in considerably deeper water, which made necessary some inside shoring of her decks by divers to avoid their collapsing under the heavy waterload on top of them when we pumped
out inside.

I had made a few dives myself on the *Frauenfels* for inspection purposes and had often visited her to check the progress of the work.
Most of the actual underwater work had been done by little Buck
Scougale, for whose energy, skill, and daring as a diver my respect
constantly increased. Buck had been aided by Dorcy, the *Intent's* only
other diver who, while he lacked Buck's skill and ability to get about
in tight places, nevertheless put everything he had into helping out
underwater. Buck and Dorcy together had done all the work inside
and outside the submerged hulk of the *Frauenfels,* a terrific job for
only two men in such a short time. To some degree, they had been
aided by a shipmate, Herald Bertolotti, "Muzzy," who was learning
to dive. "Muzzy" proved an able student, and was of considerable
assistance on the bottom.

Now the *Frauenfels* was ready for her rise.

I had no intention of a repetition of the man-killing episode on the *Liebenfels*. This time, I had a magnificent set of salvage pumps of my own, big ones as well as little ones, which the *Chamberlin* had brought out from the United States. My pumping equipment, already mounted in place on wooden platforms standing island-like on the cofferdams rising from the submerged hull of the *Frauenfels,* was topped by four huge 10-inch Jaeger pumps. These mounted, two forward and two aft, had twice the capacity each of the 6-inch pumps I had used on the *Liebenfels*—each of those 10-inch pumps could throw 3000 gallons of water a minute. Then, in addition, I had four 6-inch pumps, half-a-dozen 4-inch pumps, and finally some small 2-inch pumps which could be carried around by hand.

Accompanied by the *Resolute* and carrying Captain Reed, Lloyd Williams, all their salvage men, and the ten South Africans to help out, the *Intent* steamed into the south harbor early on October 1 to commence. I had forty-eight men all told this time; I intended to have enough to work round the clock and still let everyone get some sleep by working only in shifts.

With the *Intent* and the *Resolute* both tied to port alongside what little of the *Frauenfel's* superstructure amidships showed above the water, we started up our pumps. The effect was magnificent—the rhythmic roar of over a dozen pump engines and the huge fountains of water cascading from one end of the wreck to the other into the sea, made a scene that for sound and sight was unforgettable!

It so happened that the wreck of the *Frauenfels* lay in the exact center of the line of wrecks with her bow very close to the wreck ahead of her, the *Vesuvio,* while the stern of the *Frauenfels* hardly cleared the wreck astern of her, the *Brenta,* by ten feet. Under these conditions, I considered it best to raise her bow first, to give us a better chance of keeping her clear of the neighboring wrecks when she floated.

Consequently, we pumped to lighten her bow more than her stern. With all the pumping capacity I had, by mid-afternoon, I had the forward holds pumped far enough down so by all of Bob Steele's calculations, she should start to lift forward, but she didn't. I checked Steele's figures; they were right, but the bow wasn't lifting.

Brown, Reed, Roys, and I all knitted our brows over that puzzle, but we couldn't find the answer. However, not wishing to get so much buoyancy forward as to make the bow lift finally with a sudden jolt that might cause trouble, I slowed down all the forward pumps and speeded up those astern. We would have to lift her stern first now, in spite of hardly any clearance aft.

We did. By late afternoon, the stern started to rise and by early evening we had the afterdecks awash and rising steadily. When I had the stern high enough to insure that nothing the submerged bow might do could cause the stern to go under again, we slacked down aft and went all out on the forward pumps.

The water in the forward holds went down continuously, but the bow didn't rise. Already during the daylight hours, we had once lowered all our pumps down the cofferdams, a tough job, since those 10-inch pumps were veritable mammoths to handle in getting them down onto new scaffoldings inside the wet holds. Now to avoid losing suction forward, we had to lower away the pumps again, this time in the darkness. We managed it successfully, after which half my combined salvage forces flopped down at random on the decks of the salvage tugs, and the other half kept on servicing pumps—they were consuming huge quantities of gasoline and fresh water for their radiators.

We kept on pumping forward. We certainly had buoyancy enough to start the bow up, but obstinately it refused to lift. There was no reason apparent, there was nothing to do but to keep on pumping.

At midnight with a sudden jolt, the bow broke free of the bottom, jumped ten feet at least in a violent leap that sent water cascading off both sides of her forward in solid cataracts like twin Niagaras, and then rose hurriedly till her forward deck was fairly well out of water, at least as high up as her stern. It took a diving survey outside her to disclose the why of that performance. Then we learned the answer. The bomb exploding forward had laid part of her port side steel plating flat out some feet to port and flush with her bottom. This protrusion, buried under some five or six feet of mud in the sea floor, invisible to the divers working on her previously, had been acting as a huge anchor, holding down her bow till we had developed sufficient excess buoyancy to tear it free when the bow had come rushing up.

But as all our pumps had been well lashed down in anticipation of such trouble, no damage had resulted. We had our ship afloat fore and aft, and coming up steadily through the night as full power was put on all the pumps.

[423]

Friday morning saw the *Frauenfels,* encrusted all over with mussels like her previously risen sister, with her decks all well above water and her sides far enough up to make her look like a ship again. By early Friday afternoon, I had her far enough up to consider drying her out that night and towing her into the Naval Base Saturday morning.

But no salvage job is ever completed without unexpected trouble of some kind and the *Frauenfels* proved no exception. About the middle of the afternoon, with no warning at all, it started suddenly to blow a full gale. Hurriedly, I cast loose both the *Intent* and the *Resolute* and sent them steaming full speed through a gap in the line of wrecks to take up positions to starboard of the *Frauenfels,* the windward side, in case of trouble. Hardly had they got round to the starboard quarter and each passed us a six-inch manila hawser which, on the *Frauenfels,* I hurriedly secured to the starboard quarter bitts, when the *Frauenfels* which had been straining heavily on the old wire hawsers holding her stern in position, snapped both those long-submerged steel cables. Instantly, her stern started to swing down on the sunken bow of the *Brenta* not over ten feet astern of her.

I had a wild time on the poop of the *Frauenfels,* directing the *Intent* and the *Resolute,* straining on their manila hawsers in the midst of that howling gale, while somehow we kept from fouling the wreck of the *Brenta* till the stern of the *Frauenfels* was worked down through the narrow gap and a little to leeward to clear her of the wreck astern.

Matters now looked better. My waterlogged wreck, about as high out of the water as any ordinary ship, was streaming to her bower anchors, held up against a 50-knot gale only by the two tugs straining on the two six-inch manila lines to our quarter. Unfortunately, we had to stay nearly broadside on to the gale. For not only did the chart show a bad shoal off our port side on which our stern would certainly be piled up if we went very far around to port, but also on that side if we let her swing head into the wind to ease the strain on our manila hawsers, we should be driven broadside into the wreck of the *Vesuvio.* Either one of these catastrophes would certainly, with the wind and the sea pounding us the way they were, finish our newly salvaged ship.

None too hopefully, I watched the straining manila lines to my two tugs. I had no fears about the tugs; each had 1200 horsepower

General Motors diesels—plenty to hold against the storm as their engines drove full power into it to hold us up. What worried me was the hawsers—they were both only six-inch manila lines, the biggest either ship had, and, while new, were none too big for the job. Would they stand the strain?

For twenty minutes, perhaps, I watched those lines, taut as piano wires, while the wind shrieked by, full against our now exposed hull and superstructures, the seas pounded our starboard side, and the biting spray drove like buckshot into our half-naked hides. The gale had brought a sudden change in temperature—for the first time in my whole Massawa experience, I felt cold. But I didn't dare leave the poop to get even a shirt; and then, it struck me, what would be the use of leaving anyway? All my clothes were aboard the *Intent*, tossing like a cork a hundred fathoms off to starboard while she steamed in the heavy seas against the storm.

Then, suddenly, both six-inch hawsers snapped! With nothing any longer to hold our stern up, we started to swing to port downwind on to the shoal where I could plainly see the seas breaking over the coral reefs below. If we grounded on that, the *Frauenfels* was finished!

I had good cause to bless the marvelous maneuverability which the General Motors diesel electric drives, controlled wholly from the bridge, gave both my tugs. Like falcons, the instant those lines parted, both tugs spun about and came driving down on our quarter, while on their fantails their crews madly heaved in on their ends of the broken hawsers. Perhaps a little more favorably placed, the *Intent* got to us first and sent a heaving line whistling up on our quarter. Captain Reed and I began frantically hauling in, to drag aboard the frayed end of that broken six-inch hawser and hurriedly pass it round our bitts, well away from where it had broken. Instantly the *Intent* headed out into the wind again to get a strain on the line and stop further swinging before we hit the reef.

She succeeded, thank God! We were still clear by perhaps fifty feet. Meanwhile, the second line had come aboard again from the *Resolute* but I cast it loose. If the two lines had not before held us, it was unlikely they would again for long, especially if the gale increased in force. So, taking a chance that the single line to the *Intent* would hold us off the reef while I executed the maneuver, I both sang out and waved to the *Resolute* that we didn't want her line—she was to steam through the gap astern us, get round to our lee side, put her nose against our port quarter, and push against us, full power into the wind, where she could exert her full propeller thrust without worrying about whether her hawser might stand it.

Captain Byglin on the *Resolute* waved he understood, and circled around our stern, where he managed to squeeze in between us and the reef, come up on our lee side, and start to push. Before long, we were safely clear of the reef and with the *Intent* pulling and the *Resolute* pushing, sure to ride out the tropical storm. I felt better. It had been a remarkable exhibition of seamanship on the part of both tugs and their captains, particularly on Brown's part in so swiftly repassing his broken line.

The storm blew altogether for two hours, during which, never knowing what instant they might be piled up on a reef and the ship sunk in a storm under their feet, the salvage men aboard, mainly Reed's crew, kept all the salvage pumps going and the water pouring steadily overboard.

Finally, in the late afternoon, the wind blew itself out, the sea in the south harbor subsided, and we found ourselves still afloat but confronted by new problems. I could not stay where we were without keeping both salvage ships steaming all night to hold us clear of the wreck ahead, the wreck astern, and the reef off to port, all of which we were in danger of fouling each time the tide changed. There was nothing to do save to get the waterlogged *Frauenfels* out of that line of wrecks and anchor her for the night elsewhere. But we couldn't weigh her anchors, and if we slipped them, we should have nothing to anchor her with elsewhere.

I finally decided, nevertheless, to buoy both anchors so they could be recovered later; slip both anchor cables, retaining the inboard ends of her cables aboard; and then take her away and try mooring her to one of the mooring buoys in the south anchorage outside the line of wrecks. It would be a ticklish handling job, but I felt my two tugs could manage it.

So, with one tug heaving on a line forward, and the other tied up alongside her quarter to steer, we slipped the cables, juggled the recently risen *Frauenfels* clear of the other wrecks we had been dodging in the storm, towed her about a mile away, and managed to shackle up what was left of her starboard anchor cable to the ring of a long unused Italian mooring buoy. I could only hope that the unseen ground tackle holding that old mooring buoy was still in fair shape

There we swung all through the night, while we worked to dry out our wreck. Of course, she did some heeling in the process, but nothing like what had occurred on the *Liebenfels*, since we were never short of workable pumps, nor of men either to keep them going.

By Saturday evening, we were through. The *Frauenfels* was completely dried out, high out of water, and upright. That night, everybody, except for a small watch on the pumps, slept.

On Sunday morning, October 4, again with our solitary American flag flying over her Nazi swastika, the *S.S. Frauenfels,* another prize of war taken both from the Nazis and from the sea, was towed in triumph from the south harbor.

Around Massawa and into the naval harbor, standing high out of water, she proceeded majestically in a striking marine parade, headed by the *Intent,* which had raised her, and shepherded by the *Resolute* and the *Hsin Rocket* to help steer.

We all felt proud of the *Frauenfels* job, salvaged in eleven weeks, lifted and dried out in three days, particularly as a contrast to what had happened in the long-drawn-out operation on the *Gera,* so suddenly ended by us only the week before.

As a reward for their efforts, I sent Captain Brown and the whole crew of the *Intent* up to Asmara for a week's vacation to cool off. And as a somewhat belated vacation for Reed's men for the small Italian dock, I sent them off also.

Meanwhile, the raising of the *Frauenfels* did nothing to simplify matters for me at the Naval Base. I now had five salvaged wrecks—three ships, the *Frauenfels,* the *Gera,* and the *Liebenfels;* and two dry docks, the larger and the smaller Italian units—to work on, and a negligible force only with which to work on them.

Repairs on the *Liebenfels'* hull were completed, and Hudson, my English engineer superintendent, had her engines and boilers practically ready to go to sea again. The large Italian dry dock also was far along toward completion; but the other three wrecks were crying for work, both on their hulls and machinery and I had absolutely nobody to put on them. If only the 200 workmen promised me from Alex would arrive!

CHAPTER

49

WITH MOST OF MY SALVAGE CREWS away and no emergency jobs on the dry dock, I had a few days over the following week to get closer to affairs at the Naval Base.

I learned to my delight from Captain Morrill that Eugene Zeiner had been performing miraculously as a toolroom supervisor—our loss of tools had dropped almost to the vanishing point—and when occasionally something did disappear, Morrill told me Zeiner came to him to report it with tears in his eyes, almost as if he had lost a relative. He was proving perhaps the most valuable employee we had ashore.

And one other episode Morrill told me of did nothing to make me regret having gone all out to save Zeiner from deportation. It seems that the week or so after Zeiner had turned to in the toolroom and had inventoried and become sufficiently acquainted with his precious stock of tools to take his eyes off them a few minutes to see what else was going on around the American Naval Base, of which he now found himself a part, he had discovered the existence of the American volunteer militia companies. With great interest, he had gazed on his fellow workmen drilling in preparation for possible action against either Fascisti or Nazis.

"What do you think that Zeiner did then, Captain?" Morrill asked me. "You'd've thought he'd had a bellyful of fighting after all he's been through and been discharged from the British Army as a shell-shock case, but no! The minute I'd dismissed the company, he rushes up to me and wants to enlist. Since he isn't an American, and our orders restricted us to American volunteers only, I couldn't take him in, but I told him I'd put it up to headquarters. The answer came back No—Americans only.

"When I told that to Zeiner, it nearly broke his heart. If there was going to be any fighting around Massawa, he didn't want to be left out. I felt so sorry for the poor devil, for once I developed a bright idea! The orders said Americans only as members of the volunteer companies, but they didn't say anything about restrictions on who might train them. And here was a man who'd been through more fighting than anybody else in Eritrea, against both Eyties and Nazis and knew all their tricks! It would have hurt my conscience to risk all those raw Americans in action without the best training possible, so I gave Zeiner a uniform without any American insignia on it, rated him a drill sergeant, and any day you go out to watch 'em drill, you'll find Eugene Zeiner, Czech drill sergeant, showing our men how to lay away Nazis and Eyties without getting themselves killed! That boy's good! And, of course, Captain," concluded Morrill, "if it comes to a fight, who's going to kick if the drill sergeant has to get into it too, just to make sure his pupils haven't forgotten what he's taught 'em?"

Morrill grinned at me, and I grinned back. Without breaking any regulations, he had certainly cut the Gordian knot to everybody's benefit.

I had a little time also to inspect closely some mechanical betterments. Some of my long since commercially ordered shipyard machinery had finally come in early in September and had been set up, mainly machine shop equipment. To hold it all, we had taken what had once been the Eytie mine depot building, their largest in the Naval Base, and had converted it into a new machine shop. To that had been transferred all the ex-sabotaged Italian machine shop tools, filling one half of it, while in the other half of our new building had been erected all the lathes, the drill presses, the boring mills, the milling machines and the rest that had come to me from America.

I looked over that vast machine shop proudly; between everything the Italians had left me and what I had ordered myself in America, without doubt I now had the finest machine shop in all Africa. There we could do anything, and we were doing it too, not only for all Eritrea and for the Naval Base, but also for the Middle East Forces in Egypt for whom Austin Byrne, Master Mechanic, was executing both production and repair jobs.

But my new plate shop, my most badly needed building, which had been under construction since the previous May, wasn't ready yet to house anything. Unfortunately, priority was being given to housing for the construction forces over construction for direct war purposes.

This had an interesting result. A vast quantity of labor and materials had already been wasted on housing at Ghinda, which was now lying idle. Most of the construction workmen from there were now in Massawa, overcrowding the housing facilities at the Naval Base for useful workers for war purposes while they built for themselves, this time right on the Naval Base grounds, permanent masonry residence buildings, mess halls, and recreation rooms to serve themselves. When they got through with all that, they would then themselves move into their magnificent new quarters and start some real work toward providing the extra buildings the Naval Base really could use to expedite its war work. That is, they would, provided they weren't already too late with it. The war in the Middle East, which on my visit to Alex late in September, I could see was getting ready to swing into action and move westward in a big way, might suddenly move westward so swiftly and so far away from Eritrea as to make anything anchored to the ground there, like buildings, totally useless in the further prosecution of the war. Frankly, I was losing all interest in further construction by the contractor; we had got along quite well in Massawa without any aid from his vast construction projects; now that he was getting around to some of them in Massawa, I was sure the inversion of an early war lament—too little and too late—better fitted the case. Our contractors' vast projects in Massawa were going to be too big and too late—long before he got around from his vast housing projects to tend to war construction, the war was going to move elsewhere. And while you could move machinery, ships, cranes, and floating dry docks to where else they'd best help the war effort, masonry buildings for housing were going to stay where they were when the war moved on, like those in Ghinda, a double loss, a waste of labor when they were built, a total loss when they were abandoned.

So, if the machinery in my converted ex-Italian mine depot gave me a lift as I looked at it busily engaged on war work, all the new housing construction on the Abd-El-Kader Peninsula in Massawa gave me a sharp pain every time I looked from it to that far-from-finished plate shop. What, I wondered, had we all been sent to Massawa for—to make ourselves comfortable, or to help keep the war from being lost?

CHAPTER

50

On OCTOBER 11, MY SALVAGE MEN came back from their vacation in Asmara. I started Brown and his crew overhauling all the salvage gear used on the *Frauenfels,* about a week's job. After that, they were to go back to the south harbor to make a diving survey of the damage to the *Brenta,* the Italian wreck scuttled astern of the spot from which we had just lifted the *Frauenfels,* and then to proceed with salvaging her on a plan to be developed after I had the diving survey report.

Meanwhile, being very short on mechanics for repair work, reluctantly I turned all of Reed's crew to as repair men for a few days, his salvage mechanics to work on the topside, and his divers underneath, in repairing the smaller Italian dry dock they had salvaged. This hurt me a lot, to have to use salvage men on repairs but somebody had to rebuild the bottom of the small dry dock or we should forever be running compressors on it to keep it afloat.

For their part, the *Resolute,* with its one diver, returned temporarily to the wreck of the *Moncalieri,* and the *Chamberlin* continued its job on the *XXIII Marzo.*

A couple of days went by. Through Commander Davy, liaison officer, for some weeks I had been pressing Alexandria for the promised workmen, but with ever-decreasing hope, for I knew that while no dry-docking was going on in Alex, other repair activities were being resumed and men were being returned to Alex, now that it was certain that in the face of Montgomery's growing Eighth Army, Rommel's dream of ever breaking through at El Alamein had completely faded. But I desperately needed those men, and the brighter Montgomery's prospects became, the darker became my chances of getting any volunteers from Alex.

I was engaged in discussing this problem with Commander Davy

about the middle of the morning of October 13, when unceremoniously, Captain Reed burst into my office, his bronze face flaming.
Mad as a hornet, he exclaimed,

"You'd better get right down into the contractor's office below,
Captain! They're pulling a scandalous trick on you down there!"

"Excuse me, Davy," I said, rising immediately.

When the contractor started to do anything in Massawa, it was wise
to pay attention to what was going on. Already, Reed was on his way
out on the run. I followed him downstairs into the office on the first
floor directly below mine, used by the contractor's construction superintendent in Massawa.

An interesting sight met my eye as I entered that office. Seated at
his desk was the Massawa construction superintendent, apparently
only a spectator, while standing alongside him, about to pass out
some papers, was the contractor's Assistant Foreign Manager from
Asmara, who, being one of the contractor's major executives deeply
involved always in vast projects, rarely found time to steal a few
hours off to visit unimportant (and disagreeably hot) Massawa. If he
was in Massawa personally, something really was up.

A swift glance around the office confirmed that conclusion. Seated
along the wall were Captain Brown, Captain Byglin and Captain
Hansen, while a vacant chair alongside Hansen indicated where Captain Reed (who now remained standing) had probably been seated
when he had smelled a rat and walked out to invite me to a salvage
conference where the contractor himself had seen no value in my
presence.

What had gone on before, I never learned. But as the Assistant
Foreign Manager seemed on the point of distributing a notice of
some sort to my salvage officers, I felt entitled to one also, so reaching
out, I took one from his startled fingers before he could object. Noting
that my name was on the long list at its bottom of those who would
ultimately receive copies, I saw I had done nothing unethical in seizing mine then and there, although uninvited. So I started to read it,
while the Assistant Foreign Manager, a heavy-jowled, heavily-lidded,
heavy-set individual, built like a heavyweight pugilist, hurriedly
passed out the other copies to everyone except Reed, who, I believe,
refused to accept one.

At one time, that notice on the contractor's letterhead would have
shocked me, but now as I read it, I was shockproof:

October 10, 1942

To: The Area Engineer
    Eritrean Field Area
    Asmara, Eritrea
From: Foreign Manager
Subject: General Superintendent in Charge of Salvage Work.

Attention: Lt. Col. Ralph E. Knapp

1. Effective Tuesday, October 13, 1942, Captain Edison Brown is appointed General Superintendent of Salvage work.
2. Captain Brown will be in charge of all personnel, and equipment engaged in the salvage work, and will be in complete charge and will direct Salvage Operations.

So! In somewhat more elaborate language than the August before and with a high-sounding title to go with the new responsibilities, the contractor's Foreign Manager himself was this time relieving me of my command and appointing Brown in my place. And it being October 13, the day the order was to take effect, he had evidently dispatched the Assistant Foreign Manager, who the August before had flopped in putting it over, to Massawa to try his hand again. He should have picked a better messenger boy.

I looked around. Probably everyone had already read the notice. I looked at my watch. It was about 10 A.M.

"This is a working day, gentlemen," I observed. "Brown, you ought to be on your ship where I thought you were, instead of here. Are you responsible for this?"

"No, sir," replied Brown. "I'm not sticking my neck out!"

"Very sensible of you, Brown," I admitted. "Now, you get back aboard your ship immediately and turn to. And I warn you, Brown, if you make the slightest move to act on this paper, I'll have you court-martialed! I'm in charge of all salvage here by General Maxwell's orders, and unless and until he relieves me of that responsibility, anyone else who attempts to take over is going to get hurt. Now, Brown, you can go!"

Without a word, Brown departed.

I turned to the other salvage masters.

"I'm sorry, gentlemen, you've been dragged off your work for all this foolishness. Get back to your ships and pay no attention to this piece of paper. It means nothing. Leave this matter to me. I'll clear it up."

Very willingly they started to go, but each one of them, Reed, Hansen, and Byglin, before he left, served notice on all present that he was quitting if that order ever took effect. I waved them out.

"Don't worry, boys, it never will."

They left. I turned to the Assistant Foreign Manager, who, for whatever reason, had stood silent while his conference with my salvage captains was being taken out of his hands and summarily dissolved.

"Now, that's all," I told him. "You can go back to Asmara. I'll have the Army kill this order as dead as its predecessor, which you got out. Meanwhile, you can inform your Foreign Manager which orders you saw Brown and all the others here obey—my orders, as their Commanding Officer, or his in this paper."

"Now, Captain Ellsberg," he urged, "you'd better be sensible. This time the order'll stand up. That appointment has already been approved by the Contracting Officer for the Army and it's legal."

I manifested a doubt. After all, I knew Lieut. Colonel Knapp would never give his approval, at least without consulting me first, and I said so.

"Oh, don't count on Knapp. He's not Contracting Officer any more and he's got nothing to do with it. That job has been transferred to Cairo and Major MacAlarney there has got it now. He's already approved Brown's appointment as General Superintendent. That settles it!"

So Major MacAlarney, whom I knew slightly, was now Contracting Officer and as such in far-off Cairo had evidently approved that appointment! MacAlarney, I knew, was little acquainted with affairs in Massawa; he belonged in Cairo and had made only one brief visit casually to Massawa months before. MacAlarney had too much common sense, however, ever to have approved any such order if he had known what really was involved. I glanced at the copy of the order in my hand; MacAlarney's name was not listed among those to receive a copy. Probably, he'd never seen the actual order, didn't know what was in it when the matter of his approval was requested and had imagined he was merely approving the appointment of someone the contractor wanted to promote to a higher position, involving little else, and certainly not involving his attempting to override General Maxwell's orders in making me Officer in Charge of Salvage.

Well, Cairo was farther off than Asmara and communication with it was poor. The order had to be squelched for the record and I knew MacAlarney would do it, but this time, it would take longer. Still, there was no use arguing over that.

"Just all of you in Asmara bear in mind I'm Officer in Charge of Salvage here till I'm relieved by General Maxwell's orders," I stated flatly. "I don't take orders to surrender my naval command from any civilians. Anybody who gets in my way in carrying out my duties is going to get hurt! Unless you want Brown court-martialed, don't egg him on to try to take over!"

"Now, don't get excited, Captain," the Assistant Foreign Manager advised me. "We're not relieving you as Officer in Charge. We're merely making Brown General Superintendent of Salvage Work."

"Really?" I asked, taking another careful look at that order. "And after you've done that, what does that leave me as Officer in Charge of Salvage to do in Massawa?"

"Oh, all you'll have to do is to give us a list of the ships in the order you want 'em raised, and we'll tend to everything else."

I looked at him in astonishment. Could he possibly be serious? He seemed so. Whether he thought I was another Captain McCance or just a plain damned fool, I couldn't make out. Why, in that case, should the Navy waste one of its few senior salvage officers around Massawa at all? If that was everything being an Officer in Charge of Salvage involved, I might just as well write out the list, pack my bags, and go home where it was cooler! Turn over all control of the salvage work to a contractor who long ago had admitted to me in New York that not one of his officers knew the slightest thing about it? Ridiculous! I turned on my heel and left. There was no point in staying further to listen to such drivel.

In Asmara I was, of course, backed up both by Colonel Hodges, senior Army officer in Eritrea, who said he neither knew of nor had authorized any such order, and also by Lieut. Colonel Knapp, Area Engineer, in refusing to allow that order to go into effect. But, as neither of them was now designated as Contracting Officer, they could not order its recision—only Major MacAlarney, Contracting Officer in Cairo, technically could do that. And as Cairo was far away and the lengthy coded communication required on such a matter would only overload the radio, in spite of some fruitless correspondence, it wasn't until several weeks later that action from him could finally be ob-

[435]

tained. Then, Major MacAlarney came personally to Massawa to investigate what it was all about; after that, he immediately had the order rescinded.

But during those weeks, that order caused me plenty of trouble. Brown, as he said, wasn't sticking his neck out. He was too prudent to risk any court-martial, and did nothing to attempt to take over. But also obviously he was receptive—neither did he say or do anything to show he was in any way averse to the idea or ready to assist in scotching the contractor's ridiculous attempts to relieve me under the guise of appointing a General Superintendent.

So what happened was that during that period, every other salvage master eyed Brown malevolently, ready with most of his men to quit instantly if the contractor, as he claimed he could do, succeeded in making the order stick. Under those conditions, it can be imagined how effectively salvage operations in Massawa proceeded, with practically the whole salvage force, except Brown's own crew of twelve (and perhaps even some of them), fighting mad over what was going on and ready to quit on a moment's notice.

As best I could under these circumstances, I ignored the situation and proceeded as if I had the utmost confidence in everybody's loyalty to his work and to his obligations. Oddly enough, it was from Brown himself that I got the only set-back to my attempts to carry on effectively.

The *Intent,* as ordered, started about October 20 on the wreck of the Italian ship, *Brenta*. A few days after that, I went out to the south harbor in my boat to see how she was getting along with her diving survey. I clambered aboard her as she lay alongside to port of the *Brenta's* superstructure, about all of that wreck which was showing above the sea. I found everyone in a state of great excitement.

A few minutes before, Buck Scougale (now undressed on deck) tended on the bottom by Muzzy, also in a diving rig, had hurriedly been hauled up at his own request long before he had completed his diving inspection. No other diver now was down. Buck himself told me why.

"Cap'n," said wiry little Buck in even more rapid-fire tones than usual, "I dived a short while ago to inspect her port side from outside, and Muzzy went down with me to tend my lines on the bottom. It's about eight fathoms to the bottom—not much to bother about. We was both walking along in the mud, pretty tough going, pushing through the water close aboard her port side, when we came to a big bomb hole in her side—a hell of a big hole—opening into her number two hold.

"I took a look at that hole, with the plating blown outboard all around, and I figured I might as well use it for an entrance to see what the number two hold looked like from inside. So I put my helmet against Muzzy's and told him to stay outside and tend my lines while I went in.

"Muzzy got it, all right, so I left him and walked right on through the side of that ship from the bottom outside her, as easy as if I was going through a big garage door. Of course, the minute I went through her side, it got darker in the water inside her, with only the light coming down through the sea into that hold from her flooded cargo hatches above. But after a minute or so, my eyes got used to it so I could see well enough again and I went ahead slow through the water over her floor boards to see what might be inside that hold.

"And then, Cap'n," exclaimed Buck excitedly, "I damn near walked straight into a submarine mine! There it was, detonating horns sticking out all over it, and me about to walk smack into it in my diving rig and explode the damned thing!

"I stopped dead, took one good look to make sure, and, Cap'n, believe me, I went flying through the water out o' that hold through the hole in her side out onto the ocean floor again so fast I knocked Muzzy out there flat in the mud before he could even duck! And without waiting for Muzzy to pull himself out of it, I gave 'em four jerks on my lifeline, to haul me the hell up and out o' there right now!"

So the scuttled *Brenta* had an unexploded Italian submarine mine, not a bomb, still inside its number two hold! I knew I could believe what Buck Scougale told me—he was one of the two best divers I had in Massawa, if not absolutely the best, and subject to no nightmares on the bottom. If Buck said he had seen a mine down there, I knew he had seen a mine, not just a waterlogged cask which, distorted in the murky water, might to less practiced diving eyes than his have been imagined into anything.

Well, if we had a submarine mine inside the *Brenta,* standing in the middle of an open hold where we should have to work in patching the hole in the side of that hold, there was nothing to be done save to remove the mine before we proceeded further. But to avoid blowing up the diver in the process and probably our salvage ship too (for a mine carries about twice the explosive charge of a bomb), not to mention so damaging our wreck as to make further salvage on her fruitless even if some of us survived, it was necessary to know all about that mine before we touched it.

Particularly was this so, if by any chance the Eyties had rigged that mine up as a booby trap to destroy us, which might well be the case, seeing that a naval mine had no normal reason for being in the middle of the cargo hold of a merchant ship, even of a scuttled one. Before we went any further, I had to learn all about that mine. Buck, when I should ask him, could give me a rough idea of its size and type, I knew.

The British Navy had data on all enemy mines. From Buck's description, I could identify it on the British ordnance pamphlets and study both how to remove it without exploding it, and also everything the Eyties might have done to its mechanism to make a booby trap of it. But for the present, we had to leave it alone.

So I ordered Brown to discontinue diving on the *Brenta,* and to return with his excited crew to the Naval Base, there to cool off while I read up on Italian mines. It might take several days. Meanwhile, they could all rest. I got back into my boat, and Glen Galvin shoved off with me from the *Intent* while Brown prepared to cast off himself.

Acting through Commander Davy, liaison officer, I had the British fly an explosives officer, a Royal Navy lieutenant, from Alex, loaded with all the pamphlets the British had on enemy mines. He arrived the next evening.

From a somewhat more detailed description of that mine and its lead horns, which Buck Scougale gladly gave us, Commander Davy, the explosives lieutenant, and I were able to identify it as a specific type of Italian mine. Thanking Buck for his aid, we let him go, while the three of us started an intensive study of that mine and every detail of its mechanism and design, however insignificant—a process which took us most of the night.

The explosives lieutenant was quite excited over the situation. While he had a great deal of information on that type of mine, all obtained by British intelligence men through captured or purloined Italian documents, never had they had in their hands one of those complete mines. Here was his golden opportunity as an explosives expert. If only I could recover that mine intact for him, he wanted to dissect it—as effervescent over the prospect as an entomologist about to ensnare in his net an entirely new species of butterfly!

He warned me on all the dangers, all the possibilities of exploding that mine, kept cautioning me on how to avoid damaging it. His earnestness made me smile. It was easy to observe that, all unconsciously on his part, his concern over that mine was for an entirely different reason from my own—if we got ourselves blown up, his tears would be shed over the lost mine, not over us.

By next morning, I knew enough about that mine and how to handle it, including all its booby trap possibilities, to feel willing to go out and remove it, doing all the diving on it myself, if necessary. Pending the arrival aboard the *Intent* of Commander Davy and the explosives lieutenant, who were to go along with us, I started in to tell Brown of the preliminaries necessary, before we shoved off for the *Brenta* and the south harbor.

That was when I received my first real shock in Massawa. For the first time in all my salvage experience, I heard a salvage master saying he wouldn't tackle a salvage job because it was too dangerous! The *Intent* would not cast loose to work further on the *Brenta!*

The way Brown put it was interesting—he put the blame on his crew. They were all afraid of that mine on the *Brenta* and wouldn't go near it again; it was too dangerous. And, of course, he couldn't make them.

While Brown, the man who aspired to take over my job, was blandly telling me all that, I observed him with great interest. So here was the man who thought he was competent to take over the whole operation, claiming he was incompetent to get his own salvage crew to work in the face of danger! He wasn't refusing to go himself, only his crew wouldn't go! The situation made me laugh inwardly, but outwardly, I only listened gravely to the most astonishing statement I had ever heard from a salvage officer.

Of course, I didn't believe his crew was afraid to go if properly led. There wasn't a man in the twelve of them alongside whom I hadn't myself worked and sweated and stared danger in the face with—I knew them all. They weren't cowards. I could muster that crew on deck, point out to them I didn't believe they were the cowards their captain said they were, show them the need in the middle of a war of ignoring danger, and then lead them to work on the *Brenta,* to do the diving myself to encourage them.

But if I did that, Brown's value to me as a salvage master was going to be forever destroyed, and I had too few salvage masters in Massawa to risk losing one of them, however much of a weak-sister in some directions he was proving himself to be. Besides, all the circumstances surrounding salvage at that moment were in a distressing state, and pending action shortly expected on Major MacAlarney's arrival from Cairo, I had no desire to make them any worse.

So I merely lifted my eyebrows over Brown's strange story and told him not to be concerned over his crew. I'd let the *Brenta* go till a little later. Meanwhile, I'd send the *Intent* out on an easy job I'd been saving for a rainy day—no explosives, no bomb holes, no patching— something any salvage man should be able to do almost in his sleep. That would give his crew a chance to get over their case of nerves, and then we'd tackle the *Brenta* again.

The ship to be raised was the Italian *S.S. Tripolitania*, a moderate-sized passenger ship scuttled, not in Massawa itself, but in the Daklak Islands forty miles offshore. She was one of that group of wrecks which Lieutenant Fairbairn, our British Navy pilot, who had almost died out there, had urged long ago that I must see.

Several months before, I had decided to take Fairbairn's advice. But not wanting to waste too much time covering those widespread islands, I had accepted an invitation from Squadron Leader Featherstonehaugh of the R.A.F., liaison officer between ourselves and O.E.T.A., to fly me out over those islands in his plane while I made my survey from the air.

So, in an R.A.F. plane, I had gone out with Featherstonehaugh (popularly known among us as "Feathers") and he had very thoroughly covered the islands for me at low altitude so I could see all the wrecks. As Fairbairn had maintained, there certainly was a fine lot of wrecks out there, but the day had long gone by when looking at more wrecks developed any enthusiasm in me. I had wrecks enough in Massawa harbor. So other than noting down how many there were— six—where they lay, and their approximate depths and conditions as regards future salvage, I had paid little attention till my eyes lighted on the wreck of the *Tripolitania*. Then I became suddenly interested. For over an hour, Feathers wheeled and circled to fly me as low as he dared over that wreck while I observed her from all angles.

No explosives, I knew, had been used on any of the wrecks scuttled in the Daklak Islands—they had been sunk in as deep water as possible simply by opening seacocks. But the Eyties had certainly bungled the job on the *Tripolitania*. Easily observed from the air, she lay right on the edge of a shelf off which the water deepened suddenly. But in going down, she had hit bottom on the shelf, not off it, and there she lay with her main deck hardly awash at low tide, no holes in her. All that was necessary to lift her was to seal off seachests outside as usual, close a lot of open airports in her hull, and pump her out. Of course, the usual precautions to avoid her capsizing while she was being lifted would be required, but that was all. Almost all that was necessary to lift the *Tripolitania* was a diver to seal up outside and some buckets to bail her out with.

I came back with Feathers in his plane from the Daklak Islands with the *Tripolitania* in my mind as a job to be held in reserve for a rainy day—a task on which I should some day send out a salvage crew when my men got so worn from real wrecks in Massawa that they needed a rest.

So after listening to Brown's comments on the refusal of his crew to face the dangers on the *Brenta,* I decided a fine solution for many reasons would be to send both Brown and the *Intent* out to salvage the *Tripolitania*. No salvage man could with a straight face refuse to work on her. And while the job lasted, about a week more or less, Brown and his ship, the storm center of all my morale troubles, would be far removed in the Daklak Islands from any communication with those ingenious thinkers in Asmara till after Major MacAlarney had arrived in Massawa and squelched that morale-shattering order.

I gave Brown the *Tripolitania* job and his orders regarding her. I wasn't going out to her; there was no necessity for it on such a simple job. After loading up a barge for him with all the pumps and salvage gear he might conceivably need for the job, I sent him away toward the end of October, towing the barge, headed for the Daklak Islands and the *Tripolitania*.

Meanwhile, I had to advise Commander Davy and the explosives lieutenant that unfortunately the *Brenta* was delayed a couple of weeks; however, after that, we'd certainly recover that mine, so as not to disappoint our connoisseur in explosives. He left for Alex, to return when advised.

CHAPTER

51

ON OCTOBER 14, THE DAY AFTER THE abortive attempt of the contractor to take over control of salvage, I decided the time had come to undertake the lifting of the sunken derrick alongside the quay in the commercial harbor. This was the ex-Italian floating crane which Captain McCance had twice failed to raise, and the demolition of which he had consequently recommended to the British Admiralty. With McCance's contract canceled, the crane was now mine to salvage and I concluded that with all my salvage forces back from Asmara, I had better start on it or the British might think I was no better than McCance, who had wasted some nine months on it.

The lifting of that crane, with its main deck irreparably damaged in its watertightness and airtightness by McCance in his two failures, presented now a very unusual salvage problem. In its original undamaged condition, as it lay on the bottom scuttled with open sea valves, it might easily have been prepared for lifting and lifted by any competent salvage officer who understood the factors involved, in any one of three ways.

The simplest way would have been to have used compressed air, as I did on the two sunken dry docks, with the addition of proper air escapes to take care of decreasing outside water pressures as the hull of the crane floated up. This required considerable knowledge of how compressed air acted on a wreck.

The next simplest method would have been by a combination of pumping and compressed air, still requiring considerable skill.

The hardest method, though the one which would ordinarily be used by a man knowing little of salvage, would be by sealing up the hatches in the submerged main deck, shoring up inside, and pumping out. This was the method McCance had twice tried and twice failed on, damaging the deck of the crane badly, though a good salvage man could, with considerable intelligent diving work before lifting, have done it successfully.

But now, all three of these methods were out, for no longer could the main deck of the crane hull be made either airtight or watertight —not after McCance and his men got through with it. There was no longer any chance of making the crane buoyant, either by pumping or by using compressed air, so that it would float up of itself.

There remained only one other possible way to raise that crane— it had to be lifted from the bottom of the sea as a dead weight of some 400 to 600 tons (its exact weight was unknown to anybody). But there wasn't a crane in Massawa that could lift over 15 tons, and very few anywhere in the world that could even lift 300 tons, so using floating cranes or derricks for the lift was out. Since also there wasn't any tide in Massawa to speak of (only one to three feet rise and fall), no help could be expected of the tide (a favorite British salvage method) by using surface barges secured to the wreck at low tide and lifting with it as the tide rose.

There remained as the solitary means of raising that derrick, the use of submersible pontoons. These are huge specially built horizontal steel cylinders, which can be flooded and sunk down alongside the wreck, secured to it by cradle slings of heavy wire or chain passed under it, and then made to lift the wreck by expelling all the water from inside the pontoons with compressed air. If everything is handled properly, the buoyant pontoons will then rise to the surface, bringing up the wreck with them hanging in its cradle of slings.

It so happened that my first (and most prominent) salvage job had been the submarine *S-51* back in 1925, where I had used the pontoon method to raise a 1200-ton smashed submarine sunk in deep water in the open Atlantic off Block Island. On that difficult pioneer task, I, then a lieutenant commander, had been Salvage Officer; and interestingly enough the Officer in Charge of the Salvage Squadron, then Captain Ernest King, was now, as Admiral Ernest King, Commander-in-Chief of the Navy.

At any rate, on that task, I had learned all about pontoons and their idiosyncrasies (which are many, and which on the *S-51* nearly stumped me and my divers). After successfully raising the *S-51*, I had finished my career in the regular Navy by designing pontoons which didn't have any idiosyncrasies. It was the pontoons I had used on the

[443]

S-51, rebuilt to that design, which later were used by the Navy in lifting the sunken submarine *S-4* off Provincetown and the *Squalus* off Portsmouth. So if there was anything at all on which I might claim to be an "expert," it was on pontoons and their use. (The average salvage officer knows very little about them or their behavior in action.)

The only drawback to the use of pontoons in lifting that sunken derrick in Massawa was that there weren't any pontoons in Massawa. Nor so far as could be discovered, were there any pontoons anywhere else in Africa, nor could any be obtained from elsewhere. And it was perfectly obvious to anyone that there wasn't available anywhere the steel out of which to build pontoons either, not to mention the lack of skilled labor also. It would take a lot of both.

So the problem of raising that invaluable sunken derrick came down to raising it with pontoons that didn't exist and couldn't be built, or in not raising it at all. I suppose it was at that point in his reasoning that Captain McCance had arrived when he advised the Admiralty to demolish the crane with explosives, and at least clear the berth it was blocking.

I determined to use pontoons to lift the derrick and to provide them shortly in spite of the non-existence of pontoons and of the steel and labor needed to build any.

So, in preparation for the task, I broke the *Resolute* off the salvage job on the *Moncalieri,* and sent her around with Ervin Johnson, her solitary diver, to the commercial harbor to begin work on the sunken crane. I put Captain Reed, my most experienced and competent salvage master, in charge of the operation, gave him Captain Roys, salvage officer on the *Resolute,* as his assistant, and started them off. Their first job would be to sweep under the sunken crane four one-inch diameter steel wires which later could be used to haul under her hull the much heavier wire hawsers needed for the actual cradle slings. Getting those four messenger wires under the hull was going to be a very tough job, requiring them to be sawed back and forth through the mud, coral, and debris, on which that sunken crane was resting, till they were under her in the proper positions.

I figured that getting those wires sawed underneath would take Bill Reed and Frank Roys and the *Resolute's* whole crew a couple of weeks, by the end of which time, I'd have the pontoons necessary to go ahead with the job.

For oddly enough, all the pontoons required for that job had been lying right there in Massawa under everybody's nose for over a year, unused for anything. The difficulty had been that no one had ever recognized them as pontoons. Every time anyone looked at them (and they were so big you couldn't avoid seeing them), they had always thought they were looking at a row of huge horizontal cylindrical storage tanks for aviation gasoline.

On the edge of Massawa was the very large ex-Italian military airfield (unused since the surrender) which had received the careful attention of the R.A.F. during the bombardments from the air prior to Massawa's capitulation. Squadron Leader Featherstonehaugh himself had flown one of the attacking bombers; whether it had been he or one of his fellow pilots who had scored the hit, I didn't know. But at any rate, one of them had succeeded in scoring a direct hit with a moderate-sized bomb on one of a row of eight mammoth horizontal cylindrical tanks which the Eyties had provided on the edge of the airfield for storing their aviation gasoline.

The results of that bomb hit must have been startling. The bomb had knocked out the head of one of those eleven foot diameter by forty-five foot long cylindrical tanks, each capable of holding 30,000 gallons of gasoline, and had poured thousands and thousands of gallons of gasoline out on the ground where, of course, it promptly all ignited from the bomb. The effects of the ensuing conflagration were still visible on the seven unhit tanks. They had all been instantly enveloped in a sea of flames, which must have made them all red-hot, for the steel plates forming the upper part of every one of those cylinders was now corrugated like a gigantic washboard.

That disaster had ended the usefulness of the airfield. With no storage there for gasoline any more, the R.A.F., when it had taken over, had never seen fit to repair the gasoline storage tanks for use again, and they, together with the airfield, had lain unused now for eighteen months.

When shortly after my arrival in Massawa, my eye had first lighted on those idle gasoline tanks, I recognized them instantly for what they were to a salvage man—pontoons ready at hand for my use should I ever need any for a salvage job. Of course, they would need some modifications and repairs to fit them for use, but it would be only a minor job. Now that I needed some pontoons, there they still were waiting for me, the biggest pontoons I had ever seen, far larger than those used on submarine salvage operations. Each tank, as a pontoon, could exert a lift of a little over 100 tons.

Of course, there were drawbacks to their use. The Eyties, when building them simply as gasoline storage tanks, had neglected also to provide them with the hawsepipes necessary for their use as pontoons, with the internal bulkheads required for stability, and with the lifting eyes and the air connections required, but so much of that as was absolutely imperative, my mechanics in the Naval Base shops could easily install. That didn't concern me much.

What really was a drawback, was that I neither owned the airfield nor its gasoline storage tanks, none of which, not being on the Abd-El-Kader Peninsula, was under my jurisdiction. It must, of course, all belong now to some one of the various British military organizations in Eritrea, and I set out to learn which, so that I could obtain official permission to take the unused tanks off the airfield and use them as pontoons for a while.

I wasted three whole days trying to find out who legally owned those damaged tanks. Everybody passed. Colonel Sundius-Smith, British Army Commander in Massawa, didn't own them. Captain Lucas of the Royal Navy didn't own them. The R.A.F. senior officer in Asmara didn't own them. Neither did Brigadier Longrigg, the Military Governor of Eritrea. I finally learned they were probably under the jurisdiction of an R.A.F. lieutenant in Massawa, attached to headquarters in Cairo, where the R.A.F. air marshal was reserving them for future R.A.F. use in Egypt.

I went to see the R.A.F. lieutenant to get his permission to take the tanks for a month or so, only to learn he'd gone a few days before somewhere into the Sudan, and wouldn't be back for two or three weeks.

Since I couldn't afford to wait two or three weeks, I concluded the best solution was to steal the gasoline tanks without further ado. Since nobody owned them, nobody could give me permission to take them, but they could, and without doubt would, stop me from taking them if I were to ask any non-owner's permission. The other way, the worst that could happen if I were caught at it before I got through was to make me put them back in the airfield and if they did that, the Royal Navy would never get its floating derrick.

Now stealing half a dozen gasoline tanks, each as big as a Pullman car, is nothing lightly to be undertaken. It requires some equipment and I had none. But Pat Murphy, the first construction superintendent in Massawa, who was back on his feet again and sympathetic toward anyone still suffering in Massawa, occasionally visited the scene of his own early troubles, and I persuaded him to lend me some of the contractor's heavy equipment for a few days and say nothing about it. (Not that I made him an accomplice by informing him I was stealing the tanks.) So Pat arranged for me with his successor as construction superintendent, the loan of a couple of heavy crawler cranes, some low-bodied trucks, and the necessary men.

With all this equipment, in two days, I stole six gasoline tanks off their concrete foundations near the deserted airfield, brazenly hauled them in broad daylight some four miles down Massawa's main street, and unloaded all six of them on the quay close alongside the sunken derrick. There, with a locomotive crane belonging on the quay, I could lift them overboard into the water whenever I had the changes finished that I required to make them into pontoons.

While Bill Reed and Frank Roys were struggling to saw messenger wires under the sunken derrick, I brought Lloyd Williams and a few salvage mechanics over from repairs to the Italian dry docks and started them on making pontoons out of Italian gasoline tanks instead.

The main job was to insert vertically in each tank, one near each end, a pair of hawsepipes to take the lifting slings. These were simply eleven-foot lengths of heavy ten-inch diameter steel pipe, welded watertight top and bottom into the gasoline tanks to give a vertical hole through them through which the cradle slings might pass.

Then, we also welded lifting eyes to each end on top, securing eyes to each end on the bottom, provided connections for one-inch air hoses on top of each tank, and fitted a six-inch valve at each end on the bottom. These last were to allow the water to flow out at the bottom of the tank when we forced compressed air in at its top, thus making the tank buoyant when we wanted it to rise.

I didn't do anything to those huge gasoline tanks that wasn't absolutely necessary, keeping the work down to the barest minimum that would give me a set of six of the crudest and flimsiest pontoons that any salvage man ever saw. They would be full of idiosyncrasies when it came to handling them, but that had to be expected.

I had been working on the conversion of these tanks about a week after I had purloined them, and had even got so far as to try one of them out under the sea (with none too encouraging results either) when it occurred to me one morning that there was one other possibility of ownership I hadn't thought of. Considering that I ought to keep salvage on as reputable a basis as possible, I decided to investigate that avenue at once and, if possible, get formal authority, which long since I had learned in dealing with the formal British, was of major importance.

So, on going to my office, I called up the local representative of the Shell Oil Company, the official British source of supply in Eritrea for all petroleum products. After all, my new pontoons had once been meant for oil tanks; perhaps the Shell Oil Company knew who officially owned them.

At last, I found I had hit the right people. Strange, I had not thought of them before. Yes, Shell was acting as representative of the R.A.F. headquarters in Cairo; the Shell manager in Asmara knew all about those tanks; if I called him there, he had complete power over them.

So, with the usual delays, Mrs. Maton got the Shell manager in Asmara on the phone for me. Yes, he controlled the airfield gasoline tanks as agent for the R.A.F. in Cairo. His orders with respect to them were that in a month or two, when a ship with a big enough deck was available, he was to get them to the waterfront, load them aboard ship, and send them all to Alex, where they were to be sent by rail to some new R.A.F. airfield then building in the Sudan.

I asked him to lend six of them to me for a month for my salvage job, pointing out the great advantages that would accrue, both to the Royal Navy and to himself from such a loan. The Royal Navy would get the sunken derrick. As for himself, if he approved the loan, I would save him all the trouble of getting the tanks from the airfield down on the quay (which he had to agree would be a troublesome job), repair all the leaks in them for him, and deliver them to him all ready for use again as gasoline tanks—all this without the slightest labor on his part. That all of these things were already done to those tanks, I felt it unwise to advise him of, trembling in my boots meanwhile that he might want to come from Asmara to Massawa to look the tanks over on the airfield before deciding.

To my great relief, however, my proposal sounded so attractive to him, that as agent for the R.A.F., he gave me immediate permission to proceed to remove the tanks, which permission he would immediately confirm by letter. I thanked him and hung up. Everything with my new pontoons was now according to Hoyle; I was an honest man again. I had that most valuable of all things in dealing with military authorities—official permission from someone on high, authorized to grant it.

And none too soon either, it swiftly turned out. Hardly had I cleaned up a few other matters in my office, which took about an hour, and was preparing to return to my pontoons on the quay over in the commercial harbor for the rest of the morning, than my phone rang and Mrs. Maton, answering it, looked up at me to announce,

"Colonel Sundius-Smith wishes to speak to you, Captain Ellsberg."

Colonel Sundius-Smith commanded all the British Forces in Massawa, a very fine officer. I had had from him a most sympathetic personal letter the month before on the occasion of the death of Horace Armstrong. What, I wondered, did he want of me now?

I swiftly learned. In a very grieved voice, Colonel Sundius-Smith regretted he had to call my attention to something that pained him greatly. Six large gasoline tanks had disappeared suddenly from the airfield and it had been reliably reported to him that at that very moment, those identical gasoline tanks were in possession of my men down on the commercial quay, miles away from where they belonged. While, of course, the colonel admitted that he didn't own the tanks, still he knew very well that I didn't either, and they certainly were British property, as prizes of war. As senior British officer on the spot, it was his duty to see that such things did not go on in His Majesty's occupied territories. Much as it hurt him to say so, I must return those tanks to the airfield at once and he would overlook my dereliction.

I felt almost like the heroine in the melodrama, who is cut loose and dragged off the railroad tracks just as The Limited roars by. In the most innocent manner possible, I replied:

"Why, Colonel, you don't mean to imply you think I'd have taken those tanks without official permission, do you? Of course, I have it. Those tanks were in the custody of the Shell manager in Asmara as representative of R.A.F. headquarters in Cairo. I have the Shell manager's official permission to take those tanks. I'll see you get a copy of his official authorization for your records."

Colonel Sundius-Smith apologized handsomely for ever having given such a vicious insinuation about a brother officer the slightest credence. Yes, just so nobody else, if he were away, bothered me again over the matter, he'd be glad to have a copy of my official permission for his files. And with more profuse apologies, which I accepted, he hung up.

I wiped the sweat off my brow. Saved in the nick of time, by the grace of God! My salvage job could proceed!

I got up to leave my office.

"Mrs. Maton," I said, "as soon as that Shell man's permission comes down tomorrow from Asmara, you see that Colonel Sundius-Smith gets a copy of it immediately!"

She smiled a Mona Lisa smile, and it struck me suddenly that she very much resembled that woman. What was Mrs. Maton thinking of behind that enigmatic smile, I wondered? After all, she was the wife of the Royal Navy's intelligence officer in Massawa. How long were all the scandalous goings-on amongst us Americans going to remain a secret from the British?

CHAPTER

52

Hⓞwever, i didn't get over to the commercial harbor that morning, nor that day either.

It appeared that Captain Reed, before going over to the sunken crane that morning, had, as usual with him, paid a routine visit to the *Gera* to check on conditions aboard her. The *Gera*, for want of a better berth, now that both the *Liebenfels* and the *Frauenfels* had the only decent moorings for large ships inside the naval harbor, was temporarily tied up alongside the starboard side of the large Italian dry dock, there to await the day when I had workmen enough in Massawa to dry-dock and repair her.

On my way down to the Naval Base pier to get my boat for the trip to the commercial harbor, I met Captain Reed on his way up to my office. He looked very grave.

"Captain," he informed me, "I was just going up to get you. You'd better come out to the *Gera* right away. I think we're in danger of losing her!"

Naturally on that I went double time to the pier, as did Reed. I told Galvin to make knots with his boat for the *Gera*. Then I asked Reed what was the matter.

"That patch McCance and his limeys put on her side forward, looks to me as if it's likely to give way any minute. The upper part of it's only wood covered with canvas; she was on the bottom so long after they got the patch on before they raised her, that the teredos must have eaten most of the wood up. Anyway, the leak through it has been increasing the last few days. This morning, she's leaking so bad, a six-inch pump can hardly keep up with it. I took a look at that patch; it looks to me as if it might fall to pieces and let go any minute. If it does, the *Gera*'ll sink right alongside the big Eytie dry dock and we'll have to salvage her all over again!"

When I boarded the *Gera*, I found what Reed had said was so; to save the *Gera* from possible foundering, it was necessary to dry-dock her immediately, whether I had any mechanics to work on her or not. There was no help for it.

We had a British armed supply ship on the Persian dry dock, but at noon she would be finished and the dry dock flooded down to undock that vessel. The dry dock would then be clear. I sent word over to Spanner, the dockmaster, that instead of taking the next supply ship waiting in the outer harbor, the *Gera* would be docked instead. But because of the enormous amount of cement McCance's men had poured into her port side to form the lower parts of their patches, and also because of about 500 tons of rock ballast he had heaved into her holds during his futile attempts to make her stand up, the *Gera* was drawing quite a lot of water. The Persian dock would have to be flooded down more than normal to dock her at all. I would let Spanner know later just how far he would have to flood down to permit the *Gera* to come on.

Meanwhile, Reed was starting up salvage pumps in every hold, both as a precaution and to get her as dry and as light in draft as possible for going on the dock. While that was being done, my boat was hastily dispatched to the commercial harbor to come back with Lloyd Williams and all the salvage mechanics there. At the same time, every salvage man working on the Italian dry docks was rushed aboard the *Gera* to help stand by the pumps in case of trouble.

Water was pouring through that worm-eaten patch like a sieve, two pumps in that hold were now running all out to hold the water down. I could only hope nothing worse happened over the next couple of hours till we got the dry dock cleared and the *Gera* on it.

Another hour went by. I had a sizeable gang of my salvage men aboard the *Gera* by then, all stationed for trouble. The Persian dock was being flooded down. Lieutenant Fairbairn came into the naval harbor with his tugboats to take the supply ship out. I waved him alongside the *Gera* and advised him to come back aboard the *Gera* the moment he had the other vessel through the wrecks at the harbor entrance, and to bring back his tugs also for an emergency docking— the *Gera* was in precarious condition. He waved his acknowledgment.

Soon, the supply ship was freely afloat and Fairbairn was taking her out. On deck of the *Gera*, we began singling the hawsers holding her alongside the big dry dock, so that the moment Fairbairn got back with his tugs, we could quickly cast off and depart for docking.

Bob Steele had already been around the *Gera* in a skiff, checking at bow and stern the draft marks on her. She was going to cause us plenty of trouble in docking. She was drawing, by far, more water than any vessel we had ever taken on the Persian dry dock; considerably more, in fact, than that dry dock was built to accommodate. To drag the *Gera* into that dry dock clear of the keel blocks, the dry dock would have to be flooded down two feet deeper than it was designed to go, even more than I had taken it down when I had docked the listing *Liebenfels*.

Still, there was no help for it. A little of the dry dock, not much, would yet remain showing above water—so little, it might raise anybody's hair to look at it. But by now I knew that Persian dry dock well. I was sure I could get away with it without losing the Persian dry dock, and it was either taking a chance in doing that, or be sure of losing the *Gera*. Already, there were wrecks enough on the bottom without adding to their number. So I sent Bob Steele over to inform Spanner of the bad news—as soon as the other ship was clear, he was to flood the Persian dry dock down two whole feet more than normal and await the *Gera*. I would myself direct the docking of the *Gera* from aboard her, as I dared not leave her. If her patch let go and she started to founder before we succeeded in getting her on the dry dock, I wanted to be aboard her for what fighting chance my salvage men, Captain Reed, and I might have to keep her afloat, even though we could no longer dry-dock her immediately.

Steele had gone to convey the message and for some time since had been back with me. Fairbairn had taken the other ship out and now with three tugs, was coming in to haul us away and line us up for going on the dry dock.

I looked over toward the Persian dock, only a hundred yards off to starboard. I could see it still lacked a foot of being flooded down far enough for the job.

"Bob!" I ordered Steele. "Take my boat and get over to that dry dock at once. Tell Spanner to take her down that last foot immediately. We're about to start for the dry dock!"

"Aye, aye, sir!" Steele slid down the Jacob's ladder from the *Gera's* deck into my boat and shoved off. A tug came alongside, Fairbairn clambered aboard us to pilot us out, we began taking hawsers from the tugs. In a few minutes, the tugs were secured, Fairbairn was shrilling out signals to them on his whistle, and we had cast loose. The *Gera* was underway, to be dragged toward the harbor entrance, swung about there to point her bow for the dry dock, and then towed up to it.

I begged Fairbairn for once to throw his usual prudence to the winds and hurry; our case was desperate and every minute might mean the difference between success and disaster. If the *Gera's* patch let go while we were maneuvering in front of the dry dock, she might founder there, blocking the only approach to the dock and putting it out of commission for weeks till we could repatch and salvage the *Gera* again. He *must* hurry. Fairbairn agreed.

And then at that moment, when we had drawn well clear of our mooring, my boat ran back alongside the *Gera* and looking down into it, I could see Bob Steele waving frantically up at me. I leaned over the *Gera's* bridge rail and asked:

"What's the matter?"

"Spanner won't take the dry dock down any farther!" Steele shouted up at me to make himself heard amidst the puffing of the tugs. "He says it's too dangerous!"

Too dangerous! I was getting sick of those words. First, from my American salvage captain, now from my English dockmaster! Didn't they realize there was a war going on, and danger for everybody was part of his job? But, whereas with Brown on the *Brenta* and her mine, I could afford to be diplomatic and take a little time to iron out the situation, with Spanner and the dry dock I couldn't afford to waste a minute. The *Gera* was underway for the dry dock. In twenty minutes, she would be coming on it. The dry dock by then had to be low enough to take her aboard or catastrophe would overwhelm us all.

Savagely, I shouted down to Steele so there might be no misunderstanding of what I meant:

"Get back aboard the dry dock at once! Tell Spanner I shouldn't leave the *Gera* and I don't want to! But tell him if he doesn't take that dry dock down another foot instantly, I'm coming aboard that dry dock personally to heave him overboard! Then, I'll take the dock down myself! Don't wait for Spanner's answer, Bob. Come right back here with the boat so I can have it if I need it. I don't need to know his answer. I can see from here whether he obeys or not. I want that boat back immediately for my use in case he doesn't! Shove off now, and see Spanner doesn't misunderstand me!"

Steele waved he understood and Glen Galvin raced away with him over the short stretch of water to the dry dock, from which the *Gera* now was steadily drawing away as the tugs dragged her out toward the harbor entrance to wind her about for a proper approach. Through Fairbairn's binoculars, I saw Steele climb aboard the upper deck of the dry dock, which required only that he step from the gunwale of my boat directly onto the deck—the flooded dry dock was already so low in the water—and start talking to Spanner. Steele, I knew, I could rely on to make my meaning clear.

Steele wasted little time on it. I saw him turn abruptly from Spanner, jump back aboard the boat, and start back for the *Gera*. I could see through the glasses, Spanner standing in indecision a moment or so, then start for the dry dock control house where the flood valves were operated. I dropped the glasses. My boat was nearly back now, but I shouldn't need it. It wasn't going to be necessary for me to heave Spanner overboard. The dry dock started slowly to sink down that last all-important foot, leaving hardly any of her side walls still visible above the sea. I could keep my attention on the *Gera*.

As swiftly as the tugs could do it, Fairbairn wound the *Gera* end for end as water from the pumps below battling the leakage poured overboard, straightened her away on the approach to the dock. The *Hsin Rocket* puffed mightily ahead of her to drag her up to it.

The bow of the *Gera* nosed up to the entrance, we picked up a headline from the dry dock, and the *Hsin Rocket* sidled off to port to get clear, while the two tugs astern kept shepherding us to hold the ship properly in line as slowly our bow was dragged in between the two side walls of the dry dock.

Looking down from the *Gera's* bridge, where I then took over from Fairbairn, now that the ship was entering the dry dock, I could see what little of my Persian dock remained above the surface—what there was of it resembled two long but almost awash rafts stretching ahead to starboard and to port of me. There wasn't more than 300 tons of reserve buoyancy in that dry dock left showing above the sea. If anything went wrong now to put any load on that dry dock before we could pump her up again, the Persian dry dock would suddenly go down those last few inches like a rock, to become a salvage job herself.

Slowly, carefully, I directed the Hindoos, the Persians, and the Eritreans on those dry dock walls as they handled the hawsers to drag us forward and to help keep us centered along the line of unseen keel blocks beneath us. The *Gera* was a wide beamed ship, as well as a deep draft one. There wasn't much clearance on the sides as she dragged ahead through the water into the dock. To make matters worse, that patch on her forward, which McCance's men had clumsily put on and which was the cause of our present troubles, protruded underwater three feet from the port side, widening her beam by that much, and giving us next to no clearance at all between that patch and the port side of the dry dock as we came on.

With infinite care, I took the *Gera* into the barely afloat dry dock, praying that nothing might happen to that patch till we got her in position and the dry dock pumps started. For now, if the patch carried away for any reason, it would be worst of all. Over 1000 tons of water would pour instantaneously into the number two hold. Even if we managed to keep the *Gera* from sinking altogether, that sudden extra load would bring her down on the keel blocks, now only inches clear of her keel, and sink the dry dock right from under her, with the *Gera* most probably ending up by sinking completely herself squarely on top of it—a terrible mess to have to salvage, one wreck atop another.

Hardly daring to breathe, in which sad state I knew all my salvage men aboard the *Gera* and the dry dock crew were, as well as I, I maneuvered the *Gera* cautiously ahead. I had her three-quarters entered with everything going well when, for no apparent reason at all, she ceased moving forward. I ordered Spanner on the dry dock to heave just a bit harder on the headline, not much.

He did. The ship didn't move. Evidently that patch to port had caught on something below water inside the dry dock, either at the side or underneath. I dared not heave hard ahead for fear of tearing loose that decrepit patch, least of all now when it would do the most harm, so I ordered the headline slacked off to relieve any possible strain on that fouled patch.

Then for the next hour I went through hell as gingerly I struggled to clear that disintegrating patch of the unseen obstruction below without using any force which might collapse it. By hand only now on all our lines, we struggled as if we were walking on eggs, to haul the ship to starboard, to haul her a little astern, to get the patch clear of whatever it was hung up on. There was no obvious reason why she should have caught on anything there; already that patch had cleared three-quarters of the length of the dock. But stuck it was, and obstinately stuck it remained in the face of what trifling force I dared use to free it.

Nobody said a word. Every order I gave was instantly obeyed. Even Spanner on the port drydock wall, who must have considered this the verification of all his fears, struggled manfully and whole-heartedly to help free the recalcitrant *Gera* of whatever it was that was holding her and us in that terribly dangerous position.

Suddenly, at the end of that agonizing hour, with no reason any more apparent for her going than for her stopping before, the *Gera* moved slowly ahead once more. Breathing a prayer of thankfulness, I dragged her forward the last hundred feet into the dry dock, hurriedly centered her over the keel blocks, and waved to Spanner to start up all the dry dock pumps full power.

It took but a few turns of those powerful pumps to float the dry dock up enough to bring the keel blocks into contact with the *Gera's* keel. In a few more minutes, the *Gera* was herself slowly rising from the water while we ran in the side spur shores, hauled the side bilge blocks in under her hull for side support, and wedged up a few extra shores from the dry dock walls to the *Gera's* sides to make sure she did no listing on us while she rose.

In another hour, we had the dry dock and the *Gera* in her both high up out of water, all danger of any nature over. I looked at that exposed salvaged wreck as she rode there on the keel blocks, her two patches to port ready now to be torn away and repaired permanently with steel plating. I felt as if the dry-docking of that wreck had taken ten years off my life.

With Lloyd Williams beside me, I inspected her blasted port side for what work would be necessary on the dry dock to repair her before we could take her off again. She was sickening to contemplate. McCance's men must have spent most of their six months on her in pouring concrete into her port side double bottoms abreast the holes— there were hundreds of tons of concrete set hard as granite there. It would take us a couple of weeks at least just to remove all that concrete with what pneumatic paving busters I could get, so that we might then go ahead with the repairs to the steel hull.

Actually, if we hadn't finally used some small charges of dynamite on it to break up that mass of concrete, we might still be hammering away on that concrete mountain with our puny cement busters. As it was, it took Lloyd Williams a whole week to get rid of all that concrete, most of it unnecessary for salvage purposes. Then, with every mechanic I had left myself, whom I could throw on the job, and some I must admit I stole from the contractor's work to help, Lloyd Williams turned to to replate with steel the huge holes gaping in the side of the *Gera* where the bombs inside had exploded.

In all that steel work, I was as handicapped as I had been on the *Liebenfels* and on the *Dido* months before by the lack of my new plate shop. There was now a lovely set of masonry residence buildings, a grand mess hall, and a really cozy and spacious recreation room for the contractor's construction forces ashore. But my new plate shop, the only new building I really needed in the Naval Base to get along without back-breaking hand work every time I had a steel plate to fabricate, still gaped unfinished at the sky—roofless, sideless, frontless, and useless.

Lloyd Williams, aided by a fine new American foreman, Charley Journey, whom I had picked up wandering about jobless in the Middle East, and by my old reliable, Bill Cunningham, a tower of strength in himself when it came to steel, managed to get the job of rebuilding the *Gera's* steel sides done in about eight days after the concrete was cleared away, and that wholly without any new plate shop to back him up. I felt sure that if only Horace Armstrong were still alive to work alongside Bill Cunningham, the job might have been done in even half that time.

As it was, the *Gera* went on the dry dock on October 29. On November 14, sixteen days on the dry dock, a remarkably short period considering what had to be done, she came off, her hull completely repaired and sound.

But even so, the day she came off, we had six British supply ships anchored idly off the outer roadstead waiting for the dry dock. I had managed to stop any more from coming from the Mediterranean. I suggested to Commander Davy, pointing out that flotilla of useless ships waiting outside, that if only he could impress on Admiral Harwood's staff in Alex the importance of delivering to me some part of the mechanics, the officers, and some of the steel long since promised me, I could hurriedly put the two salvaged Italian dry docks back into commission and avoid any such holdups in docking in the future.

Perhaps that was what finally got action. At any rate, three days later, seventy British shipyard mechanics, accompanied by Commander Mole and a Royal Navy lieutenant, arrived in Massawa on November 17, all ordered to report to me for work at the U.S. Naval Repair Base in Massawa. Some steel was promised me swiftly to follow them.

For the first time, six months after it had started operations, I had a moderate force of mechanics under my control for my Naval Base, and a couple of naval assistants who knew ships. I could hardly stand it; I had become too used to getting along on a shoe string, and sometimes even without one. If I had known the day they arrived what exactly one week from that day I was to learn, I couldn't have stood it at all.

CHAPTER

53

LLOYD WILLIAMS WITH HIS MISCEL-
laneous little crew of mechanics was in the very middle of the job
on the dry dock on the *Gera,* that is, he had just cleared away the last
of the cement. With his worn-out men, he was contemplating the
formidable steel job that still lay before him. As I marked out for
him where the bomb-damaged plating was to be burned away, someone on deck the dock above shouted for me to look out to sea.

I sidled out from under the *Gera's* bottom, clambered up the high
port side wall of the dry dock to her deck, and looked seaward as
bid. There, some miles out toward the horizon, was the *Intent,* headed
for the naval harbor, with the *Tripolitania,* listed perhaps 5° to port,
in tow astern of her, and the barge full of salvage pumps, towing
astern the *Tripolitania.*

It was November 6. Hastily, I counted on my fingers. This was the
eighth day since the *Intent* had departed for the Daklak Islands.
Brown had done well; I had figured on seven working days lifting the
Tripolitania and he must have done it in six.

I left the *Gera* to Williams and ran ashore, to order out the pilot
and his three tugs—one tug to relieve Brown of that barge tailing his
tow, and the other two to help the pilot bring the newly salvaged
wreck into the naval harbor and moor her alongside the port side
of the smaller Italian dry dock. That was the last berth I had left
available for mooring a wreck. The *Liebenfels* and the *Frauenfels*
were occupying the only two safe berths afloat in the naval harbor
itself. The *Gera,* when she came off the dry dock repaired, would have
to go back to be moored off the starboard side of the large Italian
dry dock. Nothing was left for mooring another ship except that spot
alongside the smaller dock where I intended to put the *Tripolitania.*

After she was in that berth, there wouldn't be another spot in all

Massawa for mooring another salvaged ship—I would have the naval harbor all full of salvaged wrecks and no room for any more.

The only ray of light in that situation was the *Liebenfels*—completed now, with steam up and engines tried, she was ready to go to sea again to do her bit against her late owners, the Nazis, as soon as the promised crew for her arrived in Massawa. Of course, I could never dream of sending her out under her new flag still under her old name, so I had renamed her the *General Russell Maxwell* (though our commanding general in Cairo, in whose honor she was thus named, was completely unaware of it). With that name already painted on both her bows and on her stern, looking bright and new in fresh paint all over her hull, our first salvage prize of war was ready for sea—a complete product of Massawa, salvaged by my salvage forces, repaired and refitted by my Naval Base. All hands in Massawa were quite proud of the *General Russell Maxwell,* part of their contribution toward helping to defeat the Axis.

But sad to relate, I now had to admit that her room was more welcome than her company. I must start pressing for that crew for her in spite of a scarcity of merchant officers and seamen, or I should be in a devil of a predicament over where to stow away the next ship after the *Tripolitania* to be salvaged.

But that at least was for the future. As the *Intent,* dragging the salvaged *Tripolitania,* came in, we welcomed her home to Massawa with all the whistles we had, the loudest of which, interestingly enough, was that of the *General Russell Maxwell,* once herself scuttled by the Axis. The ex-*Liebenfels* sent all the steam of her powerful boilers roaring out her deep-throated whistle, to echo far and wide over all the wrecks still on the bottom in all the three harbors of Massawa, in fervent greeting to our latest anti-Axis recruit, now risen from the depths.

The *Tripolitania* was shortly secured alongside the small dry dock, and the *Intent* moved in to moor herself at her usual berth alongside the naval pier. I went back to the *Gera's* bottom to finish laying out the job there for Williams and his men.

About the middle of the afternoon, I came ashore again from the dry dock to board the *Intent.* There I congratulated Brown on his success, and told him to convey my congratulations to all his crew for a fine job, swiftly done.

Then I got down to business. I didn't mention it to Brown and there was no need of my mentioning it—such things I knew got around Massawa amazingly fast. Having been ashore already a few hours with plenty of time to talk to the contractor's local men, I knew perfectly well Brown knew what had happened during his absence in the Daklak Islands—that Major MacAlarney, contracting officer from Cairo, had been in Massawa and that the piece of paper on which it appeared some people at least had built up fond illusions, had gone into the waste basket where it belonged with other waste paper. The only Officer in Charge of Salvage in Massawa was the one so appointed by General Maxwell.

"Now, Brown," I informed him, "I'm not sending either you or your crew to Asmara for a rest after *this* salvage job. You don't need one. You're staying here in Massawa. Tomorrow, you get your ship straightened out for another job. Day after tomorrow, early, you are all going back on the *Brenta*, to tackle that mine again. You're not afraid any more that your crew is afraid of it, are you?"

"No, sir," answered Brown promptly. "They'll all go."

"That's fine, Brown. I'm certainly glad to hear it. It saves me a little trouble. I was sure a short trip to the Daklak Islands would do you all some good in getting the right point of view. Now, here's the program," and I outlined to him what we should do. I told him to inform his crew of it, send Buck Scougale up to my room that night so I could go over with him the confidential British ordnance pamphlets on that mine, and next morning, we should all start out again for the *Brenta*.

I got hold of Commander Davy when I got ashore, and he retrieved from the guarded safe in the Royal Naval Base, those highly secret documents, meanwhile advising the explosives lieutenant in Alex to start for Massawa again. That night, Buck Scougale and I went over the intricacies of that Italian mine and its potential dangers, while Davy listened.

I started by informing Buck he needn't risk his life on that mine if he didn't want to; I'd be glad to do the diving on it myself. Buck would hear of no such thing; he wanted to do it himself. He had never himself been afraid of that mine. He had been startled enough when first he had seen it, but all he wanted, like any sensible person, was to know as much as possible about the dangers involved in facing it, before he had to face them again.

And while he didn't say so, he knew that he was a far better diver than I was and that there would be considerably less chance of anybody's getting hurt under water if he tackled the mine rather than if I did. At any rate, Buck being perfectly willing to face that mine again, I let it go at that and started to instruct Buck in what every gadget he would encounter on that mine meant and what its possibilities of causing detonation were in normal operation.

After that, I showed Buck every conceivable way in which that mine might be rigged for abnormal operation as a booby trap. Buck took it all in.

The second morning, the *Intent* started back for the south harbor and the *Brenta*. If any member of her crew had ever had the slightest fear of going back there, I could find no trace of it on any of them, as we steamed around Sheikh Said Island into the south harbor and up to the line of wrecks again.

That line of wrecks had changed considerably in appearance since first I had seen it late the March before. Now, in November there were two long gaps in the line, where once had rested the ex-*Liebenfels* and the *Frauenfels*. Soon, I felt, there would be another gap, where rested the hulk of the *Brenta,* alongside which we tied up the *Intent* and prepared for diving.

Buck was dressed in his diving rig. This time he was to enter the *Brenta's* hold by going down from above through the cargo hatches, not from the ocean floor through the bomb hole.

Carefully again, I, who was manning the ship end of his diving telephone, went over his instructions with Buck before his helmet was clapped on. He was to drop down into the hold, clear of the mine, and approach it gradually. He was to examine all around it before he moved toward it to make sure there were no trip wires along the floor boards of that hold which might set off the mine if he stumbled over one. He was to get within one foot of the mine, but no closer, and he was not to touch it or any part of it. He was to measure as exactly as he could, without touching it, with a folding steel rule I gave him, its diameter and its height. He was to count the number of lead horns on the mine, note where they were located. He was to pay particular attention to the hydrostatic piston mechanism, which should be on top of that mine, and so far as he could determine, discover whether the hydrostatic piston was down inside its cylinder, or up. The location of that piston in its cylinder was an important factor in whether the mine was armed and ready to fire or not.

Finally, Buck was to check whether two lifting eyes were where they should be on the spherical mine case, and also whether the spherical mine was still secured by tie rods to the square mine case beneath it, which should be serving as its anchor.

All this, Buck was to do, and report to me over the diving telephone each item as he checked it, before proceeding to the next, while I checked off on the diagram of that mine as he reported it, each feature to make sure it corresponded with the particular mine we thought it was.

When he had done all this, and noted anything else of interest relating to that mine, still without touching the mine, he was to come up. After that, it would be decided what next to do.

Buck went over the side of the *Intent* and vanished beneath the sea, with Muzzy tending his lines from on deck. Marked by a trail of bubbles in the water, rising from his helmet, I could trace Buck's course across the well-submerged deck of the *Brenta* and then his descent into her number two hold, while Muzzy carefully fed out slack on his lifeline and airhose.

Buck hit bottom far down inside the flooded hold. Muzzy stopped paying out line. Buck reported over the telephone he could see the mine standing about a fathom off; there seemed to be no trip wires in the water; he was approaching it.

I could see by his moving bubbles that he was; then he stopped. A moment went by. Then, in the flat toneless voice of every diver under pressure, I caught his next words, quivering with excitement in spite of the heavy air pressure flattening out all tone quality.

"Cap'n, I'm close to that mine now and it's standing on three torpedo warheads!"

Three torpedo warheads in the *Brenta* as well as a submarine mine! What, in Heaven's name, were we up against? What should all those explosives be doing inside a scuttled merchantman?

But this time, in spite of the unexpected new explosives, Buck stood his ground and so long as he stood his ground alongside that mine, I could certainly stand mine on the other end of his diving telephone.

"All right, Buck," I answered. "I got it. Three torpedo warheads as well as a mine. O.K. Now, go ahead and measure the mine with that steel rule."

Down on the bottom, about a foot away from several thousand

[464]

pounds of high explosives put there by the Eyties for no good purpose so far as Buck was concerned, Buck unfolded his steel rule, held it as closely as he dared alongside that huge steel ball containing sudden death, and sighted through the face plate of his helmet both sides of the ball to check its diameter.

"Thirty-nine inches, Cap'n," came up to me in Buck's far-away flat tones.

"Thirty-nine inches," I repeated. Practically one meter in the metric system used by the Italians. That checked exactly with my diagram.

"O.K., Buck. Now the height."

It took Buck a little longer to measure the height. He had to stoop to sight top and bottom along his vertical rule; in a diving rig, not an easy thing to do when he must not fall over against one of those protruding horns, ready to kill him more quickly than any rattlesnake's fangs, should he strike one.

Buck reported the height only approximately; he couldn't get in exactly, but his figures checked fairly well with what they should be.

"Good enough, Buck. Now count the horns."

Far below me, Buck proceeded to count the horns. Those were the lead protrusions all around the steel mine case. If anything hit and bent one of them over, it broke a thin glass vial of acid inside the lead horn, the acid spilled out over a carbon and zinc cell generating instantly an electric current, the current flowed through a relay inside to fire a detonator, and the detonator exploded about half a ton of TNT, all before you could wink an eye. Of course, when that happened, no one in the vicinity would any longer be interested in winking an eye.

"Seven horns, Cap'n," reported Buck. "All in one row, spaced even around the top half o' that mine, pointing up on about a 45° angle."

"You're doing fine, Buck!" I sang out into the telephone. "It's the mine we've been studying all right! Everything checks! Now, how about that hydrostatic piston on top? Is it in or out?"

But there Buck was stumped. Peering through his helmet as well as he could without touching anything, trying to look into what should be an open cylinder on top of the mine, Buck could see the cylinder well enough but that was as far as he got.

"Can't tell you, Cap'n," he reported finally. "I can't see into that cylinder. It's not open on the top the way you said it oughta be. Looks to me as if a wood plug's been driven into it, and maybe

[465]

sawed off just a little above the cylinder."

A wood plug driven into the hydrostatic piston! No wood plug belonged there. That appeared to be some evidence of booby trapping that mine. I'd have to think that over carefully.

"Good enough, Buck," I cautioned. "Don't touch it! Now, how about those lifting eyes and the bottom tie rods to the anchor case?"

Buck checked. The lifting eyes were as they should be; the mine sphere was securely held down to its anchor. There was nothing more to be learned.

"That's everything, Buck," I told him. "Get well clear of that mine and come up!"

Buck rose to the surface with Muzzy heaving in cautiously, and we took him aboard. I learned nothing new from questioning him on deck.

What were those three torpedo warheads doing under that mine in the *Brenta?* I had no idea. Neither had anybody else, but Buck assured me neither the mine nor its anchor case was secured to them; the mine assembly was just standing on them.

But that plug driven into the hydrostatic piston cylinder bothered me a lot. It didn't belong there. That hydrostatic piston was supposed to be pushed down by the pressure of the sea to arm the mine as it sank, once it had been planted overboard in the normal manner. Had the Eyties perhaps driven in that plug to force the piston down to insure its arming? Or had they perhaps done it for another purpose? Possibly with other changes inside that hydrostatic piston which we couldn't see, had they rigged that mine so that if ever any attempt was made to lift it out, the decreasing sea pressure would make the piston work in reverse, arm, and fire the mine as it rose? No one could tell.

However, that was evidently the major danger. Buck was sure that if we gave him a sling fitted with proper hooks, he could without danger to himself, hook them into the lifting eyes so we could hoist that mine straight up and out the open cargo hatches overhead. But if it exploded on us as it came up?

I couldn't prevent its exploding, but, at least, I could avoid the explosion doing us any harm, even if I couldn't save the *Brenta* from it. I ordered Brown to rig one of the *Brenta's* forward booms, protruding above the sea, so that it plumbed the center of the number two hold. Then I took the *Intent* down the line of wrecks to the stern of the *Colombo,* lying with half her port side out of the water, capsized just astern of the *Brenta.*

Far aft on the stern of the *Colombo,* 1000 feet at least away from that number two hold on the *Brenta,* we rigged up and secured a small portable gasoline-driven winch. I told Brown to reeve off a long line from that winch set on the *Colombo's* stern, lead it the whole length of the *Colombo* and most of the length of the *Brenta,* then down through a block from the boom on the *Brenta's* plumbing the hatch.

On the end of the line, he was to provide a bridle fitted on each leg at its lower end with a pair of sister hooks to engage the eyes in the mine.

I gave him the rest of the day to get all that rigged up. Next morning, all of us would come out again and remove the mine. After that, provided we did it successfully, we would proceed to remove the warheads the same way. So I left Brown and his men to do their rigging job, while Davy and I in my boat went back to the Naval Base to ponder the matter further as to whether the Eyties might still be a jump ahead of us in the matter of booby trapping the *Brenta.*

The problem had me worried. While I had never said anything on the subject to any of my divers in Massawa, that was part of what Major Quilln in Alex had wanted to quiz me on when in late September, I had so suddenly been called off the docking of *H.M.S. Cleopatra* to go to Alex for a conference with him. Among other things, he wanted to learn how the proposed blockship might be booby trapped so that enemy divers attempting to lift it might blow themselves up and those few who escaped destruction might get discouraged and quit.

But with that part of Major Quilln's problem I had refused to have anything to do or to offer any advice. I felt that salvage men, even enemy salvage men, faced dangers enough on a wreck without trying to add to their dangers by any such damnable devices as booby traps under water. I was perfectly willing to assist in preparing a blockship so it couldn't soon or easily be raised, but that was as far as I was willing to go. I hoped never to run into any underwater booby traps myself, I told Major Quilln, and I certainly wasn't going to be any party to preparing them, even for our enemies. Now it began to look as if the Eyties in Massawa perhaps hadn't been so ethical as regards me and my men. What did that wood plug driven into the hydrostatic piston of the *Brenta's* mine mean?

I made whatever other arrangements I wanted at the Naval Base for the next day's work, and then spent the rest of the day and all of the evening with Commander Davy and the explosives lieutenant (who had meanwhile arrived from Alex), puzzling over mine pamphlets trying to solve the riddle, but we couldn't. Unless in some way it was to help in exploding the mine as it rose or after it was up, there seemed no reason for its presence. So we separated and finally turned in.

Next morning, we started out again for the *Brenta*. Aside from the *Intent*, I had need for a work boat, a shallow punt, and a skiff, and I had provided them all. The *Intent* carried the skiff. The work boat went on her own, towing the punt.

As a work boat, I selected the *Lord Grey*, whose broad shallow hull best suited my purpose, though I was certain her Eytie crew, when they learned what was wanted of them in the south harbor, would not be pleased. Still, by then it would be too late for them to rebel.

There had been some argument after everyone else had started off from the Naval Base, as between myself and Commander Davy on one side, and the explosives lieutenant on the other. At some point in the lifting proceedings, while the mine might be brought to the surface without anyone ever getting near it till then except Buck, who was to engage the lifting hooks, someone else was going actually to have to handle that mine to get it into the punt and get it ashore.

Commander Davy and I had agreed that we two being the only naval officers around, should do that without exposing anyone else to danger while we handled the mine. Now the explosives lieutenant insisted on going with us. However, we both, being much senior to him, sprang rank on him and refused to allow it. After all, two men could handle the job perfectly; there was no reason to hazard a third. Particularly was this so, we pointed out to him, in case of an unfortunate accident with the mine, when it would be desirable to have someone acquainted with the situation left over to explain to the C.-in-C. what had happened.

We would deliver the mine to him in the south harbor on a deserted beach, if we got it successfully ashore from the *Brenta*. There it would be all his to dissect at his leisure without our company, and if in that process he blew himself up, we should both be left over and glad to reciprocate by informing the C.-in-C. of what we knew about what had happened to the late lamented explosives lieutenant.

As I had four stripes and Davy had three, while the poor lieutenant had only two, he hadn't a chance in the argument with us. We both got into my boat with Glen Galvin and set out to overhaul the *Intent,* while all he could do was get into my car with Garza (which I had offered him to salve his hurt feelings) and drive around by land to the deserted beach on the south harbor a mile away from the *Brenta,* on which beach we promised him to deliver the mine.

My boat could make twice the speed of the *Intent.* We easily overhauled and passed her, as well as the *Lord Grey* and its unsuspecting crew of Eyties, and were first alongside the *Brenta.*

The *Intent* arrived shortly and rigged for diving. Buck Scougale was quickly dressed and was preparing to go overboard when the *Lord Grey,* towing the punt, arrived. I ordered the *Lord Grey* to move on to the stern of the *Colombo* and await us there.

Buck went overboard. It wasn't necessary to go over his instructions again; he knew exactly what he was to do. Carrying a thin manila line already attached to the slings dangling from the boom plumbing the hatch, he submerged, crossed the *Brenta's* deck, was lowered carefully down into the hold. As he went down, Scotty, the *Intent's* first mate, slacked away gently on the heavy manila line leading downward from the boom so that Buck would not have to pull it down with him.

As before, I manned the deck end of Buck's diving telephone. Buck reported himself on the bottom; he was moving toward the mine. He was close alongside it; we were to slack away a little more on the bridle line. We did.

Then, there was silence for about ten minutes as below us in the depths, Buck worked cautiously with his bridle to engage the sister hooks in the eyes on the mine and to seize them there with marline so they couldn't come loose, while all the while he knew and we knew that he must not bang any of the horns or anything else with his lead weights, and that he must keep his lead-soled boots off those torpedo warheads beneath it. If Buck, working engulfed in water on a slimy deck, slipped or moved carelessly, it would be very unpleasant for all hands.

Finally, Buck phoned up to tell us to take up the slack on the mine-lifting line—it was hooked up. Gingerly, we heaved in slack while Buck stood by the mine to watch that we left the line neither so slack a loop of it might foul a horn, nor so taut we swayed the mine up off its strange foundations. We got the line heaved in to suit Buck's critical eye, secured it that way, leading far aft to the winch on the *Colombo's* stern. Then Buck got clear and asked us to take him up.

The moment Buck was back aboard, without waiting to undress him, the *Intent* cast off from the *Brenta* and herself steamed back astern the wreck of the *Colombo* where she tied up.

All was now ready to proceed. There wasn't anybody closer than 1000 feet to that mine in the fore hold of the *Brenta*. If it exploded as we lifted it, the *Brenta* would be the only sufferer.

I took a position well off to port of the *Colombo's* stern, where from my boat, I could see over the *Brenta's* submerged forward decks, as well as seeing the men of the *Intent* manning the gasoline winch secured to the capsized stern of the *Colombo*.

Brown started up the gasoline winch. I signaled him to start heaving in slowly on his lifting line. Carefully Brown clutched in the winch and took up all the slack in the 1000 foot bight of line between him and the *Brenta's* boom; then when he had a strain on the line, he cautiously winched in.

Probably two or three minutes went by while he took in fifty feet of line and all hands waited for an explosion from the rising mine. Nothing happened. Then the mine, looking somewhat like the Man from Mars with its strange spherical head spiked all over with protruding horns standing atop a square mine anchor case on wheels, burst through the surface and gradually rose some six feet above it. Then I sang out to Brown:

"Avast heaving!"

Brown stopped the winch. Very gently the mine swayed on the end of its lifting line, dripping water all over.

I let the mine hang about half an hour. If there was any delay action to a mechanism intended to explode that mine when the sea pressure was off it, I was perfectly willing to give it a chance to act without coming any closer.

When at the end of half an hour, nothing had occurred, Davy and I agreed we were dealing only with an ordinary naval mine with only the usual potentialities of death and no added special features, in spite of that inexplicable wooden plug in the hydrostatic piston. So we swung into action.

I beckoned the *Lord Grey* to come alongside my boat with the punt it had in tow—a very long punt, twenty feet long, five feet in the beam, and some three feet deep inside its hull.

Very reluctantly, the Eytie coxswain did, for with that mine now swinging in the open, plainly visible, he began to suspect the worst of his strange invitation to visit the south harbor for the first time in weeks.

I explained to him his part. Towing the punt astern of him, with only Commander Davy and me in it, he was to tow us on a very long towline, directly under the hanging mine. To do that, the *Lord Grey* would have to pass over the submerged deck of the *Brenta* (dodging its not so well submerged ventilator cowls) and directly beneath the mine, but he needn't worry—he wouldn't touch anything below with his hull if he steered straight, nor anything above either if only he kept his head down.

When the punt towing astern came under the mine, he was to stop and leave the rest to us. Davy and I would take care of it while he was a long way off on the far end of the towline.

Instantly the Eytie coxswain and his whole crew began gesticulating wildly in protest, but they were up against two very hard-hearted men who paid no attention. They were not going to be in any danger, regardless of what they thought—it was only Davy and I who were going to face that. We climbed into the punt, slacked away on the long towline I had provided, and bade them get underway or it would be the worse for them.

Shepherded by Glen Galvin in my boat (which could not safely navigate that passage over the *Brenta* or I would have used it) to see that the *Lord Grey* did not suddenly cast us adrift and flee, the *Lord Grey* headed for the *Brenta* and her mine. She made a long sweep to allow her to straighten out so she could cross the submerged *Brenta* just forward of her exposed bridge and just aft her foremast, from one of the booms of which the mine was suspended.

If ever that Eytie coxswain steered a straight course, he did that day, with a sunken hull below him, a deadly mine overhead, an awash bridge to starboard, and a mast sticking up from the sea to port. Carefully, he went through over his obstacle course, with every man in his boat stretched practically flat out on the thwarts as they passed under the mine.

Once he was clear himself he began to take a more intelligent interest, as far astern of him he towed us toward the *Brenta*. We crossed her submerged port gunwale and waved to him to go very slowly till he had us directly under the mine, then we stopped him while from the punt, we lassoed the wheels of that mine to get a guide line on it.

Once we had that, we straightened the punt out so the mine hung directly amidships over us, and signaled to Brown who was now in the skiff well off to starboard where he could see both us and Scotty at the winch, to lower away gently.

Now came the pinch. That mine and its anchor weighed a ton at least. It was up to Davy and me to guide it squarely into the punt so it landed clear of everything without fouling any of those dangerous horns and bending them.

Brown signaled the winch to slack away gently. Down came the mine between us, Davy astern of it, I ahead. We grasped its wheels as soon as we could touch them, and with more delicacy than I, at least, had ever handled anything, guided that ton of high explosives downward inside the punt till we had it safely landed on the floor boards without it tipping sideways and bending those horns.

Then we cut loose the lifting slings, and Brown signaled to haul them clear, while swiftly Davy and I passed manila lashings from the mine case to the gunwales in every direction, to hold that mine firmly down and avoid any possibility of its moving any way at all into contact with anything.

When that was done, we signaled the *Lord Grey* to tow us and our mine out of there. She did. Once we were well clear of the *Brenta*, I had the *Lord Grey* back down to the bow of the punt, when, so to speak, Davy and I abandoned ship, leaving the punt unmanned while we boarded the *Lord Grey* and hastily paid out all the slack on the towline again.

Davy and I smiled at each other. Our danger was over. We towed the punt as far up toward the beach as the *Lord Grey* could safely go without grounding herself, tossed over the towline with an anchor on it to hold the punt, and waved to the explosives lieutenant on the beach that there was his mine intact and he could do with it as he pleased, including either wading or swimming out to it. We were through.

I may add here, he spent about a week dissecting it, without blow-

Down came the mine between us.

ing himself up, which is all I know about the further history of that mine, as he departed for Alex with whatever he learned, including the mystery of that wood plug in the hydrostatic piston, without my ever seeing him again.

Meanwhile, next day we cleared out the torpedo warheads, which were taken out to sea and sunk, and the *Intent* proceeded with the salvage of the *Brenta*.

CHAPTER

54

WHILE I WAS STRUGGLING WITH THE
Gera, the *Tripolitania,* and the *Brenta* and her mine, these formed
only minor interludes in what was really my main task during that
period—the salvage of the sunken crane.

By the latter part of October, I had both physically and officially
come into possession of the six pontoons I needed for the job, and had
completed the changes required to make crude pontoons out of the
first two gasoline tanks. Bill Reed and Frank Roys, in the face of
terrific obstacles, had managed to sweep four steel messenger wires
under the hull of the sunken crane, and with these, against even
fiercer difficulties, had succeeded in hauling through the actual cradle
slings needed to lift the derrick.

Those cradle slings were something to contemplate. They were of
almost the heaviest steel wire imaginable—as thick as a man's wrist,
they were of two-inch diameter steel wire—such wire as one rarely
sees. That I should ever have found such heavy wire hawsers in Massawa, I should not have believed, but all I had to do to get them was
to look into what formerly had been Captain McCance's salvage warehouse and which now was mine. It contained everything—there was
reel on reel of that massive two-inch diameter wire that even in New
York I couldn't have obtained on short notice. That warehouse was
a regular Ali Baba's cave of salvage treasures, all mine now without
asking anyone's by your leave or having even to say,

"Open sesame!"

I used that thick wire doubled to make up each cradle sling. Three
hundred feet of it, doubled up to give a finished length of 150 feet,
formed each sling, strong enough to stand a load of 300 tons before
it broke. As I intended to put a pull of only 60 tons at most on each
end of that sling, I felt assured my slings, at least, would not break

on me in the lift.

Meanwhile, with Ervin Johnson diving to find out, I learned the submerged crane hull was 100 feet long and 60 feet wide. That presented me with another problem. Since my impromptu pontoons were each 45 feet long, I could get only two of them, end to end, down alongside each side of the crane hull—that is, only four pontoons altogether, two to starboard, two to port.

Now four pontoons could lift about 420 tons. If the crane turned out to weigh 400 tons or less, I might lift it with only four pontoons; if it proved to be heavier, I couldn't do it. I should then have to use all six pontoons, and the last two pontoons could not be placed alongside—there wasn't room for them there. They would have to go down athwartships, one across the square bow and one across the square stern of that crane.

However, that would require another pair of cradle slings under the crane, hauled under her the long way of her hull. Inasmuch as dragging two pairs of slings under her athwartships, the short way, had nearly killed us all as we tugged mightily with two huge bulldozers in tandem on the quay heaving on the messenger wires to drag those massive wire slings through the debris and coral on which the heavy crane rested, I hoped and prayed to be relieved of that necessity.

Even on the short slings, many a time as we heaved with the bulldozers, the inch-thick steel messenger wires, strained taut as iron bars, had suddenly snapped, to come swirling back on us in hurtling coils that threatened to decapitate us should a coil catch us in its path.

I decided to try with only four pontoons. If I failed on that, there would be nothing for it save to stand the gaff and run through a third pair of slings fore and aft for the third pair of pontoons.

So in late October, I started to lower pontoons against a changing war background. For on the day I started, Montgomery and Alexander with the British Eighth Army opened up the long-awaited assault on Rommel's positions before El Alamein. While under the hot Red Sea sun I labored in Massawa on that crane, before far-away El Alamein, wheel to wheel for miles on end, British guns started to pound Field Marshal Rommel's whole forty mile long position between the Mediterranean and the Quattaro Depression.

The war in the Middle East was about to move westward, I felt sure. If I didn't want to be marooned in the backwash, I'd better hurry and get that crane afloat, so not only it but I also could depart for pastures new where there would be more going on shortly than there would be in Massawa.

Interrupted somewhat by the need of saving the *Gera,* taking care of the incoming *Tripolitania,* and getting the *Brenta* clear of that mine, I stuck nevertheless mainly to the problem of getting pontoons down and that crane up.

The last few days in October, with the first two pairs of cradle slings in place, I decided to try lowering the first pontoon to see how it would act. It had, I knew, every idiosyncrasy that a pontoon could have, for I had neither the materials, the men, nor the time to build inside it the intricate steel bulkheads and piping systems to make it controllable in the water, as a pontoon should be. This pontoon was devoid of all the inside compartments it required—it was as uncomplicated inside as an empty tin can, which on a huge scale, it resembled.

It acted terribly.

With the biggest locomotive crane in Massawa to lift its 15 ton bulk off the quay and overboard, we put it in the water, where completely light, it floated in deceptive docility, looking even bigger than it had on the quay.

We towed it around to the starboard side of the crane (the side away from the quay), threaded through its hawsepipes the guide wires attached below under water to the starboard ends of a pair of cradle slings, opened the flood valves at the bottom of each end of that pontoon, opened the air vents on top to let the air out as the water flowed in, and proceeded to sink the pontoon.

Meanwhile, I shackled in to the lifting eye provided on top at each end of the pontoon, a six-inch manila hawser. With those two manila hawsers, when the pontoon got heavy enough to sink, we would lower the pontoon away from alongside the *Resolute,* to whose bitts those hawsers were led.

There was, as anticipated, trouble in making the pontoon go down horizontally, that is, both ends together and level.

Anyone will swiftly determine this who cares to experiment with a soup can emptied of soup with both heads in place and with two holes punched top and bottom in one end (or in both ends if he or she prefers) floating in the bathtub so that water can enter at the bottom hole while the air inside escapes from the top hole. That soup

[477]

can will start by floating horizontally at first, but it will be impossible to get it to go down horizontally as it fills.

Regardless of how carefully you try to balance it, as soon as water enough has entered, the water will run to one end or the other, and the can will go down, not horizontally, but one end first.

With a soup can, that isn't serious. But with a pontoon as long as a four-story building is high, it is, especially when the pontoons weigh about 15 tons each, as these did.

From my previous experience, I knew I should have plenty of trouble getting that pontoon to go down horizontally, and I had all I anticipated and plenty more. My salvage men, most of whom had never seen pontoons in action before, were aghast at the antics of that leviathan alongside the *Resolute*, bent only on obeying the laws of nature and going down on end, while I insisted that it violate them and go down horizontally so that it might be of some use to me.

After various hair-raising maneuvers on the part of the pontoon (without here going into the technical details of how it was done) I outwitted the pontoon and got it sunk horizontally just above the starboard forward deck edge of the sunken crane. While from the *Resolute* with the manila hawsers we held the heavy brute from sinking further, Ervin Johnson went overboard in his diving rig and passed through the loop of wire of each cradle sling now protruding just above the tops of the two hawsepipes in that pontoon, a heavy steel pin (if it can be called such) five inches in diameter and two and a half feet long. These two massive steel pins, straddling the tops of the hawsepipes inside the loops of cradle wire, were intended to take the 100 ton lift on the slings that the pontoon would exert upwards when we blew all the water out of it.

As those pins weighed several hundred pounds each, Johnson had quite a time under water threading them through the wire loops. We helped him with lines to the surface, where we might take some of the weight off his hands.

With the locking pins in place, Johnson then had to put his life in considerable jeopardy by lying down on deck the sunken crane with that vast pontoon hanging only a foot or two above him, while he secured to its bottom a pair of wire straps already attached to the crane hull, and intended to hold that pontoon properly aligned in position just above the crane after we on the *Resolute* let go of it, and moved on to devote our attention to its companion pontoons.

If, during that time, while Johnson, down there in the water, was sandwiched in between the deck of the sunken crane and the pontoon, anything carried away on the *Resolute* or she rolled suddenly from the wash of a passing ship, the heavy pontoon would come down on Johnson and very neatly flatten him out. Johnson knew that and so did I; I took what precautions I could and Johnson trusted to me.

He succeeded in getting the pontoon secured beneath, and dragged himself out to come up for a while.

The heavy pontoon being secured from below, we held it level from the *Resolute,* while gradually I blew compressed air into it to push water out to lighten it up enough so it would just float horizontally above the derrick hull on its own buoyancy, tugging lightly upward at each end on the two wire straps Johnson had just attached to it. Each one of those wire straps would take a pull of about five tons only; they weren't intended to lift the derrick with, only to hold the slightly buoyant pontoon in position after we let go of it from the *Resolute.*

I blew in only enough compressed air so that the strain on the manila hawsers from the pontoon to the *Resolute* just vanished. The pontoon was floating now on its own buoyancy, a vast submerged cylinder just above the sunken derrick, pulling gently upward on the steel straps under it.

Johnson dived again, first to shut tight the flood valves on the bottom of the pontoon, and second to cast loose the manila lines from its top to the *Resolute.* This left the work on that pontoon completed, so that we might move the *Resolute* and proceed with the placing of the other three. Johnson came up.

These proceedings took all day and part of the early evening. Meanwhile, I had smoked up some three packages of Camels (my whole week's ration) steadying my nerves, which badly needed steadying, and if my allowance had permitted and I'd had them, I should probably have disposed that day of a whole carton.

At any rate, we were through. I swabbed off my half-naked torso with a towel and started to put on my khaki shirt so I might go back presentably to the Naval Base, when that pontoon struck back at me.

A passing ship being piloted out the commercial harbor, sent her wake sweeping across the water to rock the *Resolute* violently. I had my boat out in the harbor to stop any ship movements while Ervin Johnson was beneath the pontoon, but of course I couldn't keep harbor traffic stopped all the time.

Whether the *Resolute* now rocked or not made little difference, but that propeller wash, sweeping far below the surface, did. The current hit the side of our submerged pontoon, gave it a heavy jolt, and broke loose the pad welded at its after end to hold the securing straps there.

The after end of the now light pontoon started promptly to float surfaceward. The moment it did, all the water still inside the pontoon ran to the low end forward, and that end, suddenly heavy, even more promptly started for the bottom.

Before I could barely get in some adequate profanity to express my feelings, there was the pontoon I had just put in the whole day securing horizontally below, now in the position *it* preferred—that is, on end! In just about forty-five feet of water, there now it stood—its forward end in the mud, its after end just clear of the surface, our carefully placed heavy cradle slings dragged out of position, and everything, in plain words, in a hell of a mess!

Such, I reflected as philosophically as I could, is the life of a salvage man when he has to handle pontoons with idiosyncrasies. Oh, if only I had there in Massawa some of my own pontoons, designed so they would placidly float and sink horizontally without protest! But my properly designed pontoons were at the Submarine Base in New London, as unattainable to me in Massawa as if they'd been on the moon.

There was nothing to do except to take off my half-on khaki shirt and go to work again. All day, my men and I had worked on that pontoon—now we could work on it all night also.

We did. It took most of the night, with Ervin Johnson uncomplainingly doing all the diving in the dark water below while we struggled on deck with air compressors and airhoses, to get the pontoon cast loose of the cradle slings and floated up to the surface. There completely light and empty, it floated horizontally once more, as if trying to delude us into the belief that it might again be persuaded to do that submerged.

All we had left now to do, was to go through that fight with the bulldozers again to get our cradle slings back into position once more. But as it was already 3 A.M., and all of us were a little tired, I decided it would be better to tackle that task next morning.

However, it so happened the next day, October 29th, was the day the *Gera* elected to attempt to sink on us, so Captain Reed and I, being otherwise engaged for most of the day, weren't able to get back on the *Resolute*. Captain Roys, nothing daunted, undertook the job himself with the bulldozers and managed to carry it through in spite of the fact that in the midst of his struggles my boat arrived to take most of his men away from him to help save the sinking *Gera*.

CHAPTER

55

W̲ITH REPAIRS ON THE "GERA," NOW dry-docked, started under Lloyd Williams' direction, I came back with Captain Reed on October 30 to resume my battle with the Eytie gasoline tanks masquerading as pontoons.

As a first step, we lifted our first pontoon out of water back onto the quay, to reweld to its bottom the clip which had carried away on us and caused us all the trouble. It appeared from the break that the welder, probably weary in the hot October sun, had done none too good a welding job.

So not only did I make sure that clip was solidly welded back, but had the welder go back over all the clips with extra beads of welding on the second pontoon also to make sure that this time everything was certainly solid. Since now Lloyd Williams had nearly every man who was any sort of mechanic working on the *Gera,* it took the solitary welder I could keep on the commercial quay some days to get all the welding work done.

On November 5, we were ready to go again with the pontoons. It so happened that the night before, Montgomery smashed through Rommel's lines at El Alamein, destroyed most of his tanks, and captured about 50,000 men, mostly Italians, whom Rommel deserted as he turned to flee westward with the battered remnants of his Afrika Korps. Rommel was proving himself the military idiot I felt he was when he tossed away his golden opportunity late the June before, to grasp at Tobruk. Now he was falling back on it. Shortly he would find, I had no doubt, how worthless to him in defeat was that bauble for which he had traded decisive victory.

But what it all certainly meant was that the long war in the Middle East had finally actually started westward. And if I knew the Libyan

Desert, it was going to move that way fast. Time was running out for Massawa.

Once again I had placed my first pontoon in the water and at 6 A.M. we started in on it. We had all the troubles we'd had the first time. Whoever starts to buck the laws of nature has his hands full, and I did again with that pontoon. All morning long, I juggled it, first one end up, then the other, before finally I succeeded in getting a balance good enough to get both ends under water at once and heavy enough for it to sink. Then it took all the rest of the day to get it secured in position over the sunken crane before finally late in the evening we could cast it loose.

This time it stayed down.

While next day, Frank Roys got the second pontoon overboard and rigged for lowering, I put in my time on the *Gera,* with Lloyd Williams, a day interrupted somewhat by the need of stowing away the newly-arrived *Tripolitania* and getting the *Intent* set for renewing her attack on the *Brenta's* mine.

November 7, I was back on the *Resolute,* all set to sink the second pontoon, which was to go down to port. The second one showed all the difficulties we'd encountered on the first one, with some troubles added. At least on the first pontoon, when it was down, we could secure it in place to its cradle slings by having the diver shove a heavy steel pin through a loop in the sling, where the wire had been doubled over.

But on the second pontoon, on the port side, we couldn't do that. There the two parts of the wire near its ends lay simply side by side— there wasn't any loop. To secure the wire in place over the hawsepipe, we had to put on wire clamps—massive steel castings made to fit the lay of the two-inch diameter wire and hold two parts of it together without slipping.

For a diver to get these heavy castings fitted underwater to the wires just above the hawsepipes and bolted together with inch-and-a-half bolts is a task—poor Ervin Johnson was nearly dead before he succeeded in getting three such clamps, one above the other, on the end of each cradle sling just above the hawsepipes.

Meanwhile, since all hands on the *Resolute* were badly knocked out by their tussle with the first pair of pontoons, I decided to give them all a rest for a few days, while I myself spent them on the *Brenta* wrestling with that mine.

When I got back from the first day on the *Brenta*, I heard the best news I'd heard since December 7, 1941, when the bombs fell on Pearl Harbor.

It was November 8, 1942. My radio when I turned it on greeted me with Eisenhower's landing in North Africa that morning!

Literally I cheered! At last America had quit defending itself and had started to fight! And in North Africa! That spelled the end of Rommel and all his dreams of conquest. With Montgomery and the Eighth Army chasing him westward and Eisenhower landed in his rear, Rommel had no escape now, with his deflated Afrika Korps, except by swimming. I doubted he was any better a swimmer than he was a strategist. The end in the Middle East could now not be far off!

Later that day I received some radio orders from the Navy Department, forwarded by the War Department, that made me decidedly less happy.

I was ordered to proceed on an inspection trip from Massawa to Durban in South Africa, there to survey the needs of that port for some additional floating dry docks which would, if I decided they were needed, be built in the United States and towed to Durban.

Then when I had completed my survey in Durban, I was to proceed to Freetown in Sierra Leone on the West African Coast, and make a similar survey of the dry dock needs of that port.

After that, I was to return to Massawa, make out my report and recommendations, and send them to the Navy Department in Washington.

I reached for a map of Africa and scanned it hurriedly. I should have to go all over Africa to do that. It involved a journey of 14,000 miles from East Africa to South Africa to West Africa and back again to East Africa. Africa is a big continent. I couldn't possibly do it, even with the best air priorities I could get, in less than two to three weeks.

Badly upset, I considered those orders. What would happen in Massawa if now I should leave for even two weeks? The past record offered no consolation. The first time, in August, I had been ordered to Cairo for a conference, the contractor had seized the opportunity to try to relieve me of my command. By great good luck, I had returned only next day and squelched that before too much damage was done. The second time, in September, when I had been ordered to Alex, my dockmaster had dropped the *Cleopatra* in the dry dock,

[484]

smashing all the keel blocks, and then reported that our dry dock was going to be out of commission for from four to six weeks! And it would have been, too, had I not returned that day to squelch that situation.

Now, of all times, when I was right in the middle of the salvage of the sunken derrick, by far the most complicated salvage operation undertaken in Massawa, to be carried out by makeshift pontoons, ludicrous gasoline tanks on which I had staked everything, I was ordered to leave again. The British had failed twice on that job; the eyes of everyone in the Royal Navy from the Admiralty in London through Alex down to Captain Lucas in Massawa were on that sunken crane. I had promised them I should do it. I could trust no one else whatever to carry it through in my absence, and I didn't want to come back from traipsing all over Africa to find that through some perfectly excusable calamity all my flimsy pontoons were ruined and I had nothing left to try it over again with. That would be no excuse for me in anybody's eyes for my failure to lift that crane!

Of all the blows I had received in Massawa since first I saw the place late the previous March, those orders were the worst! Completely miserable, I scanned those orders again. I couldn't refuse to obey. But was there perhaps any out for me in them? Word by word, I went over them again, and then, thank God, my eyes lighted on two insignificant words that in my first reading had been overshadowed by Durban, Freetown, dry docks, and the important instructions in those long orders. I was to proceed on the survey "when convenient."

I began to breathe again. It wouldn't be convenient to leave Massawa till that sunken derrick was up, in one to two weeks perhaps. After that I could leave.

So I sent an answering dispatch to the Navy Department, via the War Department, stating it would not be convenient for me to leave Massawa for that survey for roughly two weeks yet; after that, if I heard nothing further, I should start as ordered. But I also pointed out that with not much more mileage to fly, an officer from Washington could make the survey, and there would be in such a case the advantage that on his return to Washington he would be available to answer any questions anyone might ask of him there. I would appreciate Washington's comments on this, but if I heard nothing further, I would in two weeks start myself.

And with that off my chest, I turned on the radio again for what later news there might be of Eisenhower's landings in North Africa.

Next morning I was out on the *Brenta* again. Commander Davy and I removed the mine from her to the beach.

For the next few days, I alternated between the *Gera* on the dry dock and the *Resolute* on the quay, where Reed and Roys, with next to no men to work with, were trying to get the changes finished on the second pair of pontoons and the cradle slings for it adjusted in place.

Then I received a reply from the Navy Department to my message. I was not to start from Massawa unless further advised. Washington would check on the availability of someone there for the survey; if a suitable officer was found, he would be sent instead of me.

I promptly forgot about Durban and Freetown. Washington was full of officers itching to get away from it and somewhere near the war zone on any pretext at all. As soon as the word got round, there would be a line of officers a block long asking for the job. If the Navy Department couldn't find a suitable one among them, it would indeed be strange.

On November 14, starting very early, I got my third pontoon down. It may have been mid-November, and back in the United States overcoats might be coming out of moth balls, but in Massawa it was still hot. Not so hot perhaps as in August—only just as hot as a midsummer day in New York on which half a dozen people die of the heat, a few dozens more are prostrated, and the Brooklyn Navy Yard shuts down and sends all its workmen home because it's too hot to work in such a heat wave.

I drank only about three gallons of iced tea and nearly wore out a slide rule figuring buoyancies while I struggled with that third pontoon. Finally I got it down and secured, and left in time in the late afternoon to get back to the Naval Base and undock the *Gera*, which that afternoon had been finished by Lloyd Williams and practically all our mechanics, salvage and otherwise, who had been working on it night and day for sixteen days.

As I dragged the repaired *Gera* off the Persian dry dock to tie her up again alongside the large Italian dock, I reflected that if there was anyone to whom the United States owed a Medal of Merit for helping along the war effort, it was certainly Lloyd Williams—always uncomplaining, always able, always ready to perform a repair miracle on a ship when it had to be done.

Then on November 15, I was back on the sunken dry dock for (I hoped) the fourth and last pontoon. It went down no easier than the first three, but the human mind and body are fortunately so constituted that once the limit of agony is reached, additional pain causes no more conscious suffering. So it was with all my crew on the *Resolute*. We got the pontoon down; we secured it in place.

All next day and the day after we spent installing heavy wire lashings to keep our pontoons and their cradle slings from sliding up and off the bow of the derrick when we raised her bow first (as happened to the unfortunate salvagers of the *Squalus*). That was a tough underwater job, requiring two divers, so Al Watson came over to help Ervin Johnson with it. We got it done fairly early in the evening of November 17; I sent all hands away then to try to get a decent night's sleep. Next day we would try to lift the derrick. The salvage crew would need all they had in the way of energy.

I was myself badly worn out, and my mind was tormented by doubts to which there could be no answers till the trial was made. To most of my men, those pontoons were pontoons, but I knew that really they were only gasoline tanks, far too lightly built. Pontoons always had steel shells much thicker than these had; they had bulkheads inside to strengthen them; their hawsepipes were much heavier to take the lifting loads; they had a big factor of safety in strength.

I had carefully calculated what the quarter-inch thick shell plating of these tanks would stand, what load the steel pipes I had improvised my hawsepipes from might carry. Normally, those gasoline tanks should stand up under the staggering load of 100 tons each I was going to put on them.

But the situation was not normal. Every one of those gasoline tanks had been through a terrific conflagration; its steel plating had been red-hot, the top of every tank was wrinkled and corrugated horribly. What effect would that lack of cylindrical symmetry have on those tanks now that they were going to be, as pontoons, subjected to strains they had never been designed for? How much had the fire those tanks had been through weakened the steel?

And finally, how much did that derrick weigh? Did it run over 400 tons, so that even if my four pontoons held together under the strain, they couldn't lift it?

Until actually I made the trial I could have no answers. Was I going to lift that derrick next day, or were my four pontoons going to be inadequate, or worst of all, were my fire-damaged tanks going to collapse on me when the lifting load came on them, leaving me with a third pathetic failure in the history of that crane to add to the two McCance had suffered on it? I could only pray. And feeling that an added prayer might well be in order, I sent that night a brief note home:

November 17, 1942

LUCY DARLING:

We have our sunken derrick with all four pontoons secured to it, and all the lashings on, to hold them in place. Tomorrow morning we shall attempt to raise it. Pray for us.

With love,

NED

I took the letter out to see it got into the outgoing mail in the morning.

Of course, I knew that long before that letter got home, it would be all over, one way or another. But at least asking for my wife's prayers for us might be a help. I felt better, and rolled wearily into my bed.

CHAPTER

56

A<small>S AN ACT OF FAITH, NEXT MORN-</small>ing, November 18, I kept the Persian dry dock clear of any vessel, so that when we brought the sunken derrick in hanging between the pontoons, we could immediately put her on the dry dock.

Early that morning, I had all Reed's crew of salvage men, all the *Resolute's* crew, and all of Lloyd Williams' salvage mechanics on the wreck of the sunken crane—some on the *Resolute's* decks, some on the quay near by, the rest in the work boats we should need.

On the Massawa quay itself close by, we had quite a gallery to watch us, mostly British, among whom could easily be picked out McCance's salvage crew who from their very audible remarks, had come to sneer our failure. (While McCance was failing, I had carefully kept all my men far away.)

A considerable number of bets were made, which my men eagerly took, for the odds offered them were very attractive. To McCance's men, who had struggled with that derrick for nine months, the idea of someone coming along with some old gasoline tanks and in four weeks walking off with the crane, seemed ridiculous. But the odds made no difference—if I knew my men, they would have taken every shilling offered at any odds at all. They had never known failure in Massawa, and nothing could make them believe they were going to get acquainted with it that day.

Ervin Johnson and Al Watson were dressed and both went down to make a final inspection underwater of our lashings, our cradle slings, and our air connections to the pontoons. They came up to report the pontoons still in place, all the underwater rigging in order.

Lloyd Williams started up the air compressors. On the quay, I had one of the 210 cubic foot Ingersoll-Rand machines from McCance's warehouse (now mine) which originally I had used in lifting the large

Italian dry dock. On the *Resolute,* I had a much smaller compressor that belonged to her. Between the two of them, we could furnish about 300 cubic feet of air a minute, enough to expel water at the rate of perhaps 6 tons a minute. That would be ample.

One at a time, I started air going into each pontoon, while Ervin Johnson, down below again in his diving rig, opened up cautiously the bottom valve at the after end only of each pontoon to make sure that the water was going *out* of it before he opened it wide. Since that happened to be the case on every one of the four pontoons, he opened the after valves all wide and came up again to rest with his helmet off till he might be needed.

I worked off the *Resolute,* lying just ahead of the bow of the crane, with a gauge before me to show the pressure inside each pontoon. My intention was to float up first the bow, then the stern, and then have the *Resolute* tow the sunken derrick away from there.

About 9 A.M., I opened the compressed air up wide to both bow pontoons, moderately to the after pontoons, and then with the gauges and the air valves before me, like an organist before a pipe organ, I began to play a tune with the compressed air flowing through the rubber hoses to my pontoons.

For one long hour the compressors throbbed heavily. In front of me, sticking up out of the water was the steel derrick structure of that sunken crane, a mass of interlaced steel standing high out of water, looking like one of the steel piers of the George Washington Bridge as it towered over our heads.

But except for that massive steel crane-work, built to support a load of 90 tons swinging from its hook high in the air, there was nothing before me but water. Below, I knew, was the sunken hull of the crane; secured just above that hull were my four ex-gasoline tanks. But all of that, one had to take on faith—nothing of it was visible.

The compressed air went down as the minutes dragged along toward the end of the hour and I watched the pressures. But Captain Reed by my side had, as always, more faith in barnacles and mussel shells as indicators than he had in gauges. He kept his one good eye glued to a mussel properly located on the waterline for his purposes.

Reed poked me in the ribs.

"She's rising, Captain!" he whispered, pointing to his mussel.

She was. Smoothly, slowly, majestically, and to me, beautifully, that tremendous mass of steel in front of me was rising out of the sea,

The scuttled 90-ton crane, pontoons attached.

exposing more and more of its barnacled steelwork till the bow ends of our two forward pontoons broke the surface and the lifting stopped. The bow was up!

Instantly I swung all the compressed air we had into the two stern pontoons, to blow them dry.

Ten minutes later, the steel derrick structure which was leaning aft at a considerable angle, with the bow end of the hull afloat and the stern still in the mud, began slowly to tilt forward toward me. The stern was rising.

In another moment, my after pair of pontoons broke surface and there were all four of my ex-gasoline tanks afloat, with the 400 ton load of that Italian derrick swinging in the wire slings between them, a perfect lifting job!

In no more time than it took to cast loose our shore air connections (which wasn't much) the *Resolute* was towing that ex-Italian *floating* crane away from there, while Jim Buzbee and Jay Smith, salvage mechanics, went racing up the steelwork of that derrick like monkeys to unfurl from a flagstaff previously rigged atop it (another act of faith) the same American flag which proudly had floated out over every wreck we had raised.

And so, leaving the gallery on the quay gasping at the quickness of it, an hour and ten minutes after we had started the lift, the Italian derrick was on its way out of the commercial harbor to the naval harbor, salvaged at last!

CHAPTER

57

We DRY-DOCKED THE CRANE. SINCE there was no damage to its underwater hull, no repairs on the dry dock were necessary, though we found its main deck as rolling as an ocean wave from what McCance and his inexpert salvagers had done to it.

All we had to do, once the derrick was landed in the dry dock, was to pump up the dock a little to take the load off the pontoons onto the dock, then cast loose our pontoons and tow them away. After that as the dry dock was lifted higher and the crane hull came completely out of water, there was nothing required except to let the water in the hull run out the opened sea valves, then close the valves again. As soon as the Eritreans had scraped and painted the underwater hull, we floated the crane off the dock, which it had occupied one day only. So far as its hull was concerned, it was perfectly ready for use again.

However, the crane machinery, submerged a year and a half, required to be taken apart and cleaned, and that job, together with the rerigging of new steel wires to its lifting winches and hooks, took some weeks. After that, the Italian floating crane went right to work unloading ships in the commercial harbor.

But I never saw it make its first lift.

For a few days after we had salvaged it, late on Saturday afternoon, November 24, I received a dispatch from the War Department, transmitted to me by General Maxwell. It had come from Washington in secret code; only a paraphrased version of it was delivered to me:

Referring to instructions issued by the War Department, Captain Edward Ellsberg is detached from the Middle East Command and will report immediately to General Eisenhower's headquarters in Algeria for duty in connection with urgent salvage work required in all North African ports. This action has been approved by the Navy Department. Air transportation has been arranged by the War Department via Khartoum and Accra. Proceed at once.

MAXWELL

My heart leaped as I read that. The war, I knew, had suddenly moved far away from Massawa. Already Montgomery had chased Rommel completely across Libya. Tobruk had long since fallen back into British hands and somewhere beyond Benghazi, Montgomery was pursuing his fleeing enemy into Tripolitania.

Massawa's day was done. Only the portable equipment—the ships, the dry docks, the floating crane, the machinery—could be moved close enough to the new theaters of war to be of any further help. All else shortly would have to be abandoned.

Hurriedly, I directed Mrs. Maton to send for all my salvage captains. I had very little time left, my plane would be going out of Asmara early next morning, Sunday.

I said good-by to all of them, after ordering all salvage work knocked off and the ships to start loading salvage gear at once to leave for the western Mediterranean via Capetown immediately they were loaded. The new American army in North Africa had urgent need of them.

I went back to my room in Building 35 and hurriedly started to pack what little I could take by air, with the rest of my belongings to go on the *Chamberlin*. Captain Morrill and Lieutenant Woods came in to help.

I turned my command of the Naval Base over temporarily to Captain Morrill. No doubt, now the Royal Navy would shortly take over.

My telephone started to ring. Colonel Sundius-Smith, Captain Lucas, other British officers, called to bid me farewell, and wish me good luck in North Africa. My shop foremen came to say good-by. I thanked them all for what they had done—more than I could ever repay them for.

I worked till 3 A.M. packing, by which time I had to quit and go. My plane was leaving Asmara early in the morning for Khartoum. Trying to sort out everything I should need in North Africa into the few things I could take by air, was troublesome. One thing after another had to be laid aside to go via the *Chamberlin*. Finally, my aviation bag was jammed, it seemed nothing more could be taken, when my eye, sweeping my bare room for the last time, lighted on our flag.

It had been retired from service the week before, too frayed, too worn to be flown safely any longer over our Naval Base. The last time it had been used was when hoisted over the Italian floating crane as we had brought her in.

Impregnated now with the coral dust of the Abd-El-Kader Peninsula, badly faded from battling the scorching rays of the Massawa sun, its days as a flag were over.

But as I remembered that day on May 20, when first we had proudly hoisted it over our Naval Base and how it had flown over our every triumph since, I felt it had to go with me. Dusty as it was, I hastily jammed it down on top of my few clothes and closed up my bag.

Below in my car, Garza was waiting to drive me to Asmara. Regretfully, I shook hands with Morrill and with Woods; no commanding officer had ever had two more able and more loyal lieutenants; it hurt me to part with them. I climbed into the car alongside Garza.

The car started away in the night under the dark stars. Out over the waters of the Red Sea, I saw the lights twinkling across a harbor full of wrecks that I had salvaged; as we moved past the open Naval Base shops, I could see in them the machinery that once had been but sabotaged junk.

Silently I gazed on everything as rapidly I slid out the Abd-El-Kader Peninsula. I wasn't sorry to leave Massawa; it was a nightmare I should be a long time getting over. What had happened in Massawa, I should never forget; Massawa had left scars on me I should carry for the rest of my life.

We drew out of Massawa and went racing away through the darkness across the hot desert toward the mountains. Soon we were climbing rapidly. I drew my long-unused overcoat around my shoulders. Now I should need it again. North Africa, in the midst of a fierce campaign, *might* prove to be more hectic than Massawa, but, at least, it certainly would be cooler.

EPILOGUE

British Admiralty Delegation,
Building T-4,
Navy Department,
Washington, D.C.

BRITISH ADMIRALTY DELEGATION
(British Supply Council in Washington)

N.1298/42   15 September, 1942.

SIR,

I am commanded by My Lords Commissioners of the Admiralty to convey to you an expression of their appreciation of the very valuable services rendered by Captain Edward Ellsberg, U.S.N., as officer in charge of salvage operations at Massawa, which have resulted in the successful raising of the floating dock sunk in that harbour.

My Lords consider that the skill and energy shown by Captain Ellsberg in carrying out this work are deserving of high praise, and would be grateful if an expression of their appreciation could be conveyed to him.

I am, Sir,

> Your obedient Servant,
> E. A. SEAL
> *Deputy Secretary of the Admiralty*
> *North America*

The Secretary of the Navy
Navy Department
Washington, D.C.

American Embassy,
London, England
March 12, 1943.

DEAR ELLSBERG:

Receipt of the enclosed letter from Sir Henry V. Markham of the Board of Admiralty, delighted me so much that I am sending it along to you with this note. Of course, a copy will go forward to the Navy Department for inclusion in your record.

The British indicate that you have done a perfectly splendid job and your aid to them constitutes a major contribution to the Allied war effort.

It is a real joy to add a "well done" to this expression of gratitude of the Board of Admiralty. I wish for you a most speedy return to good health, both for the personal happiness of you and yours, and also because of the great value of your work to the service.

Best wishes.

Keep cheerful.

Sincerely,

HAROLD R. STARK.

Captain Edward Ellsberg, U.S.N.R.,
c/o Navy Department,
Washington, D.C.

BOARD OF ADMIRALTY

London,
9 March, 1943.

ADMIRAL H. R. STARK,
Commander, U.S. Naval Forces in Europe.

DEAR ADMIRAL:

I write to let you know that the Board have had before them reports from the late Commander-in-Chief Mediterranean, of the outstanding services to the Royal Navy of Captain Edward Ellsberg, U.S.N.R., at Massawa.

At Massawa Captain Ellsberg by great skill and unflagging energy raised the two Italian Floating Docks in spite of considerable weight of opinion that this was impossible. He also salvaged a number of sunken ships and a 90 ton floating crane, which Salvage Contractors had failed to float.

By the time he left Massawa to take up an important appointment in North Africa, the harbours and the Naval Repair Base had been fully restored to use with the exception of one berth on which he was working at the time of departure. Three of H.M. Cruisers had been partially docked and repaired there under his directions, at the worst time of the year and at a period when it was impossible to deal with them elsewhere in the Near East owing to enemy activities.

Most of this work was done under the most trying climatic conditions, and without his zeal, energy, and constant direction, which were an inspiration to his salvage crews, these excellent contributions to the Allied cause could never have been realized.

This Officer's enthusiasm and drive, apart from their material result, have had an excellent effect on Allied relations.

Captain Ellsberg's knowledge and enterprise have been of the greatest value to the Royal Navy, and it is with regret that we learn that he has had temporarily to relinquish his duties on account of ill health. May I ask you to be so good as to convey to him an expression of the gratitude of the Board of Admiralty?

Believe me,

Yours very truly,

H. V. MARKHAM.

Admiral H. R. Stark,
Commander, U.S. Naval Forces in Europe.

[There have been omitted from the above letter certain commendatory statements relative to services in North Africa, which are not pertinent to Massawa.]

Upon recommendation by the War Department, the following award of the LEGION OF MERIT, then newly authorized as a decoration, was made in the spring of 1943:

THE SECRETARY OF THE NAVY

Washington

The President of the United States takes pleasure in presenting the LEGION OF MERIT to

CAPTAIN EDWARD ELLSBERG
United States Naval Reserve

for service set forth in the following CITATION:

"For exceptionally meritorious conduct in the performance of outstanding service to the Government of the United States in the establishment of a Massawa Naval Base, Eritrea, from January 8, 1942 to April 5, 1943. Working with tireless energy at a task considered in some respects as hopeless of accomplishment, Captain Ellsberg achieved remarkably successful results in the salvaging and repair of vital naval equipment. Having rehabilitated the Massawa Naval Base shops, he made possible extensive drydocking operations for the benefit of all types of Allied shipping."

For the President,
FRANK KNOX,
Secretary of the Navy.

THE END